Lecture Notes in Artificial Intelligence 11617

Subseries of Lecture Notes in Computer Science

More information about this series at http://www.springer.com/series/1244

Cezary Kaliszyk · Edwin Brady ·
Andrea Kohlhase · Claudio Sacerdoti Coen (Eds.)

Intelligent Computer Mathematics

12th International Conference, CICM 2019
Prague, Czech Republic, July 8–12, 2019
Proceedings

 Springer

Editors
Cezary Kaliszyk 🆔
University of Innsbruck
Innsbruck, Austria

Edwin Brady 🆔
University of St. Andrews
St. Andrews, UK

Andrea Kohlhase
University of Applied Sciences
Neu-Ulm, Germany

Claudio Sacerdoti Coen 🆔
University of Bologna
Bologna, Italy

ISSN 0302-9743   ISSN 1611-3349   (electronic)
Lecture Notes in Artificial Intelligence
ISBN 978-3-030-23249-8   ISBN 978-3-030-23250-4   (eBook)
https://doi.org/10.1007/978-3-030-23250-4

LNCS Sublibrary: SL7 – Artificial Intelligence

This Springer imprint is published by the registered company Springer Nature Switzerland AG
The registered company address is: Gewerbestrasse 11, 6330 Cham, Switzerland

Preface

This volume contains the contributions of the 12th Conference on Intelligent Computer Mathematics, CICM 2019. The CICM conference is dedicated to promoting the advancement of machine-supported reasoning, computation, and knowledge management in science, technology, engineering, and mathematics. This year CICM took place in Prague, Czech Republic, during July 8–12, 2019, and was hosted at the Czech Institute of Informatics, Robotics, and Cybernetics (CIIRC) of the Czech Technical University in Prague (CTU). The CICM conference series is the combination of several events that were previously held separately: the Symposium on the Integration of Symbolic Computation and Mechanized Reasoning, the International Conference on Mathematical Knowledge Management, and the Digital Mathematics Library Conference.

CICM has been held annually as a joint meeting since 2008. Previous meetings took place in Birmingham (UK, 2008), Grand Bend (Canada, 2009), Paris (France, 2010), Bertinoro (Italy, 2011), Bremen (Germany, 2012), Bath (UK, 2013), Coimbra (Portugal, 2014), Washington DC (USA, 2015), Białystok (Poland, 2016), Edinburgh (UK, 2017), and Linz (Austria, 2018).

This year CICM consisted of three tracks:

- Mathematical Knowledge Management (MKM) is an interdisciplinary research area aiming at the development of innovative and ever more sophisticated ways of managing mathematical knowledge. MKM brings together and serves several communities dealing with mathematical knowledge, foremost mathematicians, computer scientists, engineers, librarians, educators, students, and publishers.
- Calculemus is dedicated to the integration of computer algebra systems and systems for mechanized reasoning such as interactive proof assistants and automated theorem provers.
- Systems and Projects: Orthogonally, the Systems and Projects track called for descriptions of digital resources, such as data and systems, and of projects, whether old, current, or new, as well as survey papers covering any topics of relevance to the CICM community.

The Program Committee (PC) accepted 19 paper out of 41 formal submissions. Each submission was refereed by at least three PC members or external reviewers appointed by the PC members. The reviewing was done in a single-blind manner, and included a response period, in which authors could answer and clarify the points raised by the reviews. In one case, an open-ended shepherding phase was used, during which the authors were allowed to improve their paper under the guidance of a designated PC member. For the preparation of these proceedings and for the general conference and discussion management, we used Andrei Voronkov's EasyChair conference management system.

The PC was chaired by the editors of the volume. Cezary Kaliszyk served as the general PC chair. Edwin Brady, Andrea Kohlhase, and Claudio Sacerdoti Coen served as track chairs of the Calculemus, MKM, and Systems and Projects tracks, respectively. Dennis Müller was the doctoral program chair.

The conference issued a call for workshops and tutorials, of which five proposals were approved:

- OpenMath 2019 - the 30th OpenMath Workshop organized by James Davenport and Michael Kohlhase
- LML 2019 - the Large Mathematics Libraries Workshop organized by William Farmer and Dennis Müller
- FMM 2019 - the 4th Workshop on Formal Mathematics for Mathematicians organized by Karol Pąk
- FVPS 2019 - the Second Workshop on Formal Verification of Physical Systems organized by Sofiene Tahar, Osman Hasan, and Umair Siddique
- EMML 2019 - a tutorial on Exploring the Mizar Mathematical Library organized by Adam Naumowicz, Artur Kornilowicz, and Adam Grabowski

The workshop programs were managed independently by the respective organizers.

Furthermore, this year's CICM featured a doctoral program, which provided a forum for PhD students to present their research and advice from senior research members of the community serving as mentors. Finally, CICM also solicited other contributions including work-in-progress papers, demos, posters, and tutorials. These informal contributions are not a part of this volume.

In addition to the presentation of the accepted papers, CICM 2019 had three invited presentations. Makarius Wenzel gave an invited talk accompanied by a full paper on "Interaction with Formal Mathematical Documents in Isabelle/PIDE":

Isabelle/PIDE has emerged over more than 10 years as the standard Prover IDE to support interactive theorem proving in Isabelle, with numerous applications in the Archive of Formal Proofs (AFP). More recently, the scope of PIDE applications has widened toward languages that are not connected to logic and proof in Isabelle, but taken from a broader repertoire of mathematics on the computer. The present paper provides an overview of the current status of the PIDE project and its underlying document model, with built-in support for parallel evaluation and asynchronous interaction. There is also some discussion of original aims and approaches, successes and failures, later changes to the plan, and ideas for the future.

Henry Prakken gave an invited talk on: "AI Models of Argumentation and Some Applications to Mathematics":

Argumentation is the process of supporting claims with grounds and of defending the thus constructed arguments against criticism. AI researchers have for more than 30 years studied the formal and computational modelling of argumentation. This has resulted in increased understanding of argumentation and in computer tools for supporting human argumentation or performing artificial argumentation.

At first sight, the rigor of mathematical thinking would be far from the "messy" world of argumentation. However, inspired by Polya's and Lakatos's groundbreaking studies of the practice of mathematical proof, quite a few scholars have studied "mathematics in action" as a form of argumentation. Some of that work employs formal and computational tools from AI. In this talk I will first give an overview of the formal and computational study of argumentation in AI, and I will then discuss several applications to mathematical modelling and proof.

Sylvain Corlay gave an invited talk: "Jupyter: From IPython to the Lingua Franca of Scientific Computing":

Since its creation in 2011, the Jupyter notebook has exploded in popularity, with a user base growing from thousands to millions. Beyond notebooks, Jupyter is, in fact, a large collection of tools meant to facilitate workflows of researchers from the exploratory analysis to the communication of their results. In this talk, we will present the main components of the ecosystem, from JupyterLab to the interactive widgets, including Binder and JupyterHub. We will show how they work together to enable the variety of use-cases for which Jupyter is used today. Then, we will try to show where the project is going in the next few months, and present the latest updates on dashboarding tools, data visualization libraries, and new language backends.

Many people contributed to making CICM 2019 a success. We are grateful to the organizers at CIIRC, notably Jan Jakubův, Martin Suda, and Josef Urban for their support in the local organization of the meeting. We thank Serge Autexier for the publicity work. We thank all the authors of the submitted papers, participants to the conference, invited speakers, workshop organizers, and tutorial speakers.

May 2019

Cezary Kaliszyk
Edwin Brady
Andrea Kohlhase
Claudio Sacerdoti Coen

Organization

Program Committee

Akiko Aizawa	University of Tokyo, Japan
Edwin Brady	University of St Andrews, UK
Cyril Cohen	Inria, France
Howard Cohl	NIST, USA
William Farmer	McMaster University, Canada
Cezar Ionescu	Oxford University, UK
Mateja Jamnik	University of Cambridge, UK
Cezary Kaliszyk	University of Innsbruck, Austria
Fairouz Kamareddine	Heriot-Watt University, UK
Andrea Kohlhase	University of Applied Sciences Neu-Ulm, Germany
Michael Kohlhase	FAU Erlangen-Nuremberg, Germany
Laura Kovacs	Vienna University of Technology, Austria
Zoltán Kovács	JKU Linz, Austria
Adam Naumowicz	University of Białystok, Poland
Grant Passmore	Aesthetic Integration, UK
Markus Pfeiffer	University of St Andrews, UK
Florian Rabe	FAU Erlangen-Nürnberg, Germany and LRI, France
Bas Spitters	Aarhus University, Denmark
Claudio Sacerdoti Coen	University of Bologna, Italy
Freek Wiedijk	Radboud University, The Netherlands
Wolfgang Windsteiger	RISC, Linz, Austria
Abdou Youssef	The George Washington University, USA
Richard Zanibbi	Rochester Institute of Technology, USA

Additional Reviewers

Ed Ayers	Julien Narboux
Gabor Bakos	Bernard Parisse
Robert Belleman	Daniel Raggi
Katja Berčič	Jan Schaefer
Jonas Betzendahl	Zohreh Shams
Frédéric Chyzak	Dan Shiebler
Floris van Doorn	Aaron Stockdill
Daniel Huang	Laurent Théry
Joe Hurd	Benoît Viguier
Katya Komendantskaya	Duo Wang
Dennis Müller	

Contents

Interaction with Formal Mathematical Documents in Isabelle/PIDE

Makarius Wenzel[(✉)]

Augsburg, Germany
https://sketis.net

Abstract. Isabelle/PIDE has emerged over more than 10 years as the standard Prover IDE for interactive theorem proving in Isabelle. The well-established Archive of Formal Proofs (AFP) testifies the success of such applications of formalized mathematics in Isabelle/HOL. More recently, the scope of PIDE has widened towards languages that are not connected to logic and proof in Isabelle, but taken from a broader repertoire of mathematics on the computer. The present paper provides a general overview of the PIDE project and its underlying document model, with built-in parallel evaluation and asynchronous interaction. There is also some discussion of original aims and approaches, successes and failures, later changes to the plan, and ideas for the future.

1 Introduction

Isabelle/PIDE means **Prover IDE**: its implementation relies on Isabelle/Scala, and the standard front-end is Isabelle/jEdit: so all these brand names can be used interchangeably at some level of abstraction. The presentation at Schloss Dagstuhl in October 2009 [18] provides an interesting historical view of the initial concepts of Isabelle/Scala and the preliminary implementation of Isabelle/jEdit. Work on that had already started one year earlier, so the Dagstuhl presentation in August 2018 could use the title "The Isabelle Prover IDE after 10 years of development" [27]. In the years between, there have been many papers about the project, notably [3,16,19,20,22,25,28,29].

Considerable complexity of Isabelle/PIDE concepts and implementations has accumulated over time, and presenting a comprehensive overview in this paper poses a challenge. Subsequently, we start with two concrete application scenarios: standard Isabelle/jEdit (Sect. 1.1) and non-standard Isabelle/Naproche (Sect. 1.2). More systematic explanations of the PIDE document-model are given in Sect. 2. Discussion of aims and approaches of PIDE follows in Sect. 3: this provides a perspective on design decisions from the past, with projections into the future.

1.1 Isabelle/PIDE as IDE for Interactive Proof Documents

Isabelle is an interactive proof assistant (similar to Coq or HOL4), and PIDE is the Prover IDE framework for it. Isabelle/PIDE is implemented in Isabelle/ML

© Springer Nature Switzerland AG 2019
C. Kaliszyk et al. (Eds.): CICM 2019, LNAI 11617, pp. 1–15, 2019.
https://doi.org/10.1007/978-3-030-23250-4_1

(based on Poly/ML) and Isabelle/Scala (on the Java Virtual Machine). This arrangement allows to use existing IDE front-ends from the Java ecosystem, e.g. the plain text editor jEdit (http://jedit.org). The combined Isabelle/jEdit [30] is presently the most sophisticated application of PIDE, and the default user-interface for Isabelle. There are other PIDE front-ends, e.g. Isabelle/VSCode and a headless server, but non-PIDE interaction has already been discontinued in October 2014. Consequently, the classic Proof General Emacs [1] does not work for Isabelle anymore: it was based on the TTY-loop that no longer exists.

Fig. 1. The all-inclusive Isabelle/PIDE/jEdit application

Users who download[1] and run the application bundle for their respective operating-system first encounter the Isabelle/jEdit desktop application, similar to Fig. 1: it provides immediate access to documentation, examples, and libraries. All of these are *Formal Mathematical Documents* in Isabelle, which are organized as *theories* and *sessions* (i.e. collections of theories with optional document out-put). This includes the Isabelle manuals from the `Documentation` panel, which shows PDFs generated from sessions in the `$ISABELLE_HOME/src/Doc` directory.

By opening `$ISABELLE_HOME/src/Doc/JEdit/JEdit.thy` in Isabelle/jEdit, we see the theory sources of the Isabelle/jEdit manual in the Prover IDE. Its con-tent mainly consists of traditional document structure: section headings and blocks of text. Such *quotations* of informal text may also contain formal items via *antiquotations*. The latter concept was introduced to allow prose text to talk

---

[1] https://isabelle.sketis.net/Isabelle_CICM2019.

about logical terms and types, but the same mechanism is re-used to augment LaTeX by formal elements: links to files or URLs, text styles with robust nesting (bold, emphasized, verbatim, footnote), item lists as in Markdown, citation management wrt. BibTeX databases etc. (see also [30, Chapter 4]).

Beyond self-application of Isabelle/PIDE/jEdit to its own documentation, the Isabelle distribution provides libraries and applications of formalized mathematics, mostly in Isabelle/HOL (see the directory `$ISABELLE_HOME/src/HOL`). The material may be edited directly in the Isabelle/jEdit Prover IDE—except for the HOL session itself, which is preloaded as non-editable session image. Such spontaneous checking may require substantial hardware resources, though. E.g. `$ISABELLE_HOME/src/HOL/Analysis/Analysis.thy` works best with 8 CPU cores and 16 GB main memory, and still requires several minutes to complete. Note that this is not just browsing, but *semantic editing* of a live document: a checked state provides full access to the execution environment of the prover.

Development of complex proof documents requires add-on tools: a theory library usually provides new logical content together with tools for specifications and proofs. Isabelle/HOL itself is an example for that, with many *proof methods* to support (semi-)automated reasoning in Isabelle/Isar [17], and *external provers* (ATP, SMT) for use with *Sledgehammer* [5]. Isabelle/PIDE orchestrates all tools within one a run-time environment of parallel functional programming. Results are exposed to the front-end via a stream of *PIDE protocol* messages. The editor can retrieve the resulting PIDE document markup in real-time (without waiting for the prover) and use conventional GUI elements to show it to the user: e.g. as text colours, squiggly underlines, icons, tooltips, popups. Output generated by the prover can have extra markup to make it *active*: when the user clicks on it, edits will be applied to the text to continue its development, e.g. see [30, Sect. 3.9] for document-oriented interaction with Sledgehammer.

The example sessions of the Isabelle distribution are quite substantial, but most Isabelle/HOL formalizations are now maintained in **AFP**, the *Archive of Formal Proofs* [7]. AFP is organized like a scientific journal, not a repository of "code". Thus it is similar to the Mizar Mathematical Library[2], but with more flexibility and programmability of *domain-specific formal languages* [28]. That continues the original LCF/ML approach [9,10] towards active documents with full-scale Prover IDE support.

AFP version 28e97a6e4921 (April 2019) has 315 authors, 471 sessions, 4912 theories. In principle, it is possible to load everything into a single prover session for Isabelle/jEdit. But scaling is not for free, and doing that blindly requires two orders of magnitude more resources than for HOL-Analysis above. In practical development of large AFP entries, users still need some planning and manual arrangement of sessions, to restrict the focus to relevant parts of AFP.

A truly integrated development environment should do that automatically for the user, and treat Isabelle + AFP as one big mathematical document for editing (and browsing). Concrete ideas for further scaling of the PIDE technology are outlined in [26], but it will require some years to get there.

---

[2] http://mizar.org/library and http://mizar.org/fm.

1.2   Isabelle/Naproche for Automatic Proof-Checking of Ordinary Mathematical Texts

Naproche-SAD is a recent tool by Frerix and Koepke [8], based on the original *System for Automated Deduction* (SAD) by Paskevich and others [11]. It processes the *Formal Theory Language* (ForTheL), which is designed to look like mathematical text, but it is restricted to a small subset of natural language.

The tool is implemented in Haskell as a plain function from input text to output messages. A file is like a chapter of mathematical text, with a nested tree-structure of elements and sub-elements (for signatures, axiomatizations, statements, proofs). Output messages inform about the translation of mathematical text to problems of first-order logic, and indicate success or failure of external proof checking; the latter is delegated to the *E Prover* by Stephan Schulz and can take several seconds for each proof obligation.

To integrate Naproche-SAD into PIDE, Frerix and Wenzel have reworked the Haskell program over 2 months in 2018, to turn the command-line tool into a service for reactive checking of ForTheL texts. Isabelle integration was done via the new Isabelle/Haskell library and some glue code in Isabelle/Scala to register ForTheL as auxiliary file-format (extension .ftl).

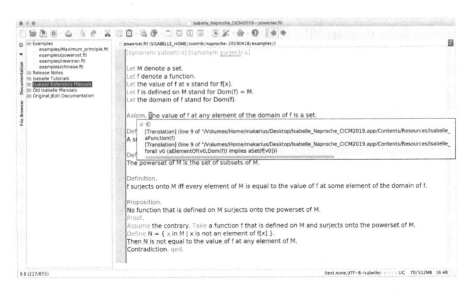

Fig. 2. Isabelle/Naproche with "ordinary mathematical text"

The resulting Isabelle/Naproche application is available as multi-platform download[3]. A running instance is shown in Fig. 2: users can directly open ForTheL files (e.g. from Documentation/Examples) and wait briefly to see output

---

[3] https://isabelle.sketis.net/Isabelle_Naproche_CICM2019.

messages attached to the text in the usual IDE manner. Further edits produce a new version of the text, which is sent in total to Naproche-SAD again. The back-end is sufficiently smart to avoid redundant checking of unchanged sub-elements: it keeps a global state with results of old versions: this is easy to implement as the program keeps running until shutdown of Isabelle/PIDE.

The general approach of using an external tool in Isabelle/PIDE like a function on input sources to output messages has been demonstrated before for `bibtex` databases [28, Sect. 5]. This technique depends on the following conditions:

- Input and output works via temporary files or anonymous streams for each invocation—no global state within the file-system.
- Source positions in output uses precise text offsets—not just line numbers: this typically requires careful inspection of text encoding and line-endings.
- The tool starts quickly and runs only briefly. As a rule of thumb for IDE reactivity, 10 ms is very fast, 100 ms is fast enough, 500 ms is getting slow.
- A long-running tool needs to be interruptible via POSIX signals: C/C++ programs often require some corrections in this respect.
- A long-running tool should output messages incrementally on a stream to let the user see approximative PIDE markup early. E.g. syntax markup immediately after parsing, and the status of semantic checking later on.

The small and quick `bibtex` program can be started afresh for each version of input text, and messages returned as a single batch extracted from the log file. In contrast, the rather heavy `Naproche-SAD` executable can spend several seconds on small mathematical texts, so the continuously running server process with its internal cache is important for reactivity; it also avoids repeated startup of a big program. To achieve that, the Haskell program had to be changed significantly, but typed functional programming helps to keep an overview of global state and interactions with the world: this makes it easy to isolate the main function for concurrent invocations of multiple server requests.

In summary, we see that Isabelle is not just Isabelle/HOL: Isabelle/Naproche uses logic in its own way, independently of the Isabelle logical framework.

2   The PIDE Document Model

Abstractly, we can understand a PIDE document as large expression of *embedded sub-languages* that can be *explored interactively* in the editor, while the prover is processing the *execution* as a parallel functional program. Continued editing by the user may cancel ongoing executions by the prover, and replace no longer relevant parts of the document by new material to be checked eventually. The communication of the editor with the prover always works via *document edits*, e.g. to insert or remove segments of *text* to produce a new *document version*. Edits also determine the *perspective* on the text: it tells the prover which parts of the document are important for the user. E.g. scrolling an editor window will update the document and refocus the execution to include uncovered text.

Document content is represented as *plain text* within editor buffers, but it is also possible to include *auxiliary files* that could be external blobs in some user-defined format (usually they are plain text as well). Both input sources and output messages are rendered in enhanced editor buffers to support text decorations and pretty-printing in the style of Oppen [13]: its formatting and line-breaking dynamically adjusts itself to font metrics and window sizes.

PIDE markup (XML) over input sources or within output pretty-trees is used for text colours, tooltips, popups etc. Thus the syntax-highlighting in jEdit is augmented by *semantics-rendering* in Isabelle/jEdit.

2.1 Document Structure and Organization: Theories and Sessions

PIDE documents follow the traditional structure of mathematical texts, which is a sequence of "definition–statement–proof" given in foundational order.

A *definition* is an atomic text element that extends the theory context: this could be a genuine definition of a constant in Isabelle/HOL, or the definition of a module in Isabelle/ML, or something else in a domain-specific formal language. A *statement* is a pending claim within the theory that requires justification by the subsequent *proof*: it could be a theorem statement in the logic or a derived definitional specification (e.g. a recursive function with termination proof). Definitions and statements can be arbitrary user-defined notions of the Isabelle application, but proofs always use the Isabelle/Isar proof language [17].

Foundational order means that the overall document elements can be seen as a well-founded sequence of elementary constructions: mutual recursion is restricted to a single definitional element, e.g. one that introduces multiple recursive functions. For better scalability, projects are usually built up as an *acyclic directed graph* of theory nodes: each theory imports existing theories and forms a canonical *merge* of the contexts before adding further material. Isabelle context management has a built-in notion of monotonicity to propagate results: after import, a well-formed term remains well-formed, a proven theorem remains proven etc. Entities from domain-specific languages need to conform to the same abstract principle of "monotonic reasoning".

A *session* consists of a sub-graph of imported theories, together with auxiliary files for document-preparation in LATEX. This roughly corresponds to a "project" in conventional IDEs for programming languages. A *session image* is a "dumped world" of the underlying Isabelle/ML process of a session, to speed-up reloading of its state. Each session image may refer to a single parent, to form an overall *tree* of session images. Merging session images is *not* supported, but a session can have multiple *session imports* to load theories from other sessions. This is not a copy of the other theory, but an inclusion that requires re-checking for the new session (often this is faster than building a complex stack of session images).

In AFP, each entry usually consists of a single session for its formal theory content, together with the LATEX setup for presentation as a journal article [7].

In addition to session documents, Isabelle2019 supports *session exports*: tools in Isabelle/ML may publish arbitrary blobs for the *session database* (with optional XZ compression). For example, the AFP entry `Buchi_Complementation` generates a functional program from its specification and exports the compiled executable. The session export mechanism avoids uncontrolled write-access to the global file-system: since PIDE document processing operates concurrently on multiple versions, writing out physical files would be ill-defined.

In *batch mode* (e.g. `isabelle build`), session sources are read from the file-system, and session exports are added to the SQLite database for this session build. Command-line tools like `isabelle export` or `isabelle build -e` can retrieve exports later on: here the session database acts like a `zip` archive.

In *interactive mode* (e.g. `isabelle jedit`), session sources are managed by the editor (with backing by the file-system), and session exports are stored in Isabelle/Scala data structures. Isabelle/jEdit provides virtual file-systems with URL prefixes `isabelle-session:` and `isabelle-export:` to access this information interactively, e.g. see the jEdit `File Browser`, menu `Favorites`, the last two items. An example is session `Tools/Haskell`, theory `Haskell`, command **export_generated_files** at the bottom: it exports generated sources of the Isabelle/Haskell library for re-use in other projects, e.g. Naproche-SAD (Sect. 1.2).

2.2   Common Syntax for Embedded Languages: Cartouches

The *outer syntax* of Isabelle theories is the starting point for user-defined language elements: the header syntax **theory** A **imports** $B_1 \ldots B_n$ is hardwired, but everything else is a defined *command* within the theory body. The Isabelle bootstrap provides the initial **ML** command: Isabelle/Pure and Isabelle/HOL are using that to define a rich collection of commands that users often understand as *the* Isabelle theory language, but it is merely a library.

A command definition requires a **keywords** declaration in the theory header, and a *command parser* with semantic *command transaction* in the theory body. All command parsers operate on the token language of Isabelle/Isar: it provides identifiers, numerals, quoted strings, embedded source etc.

Quoted string tokens are similar to string literals in ML. Some decades ago, there was no outer syntax and everything embedded into ML like that. Today we still see embedded types, terms, and propositions in that historic notation. Nested quotations do work, but require awkward backslash-escapes for quotes: the number of backslashes is exponential in the depth of nesting, so only one or two levels are seen in practice.

Embedded source tokens use the *cartouche* notation of Isabelle, which was introduced a few years ago to facilitate arbitrary nesting. The quotes are directed (like open/close parentheses) and chosen carefully to remain outside of usual application languages. The Isabelle symbols `\<open>` and `\<close>` are used for that; they are rendered in the front-end as French single-quotes: e.g. ‹*source*›. Thus a command that takes a cartouche as outer syntax remains free to use its own lexical conventions in the nested source.

For example, the subsequent ML snippet defines a term t within the ML environment of the theory; the **term**-antiquotation inside ML uses regular term notation to construct the corresponding ML datatype value; there are further nested cartouches for comments inside these domain-specific languages.

ML ⟨*val t* = **term** ⟨λx. x ≤ y + z — comment in term⟩ — comment in ML⟩

This approach of nesting languages resembles s-expressions in LISP, but the cartouche delimiters are visually less intrusive than parentheses, and the sub-expressions can be arbitrary sub-languages with their own concrete syntax. The Prover IDE helps users to understand complex nesting of languages, e.g. via text colors and popups (see Fig. 3). Isabelle/ML helps language implementors with operations for common concepts, e.g. embedded comments seen here.

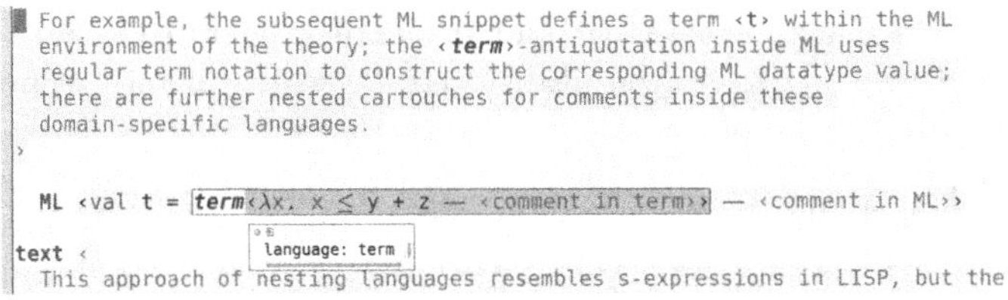

Fig. 3. PIDE exploration of nested sub-languages within this paper

2.3   Auxiliary Files with Implicit Theory Context

The outer syntax of Isabelle supports a special class of *theory load* commands: there is a single argument that refers to a file, relative to the directory where the theory file is located. Isabelle/PIDE manages the content of that file in a stateless manner: the command implementation gets its source as attachment to outer syntax tokens—there is no direct access to the file-system. In general, the editor could have unsaved buffers with changed content: the prover needs to process that intermediate state, not an old saved copy.

Embedded source via auxiliary files is more scalable than inlined car-touches. For example, consider the commands **ML** vs. **ML_file**: both incorporate Isabelle/ML definitions into the current theory context, and both are ubiquitous in the construction of Isabelle/Pure and Isabelle/HOL. **ML** is preferred for small snippets, up to one page of source text. **ML_file** is better suited for big modules: Isabelle/jEdit provides a mode for the corresponding .ML files, with static syntax tables and a SideKick parser to generate tree views.

Normally, theory load commands occur within a particular theory body to augment its content. In contrast, an *implicit theory context* helps when the file is considered stand-alone: it refers to an imported context for its language defi-nition, but the results of checking are restricted to PIDE markup shown to the user. The Isabelle/Scala programming interface allows to define a *file-format* (according to the file extension): thus PIDE knows which theory template needs to be generated internally for such auxiliary files. Example file-formats are those for `bibtex` and `Naproche-SAD` (Sect. 1.2).

Still missing is support for simultaneous loading of files by a single command, e.g. a whole sub-project in an external language. That would require the Isabelle/Scala interface to understand the syntax of the load command, beyond a single file argument. Even more ambitious would be transitive exploration of included files, to refer to a complete graph via a few root entries in the text.

2.4 Shallow Presentation of Document Sources

PIDE interaction is about creating documents, and this is taken literally for the final outcome: a traditional PDF produced via LATEX. An example is the present paper itself: document sources are edited in Isabelle/jEdit (see Fig. 3) and the batch-mode tool `isabelle build -o document=pdf` produces the typeset document for publication. This works according to a rather shallow presentation scheme going back to the early days of Isabelle/Isar (20 years ago), with a few later additions. The idea is that the source language is sufficiently close to a proper mathematical document, such that simple pretty-printing is sufficient:

- Isabelle symbols like `\<alpha>` are blindly replaced by LATEX macros: the Isabelle style files provide a meaning for that to typeset α.
- Document *markup commands* like "**section** ⟨*source*⟩" or "**text** ⟨*source*⟩" are turned into corresponding LATEX macros for sections, paragraphs etc.
- Document *markdown items* with Isabelle symbols `\<^item>`, `\<^enum>`, `\<^descr>` are turned into corresponding LATEX environments `itemize`, `enumerate`, `description`.
- *Embedded comments* like "— ⟨*source*⟩" are turned into suitable LATEX macros from the Isabelle style files.
- *Document antiquotations* are evaluated and inlined: the user-defined implementation in ML generates document output within the formal context, e.g. to pretty-print a term using its logical notation.

Note that genuine PIDE markup is not yet used for document output: it is only available in Isabelle/Scala, but document preparation works in Isabelle/ML. We can see that omission in the example of Sect. 2.2: the typeset version of Fig. 3 does not treat the ML keyword *val* specifically in LATEX, it looks like a regular identifier. Full semantic document preparation is an important area of future work: presently there are only some experiments with HTML preview in Isabelle/jEdit.

PIDE editor presentation of document sources works differently: while the prover is processing the sources, the online document model accumulates XML markup over the original sources. This can be used for painting the editor view in real-time, using whatever is available at a particular point in time; formally this is a *snapshot* of the PIDE document state. The jEdit editor is a bit limited in its visual rendering capabilities, though: a single font with small variations on style, and uniform font-size and line-height. To make the best out of that,

Isabelle/jEdit uses custom Unicode fonts derived from the DejaVu collection, with mathematical symbols taken from TEX fonts. Isabelle2019 includes a standard set of font families: `Sans Mono` (default for text buffers), `Sans` (default for GUI elements), and `Serif` (default for help texts). To emphasize the "ordinary mathematical text" format of Naproche-SAD (Sect. 1.2), the screenshot in Fig. 2 has actually used the proportional `Sans` instead of the (almost) fixed `Sans Mono`.

There are additional tricks in Isabelle/jEdit rendering to support subscript, superscript, and bold-face of the subsequent Isabelle symbol, but without nesting of font styles. Furthermore, there are some icons in the font to render special control symbols nicely, e.g. `\<^item>` for Isabelle Markdown as a square bullet, `\<^file>` as a sheet of paper, `\<^dir>` as a folder, `\<^url>` as a W3C globe.

It is interesting to see how far the jEdit text editor can be stretched, with the help of an open-ended collection of Isabelle symbols and specifically generated application fonts. Compared to that, the modest HTML5/CSS3 styling in Isabelle/VSCode is still lagging behind: the makers of VSCode are taking away most of the rendering power of the underlying Chromium browser, because they want to deliver an editor only for "code", not documents.

In the near future, there should be better convergence of offline PDF presentation and online editor rendering of PIDE documents. In particular, the Isabelle LATEX toolchain needs to be integrated into the IDE, to avoid several seconds of wait time to produce PDFs. Further ideas for renovation of Isabelle document preparation (mostly for HTML) are sketched in [26, Sect. 3.3].

3   Aims and Approaches of Isabelle/PIDE

What has Isabelle/PIDE tried to achieve over the past 10 years, what worked out and what failed? The subsequent overview of important aims and approaches summarizes **success**, **failure**, **changes** in the plan, and ideas for **future** work.

3.1   Isabelle/ML vs. Isabelle/Scala: "Mathematics" vs. "Physics"

At the bottom, Isabelle is an LCF-style proof assistant [10] that is freely programmable in Isabelle/ML. That is based on Poly/ML, which is well-tuned towards applications of symbolic logic on multicore hardware.

To complement the ultra-pure ML environment by tools and libraries from the "real" world, Isabelle/PIDE has been based on Scala/JVM from the very beginning in 2008. The JVM gives access to GUI frameworks, HTTP servers, database engines (SQLite, PostgreSQL) etc. The programming style of Isabelle/Scala follows that of Isabelle/ML to a large extent, and there are many basic libraries that are provided on both sides.

Success: The clean and efficient functional style of ML has been transferred to Scala. There are many modules on both sides that follow the typical Isabelle mindset of minimality and purity. It is feasible to move the language boundary of tool implementations, according to technical side-conditions of ML vs. Scala.

Failure: Isabelle users often find Isabelle/ML as tool implementation language already too difficult. The additional Isabelle/Scala for tool integration is beyond the multilingual capabilities of most people. This could be partly caused by common misunderstandings about both sides: Isabelle/ML is not just Standard ML, and Isabelle/Scala not just Scala—both are "Isabelle" with an idiomatic style that deviates from customs seen elsewhere.

Changes: The original conception of Isabelle/Scala as add-on library for system integration turned out insufficient. Instead, Isabelle/Scala and Isabelle/ML have become equal partners in forming the Isabelle infrastructure. Consequently, Isabelle/Pure now contains many ML and Scala modules side-by-side, sometimes with equivalent functionality (e.g. portable file and process operations), and sometimes complementary (e.g. for the PIDE protocol).

Future: Isabelle/Scala still needs proper IDE integration: its development model resembles that of Isabelle/ML in earlier decades. It is a funny paradox that the Prover IDE infrastructure is developed with a plain text editor and command-line build process. Either Scala could be integrated into PIDE as another back-end, or a regular Scala IDE could be used (e.g. IntelliJ IDEA).

3.2   Private PIDE Protocol (Untyped) vs. Public APIs (Typed)

Isabelle/PIDE resides both in Isabelle/ML and Isabelle/Scala, with typed functional programming interfaces. The PIDE implementation uses a custom-made protocol that fits tightly to the requirements of the interactive document model. Over the years, there have been frequent changes and adjustments of the protocol. The communication works over a pure byte-channel, with low overhead for structured messages and ML-like datatype values. The paper [21] explains the PIDE protocol for demonstration purposes with a back-end in Coq 8.4 (2013).

Success: Efficient and robust implementation of the bi-lingual PIDE framework in Isabelle/ML/Scala works. Easy maintenance of corresponding modules in the same directory location is feasible.

Failure: It is cumbersome to develop and maintain different PIDE implementations for different provers: the Coq/PIDE project [14] did not reach end-users and is now lagging behind years of further PIDE development.

Changes: The initial conception of the PIDE protocol was quite basic, but it acquired complexity and sophistication over time.

Future: Back-end protocol: the old idea to retarget PIDE for other provers (like Coq) could be re-opened eventually, but it requires significant personal dedication and resources to do that properly. Front-end protocol: there is already a simplified public PIDE protocol for headless interaction with the document-model. That could eventually become a client-server protocol for web applications.

3.3 Pervasive Parallelism on Multicore Hardware

Both Isabelle/ML ("pure mathematics") and Isabelle/Scala ("real physics") support parallel programming with shared memory and immutable values. User-space tools do not have to care much about it, as long as standard Isabelle programming idioms and libraries are used. Scaling of parallel programs is always a challenge: Isabelle/ML performs well into the range of 8–16 cores (on a single CPU node). Isabelle/Scala rarely uses more than 2–4 cores.

Success: Parallel Isabelle/ML became routinely available in 2008 [15], and has been refined many times [12,23]. That proved so successful that an initial motivation for PIDE was to make an IDE that can properly connect to a parallel proof engine: for the user front-end this added the aspect of asynchronous interaction, which is central to PIDE [3,24].

Failure: The predictions of CPU manufacturers in 2005 about consumer machines with many cores (32–128) have not become true, because mainstream applications cannot use so much parallelism. Instead we have seen a trend towards light-weight mobile devices (with 2–8 cores). This can confuse new Isabelle users: they think that big applications from AFP should work on e.g. 2 CPU cores and 4 GB RAM, but reality demands to double or quadruple these resources. When we see server-class machines with a lot of cores, there is often an internal division into separate CPU nodes (NUMA) with significant penalty for a shared-memory application, e.g. a machine with 64 cores might turn out as 8 nodes of 8 core CPUs with delay factor 1.6–3.2 to access data on a distant node.

Future: The Isabelle/PIDE front-end (on a small mobile device) and the back-end (on a big server) could be separated, to follow a general trend towards "cloud computing". This could be done without degrading the IDE into a mere web-browser application. Instead, the existing Isabelle/jEdit or Isabelle/VSCode desktop applications could connect to a remote version of Isabelle/PIDE, see also [26, Sect. 3.3]. Headless PIDE functionality has already been implemented and used elsewhere, e.g. to export formal content of AFP entries in Isabelle/MMT [6, Sect. 3.1]. A proper client-server environment across the Web would require substantial work, e.g. robust management of lost connections to the remote back-end.

3.4 Desktop Application Bundles on Linux, Windows, macOS

Isabelle/PIDE is available as a single download that can be unpacked and run without further ado. There is no requirement for self-assembly by end-users Isabelle does not need packaging by OS providers (e.g. Debian): it is a genuine end-user application; there can be different versions side-by-side without conflict.

Success: The majority of users is happy with the all-inclusive Isabelle application bundle (2019: 300 MB download size, 1 GB unpacked size). It works almost as smoothly as major Open Source products (e.g. Firefox, LibreOffice).

Failure: Full equality of all three platforms families has still not been achieved. Java GUI rendering on Linux is worse than on Windows and macOS; exotic Linux/X11 window managers can cause problems. Add-on tools are sometimes not as portable (and robust) on Windows: Isabelle often refers to Cygwin as auxiliary POSIX platform, but that may cause its own problems. Even for native Windows tools (e.g. via MinGW) the Unix-style orchestration of multiple processes can have timing problems (e.g. Sledgehammer provers) or fail due to antivirus software. Moreover, the recent tendency of Windows and macOS towards "application stores" makes it harder to run downloaded Isabelle bundles on the spot: users need to bypass extra vendor checks.

Changes: The initial approach was more optimistic about availability of certain "standard" components on the OS platform, notably Java and Scala. Later it became clear that almost everything needs to be bundled with Isabelle, except for the most basic system components (e.g. `libc`, `libc++`, `curl`, `perl`). Note that other projects have come to a similar conclusion, e.g. SageMath with very thorough all-inclusive bundling.

Future: The "download–unpack–run" experience of Isabelle/PIDE needs fine-tuning for first-time users. In particular, AFP needs to be included in this, to avoid manual intervention with session `ROOTS` and `ROOT` files. There could be more support for alternative applications based on the Isabelle/PIDE platform, to suppress unused components of Isabelle/HOL, e.g. see Isabelle/Naproche (Sect. 1.2).

4   Conclusion

Isabelle/PIDE is a long-term effort to support live editing of complex document structures with "active" content. Its cultural background is that of interactive theorem proving, which has high demands for execution management: interrupts, real-time requirements, parallel threads, external processes. So this provides a generous upper bound of technology for less ambitious applications of PIDE. We have seen the example of Isabelle/Naproche.

Ultimately, we may understand PIDE as a continuation and elaboration of the following approaches:

- The LCF/ML approach to interactive theorem proving by Milner et al. [9, 10].
- The Isar approach to human-readable proof documents by Wenzel [17].
- Parallel ML and future proofs by Matthews and Wenzel [12, 15, 23].
- Early prover interfaces by Aspinall [2], Bertot [4] and others.

All of that taken together amounts to decades of research: PIDE attempts to form a limit over that, to reach a new stage of semantic editing that can be taken for granted. The present paper has illustrated some applications and sketched the overall construction. It is to be hoped that builders of other mathematical tools are encouraged to re-use PIDE for their own projects.

References

1. Aspinall, D.: Proof General: a generic tool for proof development. In: Graf, S., Schwartzbach, M. (eds.) TACAS 2000. LNCS, vol. 1785, pp. 38–43. Springer, Heidelberg (2000). https://doi.org/10.1007/3-540-46419-0_3
2. Aspinall, D., Lüth, C., Winterstein, D.: A framework for interactive proof. In: Kauers, M., Kerber, M., Miner, R., Windsteiger, W. (eds.) Calculemus/MKM 2007. LNCS (LNAI), vol. 4573, pp. 161–175. Springer, Heidelberg (2007). https://doi.org/10.1007/978-3-540-73086-6_15
3. Barras, B., et al.: Pervasive parallelism in highly-trustable interactive theorem proving systems. In: Carette, J., Aspinall, D., Lange, C., Sojka, P., Windsteiger, W. (eds.) CICM 2013. LNCS (LNAI), vol. 7961, pp. 359–363. Springer, Heidelberg (2013). https://doi.org/10.1007/978-3-642-39320-4_29
4. Bertot, Y., Théry, L.: A generic approach to building user interfaces for theorem provers. J. Symbolic Comput. **11** (1996)
5. Blanchette, J.C.: Hammering away: a user's guide to Sledgehammer for Isabelle/HOL. Isabelle Documentation (2019)
6. Condoluci, A., Kohlhase, M., Müller, D., Rabe, F., Sacerdoti Coen, C., Wenzel, M.: Relational data across mathematical libraries. In: Kaliszyk, C., Brady, E., Kohlhase, A., Sacerdoti Coen, C. (eds.) Intelligent Computer Mathematics, CICM 2019, LNAI 11617, pp. 61–76. Springer, Heidelberg (2019)
7. Eberl, M., Klein, G., Nipkow, T., Paulson, L., Thiemann, R. (eds.): The Archive of Formal Proofs (AFP). https://dblp.uni-trier.de/db/journals/afp
8. Frerix, S., Koepke, P.: Automatic proof-checking of ordinary mathematical texts. In: Workshop on Formal Mathematics for Mathematicians (FMM 2018). CICM Informal Proceedings (2018). https://www.cicm-conference.org/2018/infproc/paper13.pdf
9. Gordon, M., Milner, R., Morris, L., Newey, M.C., Wadsworth, C.P.: A metalanguage for interactive proof in LCF. In: Principles of programming languages (POPL) (1978)
10. Gordon, M.J., Milner, A.J., Wadsworth, C.P.: Edinburgh LCF. A Mechanised Logic of Computation. LNCS, vol. 78. Springer, Heidelberg (1979). https://doi.org/10.1007/3-540-09724-4
11. Lyaletski, A., Paskevich, A., Verchinine, K.: Theorem proving and proof verification in the system SAD. In: Asperti, A., Bancerek, G., Trybulec, A. (eds.) MKM 2004. LNCS, vol. 3119, pp. 236–250. Springer, Heidelberg (2004). https://doi.org/10.1007/978-3-540-27818-4_17
12. Matthews, D., Wenzel, M.: Efficient parallel programming in Poly/ML and Isabelle/ML. In: ACM SIGPLAN Workshop on Declarative Aspects of Multicore Programming (DAMP 2010) (2010)
13. Oppen, D.C.: Pretty printing. ACM Trans. Program. Lang. Syst. **2**(4) (1980)
14. Tankink, C.: PIDE for asynchronous interaction with Coq. In: Benzmüller, C., Woltzenlogel Paleo, B. (eds.) User Interfaces for Theorem Provers (UITP 2014), EPTCS, vol. 167 (2014). https://doi.org/10.4204/EPTCS.167.9
15. Wenzel, M.: Parallel proof checking in Isabelle/Isar. In: Dos Reis, G., Théry, L. (eds.) ACM SIGSAM Workshop on Programming Languages for Mechanized Mathematics Systems (PLMMS 2009). ACM Digital Library (2009)
16. Wenzel, M.: Isabelle as document-oriented proof assistant. In: Davenport, J.H., Farmer, W.M., Urban, J., Rabe, F. (eds.) CICM 2011. LNCS (LNAI), vol. 6824, pp. 244–259. Springer, Heidelberg (2011). https://doi.org/10.1007/978-3-642-22673-1_17

17. Wenzel, M.: Isabelle/Isar – a generic framework for human-readable proof documents. In: Matuszewski, R., Zalewska, A. (eds.) From Insight to Proof – Festschrift in Honour of Andrzej Trybulec, Studies in Logic, Grammar, and Rhetoric, vol. 10, no. 23. University of Białystok (2007)

18. Wenzel, M.: On prover interaction and integration with Isabelle/Scala. In: Ball, T., Giesl, J., Hähnle, R., Nipkow, T. (eds.) Interaction versus Automation: the Two Faces of Deduction (Dagstuhl Seminar 09411). Schloss Dagstuhl, Germany, October 2009. http://drops.dagstuhl.de/portals/09411, https://files.sketis. net/Dagstuhl2009.pdf

19. Wenzel, M.: Asynchronous proof processing with Isabelle/Scala and Isabelle/jEdit. In: Coen, C.S., Aspinall, D. (eds.) User Interfaces for Theorem Provers (UITP 2010), FLOC 2010 Satellite Workshop. ENTCS, Elsevier, July 2010

20. Wenzel, M.: Isabelle/jEdit – a prover IDE within the PIDE framework. In: Jeuring, J., et al. (eds.) CICM 2012. LNCS (LNAI), vol. 7362, pp. 468–471. Springer, Heidelberg (2012). https://doi.org/10.1007/978-3-642-31374-5_38. https://arxiv.org/abs/1207.3441

21. Wenzel, M.: PIDE as front-end technology for Coq (2013). https://arxiv.org/abs/1304.6626

22. Wenzel, M.: READ-EVAL-PRINT in parallel and asynchronous proof-checking. In: Kaliszyk, C., Lüth, C. (eds.) User Interfaces for Theorem Provers UITP 2012, EPTCS, vol. 118 (2013). https://doi.org/10.4204/EPTCS.118.4

23. Wenzel, M.: Shared-memory multiprocessing for interactive theorem proving. In: Blazy, S., Paulin-Mohring, C., Pichardie, D. (eds.) ITP 2013. LNCS, vol. 7998, pp. 418–434. Springer, Heidelberg (2013). https://doi.org/10.1007/978-3-642-39634-2_30

24. Wenzel, M.: Asynchronous user interaction and tool integration in Isabelle/PIDE. In: Klein, G., Gamboa, R. (eds.) ITP 2014. LNCS, vol. 8558, pp. 515–530. Springer, Cham (2014). https://doi.org/10.1007/978-3-319-08970-6_33

25. Wenzel, M.: System description: Isabelle/jEdit in 2014. In: Benzmüller, C., Woltzenlogel Paleo, B. (eds.) User Interfaces for Theorem Provers, UITP 2014, EPTCS, July 2014. http://eptcs.web.cse.unsw.edu.au/paper.cgi?UITP2014:11

26. Wenzel, M.: Further scaling of Isabelle technology. In: Isabelle Workshop 2018, Oxford, UK (2018). https://files.sketis.net/Isabelle_Workshop_2018/Isabelle_2018_paper_1.pdf

27. Wenzel, M.: The Isabelle prover IDE after 10 years of development. In: Bauer, A., Escardó, M., Lumsdaine, P.L., Mahboubi, A. (eds.) Formalization of Mathematics in Type Theory (Dagstuhl Seminar 18341). Schloss Dagstuhl, Germany, August 2018. https://www.dagstuhl.de/18341, https://sketis.net/2018/the-isabelle-prover-ide-after-10-years-of-development

28. Wenzel, M.: Isabelle/jEdit as IDE for domain-specific formal languages and informal text documents. In: Masci, P., Monahan, R., Prevosto, V. (eds.) F-IDE Workshop 2018, Oxford, UK, no. 284. EPTCS (2018). http://eptcs.web.cse.unsw.edu.au/paper.cgi?FIDE2018.6

29. Wenzel, M.: Isabelle/PIDE after 10 years of development. In: User Interfaces for Theorem Provers, UITP 2018 (2018). https://sketis.net/wp-content/uploads/2018/08/isabelle-pide-uitp2018.pdf

30. Wenzel, M.: Isabelle/jEdit. Isabelle Documentation (2019)

Beginners' Quest to Formalize Mathematics: A Feasibility Study in Isabelle

Jonas Bayer[2], Marco David[1(✉)], Abhik Pal[1], and Benedikt Stock[1]

[1] Jacobs University Bremen, Campus Ring 1, 28759 Bremen, Germany
{m.david,ab.pal,b.stock}@jacobs-university.de
[2] Institut für Mathematik, Freie Universität Berlin,
Arnimallee 3, 14195 Berlin, Germany
jonas.bayer@fu-berlin.de

Abstract. How difficult are interactive theorem provers to use? We respond by reviewing the formalization of Hilbert's tenth problem in Isabelle/HOL carried out by an undergraduate research group at Jacobs University Bremen. We argue that, as demonstrated by our example, proof assistants are feasible for beginners to formalize mathematics. With the aim to make the field more accessible, we also survey hurdles that arise when learning an interactive theorem prover. Broadly, we advocate for an increased adoption of interactive theorem provers in mathematical research and curricula.

Keywords: Interactive theorem proving · Isabelle · Formalized mathematics · Hilbert's tenth problem

1 Introduction

The challenge to formalize all of mathematics, as issued by the QED Manifesto [3], might have seemed unrealistic for the 1990s but recent advances in theorem proving clearly demonstrate the feasibility of using theorem provers in mathematical research. Examples for this are the formalization of the odd-order theorem in Coq [9] and Kepler's conjecture in HOL Light [10]. Even though these tools provide the possibility of establishing mathematical truth once and for all, mathematicians are reluctant to use interactive theorem provers to verify the correctness of their proofs [5,6]. "Interactive theorem provers are written by computer scientists for computer scientists," the complaint goes, quickly followed by a comment on their infeasibility for non-experts.

In October 2017, twelve undergraduate students who just started their university studies were asked to verify a mathematical proof using an interactive theorem prover. Upon initiative of Yuri Matiyasevich, whose contribution [16] was key to solving Hilbert's tenth problem but who had no experience with proof assistants, the undergraduates set out to formalize the problem and its solution.

© Springer Nature Switzerland AG 2019
C. Kaliszyk et al. (Eds.): CICM 2019, LNAI 11617, pp. 16–27, 2019.
https://doi.org/10.1007/978-3-030-23250-4_2

Given the interactive theorem prover Isabelle [18][1] as "relatively easy to learn," the *Hilbert meets Isabelle* project was born.

Sixteen months and many ups and downs later, the project stands close to completion. The students have made many mistakes and the large workgroup has shrunk, but, most importantly, they all have learned a lot. We herewith present a feasibility study of interactive theorem provers for non-experts and disprove the concern raised earlier. From young students to senior scientists in mathematics, computer science, and engineering, everyone can pick up a proof assistant to formalize their work—it will be well worth the effort!

This paper reports about the ongoing project, reviews the tools and resources that were used, and reflects on the learning process of the group. With an emphasis placed on formalizing mathematics, we wish to analyze the hurdles of becoming a proficient user of an interactive theorem prover, scrutinize our mistakes, and share the lessons we learned in the process. We also give a list of suggestions to developers and future beginners to aid the interactive theorem proving community to grow and welcome more mathematicians in the future.

Overview. This paper is organized as follows: In Sect. 2 we provide context to the formalization. In particular, we briefly outline Hilbert's tenth problem and explain the background and motivations of those involved. Then in Sect. 3 we analyze the process of formalization, identify our key mistakes, the lessons learned from those mistakes, and things we will do differently now. The current status of the formalization is also given in this section. Finally, based on our experience of learning Isabelle, in Sect. 4 we provide recommendations to the theorem proving community and beginners interested in formalizing mathematics.

2   The Quest to Formalize

On a visit to Jacobs University Bremen one and a half years ago, Yuri Matiyasevich recruited students for a newly conceived research idea: to conduct a formal verification of his solution to Hilbert's tenth problem. In order to promote this project, he gave a series of talks on the problem, its negative solution, and related questions [13,14]. These got a collection of students curious and before long, a research group was formed. The project was co-initiated by Dierk Schleicher who supported, mentored, and supervised the workgroup.

However, neither Yuri Matiyasevich nor Dierk Schleicher had any previous experience with interactive theorem provers. Coq [4] was known as a well established, yet difficult to learn proof assistant, but Yuri Matiyasevich ultimately suggested Isabelle. Supposedly with a less steep learning curve and better documentation, this choice manifested. Thus began the quest to formalize.

---

[1] In rest of the paper we write "Isabelle" to also mean "Isabelle/HOL".

Hilbert's Tenth Problem and the MRDP Theorem. Hilbert's tenth problem comes from a list of 23 famous mathematical problems posed by the German mathematician David Hilbert in 1900 [12]. Hilbert's tenth problem asks about Diophantine equations, which are polynomial equations with integer coefficients: *Does there exist an algorithm that determines if a given Diophantine equation has a solution in the integers?* [16] The Matiyasevich–Robinson–Davis–Putnam theorem (also known as the MRDP theorem, DPRM theorem, or Matiyasevich's theorem) finished in 1970 by Yuri Matiyasevich [15], which states that every recursively enumerable subset of the natural numbers is the solution set to a Diophantine equation, implies a negative solution to Hilbert's tenth problem.

For the proof, one first needs to develop the theory of Diophantine equations. This entails showing that statements such as inequalities, disjunctions, or conjunctions of polynomial equations can be represented in terms of Diophantine polynomials. Then, as the first major step in the proof, one shows that exponentiation also has such a Diophantine representation. Next, after developing the notion of a recursively enumerable set using a Turing-complete model of computation (for instance using register machines), one shows that this computation model, which accepts exactly the elements of recursively enumerable sets, can be arithmetized, i.e. simulated using Diophantine equations and exponentiation. Since there exist recursively enumerable (semi-decidable), and hence Diophantine, sets that are not decidable, any proposed algorithm would have to solve the halting problem in order to decide an arbitrary Diophantine solution set.

Students' Background and Parallelization of Work. After the team acquainted itself with the proof, the workgroup was split accordingly: Team I worked on showing that exponentiation is Diophantine, Team II on register machines and their arithmetization. Figure 1 gives an overview of the structure of the project. For the first part, Matiyasevich [16] provides detailed proofs; however, the arguments in the second part were at a higher level of abstraction. While Team I could work on formalizing the first part with minimal Isabelle knowledge and the already detailed paper proof, the second part of the formalization turned out more challenging. The arithmetization of register machines required not only an understanding of all details omitted in the paper, it also required a good understanding of existing theories of already formalized mathematics and practice with Isabelle's tools—what definitions lend themselves to automation? What is the appropriate level of abstraction? What makes for a definition that can be used well in proofs? etc.

Especially with the diverse background of many group members, the above questions were not answered, let alone asked, immediately. The students involved were mainly first year undergraduates studying mathematics and computer science, who had not taken a course on theorem proving. Not only did the students lack any foundational knowledge in logic and type theory, some did not even have prior programming experience. Combined, these factors resulted in an approach to learning that can best be described as haphazard. However, unbeknownst to the workgroup, these also became the preconditions for a larger feasibility

Positional Notation

Register Machine (RM)

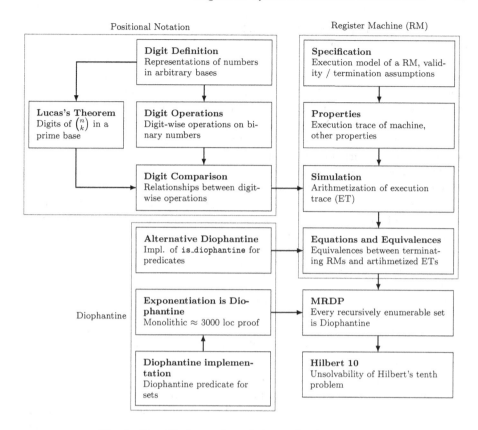

Fig. 1. Simplified overview of the project's structure.

experiment in theorem proving—how a group of inexperienced undergraduates can learn an interactive theorem prover to formalize a non-trivial mathematical result. In broader terms, the next few sections report on this feasibility study.

3 Sledgehammer Abuse, Foolish Definitions, and Reinventions

In the beginning, many definitions, functions, lemmas, and proofs were written without an overall understanding of their individual functionality and utility. Especially for proofs, a lack of this structural understanding prevented the formalization from advancing. This section reviews the gamut of work done on the formalization between October 2017 and February 2019 and analyses the key mistakes that were made in the process, as well as the lessons learned from them.

Reinventions and Sledgehammer Abuse. Due to the different nature of the two parts of the proof, the two teams progressed with different speed and success.

Team I started by implementing custom 2×2 matrices which are used frequently in the first part. Although they initially searched for a matrix datatype within existing Isabelle theories, this search turned out unsuccessful as few relevant results appeared. And the results that were found did not allow the team to infer how to use the respective implementations for their own proofs. As the formalization progressed, many other definitions and statements started relying on these custom types. Not only did this result in a dependency-blow-up of elementary properties that needed proving, they also prevented Isabelle from automating many parts of the proofs.

The reimplementation of this basic type was followed by stating and assuming intermediate lemmas without proof using Isabelle's convenient `sorry` keyword. This allowed for parallelizing the work on separate parts. The number-theoretic nature of proofs made it easier to use tools like `sledgehammer` that call external automatic theorem provers to search for proofs. The general approach to prove a given statement was the following: state an intermediate step, then check if `sledgehammer` can find a proof, otherwise introduce a simpler sub-step and repeat.

Since the paper proof was understood in full detail and the internal Isabelle libraries were sufficiently sophisticated, the `sledgehammer`-and-repeat approach worked surprisingly well. In fact, much of the entire first part was successfully formalized using this approach. This, however, had two main flaws. First, the proofs themselves were generated by automated theorem provers without human insight, hence cumbersome and almost impossible to understand. Second, since the approach worked relatively well it didn't incentivize the members to learn more about the Isabelle system and understand the functionality it provides. Remaining a mysterious tool that could automagically prove theorems, `sledgehammer`'s capabilities, limitations, and output were never actually understood.

Foolish Definitions. In parallel to the above, Team II worked on arithmetizing register machines and the results of the second part of the proof, which culminates in the statement that all recursively enumerable sets are exponentially Diophantine. The groundwork underlying this part of the implementation included a definition of register machines, in particular Minsky machines. This modeling task initially posed a major hurdle towards the formalization. In retrospect, the ideal implementation makes all variables used in the proof become readily accessible. The first implementation written was, however, the direct opposite of that as it made extensive use of lists, fold operations, and comprehensions. This approach, while easy to implement, turned out to be too unwieldy for any proofs. In the end, the implementation from Xu et al. [20] was used as model for the formalization. While they describe a Turing machine, compatible ideas were extracted and used to implement register machines.

Once a workable model of register machines was implemented, the group could set on the goal to actually prove lemmas that were only stated before. For Team II, this is where the actual challenge of learning Isabelle started all over. Although the register machine model succeeded in being strongly modular, its properties were inherently more complicated than the number-theoretic statements from the first part. In particular, most lemmas about the workings of a register machine typically required one to fix some initial state, some set of instructions as well as to assume validity of all state transitions, etc. Breaking proofs down into smaller and smaller pieces, as is commonly done also in mathematics, hence became much more difficult. In some sense, the large size of the implemented machinery posed a mental barrier to tackling the stated lemmas. Extrapolating the `sledgehammer`-and-repeat strategy of Team I, Team II initially hoped for automated theorem provers to prove very extensive lemmas without much human help. In retrospect this was a ridiculous expectation.

Expecting Intuition from Isabelle. To add to this, it turned out that the small details of intermediate proof steps were often not understood as well as the group thought. This lead to "proof-hacking" scenarios even after lemmas had been successfully split into smaller statements. Most prominently, Matiyasevich [16, Sect. 4.4.2] gives a central property of register machines without elaborate proof because it follows from an analogous special case. Due to the similarity of the properties both in writing and in function, this generalization was intuitively clear. However, collectively the team did not know how to convey this intuition to Isabelle. It took several months until a complete "paper-proof" of all intermediate steps, done by a member of the group, could suddenly give the formalization of this property new momentum. With a new straight-forward approach, its proof was seamlessly completed. Even though many proofs are conceptual, often to ease reading and understanding, every correct proof can be made formal by definition, on paper and hence in an interactive theorem prover.

Finally, the exact implementation of finite power series used in the proof posed one more difficulty. Throughout the project, three definitions of such series coexisted. One can define a finite sum directly, or alternatively define recursive functions which, in each iteration, add a term to the series from the left or right. Their equivalence can be easily proven; yet, depending on the specific use case within a proof, the right definition becomes pivotal. Exactly the above generalization benefited from an explicit definition of the power series as a finite sum, and would have taken significantly more effort with any of the other definitions. Incidentally, this is similar to conventional mathematics on paper but contrasts conventional programming where there often is no difference between two equivalent definitions.

In similar fashion, the complexity of proofs may considerably change depending on the facts which are added to the set of automatically used simplification rules. As such, both the right setup of definitions before proving as well as the right setup of the prover determine the (human) provers' success.

Current Status. With all of this at hand, the second part of the formalization was only recently advanced. Additionally, many conceptual issues were resolved earlier this year with the dedication and input from Mathias Fleury. As of writing, only few lemmas in the second part—and hence in the entire Isabelle formalization of the MRDP theorem—remain to be completed. In particular, these include more minor lemmas on register machines, proving Lucas's theorem on digit-wise representations of binomial coefficients in a prime base, and proving that certain relations like binary digit-wise multiplication are Diophantine. Table 1 lists some statistics from the current state of the formalization[2]. Once completed, the formalization is expected to be sent as a submission to the Archive of Formal Proofs [1].

Table 1. Statistics about the current progress (as of commit `bea7403d`) of the formalization.

Lines of code	7759
— of which for Register Machines	2692
— of which for Diophantine theories	3856
— of which for Positional Notation	1150
— of which for miscellaneous files	61
Number of definitions	48
Number of functions	41
Number of lemmas and theorems	295

Lessons Learned. Throughout the above story, we[3] learned many lessons which we share below. From discussions with Isabelle users of different background and at different levels, a small survey showed that these also are issues for most learners. One could call the following "trivial" and we would probably agree. However, these lessons are so essential that we recommend any future beginner to be absolutely aware of them.

1. Merely understanding the idea of a proof and knowing how it is carried out conceptually does not suffice for its formalization. As tempting as is might seem to start proving in Isabelle, the formalization should only be started after the proof has carefully been written down on paper in full detail.
2. Working with concepts that frequently pop up in mathematics, it is likely that someone else has worked on them before. Instead of reinventing the wheel, one should search the existing and extensive Isabelle libraries.
3. The exact implementations of functions and predicates can both facilitate but also impair the progress of any proof. The chosen definitions directly reflect the approach taken to the problem, which also has a big impact on

---

[2] The actual source code has been made available at https://gitlab.com/hilbert-10/dprm under the GPLv3 license.

[3] In rest of the text the authors use "we" to interchangeably refer to themselves as authors and as representatives of the workgroup.

conventional proofs. However, they additionally require an adequate level of abstraction so that human and proof assistant can work with them effectively.

What to Change Next Time. Conjointly, reflection of our method of working and learning reveals several defects, which are presented below. We suspect that these, in turn, are very likely to have systematically caused the above mistakes, or at least delayed their mending. In particular, we view the following points as definitive "not to-dos" for any formalization project using interactive theorem provers.

The most valuable source for beginners is undoubtedly Tobias Nipkow's Concrete Semantics [17]. We would have learned much quicker and with more structure, had we had strictly followed this book and its exercises. Learning Isabelle on the fly, in a *learning-by-doing* fashion, and looking up commands as needed was futile and it remains questionable if any such method of learning can be successful. Given many group member's previous programming experience, we clearly overestimated our ability to transfer this knowledge to an interactive theorem prover.

Expanding on this note, our experience suggests that relying on programming experience is helpful but should be done in tandem with an awareness of the key differences between programming and proving. Most notably, theory files are not compiled nor executed and proofs need to be written with a much more mathematical and structured mindset, as compared to programming. Interactive theorem provers are not just "yet another programming language" and our failure to realize this has only lengthened the learning process.

We became aware of the two mistakes described above after connecting with the very approachable Isabelle community. Only then we realized how naïve our initial approach to learning Isabelle was. Hence, when working on a formalization for the first time, it is very helpful to have an expert around who can be consulted when more conceptual questions arise. We agree that this may not be ideal, which is why further discussion on this issue follows in the next section.

4   Decoupling Learning from Experienced Individuals

We all have learned a lot from different members of the Isabelle community. In this ongoing process, we gradually realize that there's more to interactive theorem proving than just having one's lemmas accepted by the computer. A prime example for this is knowing what definitions are useful in which scenario. We've observed both ourselves and others, that experienced users seem fundamental to one's Isabelle education. Most of this education goes beyond mere factual information and includes understanding the Isabelle system on a deeper level, developing a systematic methodology of writing proofs, and developing a "feeling" for the proof assistant. From this, we conjecture the following.

Conjecture. Learning Isabelle currently depends on having an experienced user in reach who can regularly answer questions.

We speculate that this can be generalized to other interactive theorem provers, too. While we agree that learning from another user or developer in person is certainly efficient, this becomes unsustainable as the community grows. This naturally begs the question: *How can a beginner's learning process become more guided by resources and documentation, therein more independent?* We do not, and possibly can not, answer this question exhaustively. Nevertheless, we ask this question both to ourselves and the community and present our attempt at answering it.

Expand Documentation. Documentation plays a key role in helping new users get accustomed to a new tool. And accessible, readable and easy to navigate documentation, hence, is key to promote self-learning. As beginners our first point of contact with Isabelle's documentation system was the "Documentation" tab in the prover IDE. However, we found it difficult to navigate as there was no clear indication of which document is suitable for beginners. In retrospect we realize that working though Nipkow's tutorial [17] would have been the most ideal. However, we still feel that the current documentation system could be expanded as follows.

We identify four key parts of a systematic documentation system[4]. Tutorials that walk new users through specific parts of the Isabelle system, how-to guides for learning and using tools, topic guides that give the theoretical basis for many of the features, and finally a repository of references that document all necessary details. While the current documentation system addresses three of those parts, it still lacks a crucial link that connects them: the topic guide. This lack immediately implies that any deeper understanding of the system can only come from being around regular users – hence tightly coupling a successful learning experience to advanced users.

Maintain a Knowledge-Base. In tandem with documentation, it helps to accumulate a knowledge-base of beginner- and intermediate-level questions and answers. The Isabelle-users mailing list currently hosts the entire range of questions and is definitely appropriate for advanced questions. However, the thread archives are not suitable nor effectively searchable as a database for questions which many more are likely to have. Hence, we encourage users to ask these questions on Stack Overflow or a similar online forum. Stack Overflow, for example, aspires to become an ultimate and exhaustive knowledge base, and has achieved this for many larger communities. Conventional programming languages strongly benefit from that any basic question—as elementary it may be—has been asked and answered before. The interactive theorem proving community can do this as well.

---

[4] This identification is, by no means, original. Many large open-source software projects are aware of this structure and routinely advocate for documentation that conforms to it. See for instance the Django documentation [8] and the Write the Docs project [2].

We suggest that introductory-level resources like Concrete Semantics or the Isabelle Community Wiki main page actively encourage users to ask questions on Stack Overflow to build such a knowledge-base. This way, every question will only need to be asked and answered once, and everyone can benefit from users who share their expertise.

Develop the Isabelle Community Wiki. Thirdly, we suggest to expand the Isabelle Community Wiki in a similar fashion: by an organic community effort. In the initial stages of our project, we used an internal "Isabelle Cheat Sheet" to facilitate mutual knowledge exchange. This Cheat Sheet was meant to be a platform where common problems and their solutions could be presented to everyone. In this respect, the intention was very similar to the "Isabelle Community Wiki". Although, interestingly enough, our own Cheat Sheet and the Wiki were completely disjoint until we merged them.

While the Cheat Sheet initially only included very basic syntactical facts it was quickly extended by features of Isabelle that are not described in existing beginner-level resources, e.g. Concrete Semantics. This includes the possibility of passing arguments to `sledgehammer` or how to look up facts in the existing theories. Other facts on the Cheat Sheet include keywords that can be used for custom case distinctions. Coming back to the previous point, we found out about the latter specifically after asking the Isabelle community on Stack Overflow. The fact that the question and answer have received several upvotes indicates that questions like this are indeed relevant to a broader audience.

Adopt into University Curricula. In a larger scope, all of the aforementioned would strongly benefit from a growing user base. Having a larger community means that more people will ask questions and thereby create documentation, as well as eventually become experts themselves, working on exciting projects. As a matter of fact, knowing how to use an interactive theorem prover can be valued highly in many fields. Clearly, there is academia with mathematics and computer science which both have an interest and sometimes even a need to formally verify [10]. But uses in industry and engineering are equally compelling: formally verified robots, airplanes, rockets, and nuclear plants prove attractive to many companies and governments. Just one example of this prevailing relevance is given by the annual NASA Formal Methods Symposium.

In order to connect potential new users to the interactive theorem proving community as early as possible, we think that initiatives like *Proving for Fun* [11], i.e. "competitive proving" challenges, are a great idea to popularize the métier. Well-established competitive programming contests range from the International Informatics Olympiad to tech giant sponsored events and attract students as young as middle school from all over the world.

More radically, we suggest this subject be adapted into mathematics, computer science, and engineering curricula at universities. For wide acceptance, in particular Bachelor students need to be exposed to these tools before they specialize. Otherwise, knowledge will keep being passed on from PhD student to

PhD student within existing research groups, but not become decoupled from exactly these. Of course, this integration can happen step by step. Initially, there may be an small elective course on interactive theorem proving, or some part of a current course on logic can be dedicated to introducing an interactive theorem prover. Once this exists, much more becomes possible. In mathematics classes, there can be extra-credit problems for also formally verifying one's proof, or eventually a full exercise with this purpose. Theorem proving helps to teach what theorems and facts are precisely used in every step of a proof [7].

Some might classify this as a significant change in paradigm for university-level education. We argue that our suggestion may well be compared to computer algebra systems, which just entered Bachelor curricula less than two decades ago. In this regard, interactive theorem provers are the logical next step. With Mathematica, SAGE, and similar systems successfully assisting computation and visualization, it's now time to introduce interactive theorem provers like Isabelle to assist modelling and proving. Initially well-suited as educational tools, they might eventually also make their way into day-to-day research work.

5   Conclusion

Our experience shows that non-experts can indeed learn interactive theorem proving to an extent that allows them to formalize significant mathematical results. Within one and a half years, we gained enough Isabelle proficiency to formalize a core part of the solution to Hilbert's tenth problem. We are happy to have used Isabelle for this purpose, which we found to have a modest learning curve and be worth the time investment. To future projects of similar kind, we recommend that beginners approach learning an interactive theorem prover in a more structured way than we did. To this end, we found Tobias Nipkow's "Concrete Semantics" [17] the most helpful first introduction to Isabelle. In general, we recommend to use a single beginner-friendly resource which should also be clearly advertised as such by more experienced members of the interactive theorem proving community. For carrying out a formalization, we realize that it is most crucial to start with a detailed "paper proof" in order to then verify every single step in a proof assistant.

Moreover, we find that interactive theorem provers are attractive to many more fields and industries than their current user-base. Notably, the group we encourage most to adopt proof assistants are mathematicians, not least by incorporating them into university curricula. Our feasibility study showed that interactive theorem proving is doable and practical—now it is the time to start formalizing mathematics on a larger scale.

Acknowledgements. We want to thank the entire workgroup [19], without whose involvement we wouldn't be writing this paper; as well as Yuri Matiyasevich for initiating and guiding the project. Moreover, we would like to express our sincere gratitude to the entire welcoming and supportive Isabelle community. In particular we are indebted to Mathias Fleury for all his help with Isabelle. Thank you also to Christoph Benzmüller for mentoring us as well as Florian Rabe for suggesting this contribution and helping us prepare the final version. Furthermore, we thank everyone who replied to our small survey, sharing their experience and opinion on this topic with us. Finally, a big thank you to our supervisor Dierk Schleicher, for motivating us throughout the project, connecting us to many experts in the field, and all his comments on this article.

References

1. Archive of formal proofs. https://www.isa-afp.org/index.html
2. Write the docs. https://www.writethedocs.org/
3. Boyer, R., et al.: The QED manifesto. In: Bundy, A. (ed.) Automated Deduction – CADE 12. LNAI, vol. 814, pp. 238–251. Springer, Heidelberg (1994). http://www.cs.ru.nl/~freek/qed/qed.ps.gz
4. The Coq proof assistant (2019). http://coq.inria.fr
5. Benzmüller, C.: Towards computer aided mathematics. J. Appl. Logic **4**(4), 359–365 (2006). https://doi.org/10.1016/j.jal.2005.10.001
6. Bundy, A.: Preface. Philos. Trans.: Math. Phys. Eng. Sci. **363**(1835), 2331–2333 (2005). http://www.jstor.org/stable/30039730
7. Buzzard, K.: Xena. https://xenaproject.wordpress.com
8. Django Software Foundation, Contributors: Django documentation. https://docs.djangoproject.com/
9. Gonthier, G., et al.: A machine-checked proof of the odd order theorem. In: Blazy, S., Paulin-Mohring, C., Pichardie, D. (eds.) ITP 2013. LNCS, vol. 7998, pp. 163–179. Springer, Heidelberg (2013). https://doi.org/10.1007/978-3-642-39634-2_14
10. Hales, T., et al.: A formal proof of the Kepler conjecture. In: Forum of Mathematics, Pi 5, January 2015. https://doi.org/10.1017/fmp.2017.1
11. Haslbeck, M.P., Wimmer, S.: Proving for fun. http://competition.isabelle.systems
12. Hilbert, D.: Mathematical problems. Bull. Am. Math. Soc. **8**, 437–479 (1902). https://doi.org/10.1090/S0002-9904-1902-00923-3
13. Matiyasevich, Y.: Alfred Tarski's great algorithm: decidability of elementary algebra and geometry (talk). https://logic.pdmi.ras.ru/~yumat/talks/talks.php?istate=state_show_talk&iid=1364
14. Matiyasevich, Y.: Finite Dirichlet series with partially prescribed zeroes (talk). https://logic.pdmi.ras.ru/~yumat/talks/talks.php?istate=state_show_talk&iid=1364
15. Matiyasevich, Y.: The Diophantineness of enumerable sets. Dokl. Akad. Nauk SSSR **191**, 279–282 (1970)
16. Matiyasevich, Y.: Hilbert's Tenth Problem. MIT Press, Cambridge (1993)
17. Nipkow, T., Klein, G.: Concrete Semantics With Isabelle/HOL. Springer, Heidelberg (2014). https://doi.org/10.1007/978-3-319-10542-0
18. Nipkow, T., Wenzel, M., Paulson, L.C. (eds.): Isabelle/HOL. LNCS, vol. 2283. Springer, Heidelberg (2002). https://doi.org/10.1007/3-540-45949-9
19. Stock, B., et al.: Hilbert meets Isabelle. In: Isabelle Workshop (Federated Logic Conference) (2018). https://doi.org/10.29007/3q4s
20. Xu, J., Zhang, X., Urban, C.: Mechanising turing machines and computability theory in Isabelle/HOL. In: Blazy, S., Paulin-Mohring, C., Pichardie, D. (eds.) ITP 2013. LNCS, vol. 7998, pp. 147–162. Springer, Heidelberg (2013). https://doi.org/10.1007/978-3-642-39634-2_13

Towards a Unified Mathematical Data Infrastructure: Database and Interface Generation

Katja Berčič[1][(✉)] ⓘ, Michael Kohlhase[1][(✉)] ⓘ, and Florian Rabe[1,2][(✉)] ⓘ

[1] FAU Erlangen-Nürnberg, Erlangen, Germany
{katja.bercic,michael.kohlhase,florian.rabe}@fau.de
[2] LRI, Université Paris Sud, Orsay, France

Abstract. Data plays an increasing role in applied and even pure mathematics: datasets of concrete mathematical objects proliferate and increase in size, reaching up to 1 TB of uncompressed data and millions of objects. Most of the datasets, especially the many smaller ones, are maintained and shared in an ad hoc manner. This approach, while easy to implement, suffers from scalability and sustainability problems as well as a lack of interoperability both among datasets and with computation systems.

In this paper we present another substantial step towards a unified infrastructure for mathematical data: a storage and sharing system with math-level APIs and UIs that makes the various collections findable, accessible, interoperable, and re-usable. Concretely, we provide a high-level data description framework from which database infrastructure and user interfaces can be generated automatically. We instantiate this infrastructure with several datasets previously collected by mathematicians. The infrastructure makes it relatively easy to add new datasets.

1 Introduction and Related Work

Motivation. In general, mathematical objects are difficult to store scalably because of their rich and diverse structure. Usually, we have to focus on one aspect of mathematical objects in order to obtain representation languages that are simple enough to allow for maintenance in a scalable database. This is especially the case if we want to apply highly optimized general purpose technology like relational databases.

Mathematical data can be roughly separated into four main kinds.

1. *Symbolic data* focuses on formal expressions such as formulas, proofs, or programs. These are written in highly-structured formal languages with custom search and library management facilities.
2. *Narrative data* mixes natural language and formulas, which are usually presentation-oriented. These are written in, e.g., LATEX, published as PDF or HTML files, and queries with text or metadata-based engines.

© Springer Nature Switzerland AG 2019
C. Kaliszyk et al. (Eds.): CICM 2019, LNAI 11617, pp. 28–43, 2019.
https://doi.org/10.1007/978-3-030-23250-4_3

3. *Linked data* uses abstractions of mathematical objects that allow for optimized representations in knowledge graphs. These are stored in triple stores that allow for SPARQL-like querying.
4. Our interest here is on what we call **concrete data**, which encodes mathematical objects as simple data structures built from numbers, strings, lists, and records.

Mathematicians have constructed a wide variety of concrete datasets in terms of size, complexity, and domain. There is a vibrant and growing community of mathematicians that combine methods from experimental sciences with large scale computer support. An example of a prototypical experiment would be an algorithm that enumerates all objects of a certain kind (e.g., all finite groups up to order 2000), with measurements corresponding to computing properties (size, commutativity, normal subgroups, etc.) for each one.

While the objects themselves are typically abstract (e.g., an isomorphism class of finite groups) and involve hard-to-represent sets and functions, it is often possible to establish representation theorems that allow for unique characterization by a set of concrete properties. This allows storing even complex objects as simple data structures built from, e.g., integers, strings, lists, and records, which can be represented efficiently in standard relational databases. In the case of graphs, Brendan McKay supplies representation theorems and induced formats [McK] that are widely used to represent graphs as strings. This is typically done in combination with canonical labelings [BL83] to ensure that two graphs with different encodings are necessarily non-isomorphic. It is common to enumerate objects in order of increasing size and to let the algorithm run for as long as it scales, resulting in arbitrarily large datasets. It is not uncommon to e.g. encode the involved integers as strings because they are too big for the fixed width integer types of the underlying database.

Once the objects are stored in a database, they can be used for finding or refuting conjectures or simply as a reference table. One might want to ask questions like *"What are the Schläfli symbols of tight chiral polyhedra? or What regular polyhedra have a prime number of vertices"*. For complex hypothesis testing, the ideal solution would be an interface to a database from a computer algebra system or proof assistant system. This requires a non-trivial level of interoperability.

From the user perspective, looking up information about an object is most relevant when one does not have a lot of information about it. For example, it can be helpful to look up an object via some of its mathematical invariants. Another example is a search widget for the House of Graphs [Bri+13], which lets users draw the graph they are looking for.

State of the Art. We used a living survey of mathematical databases as a market analysis. The survey consists of a table of datasets and collections of datasets [Bera] and accompanying (unstructured) information [Berb]. At the time of writing, about a hundred datasets are recorded in about 50 table entries. The datasets range from small, with up to 100 objects, to large, with $\approx 17 \cdot 10^9$ objects. Similarly varied is the authorship: from one author producing several smaller datasets, to FindStat [Bsa14] with 69 contributors, LMFDB [LM] with 100 contributors, and the OEIS [OEIS] with thousands of contributors. Among these, the OEIS is the oldest and arguably most influential. It is notable for collecting not only mathematical objects but also symbolic data for their semantics, such as defining equations and generating functions. The most ambitious in scope in the LMFDB, a collection of mathematically related datasets that are conceptually tied together by Langland's program [Ber03].

Some databases like the OEIS and the LMFDB have become so important that substantial mathematical knowledge management (MKM) architecture has been developed for them. But most data sets are maintained in ad hoc systems such as text files with one entry per line or code that produces an array of objects for a computer algebra system. Less frequently, they are implemented as SQL databases or integrated with a computer algebra system such as SageMath, GAP, or Magma. There are multiple problems with this situation.

1. *Foundation/Documentation:* employed representation theorems can be difficult to find and apply, and there is usually no canonical representation.
2. *Database Encoding:* The data types typically available in the database cannot capture the richness of mathematical types. Thus, the original objects may be significantly different from their concrete encoding (e.g., a record of integers and booleans) that is stored in the database, and the database schema gives little information about the objects. Consequently, any query of the dataset requires not only understanding and reversing the database schema but also the possibly complex encoding.
3. *Silos:* Even if these are documented, any reuse of the dataset is tedious and error-prone in practice.

Thus, the current situation precludes developing MKM solutions that could provide, e.g., mathematical query languages (i.e., queries that abstract from the encoding), generic user interfaces, mathematical validation (e.g., type-checking relative to the mathematical types, not the database types), or cross-collection interlinking.

Vision/Goal. To host all of these services and tools, we envision a 'universal unified infrastructure for mathematical data: a – possibly federated – storage and hosting system with math-level APIs and UIs that makes the various collections findable, accessible, and interoperable, and re-usable (see [FAIR18] for a discussion). We want to establish such a system (MathDataHub) as part of the MathHub portal [MH].

Contribution. As a substantial step towards MathDataHub, we provide a high-level data description framework MDDL (Math Data Description Language), and a code generation system MBGen [MB]. Authors that describe their mathematical data collections in MDDL will be able to use MBGen to generate the necessary infrastructure extensions in MathDataHub, which can then host the data sets.

An MDDL schema consists of a set of property names with their mathematical types as well their concrete encodings in terms of low-level database types. This allows building user interface, validation, and querying tools that completely abstract from the encoding and the technicalities of the database system. The schemata are written as MMT theories, which allows for concise formalizations of mathematical types.

The automated database setup process will be of benefit to *authors* of mathematical datasets by giving them better out-of-the-box tools and by making it easier to make more datasets available. In the long run, *users* of mathematical datasets will benefit from standardized interfaces and cross-database sharing and linking. Similarly, the community as a whole will benefit from novel methods such as machine learning applied to mathematical datasets or connecting areas by observing similarities between data from different areas.

Related Work. The LMFDB collection of datasets enables authors to add their own datasets, cross-reference to existing datasets, and use a set of mature generic tools and a web-based user interface for accessing and searching their dataset. But it is limited to a specific topic, and does not systematically organize database schemata and encodings.

The House of Graphs portal is a home to a "searchable database of interesting graphs" as well as a repository, to which users can contribute their own datasets. Like the LMFDB, it is limited to a specific topic.

Some generic services exist for hosting research data, including systems like RADAR, publishers (Springer, albeit with a size limit), and EU-level infrastructures such as EUDAT and EOSC. But these have not been used extensively by mathematicians, partially due to a lack of awareness and a lack of added value they provide. Similarly unused go tools for managing and browsing general databases. These tend to be rich in features that are not useful from the perspective of mathematical datasets and have an initially steep learning curve, without features useful for mathematics at the end of it. We are somewhat surprised that even the simpler tools (based on the light-weight SQLite database, such as sqliteonline.com) appear to not be used much or at all – see [Bera].

The OpenDreamKit project developed the concepts of mathematical schemata and codecs that allow for systematically specifying the mathematical types in a dataset and their encodings [WKR17]. This provided the starting point for the present paper. These schemata and codecs used encodings as untyped JSON objects, and we had to extend them significantly for the present SQL-based approach.

The code generation system produces code for what is essentially an instance of a DiscreteZOO website. The DiscreteZOO project [BV18] itself is composed of a data repository, a website and a SageMath package. All three were developed for the use case of collections of graphs with a high degree of symmetry, but designed to be useful in a more general setting.

The MDDL Value Proposition. Given a standard set of MDDL schemata and codecs for basic mathematical objects, authors mainly need to specify the construction of objects at the mathematical level. Arguably the mathematical level of description – though formal and detailed itself – is nearer to mathematical practice and to the computational systems used to generate the data set than database schemata. In particular, the pay-off of a MDDL specification is higher than from a database schema as the APIs and UIs, that would have to be written manually, are generated by MBGen. This difference becomes more pronounced as the mathematical objects become more complex and thus the differences between the mathematical and database structures grow.

Our work was partially motivated by a collaboration with the LMFDB community. The LMFDB system was based on a JSON database, where the use of schemata was optional. As a consequence, the mathematical meaning of the fields was often unclear to all but a few experts, creating severe FAIRness problems. These problems have since partially been resolved by a community-wide database schema/math documentation effort, which can be seen as an informal, human-oriented version of MDDL.

Overview. In Sect. 2, we define our notion of a mathematical schema. In Sect. 3, we describe how to build a database instance from a set of schemata and show the user interface that we generate for the database. Section 4 concludes the paper and discusses future work.

Running Example. We use the following – intentionally simple – scenario and dataset: Joe has collected a set of integer matrices together with their trace, eigenvalues, and the Boolean property whether they are orthogonal for his Ph.D. thesis. As he wants to extend, persist, and publicize this data set, he develops a MDDL description and submits it to MathDataHub. Jane, a collaborator of Joe's, sees his MathDataHub data set and is also interested in integer matrices, in particular their characteristic polynomials. To leverage and extend Joe's data set, she provides MDDL descriptions of her extension and further extends the MathDataHub matrix data infrastructure. Table 1 gives an overview of the situation.

Table 1. Running Example: Joe's and Jane's matrix datasets

Joe's dataset				Jane's column
M	$\mathrm{Tr}(M)$	Orthogonal	σ_M	$\det(\lambda I - M)$
$\begin{pmatrix} 2 & 0 \\ 0 & 1 \end{pmatrix}$	2	yes	2, 1	$\lambda^2 - 3\lambda + 2$
$\begin{pmatrix} 2 & 1 \\ 1 & 2 \end{pmatrix}$	4	no	3, 1	$\lambda^2 - 4\lambda + 3$
$\begin{pmatrix} -1 & 0 \\ 0 & 1 \end{pmatrix}$	0	yes	1, -1	$\lambda^2 - 1$

2   Defining Schema Theories

In this section, we give an overview of MDDL, the description language for datasets. Concretely, MDDL consists of a modular collection of MMT theories describing the mathematical and database types of a data set to be supported by the system, as well as the codecs that map between them. As such, MDDL forms a nucleus of a common vocabulary for typical mathematical datatypes. These can and should eventually be linked to representation standards in other domains. For mathematical data sets, the math-specific aspects attacked by our work are the dominant factor.

We avoid a formal introduction of MMT and refer to [Rab17,RK13] for details. For our purposes, only a small fragment of the language is needed and it is more appropriate to didactically introduce it by example.

Essentially, an MMT theory is a list of declarations $c : A$, where c is a name and A is the type of c. Additionally, an MMT theory T may have a *meta-theory* M. The basic idea is that M defines the language in which the expressions in T are written and the typing rules that determine which expressions are well-typed.

In our setup, there are three levels: The mathematical domain level and two meta-levels; see the diagram on the right.

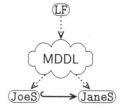

1. the database schemata are the main theories of interest, here the MDDL specifications JoeS and JaneS
   provided by Joe and Jane.
2. their meta-theory is a collection of theories that
   define
     – a selection of typical mathematical datatypes
     – codecs for these datatypes to database types
3. the meta-theory of the MDDL theories is a variant of
   the logical framework LF.

LF already exists in MMT, whereas the MDDL theories were written specifically for our system. The schema theories are intended to be written by users
for their respective databases or datasets. In essence, a schema theory defines
one typed constant $c : A$ per database column and chooses the codec to use for
that column. Table 2 gives an overview. The user describes the mathematical
concepts relevant for the datasets (the first column) in the corresponding MMT
language (second column). The MBGen system produces the database schema
(third column) as well as a website interface for it.

Table 2. Overview of concepts involved in schema theories

Mathematics	MMT	DB
Sets of objects of the same type T	Theory of T	Table
Object property c of type A	Constant $c : A$ and choice of codec for A	Column
Object	Model of theory	Row

In principle, MDDL could be written as a single theory once and for all. But
in practice, it is important to make it user-extensible: as any mathematical type
could occur in a database, MDDL will never be finished. Thus we employ a user-
extensible theory graph, user schema theories can then import what they need.
More precisely, the meta-theory of a schema theory must be some MMT theory
that extends MDDL. In the long run, we expect MDDL to grow into a large,

central, and continually growing theory graph that maximizes the integration potential for users to exchange data across databases and computation systems. For this paper however, it is more instructive to use a small self-contained theory that allows describing the functionality in depth.

MDDL consists of multiple parts that we describe in the sequel:

- the mathematical types (theory `MathData`)
- the database types (`DbData`)
- the codecs translating between them (`Codecs`).

Along the way, we develop the schema theory for our running example. All of these are available online at [ST].

Example 1 (Joe's simplified schema theory).
Joe writes a schema theory `MatrixS` for matrix data using MDDL as the meta-theory – see the listing on the right. For a start, he just writes down the names of the columns and their types. Each declaration in the theory corresponds to one of the columns in Table 1: its name and type.

```
theory MatrixS: ?MDDL =
  ID: ℤ
  mat: matrix ℤ 2 2
  trace : ℤ
  orthogonal : bool
  eigenvalues : list  ℤ
```

We will show the finished schema theory with codecs for Joe's dataset in Example 2.

2.1 Mathematical Types and Operations

The theory `MathData` (see Listings 1.1 to 1.2) defines the mathematical types that we provide for building objects. These are unlimited in principle except that a mathematical type is only usable if at least one codec for it is available. Therefore, we only present a small representative set of examples.

It is important to understand that `MathData` is *not* a symbolic library of formalized or implemented mathematics in the style of proof assistants or computer algebra systems. There are three big differences, all of which make `MathData` much simpler:

1. We do not fix a logic or programming language as the foundation of the library. Foundational questions are almost entirely irrelevant for mathematical database schemata. `MathData` should be related to foundational libraries, but this is not a primary concern.
2. We do not include any axioms or theorems and proofs. It is reasonable to include some of those at a later stage, especially when increasingly complex types are used. Currently, their only purpose would be documentation – no system component performs any reasoning.
3. We do not define any of the types or operations. Formal definitions are irrelevant because they would never be applied anyway: all computation happens in the database.

Incidentally, because we do not use proofs or definitions, it is much easier to avoid fixing a foundation: most foundational complexity, e.g., induction, is not needed at all.

For similar reasons, it is neither necessary nor helpful to describe many operations on these types. Firstly, practical schema theories make little to no use of dependent types. Therefore, operations usually do not occur in schema theories, which only have to declare types. Secondly, practical datasets store primarily concrete data, where all operations have already been computed—irreducible symbolic expressions usually are not stored in the first place.

The only reasons why we declare any operations are (i) to have constructors to build concrete objects, e.g., *nil* and *cons* for lists, (ii) to use operations in queries to the extent that we can map them to corresponding database operations.

Literals. We start with types for literals: Booleans, integers, strings, and UUIDs. The latter have no mathematical meaning but are often needed to uniquely identify objects in datasets.

For each literal type, we provide the usual basic operations such as addition of integers.

Listing 1.1. Literals from MathData

```
bool : type
int  : type   # ℤ
eq   : {a: type} a → a → bool  # 2 = 3
leq  : ℤ → ℤ → bool  # 1 ≤2
geq  : ℤ → ℤ → bool  # 1 ≥2
string : type
uuid: type
```

Collection Types. We define a few standard collection types: *List A*, *Vector A n*, and *Option A* are the usual types of arbitrary-length finite lists, fixed-length lists, and options containing objects of type *A*. We abbreviate matrices as vectors of vectors.

Listing 1.2. An excerpt from the MathData theory: collections

```
vector  : type → ℤ → type
    # vector 1 2 prec 10
empty : {a} vector a 0
single  : {a} a → vector a 1
matrix : type → ℤ → ℤ → type
    = [a,m,n] vector (vector a m) n
option : type → type
some : {a} a → option a
none : {a} option a
getOrElse : {a} option a → a → a
```

Algebraic Structures. MMT theories can be naturally used to define types of algebraic structures such as groups, rings, etc. [MRK18]. Any such theory is immediately available as a type.

Algebraic structures are difficult because they are complex, deeply structured objects. We omit the details here completely and only sketch a type of rings, which we need to build the type of polynomials.

2.2   Database Types and Operations

The theory DbData describes the most important types and operations provided by the target database, in our case PostgreSQL. This theory is fixed by PostgreSQL. However, we allow it to be extensible because PostgreSQL allows adding user-defined functions. That can be helpful to supply operations on encoded objects that match mathematical operations.

Listing 1.3. The DbData theory (simplified)

```
theory DbData : ur:?PLF =
  db_tp   : type ▌
  db_val  : db_tp → type ▕ # V 1 prec −5 ▌
  db_null : {a} V a ▌
  db_int , db_bool, db_string , db_uuid  : db_tp ▌
  db_array : db_tp → db_tp ▌
  eq   : {a} V a → V a → V db_bool ▕# 1 = 2 ▌ ...
▌
```

The types of DbData are signed 64 bit integers, double precision floating-point numbers, booleans, strings, and UUIDs as well as the null-value and (multidimensional) arrays of the above. The native PostgreSQL operations include the usual basic operations like Boolean operations and object comparisons.

2.3   Codecs: Encoding and Decoding Mathematical Objects

Overview. The theory Codecs specifies encodings that can be used to translate between mathematical and database types. A **codec** consists of

- a mathematical type A, i.e., an expression in the theory MathData,
- a database type a, i.e., an expression in the theory DbData,
- partial functions that translate back and forth between MathData-expressions of type A and DbData-expressions of type a.

Obviously, decoding (from database type to mathematical type) is a partial function—for example, an encoding of integers as decimal-notation strings is not surjective. But encoding must be a partial function, too, because only *values* and not arbitrary expressions of type A can be encoded. For example, for integers, only the literals $0, 1, −1, \ldots$ can be encoded but not symbolic expressions like $1 + 1$, let alone open expressions like $1 + x$. We do not define in general what a value is. Instead, every encoding function is partial, and we call *values* simply those expressions for which the encoding is defined.

Neither encoding nor decoding have to be injective. For example, a codec that encodes rational numbers as pairs of integer numerator and denominator might maximally cancel the fraction both during encoding and decoding. We also allow that provably equal expressions are encoded as different codes. That may be necessary for types with undecidable equality such as algebraic numbers. Similarly, we do not require that encoding *enc* and decoding *dec* are inverse functions. The only requirement we make on codecs is that for every expression e for which $enc(e)$ is defined, we have that $dec(enc(e))$ is defined and provably equal to e.

Like in [WKR17], we only *declare* but do not *implement* the codecs in MMT. It is possible in principle and desirable in the long run to implement the codecs in an soundness-guaranteeing system like a proof assistant and then generate codec implementations for various programming languages. But practical mathematical datasets for which our technology is intended often use highly optimized ad hoc encodings, where formal verification would make the project unnecessarily difficult early on. Instead, at this point we are content with a formal specification of the codec properties.

Contrary to [WKR17], we work with a *typed* database, which requires codecs to carry their database type a. Thus, we had to redevelop the notion of codecs completely.

An Initial Codec Library. We only provide a representative set of codec examples here. For each literal type, we define an identity codec that encodes literals as themselves. In the case of integers, encoding is only defined for small enough integers. For large integers, we provide a simple codec that encodes integers using strings in decimal notation.

Apart from their intended semantics as codecs, the codec expressions are normal typed MMT expressions and therefore subject to binding and type-checking. For example, *ListAsArray* is a codec operator of type

$$\Pi A : \mathsf{type}, a : db\_tp.\, codec\, A\, a \longrightarrow codec\,(list\, A)\,(db\_array\, a)$$

It takes a codec that encodes list elements of type A as database type a and returns a codec that encodes lists of type *list A* as database arrays of type *db_array a*. Similarly, we provide codec operators for all collection types.

There can be multiple codecs for the same mathematical type. The most well-known practical example where that matters is the choice between sparse and dense encodings of lists and related types such as univariate polynomials, matrices and graphs. But even basic types can have surprisingly many codecs as we have seen for integers above. For example, in the LMFDB collection, we found at least 3 different encodings of integers: the encoding is not obvious if integers are bigger than the bounded integers provided by the database.

In practice, we expect users to declare additional codecs themselves. This holds true especially when capturing legacy databases in our framework, where the existing data implicitly describes an ad-hoc encoding.

Choosing Codecs in Schema Theories. Every column (constant) $c : A$ in a schema theory must carry a codec. This must be an expression $C : codec\, A\, a$ for some database type a.

Because the choice C of codec has no mathematical meaning, we do not make it part of the type of c. Thus, A is always just the mathematical type. Instead, we use MMT's metadata feature to attach C. Any MMT declaration can carry metadata, which is essentially a key-value list, where the key is an MMT identifier and the value an MMT expression.

We use the constant *codec* as the key and the codec C as the value. The resulting concrete syntax then becomes $c : A$ *meta codec C*.

Example 2. Joe now adds codecs to his theory from Example 1 via metadata annotations as described above. Note that Joe does not need to add any new codecs, since MDDL already includes everything he needs. He also adds metadata `tag` annotations to specify databases schema and interface aspects. We will go into those in the next section.

Listing 1.4. Joe's schema theory with codecs

```
theory MatrixS : ?MDDL =
    mat: matrix ℤ 2 2 │ meta ?Codecs?codec MatrixAsArray IntIdent
        tag ?MDDL?opaque ▌
    trace : ℤ │meta ?Codecs?codec IntIdent ▌
    orthogonal: bool │ meta ?Codecs?codec BoolIdent ▌
    eigenvalues : list ℤ │meta ?Codecs?codec ListAsArray IntIdent
        tag ?MDDL?opaque ▌
▌
```

3   Database and Interface Generation

Given the MDDL framework presented above, the MBGen generator is rather
straightforward. It uses the Slick library [Slk] for functional/relational mapping
in Scala to abstract from the concrete database – we use Postgres SQL. MBGen
creates the following Slick data model and uses it to create the actual database:
For every schema theory T, MBGen generates a SQL table. The table name is
the theory name, and it has a primary key called ID[1] of type UUID. For each
declaration s in T, it generates a column, whose type is obtained from the codec
declaration.

Example 3. When Joe runs MBGen on his schema
theory from Listing 1.4, he obtains the database
schema on the right. He can directly upload his
data using the corresponding SQL INSERT statements, see the table below. Alternatively, he can
use the math-level API provided by MBGen and
specify the data at the mathematical level, i.e. as
MMT declarations.

```
   Column      |    Type
---------------+----------
ID             | uuid
MAT            | integer[]
TRACE          | integer
ORTHOGONAL     | boolean
EIGENVALUES    | integer[]
Indexes: "MatrixS_pkey"
PRIMARY KEY, btree ("ID")
```

```
        ID         |    mat     | trace | orthogonal | eigenvalues
-------------------+------------+-------+------------+-------------
e278b5e8-4404-...  | {2,0,0,1}  |   2 | t          | {2,1}
05a30ff0-4405-...  | {2,1,1,2}  |   4 | f          | {3,1}
1be3f022-4405-...  | {-1,0,0,1} |   0 | t          | {1,-1}
```

Example 4 (Jane's extension). Jane specifies her dataset via a schema theory in
Fig. 1. She includes Joe's schema theory MatrixS and references the primary key
of the corresponding database table as a foreign key. Jane has a slightly harder
time importing her data set: she needs to obtain the the ID of the respective
matrices. Fortunately, this is only an easy SQL query away, since she is using
the same matrix encoding (Table 3).

In addition to the codec, the user can provide further information about the
dataset, so that the system can produce a better user interface.

---

[1] The data set might already have a pre-existing ID-like field, which is not a UUID. In
this case we need to add a declaration for a custom index key.

```
theory MatrixWithCharacteristicS  :  ?SchemaLang =
   include  ?MatrixS ▌
   matrixID: int  │  meta ?SchemaLang?foreignKey ?MatrixS ▌
   characteristic  :  Polynomial IntegerRing │
       meta ?Codecs?codec PolynomialAsSparseArray IntIdent ▌
▌
```

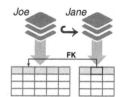

Fig. 1. Jane's extensions for matrices with characteristic polynomial

Table 3. Metadata tags

`Collection`	Collection metadata, e.g. provenance data
`Display`	Display name in the list of filters and in the results table head
`Hidden`	By default, hide in the results display
`Opaque`	Do not use for filtering

The tag `hidden` can be used when a dataset has many columns (like the graph datasets in DiscreteZOO). If there are hidden columns, the interface shows an additional widget, which lets a visitor choose which columns they want to see. If the tag `display` is not present, the column name is used for display. The tags particularly relevant for the interface the metadata tags and the tags `hidden` and `opaque`.

DiscreteZOO was already designed to work for general datasets. For the needs of MBGen, we further simplified the setup to the point where all dataset-specific information is contained in JSON files and can be hot-swapped. We also rewrote the frontend in React.JS for better performance and eventual integration into the React.JS-based MathHub front-end. The DiscreteZOO website interface was described in [BV18].

	mat	trace	orthogonal	eigenvalues
MathDataHub	orthogonal ⑦	✎	trace ⑦	
Display results	Matches found: 2			
	[[2,0],[2,0]]	2	true	2,1
	[[-1,0],[-1,0]]	0	true	1,-1

Fig. 2. Screenshot of the website for Joe and Jane's use case

Evaluation: Mirroring Existing Databases. To evaluate the setup, we have integrated the datasets currently hosted on the DiscreteZOO website in Math-DataHub using the workflows described above. They are simpler than the much smaller running example: they only contain Boolean and integer valued properties and the objects are string-encoded. All the schema theories are available online [ST] in the folder source. The website stack obtained from these theories is equivalent to the original DiscreteZOO website. The links to the websites generated for the demos are available at the project wiki [MB] (Fig. 2).

This exercise shows that an author of a dataset with uncomplicated columns and no new codecs can start from an existing schema theory and adapt it to their needs in under an hour—essentially all that is required is to change the names of the columns.

4   Conclusion and Future Work

We have presented a high-level description language MDDL for mathematical data collections. MDDL combines storage aspects with mathematical aspects and relates them via an extensible collection of codecs. Dataset authors can specify schema aspects of their data sets and use the MBGen tool to generate or extend database tables and create customized user interfaces and universal mathematics-level APIs and thus tool stacks.

We have developed the framework and system to a state, where it already provides benefits to authors of smaller or simpler datasets, particularly students. The next step will be to stabilize and scale the MBGen system, fully integrate it into the MathHub system, and establish a public data infrastructure to the mathematical community. We will now discuss some aspects of future work.

Mirroring Existing Datasets. Eventually, we hope that the system could be a useful mirror for the larger mathematical databases such as the FindStat, House of Graphs, LMFDB, and OEIS[2]. This would make (a significant subset) of the data available under a common, unified user interface, provide integrated, cross-library APIs and services like math-level search, and could bring out cross-library relations that were difficult to detect due to system borders. On the other hand, existing datasets act as goalposts for which features are needed most and thus drive MathDataHub development. Seeing which datasets can get realized in the system also serves as a measure of success.

A core library of codecs and support for common data types would lower the joining costs for MathDataHub by making MDDL schema theories straightforward to write.

Query Encoding. In the online version of MathData, we also already specify commutativity conditions, which we omit here. Their purpose will be to specify

---

[2] We can only hope to duplicate the generic parts of the user interface. Websites like the these four major mathematical database provide a lot of customized mathematical user functionality, which we cannot hope to reproduce generically.

when codecs are homomorphisms, i.e., when operations on mathematical values are correctly implemented by database operations on the encoded values. This will allow writing queries in user-friendly mathematical language, which are automatically translated to efficient executable queries in database language while guaranteeing correctness.

Extending the Data Model, User interface, and Query Languages by Provenance. The MathDataHub system should provide a general model for data provenance, and propagate this to the UI and query levels. Provenance is an often-overlooked aspect of mathematical data, which can apply to data sets (like Joe's) single properties (e.g. Jane's characteristic polynomials), or even a single datum (e.g. the proof that the Monster group is simple). Provenance is the moral equivalent to proofs in pure mathematics, but is rarely recorded. It seems that the only chance to do this is by supporting this at the system level.

MathHub/MitM Integration. The schema theories rely on the representations of mathematical objects via their "mathematical types". These are supplied e.g. by the Math-in-the-Middle (MitM) Ontology or theorem prover libraries hosted on MathHub. Using these would make specifying MDDL schema theories even simpler, and would allow the MathDataHub UI to give access the mathematical definitions of the column values – e.g. by hovering over a name to get a definition in a tooltip.

Interoperability with Computer Algebra Systems. Most mathematical data sets are computed and used in computer algebra systems. We have used the MitM framework [Koh+17] for distributed computation with the virtual theories underlying the MDDL framework [WKR17]. This needs to be reinstated for MathDataHub and scaled to the systems uses by the MathDataHub data sets.

Exploit MMT *Modularity.* MDDL is based on MMT, and we have already seen that MMT inclusions can directly be used to specify connected tables. We conjecture that MMT views correspond to database views; and would like to study how this can be exploited in the MDDL framework.

A Flexible Caching/Re-Computation Regime. Instead of storing data, we can compute them on demand; similarly, computation can be done once and the data stored for later use. The better option comes down to the trade-off between computing and storage costs. This trade-off depends on hardware power and costs on one hand and community size and usage patterns on the other. It is generally preferable to perform computation "near" where the data is stored.

Mathematical Query Languages. We have seen that the MDDL framework allows to directly derive a query interface for MathDataHub and note that this is inherently cross-dataset – a novel feature afforded by the modularity MDDL inherits from MMT. We conjecture that the framework allows the development of mathematical query languages – using e.g. [Rab12] as a starting point. The main research question is how to push computation to the database level (as opposed to the database model or the web client). The PostgreSQL database supports extensions by stored procedures. This would be one option for implementing additional filters for the website, such as enabling the condition "is prime" on integers. The stored procedures could also be used as a method for implementing "virtual columns", or columns that are computed, rather than stored.

Acknowledgements. The authors gratefully acknowledge helpful discussions with Tom Wiesing on MathHub integration and virtual theories. Discussions with Gabe Cunningham on concrete examples of questions a researcher might have and descriptions of tools that would help them helped shape our intuitions. The work presented here was supported by EU grant Horizon 2020 ERI 676541 OpenDreamKit.

References

[Bera] Berčič, K.: Math databases table. https://mathdb.mathhub.info/. Accessed 15 Jan 2019

[Berb] Berčič, K.: Math databases wiki. https://github.com/MathHubInfo/Documentation/wiki/Math-Databases. Accessed 15 Jan 2019

[Ber03] Gelbart, S., Bernstein, J. (eds.): An Introduction to the Langlands Program. Birkhäuser, Basel (2003). ISBN: 3-7643-3211-5

[BL83] Babai, L., Luks, E.M.: Canonical labeling of graphs. In: Proceedings of the Fifteenth Annual ACM Symposium on Theory of Computing, STOC 1983, pp. 171–183. ACM, New York (1983). https://doi.org/10.1145/800061.808746. ISBN: 0-89791-099-0

[Bri+13] Brinkmann, G., et al.: House of graphs: a database of interesting graphs. Discrete Appl. Math. **161**(1–2), 311–314 (2013). https://doi.org/10.1016/j.dam.2012.07.018. ISSN: 0166–218X

[Bsa14] Berg, C., Stump, C., et al.: FindStat: the combinatorial statistic finder (2014). http://www.FindStat.org. Accessed 31 Aug 2016

[BV18] Berčič, K., Vidali, J.: DiscreteZOO: a fingerprint database of discrete objects (2018). arXiv:1812.05921

[FAIR18] European Commission Expert Group on FAIR Data: Turning FAIR into reality (2018). https://doi.org/10.2777/1524

[Koh+17] Kohlhase, M., et al.: Knowledge-based interoperability for mathematical software systems. In: Blömer, J., Kotsireas, I.S., Kutsia, T., Simos, D.E. (eds.) MACIS 2017. LNCS, vol. 10693, pp. 195–210. Springer, Cham (2017). https://doi.org/10.1007/978-3-319-72453-9_14

[LM] The L-functions and modular forms database. http://www.lmfdb.org. Accessed 02 Jan 2016

[MB] MBGen description, links demos and code repositories. https://github.com/MathHubInfo/Documentation/wiki/MBGen. Accessed 05 Mar 2019

[McK] McKay, B.: Description of graph6, sparse6 and digraph6 encodings. http://users.cecs.anu.edu.au/~bdm/data/formats.txt

[MH] MathHub.info: Active mathematics. http://mathhub.info. Accessed 28 Jan 2014

[MRK18] Müller, D., Rabe, F., Kohlhase, M.: Theories as types. In: Galmiche, D., Schulz, S., Sebastiani, R. (eds.) IJCAR 2018. LNCS (LNAI), vol. 10900, pp. 575–590. Springer, Cham (2018). https://doi.org/10.1007/978-3-319-94205-6_38

[OEIS] The on-line encyclopedia of integer sequences. http://oeis.org. Accessed 28 May 2017

[Rab12] Rabe, F.: A query language for formal mathematical libraries. In: Jeur-
         ing, J., et al. (eds.) CICM 2012. LNCS (LNAI), vol. 7362, pp. 143–
         158. Springer, Heidelberg (2012). https://doi.org/10.1007/978-3-642-31374-
         5_10. arXiv: 1204.4685. ISBN: 978-3-642-31373-8
[Rab17] Rabe, F.: How to identify, translate, and combine logics? J. Logic Comput.
         27(6), 1753–1798 (2017)
 [RK13] Rabe, F., Kohlhase, M.: A scalable module system. Inf. Comput. **230**(1),
         1–54 (2013)
  [Slk] Slick, functional relational mapping for scala. http://slick.lightbend.com/.
         Accessed 16 Mar 2019
   [ST] Rabe, F., Berčič, K.: Schema theories repository for the prototyper. https://
         gl.mathhub.info/ODK/discretezoo. Accessed 14 Mar 2019
[WKR17] Wiesing, T., Kohlhase, M., Rabe, F.: Virtual theories – a uniform interface
         to mathematical knowledge bases. In: Blömer, J., Kotsireas, I.S., Kutsia, T.,
         Simos, D.E. (eds.) MACIS 2017. LNCS, vol. 10693, pp. 243–257. Springer,
         Cham (2017). https://doi.org/10.1007/978-3-319-72453-9_17

A Tale of Two Set Theories

Chad E. Brown[1] and Karol Pąk[2]([⊠]) [iD]

[1] Czech Technical University in Prague, Prague, Czech Republic
[2] University of Białystok, Bialystok, Poland
pakkarol@uwb.edu.pl

Abstract. We describe the relationship between two versions of Tarski-Grothendieck set theory: the first-order set theory of Mizar and the higher-order set theory of Egal. We show how certain higher-order terms and propositions in Egal have equivalent first-order presentations. We then prove Tarski's Axiom A (an axiom in Mizar) in Egal and construct a Grothendieck Universe operator (a primitive with axioms in Egal) in Mizar.

Keywords: Formalized mathematics · Theorem proving · Set theory · Proof checking · Mizar

1 Introduction

We compare two implemented versions of Tarski-Grothendieck (TG) set theory. The first is the first-order TG implemented in Mizar [3,15] axiomatized using Tarski's Axiom A [24,25]. The other is the higher-order TG implemented in Egal [7] axiomatized using Grothendieck universes [17]. We discuss what would be involved porting Mizar developments into Egal and vice versa.

We use Egal's Grothendieck universes (along with a choice operator) to prove Tarski's Axiom A in Egal. Consequently the Egal counterpart of each of Mizar's axioms is provable in Egal and so porting from Mizar to Egal should always be possible in principle. In practice one would need to make Mizar's implicit reasoning using its type system explicit, a nontrivial task outside the scope of this paper.

Porting from Egal to Mizar poses two challenges. One is that many definitions and propositions in Egal make use of higher-order quantifiers. In order to give a Mizar counterpart, it is enough to give a first-order reformulation and prove the two formulations equivalent in Egal. While this will not always be possible in principle, it has been possible for the examples necessary for this paper. The second challenge is to construct a Grothendieck universe operator in Mizar that satisfies the properties of a corresponding operator in Egal. We have constructed such an operator.

We give a brief introduction to Mizar and its version of first-order Tarski-Grothendieck in Sect. 2. In Sect. 3 we introduce the new system Egal and describe its version of higher-order Tarski-Grothendieck. In Sect. 4 we give a few examples

© Springer Nature Switzerland AG 2019
C. Kaliszyk et al. (Eds.): CICM 2019, LNAI 11617, pp. 44–60, 2019.
https://doi.org/10.1007/978-3-030-23250-4_4

of definitions and propositions in Egal that can be reformulated in equivalent first-order forms. These first-order versions have counterparts in Mizar. Section 5 discusses the Egal proof of Tarski's Axiom A. In Sect. 6 we discuss the construction of a Grothendieck universe operator in Mizar.[1] Possibilities for future work are discussed in Sect. 7.

2   Mizar and FOTG

The Mizar system [16] from its beginning aimed to create a proof style that simultaneously imitates informal mathematical proofs as much as possible and can be automatically verified to be logically correct. A quite simple and intuitive reasoning formalism and an intuitive soft type system play a major role in the pursuit of Mizar's goals.

The Mizar proof style is mainly inspired by Jaśkowski [18] style of natural deduction and most statements correspond to valid first-order predicate calculus formulas. Over time the Mizar community has also added support for syntax that goes beyond traditional first-order terms and formulas. In particular, Mizar supports **schemes** with predicate and function variables, sufficient to formulate the Fraenkel replacement as one axiom in Mizar. This axiom is sufficient to construct the set comprehension $\{Fx|x \in X, Px\}$ (called *Fraenkel terms*) for a given set X, function F and predicate P in the Mizar language but it is impossible to define such a functor for arbitrary X, F, P. Therefore, in response to the needs of Mizar's users, support for Fraenkel terms has been built into the system. In fact Mizar supports a generalized notation where the set membership relation $x \in X$ in the Fraenkel term has been replaced by the type membership $x : \Theta$ if the Mizar type Θ has the **sethood** property. A Mizar type has the **sethood** property if the collection of all objects of the type forms a set (as opposed to a class). Semantically, Mizar types are simply unary first-order predicates over sets that can be parameterized by sets. However, the type inference mechanisms make Mizar significantly more powerful and user-friendly. The rules available for automatic type inference are influenced by the author of a given script by choosing the **environ** (i.e., environment, see [15]). By skillfully choosing the environment, an author can make a Mizar article more concise and readable since the type system will handle many inferences implicitly. Mizar types must be inhabited and this obligation must be proven by a user directly in the definition of a given type or before the first use if a type has the form of intersection of types.

Parallel to the system development, the Mizar community puts a significant effort into building the Mizar Mathematical Library (MML) [4]. The MML is the comprehensive repository of currently formalized mathematics in the Mizar system. The foundation of the library, up to some details discussed below, is first-order Tarski-Grothendieck set theory (FOTG). This is a non-conservative extension of Zermelo–Fraenkel set theory (ZFC), where the axiom of infinity has

---

[1] At http://grid01.ciirc.cvut.cz/~chad/twosettheories.tgz one can find Egal, the Egal formalization files and the Mizar formalization files.

been replaced by Tarski's Axiom A. Axiom A states that for every set N there is a Tarski universe M such that $N \in M$. A Tarski universe is essentially a set closed under subsets and power sets with the property that every subset of the universe is either a member of the universe or equipotent with the universe. The statement of Axiom A in Mizar is shown in Fig. 1.

```
reserve N,M,X,Y,Z for set;
theorem :: TARSKI_A:1
  ex M st N in M &
      (for X,Y holds X in M & Y c= X implies Y in M) &
      (for X st X in M ex Z st Z in M & for Y st Y c= X holds Y in Z) &
      (for X holds X c= M implies X,M are_equipotent or X in M);
```

Fig. 1. Tarski's Axiom A in Mizar

FOTG was not the only foundation considered for the library. One of the main reasons it was chosen is the usefulness of Axiom A in the formalization of category theory. Namely, FOTG provides many universes that have properties analogous to those of a class of all sets. In particular, every axiom of ZFC remains true if we relativize quantifiers to the given universe.

The axiom of choice can be proven in FOTG. In fact Axiom A was used to prove Zermelo's well-ordering theorem and the axiom of choice in an early MML article [2]. Later changes to Mizar also yielded the axiom of choice in a more direct way and we briefly describe the relevant changes.

While working with category theory in the Mizar system, new constructions called *permissive* definitions were introduced (implemented in Mizar-2 in the 80's [16]). Permissive definitions allow an author to make definitions under assumptions where these assumptions can be used to justify the obligations. For example, the type morphism of a,b can be defined under the assumption that there exists a morphism from a to b. Without the assumption the definition of morphism of a,b would not be allowed since the type would not be provably inhabited (see [19,20]).

In contrast to Fraenkel terms, permissive definitions do not have an obvious semantic justification in FOTG. For any type Θ of a,b,... (depending on objects $a, b, \ldots$) a permissive definition can be used to obtain a choice operator for the type in the following way:

```
definition
    let a,b,... such that C: contradiction;
    func choose(a,b,...) → Θ of a,b,... means contradiction;
    existence by C; uniqueness by C;
end;
```

The definition states that given objects $a, b, \ldots$ (of appropriate types), the function choose will return an object of type Θ of a,b,... satisfying the condition contradiction. The definition is made under the extra assumption contradiction and it is this extra assumption (from which everything can be proven) that guarantees existence and uniqueness of an object of type Θ of a,b,... satisfying the otherwise impossible condition. After the definition is made, Mizar allows the user to make use of the term choose(a,b,...) of type Θ of a,b,... even in non-contradictory contexts.

To avoid repetition of definitions like choose, in 2012, the Mizar syntax was extended by the *explicit* operator **the** (e.g., **the** Θ **of** a,b,...). This new operator behaves similarly to a Hilbert ε-operator, which corresponds to having a global choice operator on the universe of sets (cf. p. 72 of [13]). ZFC extended with a global choice operator is known to be conservative over ZFC [12]. The situation with FOTG is analogous to that of ZFC, and we conjecture FOTG extended with a global choice operator (**the**) is conservative over FOTG. Regardless of the truth of this conjecture, we take the proper foundation of the MML to be FOTG extended with a global choice operator (see [20]).

3   Egal and HOTG

Egal [7] is a proof checker for higher-order Tarski-Grothendieck (HOTG) set theory. Since this is the first publication describing Egal, we begin by placing the system in context and discussing various design decisions.

The idea of combining higher-order logic and set theory is not new [14,21,23]. However, many of the features of existing higher-order systems (e.g., the ability to define new type constructors such as $\alpha \times \beta$) should in principle no longer be needed if one is doing higher-order set theory. Instead the higher-order logic only needs to be expressive enough to bootstrap the set theory. Once enough set theory has been developed users would work with products of sets (instead of products of types). With this in mind, Egal begins with a "higher-order logic" restricted to a simple type theory mostly in the style of Church [10], extended with limited prefix polymorphism (discussed below).

Another motivation to use as restricted a form of higher-order logic as possible is to ensure Egal satisfies the de Bruijn criterion [5]: Egal proofs should be checkable by independent small proof checkers. For this reason Egal places an emphasis on proof terms and proof checking. Proof terms are λ-calculus terms corresponding to natural deduction proofs in the Curry-Howard sense. Egal proof scripts are presented in a way similar to Coq [6] and instruct Egal how to construct a proof term. Since the underlying logic is relatively simple and the additional set theory axioms are few, the portion of the code that does type checking and proof checking is reasonably short. Of course the Egal code consists of more than just a checker. For example, the code includes a parser allowing users to give terms using mathematical notation and variable names (instead of the de Bruijn indices used internally) as well as an interpreter for proof script steps. Nevertheless we claim Egal satisfies the de Bruijn criterion in the sense that a small independent checker could easily be written to take as input serialized versions of the internal representations of Egal types, terms and proof terms and check correctness of a sequence of definitions and proofs. The de

Bruijn criterion also provides a major point of contrast between Egal and Mizar, as constructing an independent checker for Mizar proofs would be nontrivial for several reasons (e.g., the soft typing system).

The kernel of the Egal system includes simply typed λ-calculus with a type of propositions along with a λ-calculus for proof terms. There is a base type of individuals ι (thought of as sets), a based type of propositions o and function types $\sigma \to \tau$. Egal also allows the use of type variables for some purposes (e.g., defining equality or giving axioms such as functional extensionality). To simplify the presentation, we will assume there are no type variables at first and then briefly describe how type variables are treated. Without extra axioms, the logic of Egal is intentional intuitionistic higher-order logic. On top of this logic we add constants and axioms that yield an extensional classical higher-order set theory.

To be precise let $\mathcal{T}$ be the set of types generated freely via the grammar $o|\iota|\sigma \to \tau$. We use σ, τ to range over types. For each $\sigma \in \mathcal{T}$ let $\mathcal{V}_\sigma$ be a countably infinite set of variables and assume $\mathcal{V}_\sigma \cap \mathcal{V}_\tau = \emptyset$ whenever $\sigma \neq \tau$. We use $x, y, z, X, Y, f, g, p, q, P, Q, \ldots$ to range over variables. For each $\sigma \in \mathcal{T}$ let $\mathcal{C}_\sigma$ be a set of constants. We use $c, c_1, c_2, \ldots$ to range over constants. We consider only a fixed family of constants given as follows:

- ε_σ is a constant in $\mathcal{C}_{(\sigma \to o) \to \sigma}$ for each type σ.
- In is a constant in $\mathcal{C}_{\iota \to \iota \to o}$.
- Empty is a constant in $\mathcal{C}_\iota$.
- Union is a constant in $\mathcal{C}_{\iota \to \iota}$.
- Power is a constant in $\mathcal{C}_{\iota \to \iota}$.
- Repl is a constant in $\mathcal{C}_{\iota \to (\iota \to \iota) \to \iota}$.
- UnivOf is a constant in $\mathcal{C}_{\iota \to \iota}$.

No other constants are allowed. We assume none of these constants are variables.

We next define a family $(\Lambda_\sigma)_{\sigma \in \mathcal{T}}$ of typed terms as follows. We use s, t and u to range over terms.

- If $x \in \mathcal{V}_\sigma$, then $x \in \Lambda_\sigma$.
- If $c \in \mathcal{C}_\sigma$, then $c \in \Lambda_\sigma$.
- If $s \in \Lambda_{\sigma \to \tau}$ and $t \in \Lambda_\sigma$, then $(st) \in \Lambda_\tau$.
- If $x \in \mathcal{V}_\sigma$ and $t \in \Lambda_\tau$, then $(\lambda x.t) \in \Lambda_{\sigma \to \tau}$.
- If $s \in \Lambda_o$ and $t \in \Lambda_o$, then $(s \Rightarrow t) \in \Lambda_o$.
- If $x \in \mathcal{V}_\sigma$ and $t \in \Lambda_o$, then $(\forall x.t) \in \Lambda_o$.

Each member of Λ_σ is a *term of type σ*. Terms of type o are also called *propositions*. We sometimes use φ, ψ and ξ to range over propositions. It is easy to see that Λ_σ and Λ_τ are disjoint for $\sigma \neq \tau$. That is, each term has at most one type.

We omit parentheses when possible, with application associating to the left and implication associating to the right: stu means $((st)u)$ and $\varphi \Rightarrow \psi \Rightarrow \xi$ means $(\varphi \Rightarrow (\psi \Rightarrow \xi))$. Binders are often combined: $\lambda xyz.s$ means $\lambda x.\lambda y.\lambda z.s$ and $\forall xyz.\varphi$ means $\forall x.\forall y.\forall z.\varphi$. To present the types of variables concisely, we sometimes annotate variables in binders with their types, as in $\lambda x : \sigma.s$ to assert $x \in \mathcal{V}_\sigma$. When the type of a variable is omitted entirely, it is ι.

Although the only logical connectives as part of the definition of terms are implication and universal quantification, it is well-known how to define the other connectives and quantifiers in a way that even works in an intuitionistic setting [8]. For this reason we freely write propositions $(\neg\varphi)$, $(\varphi \wedge \psi)$, $(\varphi \vee \psi)$, $(\varphi \Leftrightarrow \psi)$, $(\exists x.\varphi)$ and $(s = t)$ (for $s, t \in \Lambda_\sigma$). Again, we omit parentheses and use common binder abbreviations in obvious ways.

We also use special notations for terms built using the constants. We write $s \in t$ for $\text{In } s \; t$. We write $\forall x \in s.\varphi$ for $\forall x.x \in s \Rightarrow \varphi$ and $\exists x \in s.\varphi$ for $\exists x.x \in s \wedge \varphi$. We write $\varepsilon x : \sigma.\varphi$ for $\varepsilon_\sigma(\lambda x : \sigma.\varphi)$ and $\varepsilon x \in s.\varphi$ for $\varepsilon x.x \in s \wedge \varphi$. We also write $\emptyset$ for Empty, $\bigcup s$ for $\text{Union } s$, $\wp s$ for $\text{Power } s$, $\{s | x \in t\}$ for $\text{Repl } t \; (\lambda x.s)$ and $\mathcal{U}_s$ for $\text{UnivOf } s$.

In general new names can be introduced to abbreviate terms of a given type. In many cases we introduce new corresponding notations as well. The following abbreviations are used in the statements of the axioms below:

- TransSet $: \iota \to o$ is $\lambda U.\forall X \in U.X \subseteq U$. Informally we say U *is transitive* to mean TransSet U.
- Union_closed $: \iota \to o$ is $\lambda U.\forall X \in U.\bigcup X \in U$. Informally we say U *is $\bigcup$-closed* to mean Union_closed U.
- Power_closed $: \iota \to o$ is $\lambda U.\forall X \in U.\wp X \in U$. Informally we say U *is $\wp$-closed* to mean Power_closed U.
- Repl_closed $: \iota \to o$ is $\lambda U.\forall X \in U.\forall F : \iota \to \iota.(\forall x \in X.Fx \in U) \Rightarrow \{Fx | x \in X\} \in U$. Informally we say U *is closed under replacement* to mean Repl_closed U.
- ZF_closed $: \iota \to o$ is $\lambda U.\text{Union\_closed } U \wedge \text{Power\_closed } U \wedge \text{Repl\_closed } U$. Informally we say U *is ZF-closed* to mean ZF_closed U.

The deduction system for Egal includes a set $\mathcal{A}$ of closed propositions we call axioms. The specific members of the set $\mathcal{A}$ are as follows:

Prop. Ext. $\forall PQ : o.(P \Leftrightarrow Q) \Rightarrow P = Q$,
Func. Ext. $\forall fg : \sigma \to \tau.(\forall x : \sigma.fx = gx) \Rightarrow f = g$ (for types σ and τ),
Choice $\forall p : \sigma \to o.\forall x : \sigma.px \Rightarrow p(\varepsilon x : \sigma.px)$ (for each type σ),
Set Ext. $\forall XY.X \subseteq Y \Rightarrow Y \subseteq X \Rightarrow X = Y$,
$\in$-Induction $\forall P : \iota \to o.(\forall X.(\forall x \in X.Px) \Rightarrow PX) \Rightarrow \forall X.PX$,
Empty $\neg\exists x.x \in \emptyset$,
Union $\forall Xx.x \in \bigcup X \Leftrightarrow \exists Y.x \in Y \wedge Y \in X$,
Power $\forall XY.Y \in \wp X \Leftrightarrow Y \subseteq X$,
Replacement $\forall X.\forall F : \iota \to \iota.\forall y.y \in \{Fx | x \in X\} \Leftrightarrow \exists x \in X.y = Fx$,
Universe In $\forall N.N \in \mathcal{U}_N$,
Universe Transitive $\forall N.\text{TransSet } \mathcal{U}_N$,
Universe ZF closed $\forall N.\text{ZFclosed } \mathcal{U}_N$ and
Universe Min $\forall NU.N \in U \Rightarrow \text{TransSet } U \Rightarrow \text{ZFclosed } U \Rightarrow \mathcal{U}_N \subseteq U$.

The axiom set would be finite if it were not for functional extensionality and choice. In the implementation type variables are used to specify functional extensionality and choice. Again, we delay discussion of type variables for the moment.

The notions of free and bound variables are defined as usual, as is the notion of a variable x being free in a term s. We consider terms equal up to bound variable names. As usual there are notions of capture-avoiding substitution and we write s_t^x to be the result of subsituting t for x in s. We have the usual notions of β-conversion and η-conversion: $(\lambda x.s)t$ β-reduces to s_t^x and $(\lambda x.sx)$ η-reduces to s if x is not free in s. The relation $s \sim_{\beta\eta} t$ on terms $s, t \in \Lambda_\sigma$ is the least congruence relation closed under β-conversion and η-conversion.

The underlying deduction system for Egal is natural deduction with proof terms. We do not discuss proof terms here, but give the corresponding natural deduction calculus without proof terms in Fig. 2. The calculus defines when $\Gamma \vdash \varphi$ is derivable where Γ is a finite set of propositions and φ is a proposition.

$$\text{Ax } \frac{\varphi \in \mathcal{A}}{\Gamma \vdash \varphi} \qquad \text{Hyp } \frac{\varphi \in \Gamma}{\Gamma \vdash \varphi} \qquad \beta \, \frac{\Gamma \vdash \psi \quad \psi \sim_{\beta\eta} \varphi}{\Gamma \vdash \varphi} \qquad \Rightarrow\text{I } \frac{\Gamma \cup \{\varphi\} \vdash \psi}{\Gamma \vdash \varphi \Rightarrow \psi}$$

$$\Rightarrow\text{E } \frac{\Gamma \vdash \varphi \Rightarrow \psi \quad \Gamma \vdash \varphi}{\Gamma \vdash \psi} \qquad \forall\text{I } \frac{\Gamma \vdash \varphi_y^x \quad y \in \mathcal{V}_\sigma \text{ is not free in } \Gamma \cup \{\varphi\}}{\Gamma \vdash \forall x : \sigma.\varphi}$$

$$\forall\text{E } \frac{\Gamma \vdash \forall x : \sigma.\varphi \quad t \in \Lambda_\sigma}{\Gamma \vdash \varphi_t^x}$$

Fig. 2. Natural deduction system

We now briefly discuss the role of polymorphism in Egal. We have already seen examples where type variables would be useful. Instead of having infinitely many constants ε_σ in the implementation there is one constant ε which must be associated with a type when used. Likewise, the axioms of functional extensionality and choice make use of type variables and whenever these axioms are used the instantiations for these type variables must be given. Some definitions (such as equality, existential quantification and if-then-else) as well as some theorems (such as the existential introduction rule) also make use of type variables. From the beginning Egal was designed to discourage the use of type variables in the hope of eventually eliminating them. For this reason constants, definitions, axioms and theorems can use at most three type variables. To make this precise we have three fixed type variables ν_0, ν_1 and ν_2. For $n \in \{0, 1, 2, 3\}$ we have $\mathcal{T}^n$ as the set of types freely generated from $\nu_0 | \cdots | \nu_{n-1} | o | \iota | \sigma \to \tau$. Similarly we have four families of terms $(\Lambda_\sigma^n)_{\sigma \in \mathcal{T}^n}$ and four judgments $\Gamma \vdash_n \varphi$ where Γ is a finite subset of Λ_o^n and φ is in Λ_o^n. All definitions and theorems (with proofs) are given in some type context determined by $n \in \{0, 1, 2, 3\}$. The context remains fixed throughout the declaration. If $n > 0$, then when the definition or theorem is used later (in type context $m \in \{0, 1, 2, 3\}$) it must be given along with n (explicitly given) types from $\mathcal{T}^m$ which are used to instantiate the type variables.

In addition to the constants and axioms of the system, we import a number of constructions and results from the library distributed with Egal. Some of the constructions are definitions of logical connectives, equality and existential quantification as well as basic theorems about their properties. Negation of equality, negation of set membership and subset are imported, defined in the obvious ways. We use the notation $s \neq t$, $s \notin t$ and $s \subseteq t$ for the corresponding propositions. The definitions TransSet, Union_closed, Power_closed, Repl_closed and ZF_closed are imported. In addition the following definitions are imported:

- ordinal : $\iota \to o$ is $\lambda \alpha$. TransSet $\alpha \wedge \forall \beta \in \alpha$. TransSet β. Informally we say β *is an ordinal* to mean ordinal β.
- famunion : $\iota \to (\iota \to \iota) \to \iota$ is $\lambda X F. \bigcup \{Fx | x \in X\}$. We write $\bigcup_{x \in s} t$ for famunion s $(\lambda x.t)$.

We also import the following objects in an opaque way, so that we will only be able to use properties imported from the library and not the actual definitions.

- Sep : $\iota \to (\iota \to o) \to \iota$. We write $\{x \in X | \varphi\}$ for Sep X $(\lambda x.\varphi)$. Results are imported to ensure $\forall z.z \in \{x \in X | \varphi\} \Leftrightarrow z \in X \wedge \varphi_z^x$ is provable.
- ReplSep : $\iota \to (\iota \to o) \to (\iota \to \iota) \to \iota$. We write $\{s | x \in X \text{ such that } \varphi\}$ for ReplSep X $(\lambda x.\varphi)$ $(\lambda x.s)$. Results are imported to ensure the provability of $\forall z.z \in \{s | x \in X \text{ such that } \varphi\} \Leftrightarrow \exists y \in X.\varphi_y^x \wedge z = s_y^x$.
- UPair : $\iota \to \iota \to \iota$. We write $\{x, y\}$ for UPair x y. Results are imported to ensure $\forall z.z \in \{x, y\} \Leftrightarrow z = x \vee z = y$ is provable.
- Sing : $\iota \to \iota$. We write $\{x\}$ for Sing x. Results are imported to ensure $\forall z.z \in \{x\} \Leftrightarrow z = x$ is provable.
- R : $(\iota \to (\iota \to \iota) \to \iota) \to \iota \to \iota$. The R operator is used to define functions by $\in$-recursion over the universe. Given a function $F : \iota \to (\iota \to \iota) \to \iota$ satisfying certain conditions, R F yields a function f satisfying f X $=$ F X f. Its construction is discussed in detail in [8]. It is obtained by defining the graph of R F as the least relation satisfying appropriate closure properties and then using $\in$-induction to prove (under appropriate assumptions) that this yields a functional relation. Here we will only need the fundamental property imported as Proposition 5 below. Its use will be essential in proving Tarski's Axiom A in Sect. 5.

We will freely make use of these imported terms to form new terms below.

Less than 60 results proven in the library need to be imported in order to prove the results discussed in this paper. Most of those results are basic results about logic and set theory and we will leave them implicit here. The choice axiom and the extensionality axioms make the logic extensional and classical [11]. We import excluded middle and the double negation law from the library.

The following imported results are worth making explicit:

Proposition 1. $\forall x.x \notin x$.

Proposition 2 (Regularity). $\forall Xx.x \in X \Rightarrow \exists Y \in X.\neg \exists z \in X.z \in Y$.

Proposition 3. $\forall \alpha$.ordinal $\alpha \Rightarrow \forall \beta \in \alpha$.ordinal β.

Proposition 4. $\forall \alpha \beta$.ordinal $\alpha \Rightarrow$ ordinal $\beta \Rightarrow \alpha \in \beta \vee \alpha = \beta \vee \beta \in \alpha$.

The fundamental property of R is imported from the library:

Proposition 5 (cf. Theorem 1 in [8]).

$$\forall \Phi : \iota \to (\iota \to \iota) \to \iota.(\forall X.\forall gh : \iota \to \iota.(\forall x \in X.gx = hx) \Rightarrow \Phi \ X \ g = \Phi \ X \ h)$$
$$\to \forall X.\mathsf{R} \ \Phi \ X = \Phi \ X \ (\mathsf{R} \ \Phi)$$

4   Higher-Order vs. First-Order Representations

For many concepts we cannot directly compare the formulations in Egal with those from Mizar since Egal is higher-order. On the other hand, for the cases of interest in this paper we show we can find first-order formulations which are provably equivalent in Egal and have counterparts in Mizar. In particular we will use this to compare Grothendieck universes in Egal (defined using closure under replacement) and Grothendieck universes in Mizar (defined using closure under unions of families of sets).

Tarski's Axiom A (Fig. 1) informally states that every set is in a Tarski universe. The most interesting condition in the definition of a Tarski universe is that every subset of the universe is either a member of the universe or is equipotent with the universe. The notion of equipotence of two sets can be represented in different ways. In first-order one can define when sets X and Y are equipotent as follows: there is a set R of Kuratowski pairs which essentially encodes the graph of a bijection from X to Y. In order to state Axiom A in Mizar, one must first define Kuratowski pairs and then equipotence. This first-order definition of equipotence can of course be made in Egal as well. We omit the details, except to say we easily obtain an Egal abbreviation equip of type $\iota \to \iota \to o$ with a definition analogous to the definition of equipotence in Mizar.

There is an alternative way to characterize equipotence in Egal without relying on the set theoretic encoding of pairs and functions. We simply use functions of type $\iota \to \iota$ given by the underlying simple type theory.

Let bij : $\iota \to \iota \to (\iota \to \iota) \to o$ be

$$\lambda XY.\lambda f : \iota \to \iota.(\forall u \in X.fu \in Y) \wedge (\forall uv \in X.fu = fv \Rightarrow u = v)$$
$$\wedge (\forall w \in Y.\exists u \in X.fu = w).$$

Informally we say f *is a bijection taking X onto Y* to mean bij $X \ Y \ f$.

It is straightforward to prove equip $X \ Y \Leftrightarrow \exists f : \iota \to \iota.$bij $X \ Y \ f$ in Egal. When proving Axiom A in Egal (see Theorem 5) we will use $\exists f : \iota \to \iota.$bij $X \ Y \ f$ to represent equipotence. To obtain the first-order formulation Axiom A, the equivalence of the two formulations of equipotence can be used.

A similar issue arises when considering the notion of being ZF-closed in Mizar. The definition of ZF_closed relies on Repl_closed. Repl_closed relies on the higher-order Repl operator and quantifies over the type $\iota \to \iota$. An alternative first-order definition of U being ZF-closed is to say U is $\wp$-closed and U is closed under internal family unions. The internal family union of a set I and a set f is defined as the set famunionintern $I \ f$ such that $w \in$ famunionintern $I \ f$ if and only if $\exists i \in I.\exists X.[i, X] \in f \wedge w \in X$ where $[i, X]$ is the Kuratowski pair $\{\{i\}, \{i, X\}\}$. It is easy to prove such a set exists, in both Egal and Mizar. Closure of U under internal family unions states that if $I \in U$, f is a set of Kuratowski pairs representing the graph of a function from I into U, then famunionintern $I\ f \in U$.

We say U is *ZF-closed in the FO sense* if U is $\wp$-closed and closed under internal family unions. In Egal it is straightforward to prove that for transitive sets U, U is ZF-closed if and only if U is ZF-closed in the FO sense. Grothendieck universes in Egal are transitive ZF-closed sets. Grothendieck universes in Mizar are transitive sets that are ZF-closed in the FO sense. By the equivalence result, we know these two notions of Grothendieck universes are equivalent in Egal.

5   Tarski's Axiom A in Egal

We will now describe the HOTG proof of Tarski's Axiom A in Egal.

We begin by using the recursion operator to define an operator returning the set of all sets up to a given rank: $\mathsf{V} : \iota \to \iota$ is $\mathsf{R}(\lambda X v. \bigcup_{x \in X} \wp(vx))$. We will write $\mathbf{V}_X$ for V applied to X. Using Proposition 5 it is easy to prove the following:

Theorem 1. $\forall X.\mathbf{V}_X = \bigcup_{x \in X} \cdot \wp(\mathbf{V}_x)$

It is then straightforward to prove a sequence of results.

Theorem 2. *The following facts hold.*

1. $\forall y x X. x \in X \Rightarrow y \subseteq \mathbf{V}_x \Rightarrow y \in \mathbf{V}_X$.
2. $\forall y X. y \in \mathbf{V}_X \Rightarrow \exists x \in X. y \subseteq \mathbf{V}_x$.
3. $\forall X. X \subseteq \mathbf{V}_X$.
4. $\forall XY. X \subseteq \mathbf{V}_Y \Rightarrow \mathbf{V}_X \subseteq \mathbf{V}_Y$.
5. $\forall XY. X \in \mathbf{V}_Y \Rightarrow \mathbf{V}_X \in \mathbf{V}_Y$.
6. $\forall XY. X \in \mathbf{V}_Y \vee \mathbf{V}_Y \subseteq \mathbf{V}_X$.
7. $\forall XY. \mathbf{V}_X \in \mathbf{V}_Y \vee \mathbf{V}_Y \subseteq \mathbf{V}_X$.

Proof. Parts 1 and 2 are easy consequences of Theorem 1 and properties of powersets and family unions. Part 3 follows by $\in$-induction using Part 1. Part 4 also follows by $\in$-induction using Parts 1 and 2. Part 5 follows easily from Parts 1, 2 and 4. Part 6 follows by $\in$-induction using classical reasoning and Parts 1 and 2. Part 7 follows from Parts 5 and 6.

Let $\mathsf{V\_closed}$ of type $\iota \to o$ be $\lambda U. \forall X \in U. \mathbf{V}_X \in U$. Informally we say U if $\mathbf{V}$-closed to mean $\mathsf{V\_closed}\ U$. The following theorem is easy to prove by $\in$-induction using Theorem 1.

Theorem 3. *If U is transitive and ZF-closed, then U is $\mathbf{V}$-closed.*

Using the choice operator it is straightforward to construct the inverse of a bijection taking X onto Y and obtain a bijection taking Y onto X.

Theorem 4. $\forall XY. \forall f : \iota \to \iota.\mathsf{bij}\ X\ Y\ f \Rightarrow \mathsf{bij}\ Y\ X\ (\lambda y. \varepsilon x \in X. fx = y)$.

We now turn to the most complicated Egal proof. More than half of the file ending with the proof of Axiom A is made up of the proof of Lemma 1. We outline the proof here and make some comments about the corresponding formal proof in Egal along the way. For the full proof see the technical report [9] or the Egal formalization.

Lemma 1. *Let U be a ZF-closed transitive set and X be such that $X \subseteq U$ and $X \notin U$. There is a bijection $f : \iota \to \iota$ taking $\{\alpha \in U | \text{ordinal } \alpha\}$ onto X.*

Proof. In the Egal proof we begin by introducing the local names U and X and making the corresponding assumptions.

```
let U. assume HT: TransSet U. assume HZ: ZF_closed U.
let X. assume HXsU: X c= U. assume HXniU: X /:e U.
```

We next make six local abbreviations. Let

- $\boldsymbol{\lambda}$ be $\{\alpha \in U | \text{ordinal } \alpha\}$,
- $\mathbf{P} : \iota \to \iota \to (\iota \to \iota) \to o$ be $\lambda \alpha x f. x \in X \wedge \forall \beta \in \alpha. f\beta \neq x$,
- $\mathbf{Q} : \iota \to (\iota \to \iota) \to \iota \to o$ be $\lambda \alpha f x. \mathbf{P} \ \alpha \ x \ f \wedge \forall y. \mathbf{P} \ \alpha \ y \ f \Rightarrow \mathbf{V}_x \subseteq \mathbf{V}_y$,
- $\mathbf{F} : \iota \to (\iota \to \iota) \to \iota$ be $\lambda \alpha f. \varepsilon x. \mathbf{Q} \ \alpha f x$,
- $\mathbf{f} : \iota \to \iota$ be $\mathbf{RF}$ and
- $\mathbf{g} : \iota \to \iota$ be $\lambda y. \varepsilon \alpha \in \boldsymbol{\lambda}. \mathbf{f}\alpha = y$.

In the Egal proof three of these local definitions are given as follows:

```
set lambda : set := {alpha :e U|ordinal alpha}.
...
set f : set->set := In_rec F.
set g : set->set := fun y => some alpha :e lambda, f alpha = y.
```

The following claims are then proven:

$$\forall \alpha. \mathbf{f}\alpha = \mathbf{F} \ \alpha \ \mathbf{f} \tag{1}$$

$$\forall \alpha \in \boldsymbol{\lambda}. \mathbf{Q} \ \alpha \ \mathbf{f} \ (\mathbf{f}\alpha) \tag{2}$$

$$\forall \alpha \in \boldsymbol{\lambda}. \mathbf{f}\alpha \in X \tag{3}$$

$$\forall \alpha \beta \in \boldsymbol{\lambda}. \mathbf{f}\alpha = \mathbf{f}\beta \Rightarrow \alpha = \beta \tag{4}$$

$$\text{bij } \{\mathbf{f} \ \alpha | \alpha \in \boldsymbol{\lambda}\} \ \boldsymbol{\lambda} \ \mathbf{g} \tag{5}$$

$$\boldsymbol{\lambda} = \{\mathbf{g} \ y | y \in \{\mathbf{f} \ \alpha | \alpha \in \boldsymbol{\lambda}\}\} \tag{6}$$

$$\forall x \in X. \exists \alpha \in \boldsymbol{\lambda}. \mathbf{f}\alpha = x \tag{7}$$

Note that (3), (4) and (7) imply $\mathbf{f}$ is a bijection taking $\boldsymbol{\lambda}$ onto X, which will complete the proof. Here we only describe the proof of (2) in some detail and make brief remarks about the proofs of the other cases. For example, Proposition 5 is used to prove (1).

In the Egal proof we express (2) as a claim followed by its subproof.

```
claim L1: forall alpha :e lambda, Q alpha f (f alpha).
```

The subproof is by $\in$-induction. Let α be given and assume as inductive hypothesis $\forall\gamma.\gamma \in \alpha \Rightarrow \gamma \in \boldsymbol{\lambda} \Rightarrow \mathbf{Q}\ \gamma\ \mathbf{f}\ (\mathbf{f}\gamma)$. Assume $\alpha \in \boldsymbol{\lambda}$, i.e., $\alpha \in U$ and ordinal α. Under these assumptions we can prove the following subclaims:

$$\forall\beta \in \alpha.\mathbf{Q}\ \beta\ \mathbf{f}\ (\mathbf{f}\beta) \tag{8}$$

$$\forall\beta \in \alpha.\mathbf{f}\beta \in X \tag{9}$$

$$\{\mathbf{f}\beta|\beta \in \alpha\} \subseteq X \tag{10}$$

$$\{\mathbf{f}\beta|\beta \in \alpha\} \in U \tag{11}$$

$$\exists x.\mathbf{P}\ \alpha\ x\ \mathbf{f} \tag{12}$$

$$\exists x.\mathbf{Q}\ \alpha\ \mathbf{f}\ x \tag{13}$$

$$\mathbf{Q}\ \alpha\ \mathbf{f}\ (\mathbf{F}\ \alpha\ \mathbf{f}) \tag{14}$$

We show only the proof of (13) assuming we have already established (12). Let $\mathbf{Y}$ be $\{\mathbf{V}_x|x \in X \text{ such that } \forall\beta \in \alpha.\mathbf{f}\beta \neq x\}$. By (12) there is a w such that $\mathbf{P}\ \alpha\ w\ \mathbf{f}$. That is, $w \in X$ and $\forall\beta \in \alpha.\mathbf{f}\beta \neq w$. Clearly $\mathbf{V}_w \in \mathbf{Y}$. By Regularity (Proposition 2) there is some $Z \in \mathbf{Y}$ such that $\neg\exists z \in \mathbf{Y}.z \in Z$. Since $Z \in \mathbf{Y}$ there must be some $x \in X$ such that $Z = \mathbf{V}_x$ and $\forall\beta \in \alpha.\mathbf{f}\beta \neq x$. We will prove $\mathbf{Q}\ \alpha\ \mathbf{f}\ x$ for this x. We know $\mathbf{P}\ \alpha\ x\ \mathbf{f}$ since $x \in X$ and $\forall\beta \in \alpha.\mathbf{f}\beta \neq x$. It remains only to prove $\forall y.\mathbf{P}\ \alpha\ y\ \mathbf{f} \Rightarrow \mathbf{V}_x \subseteq \mathbf{V}_y$. Let y such that $\mathbf{P}\ \alpha\ y\ \mathbf{f}$ be given. By Theorem 2:7 either $\mathbf{V}_y \in \mathbf{V}_x$ or $\mathbf{V}_x \subseteq \mathbf{V}_y$. It suffices to prove $\mathbf{V}_y \in \mathbf{V}_x$ yields a contradiction. We know $\mathbf{V}_y \in \mathbf{Y}$ since $\mathbf{P}\ \alpha\ y\ \mathbf{f}$. If $\mathbf{V}_y \in \mathbf{V}_x$, then $\mathbf{V}_y \in Z$ (since $Z = \mathbf{V}_x$), contradicting $\neg\exists z \in \mathbf{Y}.z \in Z$.

We conclude (14) by (13) and the property of the choice operator used in the definition of $\mathbf{F}$. By (14) and (1) we have $\mathbf{Q}\ \alpha\ \mathbf{f}\ (\mathbf{f}\alpha)$. Recall that this was proven under an inductive hypothesis for α. We now discharge this inductive hypothesis and conclude (2).

One can easily prove (3) and (4) from (2) and Proposition 4. From (4) and Theorem 4 we have (5) and from this we obtain (6).

Finally to prove (7) assume there is some $x \in X$ such that $\neg\exists\alpha \in \boldsymbol{\lambda}.\mathbf{f}\alpha = x$. Under this assumption one can prove $\boldsymbol{\lambda} \in \boldsymbol{\lambda}$, contradicting Proposition 1. It is easy to prove $\boldsymbol{\lambda}$ is an ordinal, so it suffices to prove $\boldsymbol{\lambda} \in U$. The proof that $\boldsymbol{\lambda} \in U$ makes use of Proposition 3, Theorem 3, Theorem 2:3, (2), (5), (6) and the closure properties of U.

We can now easily conclude Tarski's Axiom A in Egal.

Theorem 5 (Tarski A). *For each set N there exists an M such that*

1. $N \in M$,
2. $\forall X \in M.\forall Y \subseteq X.Y \in M$,
3. $\forall X \in M.\exists Z \in M.\forall Y \subseteq X.Y \in Z$ and
4. $\forall X \subseteq M.(\exists f : \iota \to \iota.\mathsf{bij}\ X\ M\ f) \vee X \in M$.

Proof. We use $U := \mathcal{U}_N$ as the witness for M. We know $N \in \mathcal{U}_N$, $\mathcal{U}_N$ is transitive and ZF-closed by the axioms of our set theory. All the properties except the last follow easily from these facts. We focus on the last property. Let $X \subseteq U$ be given. Since we are in a classical setting it is enough to assume $X \notin U$ and prove there is some bijection $f : \iota \to \iota$ taking X onto U. Since $U \subseteq U$ and $U \notin U$ (using Proposition 1), we know there is a bijection g taking $\{\alpha \in U \,|\, \text{ordinal } \alpha\}$ onto U by Lemma 1. Since $X \subseteq U$ and $X \notin U$, we know there is a bijection h taking $\{\alpha \in U \,|\, \text{ordinal } \alpha\}$ onto X by Lemma 1. By Theorem 4 there is a bijection g^{-1} taking X onto $\{\alpha \in U \,|\, \text{ordinal } \alpha\}$. The composition of g^{-1} and h yields a bijection f taking X onto U as desired.

6   Grothendieck Universes in Mizar

In this section we construct Grothendieck universes using notions introduced in the MML articles CLASSES1 and CLASSES2 [1,22]. For this purpose, first, we briefly introduce the relevant constructions from these articles. We then define the notion of a Grothendieck universe of a set A as a Mizar type, the type of all transitive sets with A as a member that are closed under power sets and internal family unions. Since Mizar types must be nonempty, we are required to construct such a universe. We finally introduce a functor GrothendieckUniverse A that returns the least set of the type. Additionally, we show that every such Grothendieck universe is closed under replacement formulating the property as a Mizar scheme.

To simplify notation we present selected Mizar operators in more natural ways closer to informal mathematical practice. In particular, we use $\emptyset$, $\in$, $\subseteq$, $\wp$, $|\cdot|$, $\bigcup$ to represent Mizar symbols as {}, in, c=, bool, card, union, respectively.

Following Bancerek, we will start with the construction of the least Tarski universe that contains a given set A. Tarski's Axiom A directly implies that there exists a Tarski set T_A that contains A where Tarski is a Mizar *attribute* (for more details see [15]) defined as follows:

    attr T **is** Tarski **means** : : CLASSES1:def 2
       T **is** subset-closed & (**for** X **holds** X $\in$ T **implies** $\wp$(X)$\in$ T) &
       for X **holds** X $\subseteq$ T **implies** X,T are_equipotent **or** X $\in$ T;

Informally we say that T is Tarski to mean T is closed under subset, power sets and each subset of T is a member of T or is equipotent with T. Then one shows that $\bigcap\{X \,|\, A \in X \subseteq T_A, X$ is Tarski set$\}$ is the least (with respect to inclusion) Tarski set that contains A, denoted by Tarski-Class A.

By definition it is easy to prove the following:

Theorem 6. *The following facts hold.*

1. $\forall A.\ A \in$ Tarski-Class A,
2. $\forall A\, X\, Y.\ Y \subseteq X \wedge X \in$ Tarski-Class $A \Rightarrow Y \in$ Tarski-Class A,
3. $\forall A\, X.\ Y \in$ Tarski-Class $A \Rightarrow \wp(X) \in$ Tarski-Class A,
4. $\forall A\, X.\ X \subseteq$ Tarski-Class $A \wedge |X| < |$Tarski-Class $A| \Rightarrow X \in$ Tarski-Class A.

Tarski universes, as opposed to Grothendieck universes, might not be transitive (called epsilon-transitive in the MML) but via transfinite induction. By Theorems 22 and 23 in [1] we know Tarski-Class A is transitive if A is transitive. Therefore, in our construction we take the transitive closure of A prior to the application of the Tarski-Class functor. Using a recursion scheme we know for a given set A there exists a recursive sequence f such that $f(0) = A$ and $\forall k \in \mathbb{N}.\ f(k+1) = \bigcup f(k)$. For such an f, $\bigcup\{f(n)|n \in \mathbb{N}\}$ is the least (with respect to the inclusion) transitive set that includes A (or contains A if we start with $f(0) = \{A\}$). The operator is defined in [1] as follows:

func the_transitive-closure_of A $\to$ **set means** :: CLASSES1:def 7
    for x **holds** x $\in$ it **iff ex** f **being** Function, n **being** Nat **st**
      x $\in$ f.n & dom f $= \mathbb{N}$ & f.0 $= A$ & **for** k **being** Nat **holds** f.(k+1) $= \bigcup$ f.k;

We now turn to a formulation of ZF-closed property in Mizar. It is obvious that $\wp$-closed, $\bigcup$-closed properties can we expressed as two Mizar types as follows:

attr X **is** power-closed **means for** A **being set st** A $\in$ X **holds** $\wp(A) \in$ X;
attr X **is** union-closed **means for** A **being set st** A $\in$ X **holds** $\bigcup(A) \in$ X;

Note that we cannot express the closure under replacement as a Mizar type since each condition that occurs after **means** has to be a first-order statement. We must therefore use an alternative approach that uses closure under internal family unions using the notion of a function as well as its domain (dom) and range (rng) as follows:

attr X **is** FamUnion-closed **means**
    for A **being set for** f **being** Function **st** dom f $= A$ & rng f $\subseteq$ X & A $\in$ X
    holds $\bigcup$ rng f $\in$ X;

Comparing the properties of Tarski and Grothendieck universes we can prove the following:

Theorem 7. *The following facts hold.*

1. $\forall X.X$ *is* Tarski $\Rightarrow X$ *is* subset-closed power-closed,
2. $\forall X.X$ *is* epsilon-transitive Tarski $\Rightarrow X$ *is* union-closed,
3. $\forall X.X$ *is* epsilon-transitive Tarski $\Rightarrow X$ *is* FamUnion-closed.

Proof. Part 1 is an easy consequences of the Tarski definition and properties of powersets. Part 2 is a direct conclusion of the MML theorem CLASSES2:59. To prove 3 let X be an epsilon-transitive Tarski set, A be a set and f be a function such that dom $f = A$, rng $f \subseteq X$, $A \in X$. Since X is subset-closed as a Tarski set and $A \in X$, we know that $\wp(A) \subseteq X$. By Cantor's theorem we conclude that $|A| < |\wp(A)|$ and consequently $|A| < |X|$. Since $|\text{rng } f| \leq |\text{dom } f| = |A|$, we know that rng f is not equipotent with X. Then rng $f \in X$ since X is Tarski and rng $f \subseteq X$, and finally $\bigcup \text{rng } f \in X$ by Part 2.

We can now easily infer from Theorem 7 that the term:

$$\textsf{Tarski-Class(the\_transitive-closure\_of \{A\})} \tag{15}$$

is suitable to prove that the following Mizar type is inhabited:

mode Grothendieck **of** A $\rightarrow$ set **means**
    A $\in$ **it** & **it** **is** epsilon-transitive power-closed FamUnion-closed;

Now it is a simple matter to construct the Grothendieck universe of a given set A (GrothendieckUniverse A) since $\bigcap\{X|X \subseteq G_A, X$ is Grothendieck **of** $A\}$ is the least (with respect to the inclusion) Grothendieck **of** A, where G_A denotes the term (15).

As we noted earlier, we cannot express the closure under replacement property as a Mizar type or even assumption in a Mizar theorem. However we can express and prove that every Grothendieck **of** A satisfies this property as a scheme as follows:

scheme ClosedUnderReplacement
    {A() $\rightarrow$ set, U() $\rightarrow$ Grothendieck **of** A(),F(set) $\rightarrow$ set}:
    {F(x) **where** x **is** Element **of** A(): x $\in$ A()} $\in$ U()
provided
    for X **being** set **st** X $\in$ A() **holds** F(X) $\in$ U()

The proof uses a function that maps each x in A() to $\{F(x)\}$.[2]

7   Future Work

The present work sets the stage for two future possibilities: translating Mizar's MML into Egal and translating Egal developments into Mizar articles. Translating the MML into Egal is clearly possible in principle, but will be challenging in practice. The "obvious" inferences allowed by Mizar would need to be elaborated for Egal. Furthermore, the implicit inferences done by Mizar's soft typing system would need to be made explicit for Egal. A general translation from Egal developments to Mizar articles is not possible in principle (since Egal is higher-order) although we have shown it is often possible in practice (by handcrafting equivalent first-order formulations of concepts). There is no reason to try to translate the small Egal library to Mizar, but it might be useful to have a partial translation for Egal developments that remain within the first-order fragment. With such a translation a user could formalize a mathematical development in Egal and automatically obtain a Mizar article.

8   Conclusion

We have presented the foundational work required in order to port formalizations from Mizar to Egal or Egal to Mizar. In Egal this required a nontrivial proof of

---

[2] Note that in Mizar schemes, schematic variables such as A must be given as A() to indicate A is a term with no dependencies.

Tarski's Axiom A, an axiom in Mizar. In Mizar this required finding equivalent first-order representations for the relevant higher-order terms and propositions used in Egal and then constructing a Grothendieck universe operator in Mizar.

Acknowledgment. This work has been supported by the European Research Council (ERC) Consolidator grant nr. 649043 *AI4REASON* and the Polish National Science Center granted by decision n°DEC-2015/19/D/ST6/01473.

References

1. Bancerek, G.: Tarski's classes and ranks. Formalized Math. **1**(3), 563–567 (1990)
2. Bancerek, G.: Zermelo theorem and axiom of choice. Formalized Math. **1**(2), 265–267 (1990)
3. Bancerek, G., et al.: Mizar: state-of-the-art and beyond. In: Kerber, M., Carette, J., Kaliszyk, C., Rabe, F., Sorge, V. (eds.) CICM 2015. LNCS (LNAI), vol. 9150, pp. 261–279. Springer, Cham (2015). https://doi.org/10.1007/978-3-319-20615-8_17
4. Bancerek, G., et al.: The role of the Mizar Mathematical Library for interactive proof development in Mizar. J. Autom. Reason. **61**(1–4), 9–32 (2018). https://doi.org/10.1007/s10817-017-9440-6
5. Barendregt, H., Wiedijk, F.: The challenge of computer mathematics. R. Soc. Lond. Trans. Ser. A **363**, 2351–2375 (2005)
6. Bertot, Y.: A short presentation of Coq. In: Mohamed, O.A., Muñoz, C., Tahar, S. (eds.) TPHOLs 2008. LNCS, vol. 5170, pp. 12–16. Springer, Heidelberg (2008). https://doi.org/10.1007/978-3-540-71067-7_3
7. Brown, C.E.: The Egal manual, September 2014
8. Brown, C.E.: Reconsidering pairs and functions as sets. J. Autom. Reason. **55**(3), 199–210 (2015). https://doi.org/10.1007/s10817-015-9340-6
9. Brown, C.E., Pąk, K.: A tale of two set theories (2019). http://alioth.uwb.edu.pl/~pakkarol/publications.html
10. Church, A.: A formulation of the simple theory of types. J. Symb. Log. **5**, 56–68 (1940)
11. Diaconescu, R.: Axiom of choice and complementation. Proc. Am. Math. Soc. **51**, 176–178 (1975)
12. Felgner, U.: Comparison of the axioms of local and universal choice. Fundamenta Mathematicae **71**(1), 43–62 (1971)
13. Fraenkel, A.A., Bar-Hillel, Y., Lévy, A.: Foundations of Set Theory. North-Holland Pub. Co. (1973)
14. Gordon, M.: Set theory, higher order logic or both? In: Goos, G., Hartmanis, J., van Leeuwen, J., von Wright, J., Grundy, J., Harrison, J. (eds.) TPHOLs 1996. LNCS, vol. 1125, pp. 191–201. Springer, Heidelberg (1996). https://doi.org/10.1007/BFb0105405
15. Grabowski, A., Korniłowicz, A., Naumowicz, A.: Mizar in a Nutshell. J. Formalized Reason. **3**(2), 153–245 (2010)
16. Grabowski, A., Korniłowicz, A., Naumowicz, A.: Four decades of Mizar. J. Autom. Reason. **55**(3), 191–198 (2015). https://doi.org/10.1007/s10817-015-9345-1
17. Grothendieck, A., Verdier, J.L.: Théorie des Topos et Cohomologie Etale des Schémas. LNM, vol. 269, 1st edn. Springer, Heidelberg (1972). https://doi.org/10.1007/BFb0081551
18. Jaśkowski, S.: On the rules of suppositions. Studia Logica **1**, 32 p. (1934)

19. Kaliszyk, C., Pąk, K.: Presentation and manipulation of Mizar properties in an Isabelle object logic. In: Geuvers, H., England, M., Hasan, O., Rabe, F., Teschke, O. (eds.) CICM 2017. LNCS (LNAI), vol. 10383, pp. 193–207. Springer, Cham (2017). https://doi.org/10.1007/978-3-319-62075-6_14

20. Kaliszyk, C., Pąk, K.: Semantics of Mizar as an Isabelle object logic. J. Autom. Reason. (2018). https://doi.org/10.1007/s10817-018-9479-z

21. Kirst, D., Smolka, G.: Categoricity results and large model constructions for second-order ZF in dependent type theory. J. Autom. Reason. (2018). https://doi.org/10.1007/s10817-018-9480-6. Accessed 11 Oct 2018

22. Nowak, B., Bancerek, G.: Universal classes. Formalized Math. **1**(3), 595–600 (1990)

23. Obua, S.: Partizan games in Isabelle/HOLZF. In: Barkaoui, K., Cavalcanti, A., Cerone, A. (eds.) ICTAC 2006. LNCS, vol. 4281, pp. 272–286. Springer, Heidelberg (2006). https://doi.org/10.1007/11921240_19

24. Tarski, A.: Über Unerreichbare Kardinalzahlen. Fundamenta Mathematicae **30**, 68–89 (1938)

25. Trybulec, A.: Tarski Grothendieck set theory. J. Formalized Math. Axiomatics (2002). Released 1989

Relational Data Across Mathematical Libraries

Andrea Condoluci[1][✉], Michael Kohlhase[2][✉], Dennis Müller[2][✉],
Florian Rabe[2,3][✉], Claudio Sacerdoti Coen[1][✉], and Makarius Wenzel[4][✉]

[1] Università di Bologna, Bologna, Italy
`andrea.condoluci@unibo.it`, `sacerdot@cs.unibo.it`
[2] Computer Science, FAU Erlangen-Nürnberg, Erlangen, Germany
`{michael.kohlhase,dennis.mueller,florian.rabe}@fau.de`
[3] LRI, Université Paris Sud, Orsay, France
[4] Augsburg, Germany
`makarius@sketis.net`
`https://sketis.net`

Abstract. Formal libraries are treasure troves of detailed mathematical knowledge, but this treasure is usually locked into system- and logic-specific representations that can only be understood by the respective theorem prover system. In this paper we present an ontology for using relational information on mathematical knowledge and a corresponding data set generated from the Isabelle and Coq libraries. We show the utility of the generated data by setting a relational query engine that provides easy access to certain library information that was previously hard or impossible to determine.

1 Introduction and Related Work

Overview and Contribution. For many decades, the development of a universal database of all mathematical knowledge, as envisioned, e.g., in the QED manifesto [Qed], has been a major driving force of computer mathematics. Today a variety of such libraries are available. However, integrating these libraries, or even reusing or searching in a single library can be very difficult because it currently requires understanding both the formal logic underlying it and the proof assistant used to maintain it.

We support these goals by extracting from the libraries semantic web-style relational representations, for which simple and standardized formalisms such as OWL2 [MPPS09], RDF [RDF04], and SPARQL [W3c] as well as highly scalable tools are readily available. Now it is well-known that relational formalisms are inappropriate for symbolic data like formulas, algorithms, and proofs. But our key observation is that if we systematically abstract all symbolic data away and only retain what can be easily represented relationally, we can already realize many benefits of library integration, search, or reuse.

Concretely, our contribution is threefold. Firstly, in Sect. 2, we design ULO, an upper library ontology for mathematical knowledge. We make ULO available

© Springer Nature Switzerland AG 2019
C. Kaliszyk et al. (Eds.): CICM 2019, LNAI 11617, pp. 61–76, 2019.
https://doi.org/10.1007/978-3-030-23250-4_5

as OWL2 XML file and propose it as a standard ontology for exchanging high-level information about mathematical libraries.

Secondly, in Sect. 3, we generate ULO data from concrete libraries in RDF format. For this paper we restrict ourselves to Coq and Isabelle as representative example libraries. Both datasets are massive, resulting in $\approx 10^7$ RDF triples each, requiring multiple CPU-hours to generate. We have OMDoc/MMT exports for about a dozen other libraries, including Mizar, HOLLight, TPS, PVS, from which we can generate ULO exports as well, but leave that to future work.

Thirdly, we demonstrate how to leverage these lightweight, high-level representations in practice. As an example application, in Sect. 4, we set up a relational query engine based on Virtuoso. It answers complex queries instantaneously, and even simple queries allow obtaining information that was previously impossible or expensive to extract. Example queries include asking for all theorems of any library whose proof uses induction on $\mathbb{N}$, or all authors of theorems ordered by how many of the proofs are incomplete, or all dependency paths through a particular library ordered by cumulative check time (which would enable optimized regression testing).

Other applications enabled by our work include, e.g., graph-based visualization, cross-referencing between libraries, or integrating our formal library metadata with other datasets such as publication metadata or Wikidata.

Related Work. The problem of retrieving mathematical documents that contain an instance or a generalization of a given formula has been frequently addressed in the literature [GC16]. The main difficulty is the fact that the formula structure is fundamental, but at the same time the matching must be up to changes to this structure (e.g. permutation of hypothesis, re-arrangement of expressions up to commutativity and associativity).

One solution is the technique presented in [Asp+06, AS04] that was applied to the Coq library. It consists in computing RDF-style triples that described the formula structure approximately, so that instantiation is captured by the subset relation of set of triples and matching up-to structural changes comes for free because the triples only record approximate shapes. Such a description is completely logic-independent, can be applied as well to other systems, and can be integrated with constraints over additional triples (e.g. over keywords, author, dependencies, etc). The Whelp search engine implemented the technique but is no longer maintained.

[Lan11] explores using the linked open data language and tool stack for representing mathematical knowledge. In particular, it presents various OWL ontologies, which are subsumed by the ULO, but does not have the data exports for the theorem prover libraries, which severely limited the reach of applications.

General purpose query languages for mathematical libraries data were previously introduced in [ADL12, Rab12]. Our experience is that the key practicality bottleneck for such languages is not so much the detailed definition of the language but the availability of large datasets for which querying is implemented scalably. This is the idea behind the approach we take here.

2   ULO: The Upper Library Ontology

We use a simple data representation language for upper-level information about libraries. This **Upper Library Ontology** (ULO) describes objects in theorem prover libraries, their taxonomy, and relations as well as organizational and information. The ULO allows the export of upper-level library data from theorem prover libraries as RDF/XML files (see Sect. 3), and gives meaning to them. The ULO is implemented as an OWL2 ontology, and can be found at https://gl. mathhub.info/ulo/ulo/blob/master/ulo.owl. All new concepts have URIs in the namespace https://mathhub.info/ulo, for which we use the prefix ulo: below.

In the sequel we give an overview of the ULO, and we refer to [ULO] for the full documentation. For each concept, little icons indicate whether our extractors for Isabelle "⚫" and Coq "⚫" provide at least partial support (see also Sect. 3).

2.1   Individuals

Individuals are the atomic objects relevant for mathematical libraries. Notably, they do not live in the ulo namespace but in the namespace of their library.

These include in particular all globally named objects in the library such as theories/modules/etc, types, constants, functions, predicates, axioms, theorems, tactics, proof rules, packages, directories, files, sections/paragraphs, etc. For each library, these individuals usually share a common namespace (an initial segment of their URI) and then follow a hierarchic schema, whose precise semantics depends on the library.

Additionally, the individuals include other datasets such as researchers as given by their ORCID or real name, research articles as given by their DOI, research software systems as given by their URI in swMATH[1], or MSC[2] and ACM[3] subject classes as given by their respective URIs. These individuals are not generated by our export but may occur as the values of key-value attributions to the individuals in prover libraries.

2.2   Classes

Classes can be seen as unary predicates on individuals, tags, or soft types. The semantic web conventions tend to see them simply as special individuals that occur as values of the is-a property of other individuals. Figure 1 gives an overview of the most important classes in the ULO.

Logical Role. The logical classes describe an individual's formal role in the logic, e.g., the information that $\mathbb{N}$ is a type but 0 an object.

ulo:theory⚫⚫ refers to any semantically meaningful group of named objects (declarations). There is a wide range of related but subtly different concepts

---

[1]   https://swmath.org/software/NUMBER.

[2]   http://msc2010.org/resources/MSC/2010/CLASS.

[3]   https://www.acm.org/publications/class-2012.

using words such theory, class, signature, module type, module, functor, locale, instances, structure, locale interpretation, etc.

Inside theories, we distinguish five classes of declarations depending on what kind of entity is constructed by an individual: `ulo:type` ⬡⬥ if it constructs types or sorts like ℕ or *list*; `ulo:function` ⬡⬥ if it constructs inhabitants of types like + or *nil*; `ulo:predicate` ⬡⬥ if it constructs booleans/propositions such as = or nonEmpty; `ulo:statement` ⬡⬥[4] if it establishes the truth of a proposition such as any axioms, theorem, inference rule; and finally `ulo:universe` ⬡⬥ if it constructs collections of types such as Set or Class.

Note that while we hold the distinction of these five classes to be universal, concrete logics may not always distinguish them syntactically. For example, HOL identifies functions and predicates, but the extractor can indicate whether a declaration's return type is the distinguished type of booleans. Similarly, Curry-Howard-based systems identity predicates and types as well as statements and objects, which an extractor may choose to separate.

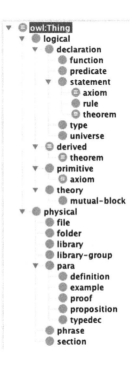

Fig. 1. ULO classes

Orthogonally to the above, we distinguish declarations by their definition status: `ulo:primitive` ⬡⬥ if it introduces a new concept without a definition such as an urelement or an axiom; and `ulo:derived` ⬡⬥ if it can be seen as an abbreviation for an existing concept like a defined operator or a theorem. For example, intersecting the classes `ulo:statement` and `ulo:derived`, we capture all theorems.

While the primitive-derived distinction is clear-cut for definition-based systems like Coq, it is trickier for axiom-based systems like Isabelle: an Isabelle definition actually consists of a primitive concept with a defining axioms for it. For that purpose, we introduce the `ulo:defines` property in Sect. 2.3.

Physical Role. The physical classes describe an individual's role in the physical organization of a library. This includes for an individual *i*:

- `ulo:section` ⬡ if *i* is an informal grouping inside a file (chapter, paragraph etc.)
- `ulo:file` ⬥ if *i* is a file

---

[4] We have reconsidered the name of this class many times: all suggested names can be misunderstood. The current name stems from the intuition that axioms and theorems are the most important named truth-establishing declarations, and *statement* is a common way to unify them. Arguably more systematic would be *proof*: anything that establishes truth is formalized as an operator that constructs a proof.

- ulo:folder⟩ if i is a grouping level above source files inside a library, e.g., a folder, sub-package, namespace, or session
- ulo:library⟩ if i is a library. Libraries have logical URIs and serve as the root objects containing all other individuals. A library is typically maintained and distributed as a whole, e.g., via a GitHub repository. A library has a logical URI and the URIs of individuals are typically formed relative to it.
- ulo:library-group⟩ if i is a group of libraries, e.g., a GitHub group.

In addition we define some classes for the lowest organizational level, called *logical paragraphs*. These are inspired by definition–example–theorem–proof seen in informal mathematics and often correspond to LaTeX environments. In formal libraries, the individuals of these classes may be the same as the ones for the logical classes or different ones. For example, a document-oriented system like Isabelle could assign a physical identifier to a paragraph and a different logical one to the formal theorem inside it. These identifiers could then have classes ulo:proposition and ulo:statement respectively. A purely formal system could omit the physical class or add it to the logical identifier, e.g., to mark a logical definition as an ulo:example⟩ or ulo:counter-example. Some of these, in particular, theorems given informal classes like "Lemma" or "Hauptsatz", a string which can be specified by the ulo:paratype relation (see below).

2.3 Properties

All properties are binary predicates whose first argument is an individual. The second argument can be an individual (**object property**) or a value (**data property**). Unless mentioned otherwise, we allow the same property to be used multiple times for the same individual.

The two kinds are often treated differently. For example, for visualization as a graph, we can make individuals nodes (using different colors, shapes etc. depending on which classes a node has) and object properties edges (using different colors, shapes, etc. for different properties). The data properties on the other hand would be collected into a key-value list and visualized at the node. Another important difference is during querying: object properties are relations between individuals and thus admit relational algebra such as union and intersection or symmetric and transitive closure. Data properties on the other hand are usually used with filters that select all individuals with certain value properties.

Library Structure. Individuals naturally form a forest consisting e.g., of (from roots to leafs) library groups, libraries, folders, files, section, modules, groups of mutual recursive objects, constants. Moreover, the dependency relation between individuals (in particular between the leaves of the forest) defines an orthogonal structure.

ulo:specifies(i, j)⟩ expresses that j is a child of i in the forest structure. Thus, taking the transitive closure of ulo:specifies starting with a library, yields all individuals declared in a library.

`ulo:uses`(i, j)⊛ expresses that j was used to check i, where j may include extra-logical individuals such as tactics, rules, notations. A very frequent case is for j to be an occurrence of a logical individual (e.g. a constant or a theorem). The case of occurrences leads to the question about what information can be attached to an occurrence. Examples could be: the number of repetitions of the occurrence; whether the occurrence of a constant induces a dependency on the type only, or on the actual definition as well; where the occurrence is located (e.g. in the statement vs proof, in the type vs body or in more specific positions, like as the head symbol of the conclusion, see [Asp+06] for a set of descriptions of positions that is useful for searching up to instantiation). For now we decided to avoid to specify occurrences in the ontology, for the lack of a clear understanding of what properties will really be useful for applications. Integrating the ULO ontology with occurrenes is left for future work towards ULO 1.0.

Semantic Relations between Declarations. Relational representations treat individuals as black boxes. But sometimes it is helpful to expose a little more detail about the internal structure of a declaration. For that we define the following properties:

- `ulo:defines`(i, j) is used to relate a declaration j to its definition i if the two have different identifiers, e.g., because they occur in different places in the source file, or because i is a defining axiom for a constant j.
- `ulo:justifies`(i, j)⊛ relates any kind of argument i to the thesis j it supports. The most important example is relating a proof to its theorem statement if the two have different identifiers.
- `ulo:instance-of`(i, j)⊛ relates a structuring declaration j to the theory-like entity i that realizes, e.g., a module to its module type, an instance to its (type) class, a model to its theory, or an implementation to its specification.
- `ulo:generated-by`(i, j) expresses that i was generated by j, e.g., the user may define an inductive type j and the systems automatically generated an induction schema i.
- `ulo:inductive-on`(i, j)⊛ expresses that i is defined/proved by induction on the type j.

Informal Cross-References. First we define some self-explanatory cross-references that are typically (but not necessarily) used to link individuals within a library. These include `ulo:same-as`, `ulo:similar-to`, `ulo:alternative-for`, `ulo:see-also`, `ulo:generalizes`, and `ulo:antonym-of`.

Second we define some cross-references that are typically used to link a knowledge item in a library to the outside. Of particular relevance are:

- `ulo:formalizes`(i, j) indicates that j is an object in the informal realm, e.g., a theorem in an article, that is formalized/implemented by i.
- `ulo:aligned-with`(i, j) indicates that i and j formalize/implement the same mathematical concept (but possibly in different ways).

Data Properties. All properties so far were object properties. Data properties are mostly used to attach metadata to an individual. We do not introduce new names for the general-purpose metadata properties that have already been standardized in the Dublin Core such as `dcterms:creator`, `dcterms:title`, `dcterms:contributor`, `dcterms:description`, `dcterms:date`, `dcterms:is VersionOf`, `dcterms:source`, `dcterms:license`. But we define some new data properties that are of particular interest for math libraries:

- `ulo:name`(i, v)⚫ attributes a string v to a declaration that expresses the (user-provided) name as which it occurs in formulas. This is necessary in case an individual generated URI is very different from the name visible to users, e.g., if the URI is generated from an internal identifier or if the name uses characters that are illegal in URIs.
- `ulo:sourceref`(i, v)⚫ expresses that v is the URI of the physical location (e.g., file, line, column in terms of UTF-8 or UTF-16 characters) of the source code that introduced i.
- `ulo:docref`(i, v) expresses that v is the URI reference to a place where f is documented (usually in some read-only rich text format).
- `ulo:check-time`(i, v)⚫ expresses that v is the time (a natural number giving a time in milliseconds) it took to check the declaration that introduced i.
- `ulo:external-size`(i, v)⚫ expresses that v measures the source code of i (similar to positions above).
- `ulo:internal-size`(i, v) expresses that v is the number of bytes in the internal representation of i including inferred objects and generated proofs.
- `ulo:paratype`(i, v)⚫ gives the "type" of a logical paragraph, i.e. something like "Lemma", "Conjecture", ... This is currently a string, but will become a finite enumeration eventually.

Locations, sizes, and times may be approximate.

Organizational Status. Finally, we define a few (not mutually exclusive) classes that library management–related information such as being experimental or deprecated. Many of these are known from software management in general. The unary properties are realized as data properties, where the object is an explanatory string, the binary relations as object properties. An important logic-specific class is `ulo:automatically-proved` — it applies to any theorem, proof step, or similar that was discharged automatically (rather than by an interactive proof).

3 Exporting ULO Data from Prover Libraries

3.1 Exporting from Isabelle

Overview. Isabelle is generally known for its Isabelle/HOL library, which provides many theories and add-on tools (implemented in Isabelle/ML) in its `Main` theory and the `main` group of library sessions. Some other (much smaller) Isabelle logics are FOL, LCF, ZF, CTT (an old version of Martin-Löf Type Theory), but today most Isabelle applications are based on HOL. User contributions are centrally maintained in AFP, the *Archive of Formal Proofs* (https://www.isa-afp.org): this will provide substantial example material for the present paper (see Sect. 3.3).

The foundations of Isabelle due to Paulson [Pau90] are historically connected to *logical frameworks* like Edinburgh LF: this fits nicely to the LF theory of MMT [RK13]. The Isabelle/MMT command-line tool [Wen18b] exports the λ-calculus of Isabelle/Pure into MMT as LF terms, with some add-on structures.

From a high-level perspective, Isabelle is better understood as *document-oriented proof assistant* or *document preparation system* for domain-specific formal languages [Wen18a]. It allows flexible nesting of sub-languages, and types, terms, propositions, and proofs (in Isabelle/Isar) are merely a special case of that. The result of processing Isabelle document sources consists of internal data structures in Isabelle/ML that are private to the language implementations. Thus it is inherently difficult to observe Isabelle document content by external tools, e.g. to see which λ-terms occur in nested sub-languages.

PIDE is an approach by Wenzel to expose *aspects* of the ML language environment to the outside world, with the help of the Isabelle/Scala library for "Isabelle system programming". A major application of Isabelle/Scala/PIDE is Isabelle/jEdit, which is a Java-based text editor that has been turned into a feature-rich Prover IDE over 10 years of development [Wen18c]. To implement Isabelle/MMT [Wen18b], Wenzel has upgraded the Headless PIDE server of Isabelle2018 to support theory exports systematically. The Isabelle/MMT command-line tool uses regular Scala APIs of MMT (without intermediate files), and results are written to the file-system in OMDoc and RDF/XML format.

Isabelle2019 exports *logical foundations* of theory documents (types, consts, facts, but *not* proof terms), and aspects of *structured specifications* (or "little theories"): locales and locale interpretations, which also subsumes the logical content of type classes. Isabelle/MMT (repository version e6fa4b852bf9) turns this content into OMDoc and RDF/XML. This RDF/XML extractor supports both DC (Dublin Core Meta Data) and our ULO ontology (Sect. 2).

Individuals. Formal entities are identified by their *name* and *kind* as follows:

- The name is a long identifier (with dot as separator, e.g. `Nat.Suc`) that is unique within the current theory context (including the union of all theory imports). Long names are managed by namespaces within the formal context to allow partially qualified names in user input and output (e.g. `Suc`). The structure of namespaces is known to the prover, and not exported.
- The kind is a short identifier to distinguish the namespaces of formal entities, e.g. `type` for type constructors, `const` for term constants, `fact` for lists of theorems that are recorded in the context, but also non-logical items like `method` (Isar proof methods), `attribute` (Isar hint language) etc.

This name/kind scheme is in contrast to usual practice in universal λ-calculus representations like MMT/LF, e.g. there could be a type `Nat.nat` and a separate term constant of the same name. Moreover the qualification in long names only uses theory base names, not their session-qualified long name (which was newly introduced in Isabelle2017). So in order to support one big space of individuals over all Isabelle sessions and theories, we use the subsequent URI format that essentially consists of a triple (*long-theory-name*, *entity-name*, *entity-kind*):

> `https://isabelle.in.tum.de?`*long-theory-name*`?`*entity-name*`|`*entity-kind*

For example, `https://isabelle.in.tum.de?HOL.Nat?Nat.nat|type` refers to the type of natural numbers in the Isabelle/HOL.

Logic. The primitive logical entities of Isabelle/Pure are types, terms, and theorems (facts). Additionally, Isabelle supports various theory-like structures. These correspond our declaration classes as follows:

- `ulo:theory` refers to global **theory** and local **locale** contexts. There are various derivatives of **locale** that are not specifically classified, notably **class** (type classes) and **experiment** (locales with inaccessible namespace).
- `ulo:type` refers to *type constructors* of Isabelle/Pure, and object-logic types of many-sorted FOL or simply-typed HOL. These types are syntactic, and not to be confused with the "propositions-as-types" approach in systems like Coq. Dependent types are represented as terms in Isabelle.
- `ulo:function` refers to *term constants*, which are ubiquitous in object-logics and applications. This covers a broad range of formal concepts, e.g. logical connectives, quantifiers (as operators on suitable λ-terms), genuine constants or mathematical functions, but also recursion schemes, or summation, limit, integration operators as higher-order functions.
- `ulo:statement` refers to individual theorems, which are projections from the simultaneous `fact` lists of Isabelle. Only the head statement of a theorem is considered, its proof body remains abstract (as reference Isar to proof text). Theorems that emerge axiomatically (command **axiomatization**) are marked as `ulo:primitive`, properly proven theorems as `ulo:derived`, and theorems with unfinished proofs (command **sorry**) as `ulo:experimental`.

The `ulo:specifies` and `ulo:specified-in` relations connect theories and locales with their declared individuals. The `ulo:uses` relation between those represents syntactic occurrence of individuals in the type (or defining term) of formal entities in Isabelle: it spans a large acyclic graph of dependencies. Again, this excludes proofs: in principle there could be a record of individuals used in the proof text or by the inference engine, but this is presently unimplemented.

The `ulo:source-ref` property refers to the defining position of formal entities in the source. Thanks to Isabelle/PIDE, this information is always available and accurate: the Prover IDE uses it for highlighting and hyperlinks in the editor view. Here we use existing URI notation of MMT, e.g. https://isabelle.in.tum.de/source/FOL/FOL/FOL.theory#375.19.2:383.19.10 with offset/line/column of the two end-points of a text interval.

The `ulo:check-time` and `ulo:external-size` properties provide some measures of big theories in time (elapsed) and space (sources). This is also available for individual commands, but it is hard to relate to resulting formal entities: a single command may produce multiple types, consts, and facts simultaneously.

Semi-formal Documents. We use `ulo:section` for the six levels of headings in Isabelle documents: **chapter**, **section**, ..., **subparagraph**. These are turned into dummy individuals (which are counted consecutively for each theory).

`ulo:file`, `ulo:folder`, `ulo:library` are presently unused. They could refer to the overall project structure Isabelle document sources in the sense of [Wen18a], namely as *theories* (text files), *sessions* (managed collections of theories), and *project directories* (repository with multiple session roots).

For document metadata, we use the Dublin Core ontology. The Isabelle command language has been changed to support a new variant of *formal comment*. By writing "✐⟨*marker*⟩", the presentation context of a command may be augmented by arbitrary user-defined marker expressions. Isabelle/Pure already provides `title`, `creator`, `contributor` etc. from Sect. 2.3: they produce PIDE document markup that Isabelle/MMT can access and output as corresponding RDF.

This approach allows to annotate theory content *manually*: a few theories of `HOL-Algebra` already use ✐⟨contributor ...⟩ sporadically. For automatic marking, metadata of AFP entries is re-used for their theories. One could also digest comments in theory files about authors, but this is presently unimplemented.

3.2   Exporting from Coq

Coq is one of the major interactive theorem provers in use. Many large libraries have been developed for Coq, covering both mathematics (e.g. the MathComp library that includes the proof of Feit-Thompson theorem; the CoRN library that covers many results in constructive analysis) and computer science (e.g. the proof of soundness of the CompCert compiler; the Color library about rewriting theory). We discuss some architectural choices for the extraction of RDF triples.

Libraries and URIs. In contrast to Isabelle/AFP, there is no centralized maintenance of Coq libraries. There is even no index of publicly accessible libraries, even if many are nowadays hosted on GitHub or at least have a downloadable tarball. Moreover, Coq does not even has a proper notion of library: the Coq compiler processes individual `.v` files and a library is usually a bunch of Coq files together with a `Makefile` to compile them in the right order. However, Coq has a notion of *logical* names: when a file is compiled, the compiler is invoked passing a logical name like `mathcomp.field` and every object declared in the file will be given a logical name whose prefix is `mathcomp.field`. For technical reasons (e.g. to address sub-objects or things that are not Coq objects) the URIs we use are not logical names, but we try to keep a correspondence where possible. For example `cic:/mathcomp/field/falgebra/SubFalgType/A.var` is the URI of a variable declared into the `SubFalgType` section of the file `falgebra.v` compiled with logical name prefix `mathcomp.field`.

Opam Packages. There is a recent effort by the Coq team to push developers of libraries to release *opam* packages for them. Opam is a package manager for ocaml libraries that can be (ab)used to automatically download, compile and install Coq libraries as well. Moreover, to release an opam package some Dublin-core like metadata like author and synopsis must be provided. Other interesting mandatory metadata are license and version. Finally, opam packages specify the exact Coq version they depend on, granting that compilation will succeed.

To make Coq libraries accessible to other tools, Sacerdoti Coen wrote a fork of Coq 8.9.0[5] (the current stable release) that can be automatically invoked by opam and that behaves exactly as the standard Coq, but for the fact that it produces multiple XML files that describe the content of the Coq library. The XML files encode the information present in Coq kernel augmented with additional data coming from the sources or computed when the Coq sources are elaborated. In the remainder of the paper we identify the notion of library (that Coq lacks) with that of an opam package: all libraries without a package will be ignored. The exported files are collected in Git repositories in one-to-one correspondence with opam packages[6].

Coqdoc Output. Coq comes with a standard tool, named `coqdoc`, to automatically generate a Web site that documents a library. The Web pages contain pretty-printed and syntax highlighted copies of the sources where additionally hyperlinks are introduced for every identifier defined in the library. In particular, each object in the library is given an HTML anchor in some HTML page. Finally, the pages also include markup automatically generated from special comments that the user adds to the source files.

After extracting opam packages to XML we run coqdoc over the union of all the extracted libraries, obtaining the Web site that documents all the exported libraries (available at https://coq.kwarc.info/).

RDF Triples. We generate RDF triples from three different sources. The first source is the description of the opam packages. Each package is given a URI that mangles its name and version. Triples map this URI to the available opam metadata.

The second source are the (compressed) XML files exported by Sacerdoti Coen's fork [Sac19]. In particular we run Python scripts over the XML files to collect all the ULO triples related to Coq objects (definitions, theorems, modules, sections, etc.). Each object is represented on disk either as a directory (if it contains other objects) plus additional XML files (to attach additional data) or to an XML file on disk (if it is atomic). The physical structure on the filesystem is exactly the URI structure: the file `A.var.xml.gz` whose URI is `cic:/mathcomp/field/falgebra/SubFalgType/A.var` is stored in the `mathcomp/field/falgebra/SubFalgType` directory of the `coq-mathcomp -field-1.7.0` Git repository. The repository was generated exporting from the

---

[5] https://github.com/sacerdot/coq.
[6] https://gl.mathhub.info/Coqxml.

opam package `coq-mathcomp-field`, version 1.7.0. The scripts themselves are therefore quite straightforward: for each Git package, they just recursively traverse the filesystem and the XML trees collecting the triples and adding them to the repository.

The third source is the coqdoc generated website: `ulo:docref` maps URIs to relative URLs pointing to website. E.g. `cic:/mathcomp/field/falgebra/SubFalgType/A.var` is mapped to `mathcomp.field.falgebra.html#SubFalgType.A`.

Precision. The ULO ontology is useful as long as it is reused for different systems and it is the result of a compromise. For instance, multiple structuring notions like Coq modules, functors, module types and sections are all mapped to `ulo:theory`. It is in principle possible to also export Coq-specific triples to run Coq-specific queries, but we have not followed this direction.

Coverage. There is a certain number of ULO relations that are currently not generated for Coq. We classify them into three classes. The first one is information that is inferrable from the XML sources, but requires non-trivial computations (e.g. computing the type of some lambda-term to decide if it encodes a proof via Curry-Howard or otherwise is a proper term). The second class is information that is not recorded in the XML files but that could be recorded modifying the XML exporter (e.g. `ulo:external-size`, `ulo:check-time` or `ulo:simplification-rule`). The third class is information that must be user provided (e.g. `ulo:similar-to`, `ulo:formalizes` or `ulo:aligned-with`) and that is completely absent from Coq sources.

Future Work. As future work we plan to improve the Coq XML exporter and the RDF scripts to achieve full coverage of the first two classes. To cover the third class, we would badly need an extension of the input language of Coq to let the user add machine-understandable metadata to the sources, like Isabelle does. The extension would need to be official accepted upstream and adopted by users before information belonging to the third class can be exported automatically.

3.3 Statistics

Here are some statistics for both Isabelle[7] and Coq, referring to various subsets of the available libraries. This gives an idea about overall size and scalability of the export facilities so far. The datasets are publicly available from https://gl.mathhub.info/Isabelle and https://gl.mathhub.info/Coqxml/coq.8.9.0.

Library	Individuals	Relations	Theories	Locales	Types	Constants	Statements	RDF/XML file size	elapsed time
Distribution only group main	103,873	2,310,704	535	496	235	8,973	88,960	188 MB	0.5h
Distribution+AFP without very_slow	1,619,889	36,976,562	6,185	4,599	10,592	215,878	1,359,297	3,154 MB	16.5h
All 49 Libraries	383,527	11,516,180	1,979	-	6,061	-	161,736	452 MB	

---

[7] Versions: Isabelle/9c60fcfdf495, AFP/d50417d0ae64, MMT/e6fa4b852bf9.

4 Applications

In this section, we evaluate the ULO framework, i.e. the ULO ontology and the generated RDF data by showing how they could be exploited using standard tools of the Semantic Web tool stack.

x	y
cic:/Coq/Init/Nat/add.con	cic:/Coq/Init/Datatypes/nat.ind
cic:/Coq/Init/Nat/mul.con	cic:/Coq/Init/Datatypes/nat.ind
cic:/Coq/Init/Nat/eqb.con	cic:/Coq/Init/Datatypes/nat.ind
cic:/Coq/Init/Nat/div2.con	cic:/Coq/Init/Datatypes/nat.ind
cic:/Coq/Init/Nat/compare.con	cic:/Coq/Init/Datatypes/nat.ind
cic:/Coq/Init/Nat/divmod.con	cic:/Coq/Init/Datatypes/nat.ind
cic:/Coq/Init/Nat/even.con	cic:/Coq/Init/Datatypes/nat.ind
cic:/Coq/Init/Nat/gcd.con	cic:/Coq/Init/Datatypes/nat.ind
https://isabelle.in.tum.de?HOL.List?List.replicate|const	https://isabelle.in.tum.de?HOL.Nat?Nat.nat|type

Fig. 2. Virtuoso output for the example query using alignments

We have set up an instance of Virtuoso Open-Source Edition[8], which reads the exports described in Sect. 3 and provides a web interface with a SPARQL endpoint to experiment with the ULO dataset. Then we have tried several queries with promising results (just one shown below for lack of space). The queries are not meant to be a scientific contribution per se: they just show how much can be accomplished with the ULO dataset with standard tools in one afternoon.

Example Query: All Recursive Functions on $\mathbb{N}$. For this, we use the ulo:inductive−on relation to determine inductive definitions on a type ?y, which we restrict to one that is aligned with the type nat_lit of natural numbers from the interface theory NatLiterals in the Math-in-the-Middle Ontology.

SELECT ?x ?y WHERE {
  ?x ulo:inductive−on ?y .
  http://mathhub.info/MitM/Foundation?NatLiterals?nat_lit ulo:aligned−with ?y . }

Note that we use alignments [Mül+17] with concepts from an interface theory as a way of specifying "the natural numbers" across theorem prover libraries. The result is a list of pairs: each pair combines a specific implementation of natural numbers (Isabelle has several, depending on the object-logic), together with a function defined by reduction on it. A subset of the results of this query are shown in Fig. 2.

---

[8] https://github.com/openlink/virtuoso-opensource.

o	dist
cic:/Coq/setoid_ring/Ring_theory/semi_ring_theory.ind	1
cic:/Bignums/BigN/BigN/BigN/mul_comm.con	1
cic:/Bignums/BigN/BigN/BigN/mul_assoc.con	1
cic:/Bignums/BigN/BigN/BigN/mul_add_distr_r.con	1
cic:/Bignums/BigN/BigN/BigN/mul_1_l.con	1
cic:/Bignums/BigN/BigN/BigN/mul_0_l.con	1
cic:/Bignums/BigN/BigN/BigN/add_comm.con	1
cic:/Bignums/BigN/BigN/BigN/add_assoc.con	1
cic:/Bignums/BigN/BigN/BigN/add_0_l.con	1
cic:/Bignums/BigN/BigN/BigN/one.con	1
cic:/Bignums/BigN/BigN/BigN/zero.con	1
cic:/Bignums/BigN/BigN/BigN/t.con	1
cic:/Bignums/BigN/BigN/BigN/mul.con	1
cic:/Bignums/BigN/BigN/BigN/eq.con	1
cic:/Bignums/BigN/BigN/BigN/add.con	1
cic:/Coq/setoid_ring/Ring_theory/DEFINITIONS/R.var	2
cic:/Coq/setoid_ring/Ring_theory/DEFINITIONS/rO.var	2
cic:/Coq/setoid_ring/Ring_theory/DEFINITIONS/rmul.var	2
cic:/Coq/setoid_ring/Ring_theory/DEFINITIONS/rI.var	2
cic:/Coq/setoid_ring/Ring_theory/DEFINITIONS/req.var	2
cic:/Coq/setoid_ring/Ring_theory/DEFINITIONS/radd.var	2
cic:/rO.var	2
cic:/rmul.var	2
cic:/rI.var	2
cic:/radd.var	2
cic:/req.var	2
cic:/R.var	2

Fig. 3. Virtuoso output for the transitive example query

Transitive Queries. The result of the query above only depends on the explicitly generated RDF triples. Semantic Web tools that understand OWL allow more complex queries. For example, Virtuoso implements custom extensions that allow for querying the transitive closure of a relation. The resulting query syntax is a little convoluted, and we omit some details in the example below.

```
SELECT ?o ?dist WHERE { {
    SELECT ?s ?o WHERE { ?s ulo:uses ?o }
  }
  OPTION ( TRANSITIVE, t_distinct, t_in(?s), t_out(?o), t_min (1),
          t_max (10), t_step ('step_no') as ?dist ) .
  FILTER ( ?s = <cic:/Bignums/BigN/BigN/BigNring.con> )
}
ORDER BY ?dist DESC 2
```

The above code queries for all symbols recursively used in the (effectively randomly chosen) Lemma `BigNring` stating that the ring of arbitrary large natural numbers in base 2^{31} is a semiring; the output for that query is shown in Fig. 3.

Interesting examples of library management queries which can be modeled in SPARQL (and its various extensions, e.g. by rules) are found in [ADL12]. Instead [Asp+06, AS04] show examples of interesting queries (approximate search of formulae up to instantiation or generalization) that can be implemented over RDF triples, but that requires an extension of SPARQL with subset and superset predicates over sets.

5 Conclusion and Future Work

We have introduced an upper ontology for formal mathematical libraries (ULO), which we propose as a community standard, and we exemplified its usefulness at a large scale. Consequently, future work will be strongly community-based.

We envision ULO as an interface layer that enables a separation of concerns between library maintainers and users/application developers. Regarding the former, we have shown how ULO data can be extracted from the libraries of Isabelle and Coq. We encourage other library maintainers to build similar extractors. Regarding the latter, we have shown how powerful, scalable applications like querying can be built with relative ease on top of ULO datasets. We encourage other users and library-near developers to build similar ULO applications, using our publicly available datasets for Isabelle and Coq, or using future datasets provided for other libraries.

Finally, we expect our own and other researchers' applications to generate feedback on the specific design of ULO, most likely identifying various omissions and ambiguities. We will collect these and make them available for a future release of ULO 1.0, which should culminate in a standardization process.

Acknowledgement. The authors were supported by DFG grants RA-18723-1 and KO-2428/13-1 OAF and EU grant Horizon 2020 ERI 676541 OpenDreamKit.

References

[ADL12] Aspinall, D., Denney, E., Lüth, C.: A semantic basis for proof queries and transformations. In: McMillan, K., Middeldorp, A., Voronkov, A. (eds.) LPAR 2013. LNCS, vol. 8312, pp. 53–70. Springer, Heidelberg (2013). https://doi.org/10.1007/978-3-642-45221-5_4

[AS04] Asperti, A., Selmi, M.: Efficient retrieval of mathematical statements. In: Asperti, A., Bancerek, G., Trybulec, A. (eds.) MKM 2004. LNCS, vol. 3119, pp. 17–31. Springer, Heidelberg (2004). https://doi.org/10.1007/978-3-540-27818-4_2

[Asp+06] Asperti, A., Guidi, F., Sacerdoti Coen, C., Tassi, E., Zacchiroli, S.: A content based mathematical search engine: whelp. In: Filliâtre, J.-C., Paulin-Mohring, C., Werner, B. (eds.) TYPES 2004. LNCS, vol. 3839, pp. 17–32. Springer, Heidelberg (2006). https://doi.org/10.1007/11617990_2

[GC16]   Guidi, F., Coen, C.S.: A survey on retrieval of mathematical knowledge. Math. Comput. Sci. **10**(4), 409–427 (2016). https://doi.org/10.1007/s11786-016-0274-0

[Lan11] Lange, C.: Enabling Collaboration on Semiformal Mathematical Knowledge by Semantic Web Integration. Studies on the Semantic Web 11. AKA Verlag and IOS Press, Heidelberg and Amsterdam (2011)

[MPPS09] Motik, B., Parsia, B., Patel-Schneider, P.F.: OWL 2 Web Ontology Language: XML Serialization. W3C Recommendation. World Wide Web Consortium (W3C), 27 October 2009. http://www.w3.org/TR/2009/REC-owl2-xml-serialization-20091027/

[Mül+17] Müller, D., Gauthier, T., Kaliszyk, C., Kohlhase, M., Rabe, F.: Classification of alignments between concepts of formal mathematical systems. In: Geuvers, H., England, M., Hasan, O., Rabe, F., Teschke, O. (eds.) CICM 2017. LNCS (LNAI), vol. 10383, pp. 83–98. Springer, Cham (2017). https://doi.org/10.1007/978-3-319-62075-6_7

[Pau90] Paulson, L.C.: Isabelle: the next 700 theorem provers. In: Odifreddi, P. (ed.) Logic and Computer Science, pp. 361–386. Academic Press, Cambridge (1990)

[Qed]   The QED Project (1996). http://www-unix.mcs.anl.gov/qed/

[Rab12] Rabe, F.: A query language for formal mathematical libraries. In: Jeuring, J., et al. (eds.) CICM 2012. LNCS (LNAI), vol. 7362, pp. 143–158. Springer, Heidelberg (2012). https://doi.org/10.1007/978-3-642-31374-5_10. arXiv:1204.4685 [cs.LO]

[RK13]   Rabe, F., Kohlhase, M.: A scalable module system. Inf. Comput. **230**, 1–54 (2013). http://kwarc.info/frabe/Research/mmt.pdf

[ULO]   ULO Documentation. https://ulo.mathhub.info/. Accessed 03 Nov 2019

[W3c]   SPARQL 1.1 Overview. W3C Recommendation. World Wide Web Consortium (W3C), 23 March 2013. https://www.w3.org/TR/sparql11-overview/

[Wen18a] Wenzel, M.: Isabelle/jEdit as IDE for domain-specific formal languages and informal text documents. In: Masci, P., Monahan, R., Prevosto, V. (eds.) 4th Workshop on Formal Integrated Development Environment, F-IDE 2018 (2018). https://sketis.net/wp-content/uploads/2018/05/isabelle-jedit-fide2018.pdf

[Wen18b] Wenzel, M.: Isabelle/MMT: export of Isabelle theories and import as OMDoc content. Blog entry (2018). https://sketis.net/2018/isabelle-mmt-export-of-isabelle-theories-and-import-as-omdoc-content

[Wen18c] Wenzel, M.: Isabelle/PIDE after 10 years of development. Presented at the UITP Workshop: User Interfaces for Theorem Provers (2018). https://sketis.net/wp-content/uploads/2018/08/isabelle-pide-uitp2018.pdf

[RDF04] RDF Core Working Group of the W3C. Resource Description Framework Specification (2004). http://www.w3.org/RDF/

[Sac19] Coen, C.S.: A plugin to export Coq libraries to XML. In: 12th International Conference on Intelligent Computer Mathematics (CICM 19). LNAI (2019)

Variadic Equational Matching

Besik Dundua[1,2], Temur Kutsia[3(✉)], and Mircea Marin[4]

[1] CTE, International Black Sea University, Tbilisi, Georgia
[2] VIAM, Ivane Javakhishvili Tbilisi State University, Tbilisi, Georgia
[3] RISC, Johannes Kepler University, Linz, Austria
Kutsia@risc.jku.at
[4] West University of Timişoara, Timişoara, Romania

Abstract. In this paper we study matching in equational theories that specify counterparts of associativity and commutativity for variadic function symbols. We design a procedure to solve a system of matching equations and prove its soundness and completeness. The complete set of incomparable matchers for such a system can be infinite. From the practical side, we identify two finitary cases and impose restrictions on the procedure to get an incomplete terminating algorithm, which, in our opinion, describes the semantics for associative and commutative matching implemented in the symbolic computation system Mathematica.

1 Introduction

In variadic languages, function symbols do not have a fixed arity. They can take arbitrary number of arguments. In the literature, such symbols are known by different names: flexary, of flexible arity, polyadic, multi-ary, unranked. They are a convenient and useful tool for formalizing mathematical texts, representing symbolic computation data structures, modeling XML documents, expressing patterns in declarative programming, etc. Usually, variadic languages contain variables not only for individual terms, but also for finite sequences of terms, which help to take the full advantage of flexibility of such languages.

On the other hand, the increased expressiveness of variadic languages has its price, from the computational perspective. Solving equations involving sequence variables is a nontrivial task [15,16] and pattern matching, a very common operation in the above-mentioned applications, becomes pretty involved.

In this paper we address the problem of pattern matching in variadic languages, where some function symbols satisfy (the variadic counterparts of) the commutativity (C) and associativity (A) properties. Equational matching in these theories has been intensively studied in languages with ranked alphabets (see, e.g., [2,7,8,11]). Variadic equational matching so far attracted less attention.

We try to address this shortcoming, approaching the problem both from the theoretical and application points of view. From the theoretical side, we propose a modular rule-based system for solving matching equations with A, C, and AC function symbols. Our focus was not on coming up with an optimized, efficient

© Springer Nature Switzerland AG 2019
C. Kaliszyk et al. (Eds.): CICM 2019, LNAI 11617, pp. 77–92, 2019.
https://doi.org/10.1007/978-3-030-23250-4_6

procedure, especially since A-matching problems might even have infinitely many incomparable solutions. Rather, we chose a declarative, modular approach, which makes proving properties easier. From the application perspective, we show how some intuitive modifications of the rules can lead to terminating cases.

The final part of the paper is devoted to the analysis of the behavior of equational variadic matching algorithm implemented in the symbolic computation system Mathematica [22]. Its programming language, called Wolfram, has a powerful matching engine, using sequence variables and working modulo A and C theories, called there flat and orderless theories, respectively. The matching mechanism is explained in tutorials and help files, but to the best of our knowledge, its formal description has never been published. We try to fill this gap, proposing rules which, in our opinion, describe the input-output behavior and properties of Mathematica's flat and orderless pattern matching.

Related Work. In [17], a procedure for flat (A) matching was described and its relation to the correspondent algorithm in Mathematica was discussed. The current work builds on it and extends the results from that paper. Recently, a library to extend Python with variadic matching and sequence variables has been developed [13]. Pattern matching compiler Tom supports associative matching [4]. Usefulness of variadic operators and sequence variables in logical frameworks has been discussed in [9,10]. Variadic matching with sequence variables has been used in the mathematical assistant system Theorema [3], rule-based systems PρLog [6] and its predecessor FunLog [20], programming package Sequentica [21], XML processing language CLP(Flex) [5]. Variadic matching with regular expression types was studied in [19]. Common Logic (CL) [12] is a framework for a family of logic-based languages, designed for knowledge exchange in a heterogeneous network. It comes with variadic symbols and sequence markers (a counterpart of our sequence variables). Syntactic matching for CL was studied in [18].

2   Preliminaries

We assume some familiarity with the standard notions of unification theory [1]. We consider four pairwise disjoint sets: function symbols $\mathcal{F}$, individual variables $\mathcal{V}_{\text{Ind}}$, sequence variables $\mathcal{V}_{\text{Seq}}$, and function variables $\mathcal{V}_{\text{Fun}}$. All the symbols in $\mathcal{F}$ are *variadic*, i.e., their arity is not fixed. We will use x, y, z for individual variables, $\overline{x}, \overline{y}, \overline{z}$ for sequence variables, X, Y, Z for function variables, and a, b, c, f, g, h for function symbols. The set of variables $\mathcal{V}_{\text{Ind}} \cup \mathcal{V}_{\text{Seq}} \cup \mathcal{V}_{\text{Fun}}$ is denoted by $\mathcal{V}$. *Terms* t and *sequence elements* s are defined by the grammar:

$$t ::= x \mid f(s_1, \ldots, s_n) \mid X(s_1, \ldots, s_n), \quad n \geq 0, \qquad s ::= t \mid \overline{x}.$$

When it is not ambiguous, we write f for the term $f()$ where $f \in \mathcal{F}$. In particular, we will always write a, b, c for $a(), b(), c()$. Terms are denoted by t, r and sequence elements by s, q. Finite, possibly empty sequences of terms are denoted by $\tilde{t}, \tilde{r}$, while $\tilde{s}, \tilde{q}$ are used to denote sequences of sequence elements.

The *set of variables* of a term t is denoted by $\mathcal{V}(t)$. We can use the subscripts Ind, Seq, and Fun to indicate the sets of individual, sequence, and function variables of a term, respectively. A *ground* term is a term without variables. The size of a term t, denoted $size(t)$, is the number of symbols in it. These definitions are generalized for any syntactic object throughout the paper. The *head* of a term is its root symbol. The head of a variable is the variable itself.

A *substitution* is a mapping from individual variables to terms, from sequence variables to finite sequences of sequence elements, and from function variables to function symbols or function variables, such that all but finitely many variables are mapped to themselves. (We do not distinguish between a singleton term sequence and its sole element.) We will use lower case Greek letters for substitutions, with ε reserved for the identity substitution.

For a substitution σ, the domain is the set of variables $dom(\sigma) = \{v \in \mathcal{V} \mid \sigma(v) \neq v\}$. A substitution can be represented explicitly as a function by a finite set of bindings of variables in its domain: $\{v \mapsto \sigma(v) \mid v \in dom(\sigma)\}$. For readability, we put term sequences in parentheses. For instance, the set $\{x \mapsto f(a,\overline{y}), \overline{x} \mapsto (), \overline{y} \mapsto (a, X(f(b)), x), X \mapsto g\}$ is such a representation of the substitution, which maps x to the term $f(a,\overline{y})$, $\overline{x}$ to the empty sequence, $\overline{y}$ to the sequence of three elements $(a, X(f(b)), x)$, and X to g.

Instances of a sequence element s and a sequence $\tilde{s}$ under a substitution σ, denoted, respectively, by $s\sigma$ and $\tilde{s}\sigma$, are defined as follows:

$$x\sigma = \sigma(x), \qquad \overline{x}\sigma = \sigma(\overline{x}), \qquad (f(s_1,\ldots,s_n))\sigma = f(s_1\sigma,\ldots,s_n\sigma),$$
$$(X(s_1,\ldots,s_n))\sigma = \sigma(X)(s_1\sigma,\ldots,s_n\sigma), \qquad (s_1,\ldots,s_n)\sigma = (s_1\sigma,\ldots,s_n\sigma).$$

Example 1. Let $\sigma = \{x \mapsto f(a), \overline{x} \mapsto (b,c), \overline{y} \mapsto (), X \mapsto g\}$. Then $(X(x,\overline{x},f(\overline{y})), \overline{x},\overline{y},x)\sigma = (g(f(a),b,c,f),b,c,f(a))$. This example also shows that nested sequences are not allowed: they are immediately flattened.

Composition of two substitutions σ and ϑ, written $\sigma\vartheta$, is a substitution defined by $(\sigma\vartheta)(v) = \vartheta(\sigma(v))$ for all $v \in \mathcal{V}$.

An *equation* is a pair of terms. Given a set E of equations over $\mathcal{F}$ and $\mathcal{V}$, we denote by $\doteq_E$ the least congruence relation on the set of finite sequences of sequence elements (over $\mathcal{F}$ and $\mathcal{V}$) that is closed under substitution application and contains E. The set $\doteq_E$ is called an *equational theory* defined by E. Slightly abusing the terminology, we will also call the set E an equational theory or an E-theory. The *signature* of E, denoted $sig(E)$, is the set of all function symbols occurring in E. A function symbol is called *free* with respect to E if it does not occur in $sig(E)$.

A substitution σ is *more general* than a substitution ϑ on a set of variables V modulo an equational theory E, denoted $\sigma \leq_E^V \vartheta$, if there exists a substitution φ such that $\chi\sigma\varphi \doteq_E \chi\vartheta$ for all individual and sequence variables $\chi \in V$, and $X()\sigma\varphi \doteq_E X()\vartheta$ for all function variables $X \in V$.

Solving equations in an equational theory E is called *E-unification*. If one of the sides of an equation is ground, then it is called a *matching equation*, and solving such equations in a theory E is called *E-matching*. We write *E-matching* equations as $s \ll_E t$, where t is ground. An *E-matching problem* over $\mathcal{F}$ is a finite set of E-matching equations over $\mathcal{F}$ and $\mathcal{V}$, which we usually denote by Γ: $\Gamma = \{s_1 \ll_E t_1, \ldots, s_n \ll_E t_n\}$.

An *E-matcher* of Γ is a substitution σ such that $s_i\sigma \doteq_E t_i$ for all $1 \leq i \leq n$. The set of all E-matchers of Γ is denoted by $match_E(\Gamma)$. Γ is *E-matchable*, or *E-solvable*, if $match_E(\Gamma) \neq \emptyset$.

A *complete set of E-matchers* of Γ is a set S of substitutions with the following properties:

1. (Correctness) $S \subseteq match_E(\Gamma)$, i.e., each element of S is an E-matcher of Γ;
2. (Completeness) For each $\vartheta \in match_E(\Gamma)$ there exists $\sigma \in S$ with $\sigma \leq_E^{\mathcal{V}(\Gamma)} \vartheta$.

The set S is a *minimal complete set of matchers* of Γ with respect to $\mathcal{V}(\Gamma)$ if it is a complete set of matchers satisfying the minimality property:

3. (minimality) If there exist $\sigma, \vartheta \in S$ such that $\sigma \leq_E^{\mathcal{V}(\Gamma)} \vartheta$, then $\sigma = \vartheta$.

In this paper we consider equational theories that specify pretty common properties of variadic function symbols: counterparts of *associativity* and *commutativity*. They are defined by the axioms below (for a function symbol f):

$$f(\overline{x}, f(\overline{y}), \overline{z}) \doteq f(\overline{x}, \overline{y}, \overline{z}) \qquad \text{variadic associativity for } f$$
$$f(\overline{x}, x, \overline{y}, y, \overline{z}) \doteq f(\overline{x}, y, \overline{y}, x, \overline{z}) \qquad \text{variadic commutativity for } f$$

For an f, we denote these axioms respectively by $\mathsf{A}(f)$ and $\mathsf{C}(f)$. The $\mathsf{A}(f)$ axiom asserts that the nested occurrences of f can be flattened out. The $\mathsf{C}(f)$ says that the order of arguments of f does not matter. Below we often omit the word "variadic" and write associativity and commutativity instead of variadic associativity and variadic commutativity. We also say f is A, C, or AC if, respectively, only $\mathsf{A}(f)$, only $\mathsf{C}(f)$, or both $\mathsf{A}(f)$ and $\mathsf{C}(f)$ hold for f.

An associative normal form (A-normal form) of a term is obtained by applying to it the associativity axiom from left to right as a rewrite rule as long as possible. The notion of normal form extends to substitutions straightforwardly.

In A- and AC-theories there exist matching problems that have infinitely many solutions. This is related to the flatness property of variadic associative symbols, and originates from flat matching [14,17]. The simplest such problem is $f(\overline{x}) \ll_E f()$, where $\mathsf{A}(f) \in E$. Its complete solution set is $\{\{\overline{x} \mapsto ()\}, \{\overline{x} \mapsto f()\}, \{\overline{x} \mapsto (f(), f())\}, \ldots\}$, which is based on the fact that $f(f(), \ldots, f()) \doteq_E f()$ when $\mathsf{A}(f) \in E$. It, naturally, implies that any matching procedure that directly enumerates a complete set of A- or AC-matchers is non-terminating.

In general, our matching problems are formulated in a theory that may contain several A, C, or AC-symbols.

3   Matching Procedure

We formulate our matching procedure in a rule-based manner. The rules operate on a matching equation and return a set of matching equations. They also produce a substitution, which is denoted by ϑ in the rules and is called the local substitution. The matching procedure defined below will be based on a certain strategy for rule application. It is important to note that terms in the rules are kept in normal forms with respect to associativity. The transformation rules are divided into three groups: the common rules, rules for associative symbols, and the permutation rule that deals with commutativity.

Common Rules. In the common rules there are no restriction on the involved function symbols. They can be free, associative, commutative, or AC.

T: **Trivial**

$$s \ll_E s \leadsto_\varepsilon \emptyset.$$

S: **Solve**

$$x \ll_E t \leadsto_\vartheta \emptyset, \qquad \text{where } \vartheta = \{x \mapsto t\}.$$

FVE: **Function Variable Elimination**

$$X(\tilde{s}) \ll_E f(\tilde{t}) \leadsto_\vartheta \{f(\tilde{s}) \ll_E f(\tilde{t})\}, \qquad \text{where } \vartheta = \{X \mapsto f\}.$$

Dec: **Decomposition**

$$\{f(s, \tilde{s}) \ll_E f(t, \tilde{t})\} \leadsto_\varepsilon \{s \ll_E t, \ f(\tilde{s}) \ll_E f(\tilde{t})\}, \qquad \text{if } s \notin \mathcal{V}.$$

IVE: **Individual Variable Elimination**

$$f(x, \tilde{s}) \ll_E f(t, \tilde{t}) \leadsto_\vartheta \{f(\tilde{s}\vartheta) \ll_E f(\tilde{t})\}, \qquad \text{where } \vartheta = \{x \mapsto t\}.$$

SVP: **Sequence Variable Projection**

$$f(\overline{x}, \tilde{s}) \ll_E f(\tilde{t}) \leadsto_\vartheta \{f(\tilde{s}\vartheta) \ll_E f(\tilde{t})\}, \qquad \text{where } \vartheta = \{\overline{x} \mapsto ()\}.$$

SVW: **Sequence Variable Widening**

$$f(\overline{x}, \tilde{s}) \ll_E f(t, \tilde{t}) \leadsto_\vartheta \{f(\overline{x}, \tilde{s}\vartheta) \ll_E f(\tilde{t})\}, \qquad \text{where } \vartheta = \{\overline{x} \mapsto (t, \overline{x})\}.$$

Rules for Associative Symbols. These rules apply when the involved function symbol satisfies the associativity axiom, i.e., if it is A or AC.

IVE-AH: **Individual Variable Elimination under Associative Head**

$$f(x, \tilde{s}) \ll_E f(\tilde{t}_1, \tilde{t}_2) \leadsto_\vartheta \{f(\tilde{s}\vartheta) \ll_E f(\tilde{t}_2)\},$$
where $\mathsf{A}(f) \in E$ and $\vartheta = \{x \mapsto f(\tilde{t}_1)\}$.

FVE-AH: **Function Variable Elimination under Associative Head**

$$f(X(\tilde{s}_1), \tilde{s}_2) \ll_E f(\tilde{t}) \leadsto_\vartheta \{f(\tilde{s}_1, \tilde{s}_2)\vartheta \ll_E f(\tilde{t})\},$$
where $\mathsf{A}(f) \in E$ and $\vartheta = \{X \mapsto f\}$.

SVW-AH: **Sequence Variable Widening under Associative Head**

$$f(\overline{x}, \tilde{s}) \ll_E f(\tilde{t}_1, \tilde{t}_2) \leadsto_\vartheta \{f(\overline{x}, \tilde{s}\vartheta) \ll_E f(\tilde{t}_2)\},$$
where $\mathsf{A}(f) \in E$ and $\vartheta = \{\overline{x} \mapsto (f(\tilde{t}_1), \overline{x})\}$.

Permutation Rule. This is a straightforward rule which permutes arguments of a C or AC function symbol:

Per: **Permutation**

$$f(\tilde{s}) \ll_E f(t_1, \ldots, t_n) \rightsquigarrow_\varepsilon \{f(\tilde{s}) \ll_E f(t_{\pi(1)}, \ldots, t_{\pi(n)})\},$$

where $C(f) \in E$ and π is a permutation of $(1, \ldots, n)$.

The Matching Procedure. The matching procedure $\mathfrak{M}$ works on triples $\Gamma_1; \Gamma_2; \sigma$. It selects an equation from Γ_1 or from Γ_2 and applies one of the rules above to it. If several rules are applicable, one is chosen nondeterministically (unless the control defined below forbids it). Such a nondeterminism introduces branching in the derivation tree. Assume the rule transforms $s \ll_E t \rightsquigarrow_\vartheta \Gamma$. One step of $\mathfrak{M}$ is performed as follows:

- If the selected equation is from Γ_1 and the applied rule is the Per rule, Γ contains a single equation, which is moved to Γ_2:

$$\{s \ll_E t\} \uplus \Gamma_1'; \Gamma_2; \sigma \rightsquigarrow \Gamma_1'; \Gamma_2 \cup \Gamma; \sigma.$$

It is forbidden to apply any other rule to $s \ll_E t$ in Γ_1 if Per is applicable to it. However, Per rule itself can be applied nondeterministically with different permutations, i.e., only Per can cause branching in this case.
- If the selected equation is from Γ_1, Per is not applicable, and a common or associative rule applies to it, then the new equations remain in Γ_1:

$$\{s \ll_E t\} \uplus \Gamma_1'; \Gamma_2; \sigma \rightsquigarrow (\Gamma_1' \cup \Gamma)\vartheta; \Gamma_2\vartheta; \sigma\vartheta.$$

- If the selected equation is from Γ_2, then the Per rule does not apply. The equation should be transformed by common or associative rules. Any rule except Dec leaves the new equations in Γ_2:

$$\Gamma_1; \{s \ll_E t\} \uplus \Gamma_2'; \sigma \rightsquigarrow \Gamma_1\vartheta; (\Gamma_2' \cup \Gamma)\vartheta; \sigma\vartheta.$$

If the applied rule is Dec, then the first new equation moves to Γ_1, and the second one (whose head does not change) remains in Γ_2:

$$\Gamma_1; \{f(s, \tilde{s}) \ll_E f(t, \tilde{t})\} \uplus \Gamma_2'; \sigma \rightsquigarrow \Gamma_1 \cup \{s \ll_E t\}; \Gamma_2' \cup \{f(\tilde{s}) \ll_E f(\tilde{t})\}; \sigma.$$

Hence, to summarize, $\mathfrak{M}$ applies common and associative rules to Γ_1 if the head of the involved equation is not commutative or associative-commutative. Otherwise, the equation is transformed by the permutation rule, moved to Γ_2 and is processed there by common or associative rules. Only the equations generated by decomposition can go back to Γ_1. This process roughly can be described as "permute the arguments of C- and AC-symbols and apply syntactic and A-matching rules." It is a sound and complete approach (as we will show below), but not necessarily the most efficient one.

Given a matching problem Γ, we create the initial system $\Gamma; \emptyset; \varepsilon$ and start applying the described procedure. The process stops either at $\emptyset; \emptyset; \sigma$ (success), or at $\Gamma_1; \Gamma_2; \sigma$ such that $\mathfrak{M}$ can not make a step (failure). The procedure might also run forever. The substitution σ at the success leaf $\emptyset; \emptyset; \sigma$ is called an *answer of* Γ *computed by* $\mathfrak{M}$, or just a *computed answer* of Γ. We denote by $comp(\Gamma)$ the set of answers of Γ computed by the matching procedure $\mathfrak{M}$.

Recall that our matching problems are formulated in a theory that may contain one or more A, C, or AC-symbols. In the soundness and completeness theorems below, the equational theory E in $match_E(\Gamma)$ refers to such a theory.

Theorem 1 (Soundness). $comp(\Gamma) \subseteq match_E(\Gamma)$ *for any E-matching problem* Γ.

Proof (sketch). The theorem follows from the fact that each transformation rule is sound: If $\Gamma_1; \Gamma_2; \sigma \Longrightarrow_R \Gamma_1'; \Gamma_2'; \sigma\vartheta$ by a transformation rule R, and $\varphi \in match_E(\Gamma_1' \cup \Gamma_2')$, then $\vartheta\varphi \in match_E(\Gamma_1 \cup \Gamma_2)$. This in itself is not difficult to check: a straightforward analysis of rules suffices.   □

Theorem 2 (Completeness). *Let* Γ *be an E-matching problem. Assume* $\sigma \in match_E(\Gamma)$ *and it is in the* A-*normal form. Then* $\sigma \in comp(\Gamma)$.

Proof. We prove the theorem by constructing the derivation that starts from $\Gamma; \emptyset; \varepsilon$ and ends with $\emptyset; \emptyset; \sigma$. We denote such a derivation by $\mathcal{D}(\Gamma; \emptyset \rightsquigarrow \sigma)$.

The proof idea is as follows: We associate a complexity measure $M(\Gamma_1; \Gamma_2; \gamma)$ to each system $(\Gamma_1; \Gamma_2; \gamma)$ where $\gamma \in match_E(\Gamma_1 \cup \Gamma_2)$. Measures are ordered by a well-founded ordering. Then we use well-founded induction to prove that $\mathcal{D}(\Gamma; \emptyset \rightsquigarrow \sigma)$ exists: First, assume that for all $\Gamma_1; \Gamma_2; \gamma$ with $\gamma \in match_E(\Gamma_1 \cup \Gamma_2)$ and $M(\Gamma; \emptyset; \sigma) > M(\Gamma_1; \Gamma_2; \gamma)$ there exists a derivation $\mathcal{D}(\Gamma_1; \Gamma_2 \rightsquigarrow \gamma)$. Then, analyzing the selected equation in Γ, we prove that there is a matching rule R getting us (maybe after an application of Per rule) to one of such $\Gamma_1; \Gamma_2$'s, say, to $\Gamma_1'; \Gamma_2'$, from which there is a derivation $\mathcal{D}(\Gamma_1'; \Gamma_2' \rightsquigarrow \sigma')$, which is a part of σ. Combining the step R with $\mathcal{D}(\Gamma_1'; \Gamma_2' \rightsquigarrow \sigma')$ (and, maybe, with Per), we construct the desired derivation $\mathcal{D}(\Gamma; \emptyset \rightsquigarrow \sigma)$.

The above mentioned complexity measure is defined as a pair of multisets $M(\Gamma_1; \Gamma_2; \gamma) = (M_1, M_2)$, where $M_1 = \{size(v\gamma) \mid v \in dom(\gamma)\}$ and $M_2 = \{size(r) \mid l \ll_E r \in \Gamma_1 \cup \Gamma_2\}$. Measures are ordered by the lexicographic combination of two multiset extensions of the standard natural number ordering.

Let Γ have the form $\{s \ll_E t\} \uplus \Gamma'$. We proceed by induction as described above. It has to be shown that there is at least one matching rule that transforms the selected equation $s \ll_E t$. We distinguish between two alternatives: either s and t have the same heads, or they do not.

Case 1: $head(s) = head(t)$. The case when $s = t$ is trivial. Assume $s \neq t$ and their common head satisfies the associativity and commutativity axioms. (For free or commutative symbols, the reasoning is similar and we do not spell out its details.) Let $s = f(s_1, \tilde{s})$ and $t = f(t_1, \dots, t_n)$. Then $s\sigma$ tells us which permutation of t we should take. Performing Per with that permutation π, we get $\Gamma'; \{s \ll_E f(t_{\pi(1)}, \dots, t_{\pi(n)})\}; \varepsilon$. To construct the desired derivation we should look at s_1. If it is neither a variable nor a term whose head is a function variable, we apply the Dec rule, which gives $\Gamma_1' \cup \{s_1 \ll_E t_{\pi(1)}\}; \{f(\tilde{s}) \ll_E f(t_{\pi(2)}, \ldots, t_{\pi(n)})\}; \varepsilon$. The complexity measure of the system is strictly smaller than of the previous one, therefore, by the IH we can construct the desired derivation. If s_1 is a sequence variable, then $s_1\sigma$ tells us whether we should use SVP, SVW, SVW-AH rule. For instance, if $s_1\sigma = (f(t_{\pi(1)}, \ldots, t_{\pi(k)}), t_{\pi(k+1)}, \ldots, t_{\pi(m)})$, $m \leq n$, we use the rule SVW-AH with $\vartheta = \{s_1 \mapsto (f(t_{\pi(1)}, \ldots, t_{\pi(k)}), s_1)\}$ and get $\Gamma_1'\vartheta; \{f(s_1, \tilde{s}) \ll_E f(t_{\pi(k+1)}, \ldots, t_{\pi(n)})\}$. It has a matcher $\gamma = (\sigma \setminus \{s_1 \mapsto ((f(t_{\pi(1)}, \ldots, t_{\pi(k)}), s_1))\}) \cup \{s_1 \mapsto (t_{\pi(k+1)}, \ldots, t_{\pi(m)})\}$. Then the complexity measure of the obtained system is strictly smaller that the current one and we can use the IH again. If s_1 is an individual variable, we proceed similarly, using either IVE or IVE-AH. If the head of s_1 is a function variable X, we use FVE-AH or Dec, depending on $X\sigma$. In all cases, we can construct the desired derivation by using the IH.

Case 2: head(s) $\neq$ head(t). Then we use IVE or FVE. They decrease the complexity measure of the involved systems and we can again use the IH.   □

4   Finitary Fragment and Variant

A *fragment* of equational matching is obtained by restricting the form of the input, while *variants* require computing solutions of some special form without restricting the input. It is obvious that the procedure $\mathfrak{M}$ stops for any matching problem that does not contain sequence variables, but there are some other interesting terminating fragments and variants as well.[1]

4.1   Bounded Fragment

We start with a fragment that restricts occurrences of sequence variables.

Definition 1. *Let Γ be a matching problem. A sequence variable $\overline{x}$ is called bounded in Γ if it occurs under at least two different function symbols or only under free symbol in a subterm of Γ. The problem Γ is called bounded if all sequence variables occurring in Γ are bounded in it.*

Example 2. Let $E = \{A(f), C(f), A(g), C(g)\}$. The following matching problems are bounded:

- $\{f(\overline{x}) \ll_E f(a, g(b)), g(\overline{x}) \ll_E g(f(a), b)\}$, which has two solutions $\{\overline{x} \mapsto (f(a), g(b))\}$ and $\{\overline{x} \mapsto (g(b), f(a))\}$.
- $\{f(\overline{x}) \ll_E f(g(), g()), g(\overline{x}) \ll_E g(f(), f(), f())\}$, which has 120 solutions: $\{\{\overline{x} \mapsto \tilde{t}\} \mid \tilde{t}$ is a permutation of $(g(), g(), f(), f(), f())\}$.

---

[1] It is also possible to modify $\mathfrak{M}$ so that it terminates and computes a finite representation of the infinite set of matchers with the help of regular expressions over substitution composition. For associative (flat) matching, an implementation of such a procedure can be found at https://www3.risc.jku.at/people/tkutsia/software.html.

An important property of bounded matching problems is the existence of a bound on the size of their solutions. More precisely, the following lemma holds:

Lemma 1. *Let Γ be a bounded matching problem and σ be its solution. Assume that the terms in the range of σ are* A*-normalized. Then for every variable $v \in \mathcal{V}(\Gamma)$, we have $size(v\sigma) \leq \sum_{s \ll_E t \in \Gamma} size(t)$.*

Proof. Since Γ is bounded, there will be an occurrence of v in some $s \ll_E t \in \Gamma$ such that $v\sigma$ is not flattened in $s\sigma$. If the inequality does not hold, we will have $size(s\sigma) \geq size(v\sigma) > size(t)$, contradicting the assumption that σ solves Γ. $\square$

To design a terminating procedure for bounded matching problems, we just add an extra failure check. Let Γ be the initial matching problem and $m = \sum_{s \ll_E t \in \Gamma} size(t)$. For any system $\Gamma_1; \Gamma_2; \sigma$ obtained during the run of the matching procedure, we check whether there exists $v \in \mathcal{V}(\Gamma)$ such that $size(v\sigma) > m$. The check is performed before any rule applies to the system. If it succeeds, we terminate the development of that derivation. Otherwise, we continue as usual. In this way, no solution will be missed, and the search tree will be finite. Let us call this procedure $\mathfrak{M}_B$. We conclude that the following theorem holds:

Theorem 3. *The bounded fragment admits a terminating sound and complete matching procedure $\mathfrak{M}_B$.*

4.2 Strict Variant

Infinitely many solutions to our matching problems are caused by sequences of $f()$'s in the matchers, where f is an A or AC function symbol. But one might be interested in solutions, which do not introduce such extra $f()$'s.

For a precise characterization, we modify the variadic associativity axiom into variadic strict associativity: $f(\overline{x}, f(\overline{y}_1, y, \overline{y}_2), \overline{z}) \doteq f(\overline{x}, \overline{y}_1, y, \overline{y}_2, \overline{z})$. For an f, this axiom is denoted by $A_s(f)$ and we use A_s for the corresponding equational theory. Obviously, any solution of a matching problem modulo A_s or A_sC is also a solution modulo A or AC. Hence, we can say that we are aiming at solving a variant of A or AC-matching. We call it the *strict* variant and adapt $\mathfrak{M}$ to compute matchers for it. The adaptation is done by small changes in the associative rules:

- We change IVE-AH and SVW-AH, adding the condition that $\tilde{t}_1$ is not the empty hedge. The modified rules are called IVE-AH-strict and SVW-AH-strict.
- In the rule FVE-AH, we add the condition that $\tilde{s}_1$ is not the empty hedge, obtaining the FVE-AH-strict rule.

Replacing the associative rules by the strict associative rules, we obtain a matching procedure denoted by $\mathfrak{M}_S$.

Example 3. If $E = \{A(f)\}$, the matching problem $f(\overline{x}) \ll_E f(a, a)$ has infinitely many solutions. If $E = \{A_s(f)\}$, there are five matchers: $\{\overline{x} \mapsto (a, a)\}$, $\{\overline{x} \mapsto f(a, a)\}$, $\{\overline{x} \mapsto (f(a), a)\}$, $\{\overline{x} \mapsto (a, f(a))\}$, $\{\overline{x} \mapsto (f(a), f(a))\}$.

Theorem 4. *The procedure $\mathfrak{M}_S$ is sound and terminating.*

Proof. Soundness means that the procedure only computes strict solutions. That it computes solutions, follows from Theorem 1. Strictness of the computed solutions follows from the fact that no rule introduces terms like $f()$ in the matchers if these terms do not appear in the right hand sides of matching equations.

For termination, we associate to each matching problem Γ its complexity measure: a triple $\langle n, M_{ntr}, M_l \rangle$, where n is the number of distinct variables in Γ, M_{ntr} is the multiset $M_{ntr} = \{size(t) \mid s \ll_E t \in \Gamma \text{ for some } s, \text{ and } t \text{ does not have the form } f()\}$, and M_l is the multiset $M_l = \{size(s) \mid s \ll_E t \in \Gamma \text{ for some } t\}$.

The measures are compared lexicographically, yielding a well-founded ordering. The following table shows that each rule in $\mathfrak{M}_S$ except Per, strictly decreases the measure. Permutation is applied only finitely many times, because it produces permutations for each subterm of the right hand sides of matching equations with commutative head. It implies that $\mathfrak{M}_S$ is terminating:

Rule	n	M_{ntr}	M_l
T	$\geq$	$\geq$	$>$
Dec, SVW, SVW-AH-strict	$=$	$>$	
S, IVE, FVE, SVP, IVE-AH-strict, FVE-AH-strict	$>$		

□

The set of strict matchers computed by $\mathfrak{M}_S$ is also minimal. Note that the size of matchers is bounded by the size of the right-hand side of matching equations both for bounded fragment and strict variant.

4.3   Complexity

Both bounded fragment and strict variant are NP-complete problems. Membership in NP is trivial, and hardness follows from the hardness of syntactic variadic matching problem. The latter can be shown by encoding systems of linear Diophantine equations over natural numbers: An equation $A_1 x_1 + \cdots + A_n x_n = B$ is encoded as a syntactic matching equation $g(\overline{x}_1, \ldots, \overline{x}_1, \ldots, \overline{x}_n, \ldots, \overline{x}_n) \ll_E g(b, \ldots, b)$, where each $\overline{x}_i$ appears A_i times, $1 \leq i \leq n$, and b appears B times. To encode a system, we take matching equations $s_1 \ll_E t_1, \ldots, s_k \ll_E t_k$ and form a single matching equation as usual, using a free function symbol: $g(s_1, \ldots, s_k) \ll_E g(t_1, \ldots, t_k)$. We can obtain a solution of the original Diophantine system from a solution σ of the matching equation: For all $1 \leq i \leq n$, if $\overline{x}_i \sigma = \tilde{t}$, then $x_i = length(\tilde{t})$ gives a solution of the Diophantine system, where $length(\tilde{t})$ is the number of elements in the sequence $\tilde{t}$.

5   Experimenting with the Mathematica Variant

The programming language of Mathematica, called Wolfram, supports equational variadic matching in A, C, AC theories with individual and sequence variables. The terminology is a bit different, though. Variadic associative symbols there are called *flat* and commutative ones *orderless*. Individual variables correspond to patterns like x_, and sequence variables to patterns like y___.

The matching variants used in Mathematica are efficiently implemented, but the algorithm is not public. In this section we first show Mathematica's behavior on some selected characteristic examples and then will try to imitate it by variants of our rules. In the experiments we used the Mathematica built-in function ReplaceList[expr,rules], which attempts to transform the entire expression expr by applying a rule or list of rules in all possible ways, and returns a list of the results obtained. In transformation, Mathematica tries to match rules to expr, exhibiting the behavior of the built-in matching mechanism. The equational theories can be specified by setting attributes (flat, orderless) to symbols.

The examples below are used to illustrate the behavior of Mathematica, but we prefer to write those examples in the notation of this paper. We compare it to our strict variant, because it also does not compute extra $f()$'s in the answer. However, they are not the same, as the examples below show. We report only sets of matchers, ignoring their order and how many times the same (syntactically or modulo an equational theory) matcher was computed.

Problem:	$f(\overline{x}) \ll_E f(a)$, f is A or AC.	(1)
Strict matchers:	$\{\overline{x} \mapsto a\}, \{\overline{x} \mapsto f(a)\}$.	
Mathematica:	$\{\overline{x} \mapsto a\}$.	
Problem:	$f(f()) \ll_E f()$, f is A or AC.	(2)
Strict matchers:	No solutions.	
Mathematica:	ε.	
Problem:	$f(x, y) \ll_E f(a, b)$, f is AC.	(3)
Strict matchers:	$\{x \mapsto t_1, y \mapsto t_2\}$, with $t_1 \in \{a, f(a)\}, t_2 \in \{b, f(b)\}$,	
	$\{x \mapsto t_1, y \mapsto t_2\}$, with $t_1 \in \{b, f(b)\}, t_2 \in \{a, f(a)\}$.	
Mathematica:	$\{x \mapsto f(a), y \mapsto f(b)\}, \{x \mapsto a, y \mapsto b\}$,	
	$\{x \mapsto f(b), y \mapsto f(a)\}, \{x \mapsto b, y \mapsto a\}$	
Problem:	$f(\overline{x}, \overline{y}) \ll_E f(a, b)$, f is AC.	(4)
Strict matchers:	$\{\overline{x} \mapsto (), \overline{y} \mapsto (t_1, t_2)\}$, with $t_1 \in \{a, f(a)\}, t_2 \in \{b, f(b)\}$,	
	$\{\overline{x} \mapsto (), \overline{y} \mapsto (t_1, t_2)\}$, with $t_1 \in \{b, f(b)\}, t_2 \in \{a, f(a)\}$,	
	$\{\overline{x} \mapsto (), \overline{y} \mapsto t\}$, with $t \in \{f(a, b), f(b, a)\}$,	
	$\{\overline{x} \mapsto (t_1, t_2), \overline{y} \mapsto ()\}$, with $t_1 \in \{a, f(a)\}, t_2 \in \{b, f(b)\}$,	
	$\{\overline{x} \mapsto (t_1, t_2), \overline{y} \mapsto ()\}$, with $t_1 \in \{b, f(b)\}, t_2 \in \{a, f(a)\}$,	
	$\{\overline{x} \mapsto t, \overline{y} \mapsto ()\}$, with $t \in \{f(a, b), f(b, a)\}$,	
	$\{\overline{x} \mapsto t_1, \overline{y} \mapsto t_2\}$, with $t_1 \in \{a, f(a)\}, t_2 \in \{b, f(b)\}$,	

	$\{\overline{x} \mapsto t_1, \overline{y} \mapsto t_2\}$, with $t_1 \in \{b, f(b)\}, t_2 \in \{a, f(a)\}$,
Mathematica:	$\{\overline{x} \mapsto a, \overline{y} \mapsto b\}, \{\overline{x} \mapsto b, \overline{y} \mapsto a\}$,
	$\{\overline{x} \mapsto (a, b), \overline{y} \mapsto ()\}, \{\overline{x} \mapsto (), \overline{y} \mapsto (a, b)\}$,
Problem:	$f(x, \overline{y}) \ll_E f(a, b, c)$, f is A. (5)
Strict matchers:	$\{x \mapsto a, \overline{y} \mapsto f(b, c)\}, \{x \mapsto f(a), \overline{y} \mapsto f(b, c)\}$,
	$\{x \mapsto f(a, b), \overline{y} \mapsto c\}, \{x \mapsto f(a, b), \overline{y} \mapsto f(c)\}$.
	$\{x \mapsto t_1, \overline{y} \mapsto (t_2, t_3)\}$,
	with $t_1 \in \{a, f(a)\}, t_2 \in \{b, f(b)\}, t_3 \in \{c, f(c)\}$,
	$\{x \mapsto f(a, b, c), \overline{y} \mapsto ()\}$.
Mathematica:	$\{x \mapsto a, \overline{y} \mapsto (b, c)\}, \{x \mapsto f(a), \overline{y} \mapsto (b, c)\}$,
	$\{x \mapsto f(a, b), \overline{y} \mapsto c\}, \{x \mapsto f(a, b, c), \overline{y} \mapsto ()\}$.
Problem:	$g(f(\overline{x}), \overline{x}) \ll_E g(f(a), f(a))$, f is A or AC, g is free. (6)
Strict matchers:	$\{\overline{x} \mapsto f(a)\}$.
Mathematica:	No solutions.
Problem:	$g(f(\overline{x}), g(\overline{x})) \ll_E g(f(b, a), g(b, a))$, f is C, g is free. (7)
Strict matchers:	$\{x \mapsto (b, a)\}$.
Mathematica:	No solutions.

In (2), strictness does not allow to flatten the left hand side, but Mathematica does not have this restriction and transforms the term into $f()$.

Interestingly, the behavior of Mathematica's matching changed from the version 6.0 to the version 11.2. As it was reported in [17], for the problem (5), Mathematica 6.0 would return three out of four substitutions reported above. It would not compute $\{x \mapsto a, \overline{y} \mapsto (b, c)\}$.

In problems like (3) Mathematica does not compute a matcher in which one individual variable is mapped to a subterm from the right hand side, and the other one is instantiated by f applied to a *single* subterm from the right hand side. (The same is true when f is A.) Examining more examples, e.g. $f(x, y, z) \ll_E f(a, b, c, d)$, for f being AC, confirms this observation. One can see there matchers like $\{x \mapsto a, y \mapsto b, z \mapsto f(c, d)\}$ and $\{x \mapsto f(a), y \mapsto f(b), z \mapsto f(c, d)\}$ (and many more, the solution set consists of 72 matchers), but not $\{x \mapsto a, y \mapsto f(b), z \mapsto f(c, d)\}$ or similar.

It is interesting to see how sequence variables behave in such a situation. Example (4) shows that in Mathematica matchers, f is not applied to terms from the right hand side. Besides, when a sequence variable is instantiated by a sequence, the order of elements in that sequence coincide with their relative order in the *canonical form* of the right hand side of the equation. For instance, in (4) Mathematica does not return $\{\overline{x} \mapsto (b, a), \overline{y} \mapsto ()\}$. Note that if f were only C in (4), Mathematica would still compute exactly the same set of matchers.

The canonical form of the right hand side is important. There is a so called canonical order imposed on all Mathematica expressions,[2] and whenever there is a commutative symbol, the system rearranges its arguments according to this order. This is why Mathematica returns $\{\overline{x} \mapsto (a, b)\}$ to the matching problem $f(\overline{x}) \ll_E f(b, a)$, when $\mathsf{C}(f) \in E$. The arguments of $f(b, a)$ are first rearranged by the canonical order into $f(a, b)$, and matching is performed afterwards. These issues affect solvability of problems, as one can see in (7). It also indicates that imitating Mathematica's nonlinear matching (i.e. when the same variable occurs more than once in matching equations) is not trivial.

The final set of examples concerns function variables. One can see from the examples that even if a function variable gets instantiated by an equational symbol, Mathematica treats that instance as a free symbol (in (9) and (10), $f(b, a)$ is first normalized to $f(a, b)$):

Problem:	$X(x) \ll_E f(a)$, f is A or AC.	(8)
Strict matchers:	$\{X \mapsto f, x \mapsto a\}, \{X \mapsto f, x \mapsto f(a)\}$.	
Mathematica:	$\{X \mapsto f, x \mapsto a\}$.	
Problem:	$X(x) \ll_E f(a, b)$, f is AC.	(9)
Strict matchers:	$\{X \mapsto f, \, x \mapsto f(a, b)\}$.	
Mathematica:	No solutions.	
Problem:	$X(a, b) \ll_E f(b, a)$, f is C.	(10)
Strict matchers:	$\{X \mapsto f\}$.	
Mathematica:	$\{X \mapsto f\}$.	
Problem:	$X(b, a) \ll_E f(b, a)$, f is C.	(11)
Strict matchers:	$\{X \mapsto f\}$.	
Mathematica:	No solutions.	
Problem:	$f(x, X(b, c)) \ll_E f(a, b, c), f$ is A or AC.	(12)
Strict matchers:	$\{X \mapsto f\}$.	
Mathematica:	No solutions.	

These observations suggest that an algorithm that tries to imitate Mathematica's equational matching behavior should first linearize the matching problem by giving unique names to all variable occurrences, try to solve the obtained linear problem, and at the end check whether the obtained solutions are consistent with the original variable names, i.e, if v_1 and v_2 were the unique copies of the same variable, then the computed matcher should map v_1 and v_2 to the same expression. Linearization makes substitution application to the remaining matching problems unnecessary.

---

[2] Roughly, the canonical order orders symbols alphabetically and extends to trees with respect to left-to-right pre-order.

To model the behavior of Mathematica's equational matching, we need to look into the behavior of each kind of variable.

Imitating the Behavior of Individual Variables Under A *and* AC *Symbols.* This concerns equations of the form $f(\tilde{s}) \ll_E f(\tilde{t})$, where $A(f) \in E$. As we observed, if individual variables x and y occur as arguments of $f(\tilde{s})$, and t_1 and t_2 are two terms among $\tilde{t}$, then for the same matcher σ it can not happen that $x\sigma = t_1$ and $y\sigma = f(t_2)$: Either $x\sigma$ should also have the head f, or $y\sigma$ should have more arguments. This is what Mathematica does.

To imitate this behavior, we introduce markings for equations of the form $f(\tilde{s}) \ll_E f(\tilde{t})$, where $A(f) \in E$. Initially, they are not marked. If IVE transforms such an unmarked equation, the obtained equation is marked by 0. IVE-AH-strict introduces marking 1, if $\tilde{t}_1$ is a single term in this rule. Otherwise, it does not mark the obtained equation. Further, if an equation is marked by 1, then IVE can not apply to it, while IVE-AH-strict can. If an equation is marked by 0, IVE-AH-strict may not use a singleton sequence $\tilde{t}_1$: more terms should be put in it. The equation can be also transformed by IVE.

Imitating the Behavior of Sequence Variables Under A *and* AC *Symbols.* For equations $f(\tilde{s}) \ll_E f(\tilde{t})$, where $A(f) \in E$ and a sequence variable $\overline{x}$ appears in its solution σ, no element of the sequence $\overline{x}\sigma$ should have f as its head. For this, we simply drop SVW-AH-strict.

Imitating the Behavior of Function Variables. Equations of the form $X(\tilde{s}) \ll_E f(\tilde{t})$ are transformed by a new rule, which we denote by FVE-M: $X(\tilde{s}) \ll_E f(\tilde{t}) \leadsto_\vartheta \{g(\tilde{s}) \ll_E g(\tilde{t})\}$, where $\vartheta = \{X \mapsto f\}$ and g is free. At the same time, if $C(f) \in E$, then $g(\tilde{t})$ is brought to the canonical form. FVE-M replaces FVE. Besides, FVE-AH-strict is dropped.

We denote the obtained algorithm by $\mathfrak{M}_{\mathrm{Mma}}$ to indicate that it (tries to) imitate the Mathematica variant of variadic equational matching.

Example 4. We apply $\mathfrak{M}_{\mathrm{Mma}}$ to the problem (3): $f(x,y) \ll_E f(a,b)$ with $E = \{A(f), C(f)\}$. Consider only the branch generated by applying Per with the identity permutation. IVE marks the obtained equation $f(y) \ll_E f(b)$ by 0 and records substitution $\{x \mapsto a\}$. To $f(y) \ll_E f(b)$, we can not apply IVE-AH-strict, because the marker is 0 and $f(b)$ does not have enough arguments this rule could assign to y. Therefore, IVE applies again, returning the matcher $\{x \mapsto a, y \mapsto b\}$.

On the alternative branch, IVE-AH-strict gives the substitution $\{x \mapsto f(a)\}$ and marks $f(y) \ll_E f(b)$ by 1. In the next step only the same rule applies and we get $\{x \mapsto f(a), y \mapsto f(b)\}$.

Example 5. Let the equation be $g(X(x,y), X(y,x)) \ll_E g(f(a,b), f(b,a))$, where $E = \{C(f)\}$. Linearization and decomposition give two matching equations $X_1(x_1, y_1) \ll_E f(a,b)$ and $X_2(y_2, x_2) \ll_E f(b,a)$. The first one gives the solution $\sigma_1 = \{X_1 \mapsto f, x_1 \mapsto a, y_1 \mapsto b\}$. In the second one, normalization changes the right hand side into $f(a,b)$ and the solution is $\sigma_2 = \{X_2 \mapsto f, x_2 \mapsto b, y_2 \mapsto a\}$. Since $x_1\sigma_1 \neq x_2\sigma_2$, the solutions are inconsistent and the problem is not solvable.

6 Discussion and Conclusion

We studied matching in variadic equational theories for associativity, commutativity, and their combination. A-matching is infinitary, which leads to a nonterminating procedure. It is still possible to have a terminating algorithm, which produces a finite representation of the infinite minimal complete set of matchers, but we did not consider this option in this paper. Instead, we formulated a modular procedure, which combines common and associative matching rules and deals with commutativity by permutation. The procedure can be easily changed to obtain special terminating cases. We illustrated two such cases: bounded fragment and strict variant. Further modifying the latter, we tried to imitate the behavior of the powerful equational matching algorithm of the Mathematica system.

Acknowledgments. This research has been partially supported by the Austrian Science Fund (FWF) under the project 28789-N32 and the Shota Rustaveli National Science Foundation of Georgia (SRNSFG) under the grant YS-18-1480.

References

1. Baader, F., Snyder, W.: Unification theory. In: Robinson, J.A., Voronkov, A. (eds.) Handbook of Automated Reasoning (in 2 volumes), pp. 445–532. Elsevier and MIT Press (2001)
2. Benanav, D., Kapur, D., Narendran, P.: Complexity of matching problems. J. Symb. Comput. **3**(1/2), 203–216 (1987). https://doi.org/10.1016/S0747-7171(87)80027-5
3. Buchberger, B., et al.: Theorema: towards computer-aided mathematical theory exploration. J. Appl. Logic **4**(4), 470–504 (2006). https://doi.org/10.1016/j.jal.2005.10.006
4. Cirstea, H., Kirchner, C., Kopetz, R., Moreau, P.E.: Anti-patterns for rule-based languages. J. Symb. Comput. **45**(5), 523–550 (2010). https://doi.org/10.1016/j.jsc.2010.01.007
5. Coelho, J., Florido, M.: CLP(Flex): constraint logic programming applied to XML processing. In: Meersman, R., Tari, Z. (eds.) OTM 2004. LNCS, vol. 3291, pp. 1098–1112. Springer, Heidelberg (2004). https://doi.org/10.1007/978-3-540-30469-2_17
6. Dundua, B., Kutsia, T., Reisenberger-Hagmayer, K.: An overview of PρLog. In: Lierler, Y., Taha, W. (eds.) PADL 2017. LNCS, vol. 10137, pp. 34–49. Springer, Cham (2017). https://doi.org/10.1007/978-3-319-51676-9_3
7. Eker, S.: Single elementary associative-commutative matching. J. Autom. Reason. **28**(1), 35–51 (2002). https://doi.org/10.1023/A:1020122610698
8. Eker, S.: Associative-commutative rewriting on large terms. In: Nieuwenhuis, R. (ed.) RTA 2003. LNCS, vol. 2706, pp. 14–29. Springer, Heidelberg (2003). https://doi.org/10.1007/3-540-44881-0_3
9. Horozal, F.: A framework for defining declarative languages. Ph.D. thesis, Jacobs University Bremen (2014)
10. Horozal, F., Rabe, F., Kohlhase, M.: Flexary operators for formalized mathematics. In: Watt, S.M., Davenport, J.H., Sexton, A.P., Sojka, P., Urban, J. (eds.) CICM 2014. LNCS (LNAI), vol. 8543, pp. 312–327. Springer, Cham (2014). https://doi.org/10.1007/978-3-319-08434-3_23

11. Hullot, J.: Associative commutative pattern matching. In: Buchanan, B.G. (ed.) Proceedings of the Sixth International Joint Conference on Artificial Intelligence, IJCAI 1979, Tokyo, Japan, 20–23 August 1979, 2 Volumes, pp. 406–412. William Kaufmann (1979)

12. International Organization for Standardization: Information technology—Common Logic (CL)—a framework for a family of logic-based languages. International Standard ISO/IEC 24707:2018(E) (2018). https://www.iso.org/standard/66249.html

13. Krebber, M., Barthels, H., Bientinesi, P.: Efficient pattern matching in python. In: Schreiber, A., Scullin, W., Spotz, B., Thomas, R. (eds.) Proceedings of the 7th Workshop on Python for High-Performance and Scientific Computing. ACM (2017)

14. Kutsia, T.: Solving and proving in equational theories with sequence variables and flexible arity symbols. RISC Report Series 02–09, RISC, Johannes Kepler University Linz (2002)

15. Kutsia, T.: Unification with sequence variables and flexible arity symbols and its extension with pattern-terms. In: Calmet, J., Benhamou, B., Caprotti, O., Henocque, L., Sorge, V. (eds.) AISC/Calculemus -2002. LNCS (LNAI), vol. 2385, pp. 290–304. Springer, Heidelberg (2002). https://doi.org/10.1007/3-540-45470-5_26

16. Kutsia, T.: Solving equations with sequence variables and sequence functions. J. Symb. Comput. **42**(3), 352–388 (2007). https://doi.org/10.1016/j.jsc.2006.12.002

17. Kutsia, T.: Flat matching. J. Symb. Comput. **43**(12), 858–873 (2008). https://doi.org/10.1016/j.jsc.2008.05.001

18. Kutsia, T., Marin, M.: Solving, reasoning, and programming in Common Logic. In: Voronkov, A., et al. (eds.) 14th International Symposium on Symbolic and Numeric Algorithms for Scientific Computing, SYNASC 2012, Timisoara, Romania, 26–29 September 2012, pp. 119–126. IEEE Computer Society (2012). https://doi.org/10.1109/SYNASC.2012.27

19. Kutsia, T., Marin, M.: Regular expression order-sorted unification and matching. J. Symb. Comput. **67**, 42–67 (2015). https://doi.org/10.1016/j.jsc.2014.08.002

20. Marin, M., Kutsia, T.: On the implementation of a rule-based programming system and some of its applications. In: Konev, B., Schmidt, R. (eds.) Proceedings 4th International Workshop on the Implementation of Logics, WIL 2003, pp. 55–68 (2003)

21. Marin, M., Tepeneu, D.: Programming with sequence variables: the Sequentica package. In: Proceedings of the 5th International Mathematica Symposium on Challenging the Boundaries of Symbolic Computation, pp. 17–24. World Scientific (2003)

22. Wolfram, S.: The Mathematica Book, 5th edn. Wolfram Media (2003)

Comparing Machine Learning Models to Choose the Variable Ordering for Cylindrical Algebraic Decomposition

Matthew England$^{(\boxtimes)}$ and Dorian Florescu

Faculty of Engineering, Environment and Computing, Coventry University,
Coventry CV1 5FB, UK
{Matthew.England,Dorian.Florescu}@coventry.ac.uk

Abstract. There has been recent interest in the use of machine learning (ML) approaches within mathematical software to make choices that impact on the computing performance without affecting the mathematical correctness of the result. We address the problem of selecting the variable ordering for cylindrical algebraic decomposition (CAD), an important algorithm in Symbolic Computation. Prior work to apply ML on this problem implemented a Support Vector Machine (SVM) to select between three existing human-made heuristics, which did better than anyone heuristic alone. Here we extend this result by training ML models to select the variable ordering directly, and by trying out a wider variety of ML techniques.

We experimented with the NLSAT dataset and the Regular Chains Library CAD function for Maple 2018. For each problem, the variable ordering leading to the shortest computing time was selected as the target class for ML. Features were generated from the polynomial input and used to train the following ML models: k-nearest neighbours (KNN) classifier, multi-layer perceptron (MLP), decision tree (DT) and SVM, as implemented in the Python scikit-learn package. We also compared these with the two leading human-made heuristics for the problem: the Brown heuristic and sotd. On this dataset all of the ML approaches outperformed the human-made heuristics, some by a large margin.

Keywords: Computer algebra · Symbolic computation ·
Non-linear real arithmetic · Cylindrical algebraic decomposition ·
Machine learning

1 Introduction

A logical statement is *quantified* if it involves the universal quantifier $\forall$ or the existential quantifier $\exists$. The *Quantifier Elimination* (QE) problem is to derive from a quantified formula an equivalent un-quantified one. A simple example would be that the quantified statement, "$\exists x.\, x^2 + bx + c = 0$" is equivalent to the unquantified statement "$b^2 - 4c \geq 0$", when working over the real numbers.

© Springer Nature Switzerland AG 2019
C. Kaliszyk et al. (Eds.): CICM 2019, LNAI 11617, pp. 93–108, 2019.
https://doi.org/10.1007/978-3-030-23250-4_7

QE is one definition for simplifying or solving a problem. The tools involved fall within the field of Symbolic Computation, implemented in Computer Algebra Systems (or more recently in SMT-solvers).

Our work is on Quantifier Elimination over the reals. Here the logical statements are expressed as *Tarski formulae*, Boolean combinations $(\wedge, \vee, \neg, \rightarrow)$ of statements about the signs of polynomials with integer coefficients. QE in this theory was first shown to be soluble by Tarski [53] in the 1940s. However, the only implemented general real QE procedure has algorithmic complexity doubly exponential in the number of variables [22], a theoretical result experienced in practice. For many problem classes QE procedures will work well at first, but as the problem size increases the doubly exponential wall is inevitably hit. It is hence of critical importance to optimise QE procedures and the formulation of problems, to "push the doubly exponential wall back" and open up a wider range of tractable applications.

QE procedures can be run in multiple ways to solve a given problem: they can be initialized with different options (e.g. variable ordering [23], equational constraint designation [10]); tasks can be completed in different orders (e.g. order of constraint analysis [26]); and the problem itself may be expressible in different formalisations [56]. Changing these settings can have a substantial effect on the computational costs (both time and memory) but does not effect the mathematical correctness of the output. They are thus suitable candidates for machine learning: tools that allow computers to make decisions that are not explicitly programmed, via the statistical analysis of large quantities of data.

We continue in Sect. 2 by introducing background material on the particular decision we study: the variable ordering for Cylindrical Algebraic Decomposition. Here we also outline prior attempts to solve this problem; and prior applications of machine learning to computer algebra. Then in Sect. 3 we describe our methodology covering datasets, software, features extracted from the problems, machine learning models tests, and how we test against human-made heuristics. We present our results in Sect. 4 and final thoughts in Sect. 5.

2   Variable Ordering for CAD

2.1   Cylindrical Algebraic Decomposition

A *Cylindrical Algebraic Decomposition* (CAD) is a *decomposition* of ordered $\mathbb{R}^n$ space into cells arranged *cylindrically*: meaning the projections of any pair of cells with respect to the variable ordering are either equal or disjoint. The cells are (semi)-algebraic meaning each cell can be described with a finite sequence of polynomial constraints. A CAD is produced to be invariant relative to an input, i.e. *truth-invariant* for a logical formula (so the formula is either true or false throughout each cell). Such a decomposition can then be used to perform quantifier elimination on the formula by testing a finite set of sample points and constructing a quantifier-free formula from the semi-algebraic cell descriptions.

CAD was introduced by Collins in 1975 [19] and works relative to a set of polynomials. Collins' CAD produces a decomposition so that each polynomial has constant sign on each cell (thus truth invariant for any formula built with those polynomials). The algorithm first projects the polynomials into smaller and smaller dimensions; and then uses these to lift − to incrementally build decompositions of larger and larger spaces according to the polynomials at that level. For full details on the original CAD algorithm see [3].

QE has numerous applications throughout science and engineering (see for example the survey [52]). New applications are found regularly, such as the derivation of optimal numerical schemes [31], and the validatation of economic hypotheses [45, 46]. CAD has also found application independent of QE, such as reasoning with multi-valued functions [21] (where we decompose to see where simplification rules are valid); and biological networks [7, 29] where we decompose to identify regions in parameter space where multi-stationarity can occur.

The definition of cylindricity and both stages of the algorithm are relative to an ordering of the variables. For example, given polynomials in variables ordered as $x_n \succ x_{n-1} \succ \ldots, \succ x_2 \succ x_1$ we first project away x_n and so on until we are left with polynomials univariate in x_1. We then start lifting by decomposing the x_1−axis, and then the (x_1, x_2)−plane and so so on. The cylindricity condition refers to projections of cells in $\mathbb{R}^n$ onto a space $(x_1, \ldots, x_m)$ where $m < n$.

There have been numerous advances to CAD since its inception, for example: on how best to implement the projection [12, 34, 43, 44]; avoiding the need for full CAD [20, 55]; symbolic-numeric lifting schemes [38, 50]; adapting to the Boolean structure in the input [8, 9, 27]; and local projection approaches [15, 51]. However, in all cases, the need for a fixed variable ordering remains.

2.2   Effect of the Variable Ordering

Depending on the application requirements the variable ordering may be determined, constrained, or entirely free. The most common application, QE, requires that the variables be eliminated in the order in which they are quantified in the formula but makes no requirement on the free variables. For example, we could eliminate the quantifier in $\exists x.\, ax^2 + bx + c = 0$ using any CAD which eliminates x first; giving six possible orderings to choose from. A CAD for the polynomial under ordering $a \prec b \prec c$ has only 27 cells, but needs 115 for the reverse ordering.

Note that since we can switch the order of quantified variables in a statement when the quantifier is the same, we also have some choice on the ordering of quantified variables. For example, a QE problem of the form $\exists x \exists y \forall a\, \phi(x, y, a)$ could be solved by a CAD under either ordering $x \succ y \succ a$ or ordering $y \succ x \succ a$.

The choice of variable ordering has been long known to have a great effect on the time and memory use of CAD, and the number of cells in the output. In fact, Brown and Davenport presented a class of problems in which one variable ordering gave output of double exponential complexity in the number of variables and another output of a constant size [14].

2.3   Prior Work on Choosing the Variable Ordering

Heuristics have been developed to choose a variable ordering, with Dolzmann et al. [23] giving the best known study. After analysing a variety of metrics they proposed a polynomial degree based heuristic (the heuristic sotd defined later). However the second author demonstrated examples for which that heuristic could be misled in CICM 2013 [10]; showed that tailoring it to an implementation could improve its performance in ICMS 2014 [28]; and in CICM 2014 [37] reported that a computationally cheaper heuristic by Brown actually outperforms sotd.

In CICM 2014 [37] we used a support vector machine (SVM), an ML model widely used for non-linear classification, to choose which of three human-made heuristics to believe when picking the variable ordering. The experiments in [37] identified substantial subclasses on which each of the three heuristics made the best decision, and demonstrated that the machine learned choice did significantly better than any one heuristic overall. This motivated the present study where we consider a wider range of machine learning models and have these pick the ordering directly from the full range of choices.

2.4   Other Applications of ML to Mathematical Software

The CICM 2014 paper was the first to document the application of machine learning to CAD, or in fact to any symbolic computation algorithm/computer algebra system. Since then there have been two further studies:

– The same authors studied a different choice related to CAD (whether to precondition the input with Gröbner bases) in [35,36], again finding that a support vector machine could make the choice more accurately than the human-made heuristic (if features of the Gröbner Basis could be used).
– At MACIS 2016 there was a study applying a support vector machine to decide the order of sub-formulae solving for a QE procedure [40].

The survey paper [25] and the ICMS 2018 Special Session on Machine Learning for Mathematical Software demonstrated the wide range of other potential applications. As discussed there, while the use of machine learning in computer algebra is rare it has become a key tool in other mathematical software development. Most notably automated reasoning [2,11,41,54]; but also satisfiability checking [42,59].

3   Methodology

3.1   Dataset

Despite its long history and significant software contributions the Computer Algebra community had a lack of substantial datasets [33]: a significant barrier to machine learning. Despite efforts to address this[1], the most substantial dataset of problems designed for CAD is [58] with less than 100 examples.

---

[1] E.g. the PoSSo and FRISCO projects in the 90s and the SymbolicData Project [32].

However, CAD has recently found prominence in a new area: Satisfiability Modulo Theories (SMT). Here, efficient algorithms for the Boolean SAT problem study the Boolean skeleton of a problem, with a theory solver then checking if a satisfying Boolean assignment is valid in the domain (learning new clauses if not) [4]. For the SMT domain of Non-linear Real Arithmetic (NRA), CAD can play the role of such theory solvers[2], and so their test problems may be used to evaluate CAD. We use the `nlsat` dataset[3] produced to evaluate the work in [39]. The main sources of the examples are: METITARSKI [47], an automatic theorem prover for theorems with real-valued special functions (it applies real polynomial bounds and then using QE tools like CAD); problems originating from attempts to prove termination of term-rewrite systems; verification conditions from Keymaera [49]; and parametrized generalizations of geometric problems.

The problems in the `nlsat` dataset are all fully existential (the only quantifier is $\exists$) which is why they may be studied by SAT solvers. Although CAD can make adaptions based on the quantifiers in the input (most notably via Partial CAD [20]) the conclusions drawn are likely to be applicable outside of the SAT context.

We extracted 6117 problems with 3 variables from this database, meaning each has a choice of six different variable orderings. We randomly divided them into two datasets for training (4612) and testing (1505). The training dataset was used to tune the parameters of the ML models. The testing dataset was unknown to the models during training, and is used to compare the performance of the different ML models and the human-made heuristics.

3.2   Software

We experimented using the CAD routine `CylindricalAlgebraicDecompose` which is part of the `RegularChains` Library for MAPLE. This algorithm builds decompositions first of n-dimensional complex space before refining to a CAD of $\mathbb{R}^n$ [6,17,18]. We ran the code in Maple 2018 but used an updated version of the `RegularChains` Library downloaded from http://www.regularchains.org, which contains bug fixes and additional functionality. We ignored the quantifiers and logical connectives, using only the polynomials as input to CAD. The function thus returned a sign-invariant CAD for the polynomials.

The training and evaluation of the machine learning models was done using the `scikit-learn` package [48] v0.20.2 for Python 2.7. The features for machine learning were extracted using code written in the `sympy` package v1.3 for Python 2.7, as was the Brown heuristic. The sotd heuristic was implemented in MAPLE as part of the `ProjectionCAD` package [30].

3.3   Timings

CAD construction was timed in a Maple script that was called using the *os* package in Python for each CAD, to avoid Maple caching of results.

---

[2] However, as discussed by [1] a more custom approach is beneficial.

[3] http://cs.nyu.edu/~dejan/nonlinear/.

The target variable ordering for ML was defined as the one that minimises the computing time for a given SAT problem. All CAD function calls included a time limit. The problems in the training dataset were processed with an initial time limit of 4 s on all variable orderings. The time limit was doubled if all 6 orderings timed out. The process stopped when the CAD routine was completed for at least one ordering. All problems in the training dataset could be assigned a target variable ordering using time limits smaller than 64 s.

The problems in the testing dataset were processed with a larger time limit of 128 s for all orderings. This was in order to allow a better comparison of the computing times for the ML and the heuristics. When a variable ordering timed out, the computing time was considered equal to 128 s.

3.4   Features

We computed the same set of 11 features for each SAT problem as [37], which are listed in Table 1. All these features could be computed from the input polynomials immediately. A possibility for future work is to consider features that are more expensive, such as those from post-processing as in [35], those from the end of CAD projection as sotd does, or perhaps even going further into partial lifting as in [57]. The ML models associate a predicted variable ordering to each set of 11 features. The training and testing feature set were normalised using the mean and standard deviation of the training set.

Table 1. The features used by ML to predict variable orderings.

Feature number	Description
1	Number of polynomials
2	Maximum total degree of polynomials
3	Maximum degree of x_0 among all polynomials
4	Maximum degree of x_1 among all polynomials
5	Maximum degree of x_2 among all polynomials
6	Proportion of x_0 occuring in polynomials
7	Proportion of x_1 occuring in polynomials
8	Proportion of x_2 occuring in polynomials
9	Proportion of x_0 occuring in monomials
10	Proportion of x_1 occuring in monomials
11	Proportion of x_2 occuring in monomials

3.5   ML Models

Four of the most commonly used deterministic ML models were tuned on the training data (for details on the methods see for example the textbook [5]):

- The K−Nearest Neighbours (KNN) classifier [5, §2.5].
- The Multi-Layer Perceptron (MLP) classifier [5, §2.5].
- The Decision Tree (DT) classifier [5, §14.4].
- The Support Vector Machine (SVM) classifier with RBF kernel [5, §6.3].

The KNN classifier is a type of *instance-based* classifier, i.e. it does not construct an internal model of the data but stores all the instances in the training data for prediction. So for each new data instance the model selects the nearest k training instances. Selection can be performed by weighting instances equally, or by weighting a training instance inversely proportional to its distance from the new instance. The prediction is given by the class with the highest count among those training instances. Three algorithms are typically used to train KNN: the *brute force* algorithm computes the distances between all pairs of points, the *k-dimensional tree* algorithm partitions the data along Cartesian axes, and the *ball tree* algorithm partitions the data in a series of nesting hyper-spheres.

The DT is a non-parametric model that uses a tree-like model of decisions and their possible consequences. Each node in the tree represents a test on an attribute, each branch the outcome of the test. The *leaves* are the end points of each branch, representing the predicted class label. There are two common criteria used to assess the quality of a split in the DT. The Gini impurity criterion verifies how often a randomly chosen element would be correctly labelled if it were randomly labeled according to the distribution of labels in the subset. The entropy criterion assesses the information gain after each split.

The SVM is a model that can perform linear and non-linear classification, by selecting an appropriate kernel. It is also known as a maximum-margin classifier, because it identifies a hyperplane in the feature space that maximises the distance to the nearest data points 5. The SVM kernel acts as a similarity function between the training examples and a few predefined *landmarks*, that can offer additional computing performance. The most common kernels are: *linear*, *polynomial*, *sigmoidal* and *radial basis function* (RBF). The RBF kernel is one of the most common kernel choices, given by

$$\mathcal{K}(\mathbf{x}, \boldsymbol{\ell}) = e^{-\gamma \cdot \|\mathbf{x} - \boldsymbol{\ell}\|^2},$$

where γ is the kernel hyperparameter, and $\ell \in \mathbb{R}^n$ is a predefined *landmark*, and $\mathbf{x} \in \mathbb{R}^n$ is the training vector with n features.

The MLP is a class of feedforward artificial neural networks. It consists of a minimum of 3 layers: the input, hidden and output layer. Both the hidden and output layers use a nonlinear activation function that can be selected during cross-validation. Some of the common activation functions are: *identity*, *logistic*, *hyperbolic tangent*, and *rectified linear*.

3.6 Training

Each model was trained using grid search 5-fold cross-validation. Specifically, the training feature set was randomly divided in 5 equal parts. Each of the possible

Table 2. The hyperparameters of the ML models optimised with 5-fold cross-validation on the training dataset.

Model	Hyperparameter	Value
Decision Tree	Criterion	Gini impurity
	Maximum tree depth	17
K-Nearest Neighbours	Train instances weighting	Inversely proportional to distance
	Algorithm	Ball Tree
Support Vector Machine	Regularization parameter C	316
	Kernel	Radial basis function
	γ	0.08
	Tolerance for stopping criterion	0.0316
Multi-Layer Perceptron	Hidden layer size	18
	Activation function	Hyperbolic tangent
	Algorithm	Quasi-Newton based optimiser
	Regularization parameter α	$5 \cdot 10^{-5}$

combinations of 4 parts was used to tune the model parameters, leaving the last part for fitting the hyperparameters by cross-validation. For each of the models, the grid search was performed for an initially large range for each hyperparameter. This range was increased until all optimal hyperparameters were inside the range, and not on the edge. Subsequently, the range was gradually decreased to home in on each optimal hyperparameter, until the performance plateaued. Each grid search lasted from a few seconds for simpler models like KNN to a few minutes for more complex models like MLP. The optimal hyperparameters selected during cross-validation are in Table 2.

3.7 Comparing with Human-Made Heuristics

The ML approaches were compared in terms of prediction accuracy and resulting CAD computing time against the two best known human-made heuristics.

Brown. This heuristic chooses a variable ordering according to the following criteria, starting with the first and breaking ties with successive ones:
(1) Eliminate a variable first if it has lower overall degree in the input.
(2) Eliminate a variable first if it has lower (maximum) total degree of those terms in the input in which it occurs.
(3) Eliminate a variable first if there is a smaller number of terms in the input which contain the variable.
It is named after Brown who documented it only in the notes of a tutorial[4].

---

[4] https://www.usna.edu/Users/cs/wcbrown/research/ISSAC04/handout.pdf.

sotd. This heuristic constructs the full set of projection polynomials for each permitted ordering and selects the ordering whose corresponding set has the lowest sum of total degrees for each of the monomials in each of the polynomials. It was the reccommendation made after the study [23].

Unlike the ML models, these human-made heuristics can end up predicting several variable orderings (i.e. when they cannot discriminate). In practice if this were to happen the heuristic would select one randomly (or perhaps lexicographically), however that final pick is not particularly meaningful for an evaluation. To accommodate this, for each problem, the prediction accuracy of such a heuristic is judged to be the percentage of its predicted variable orderings that are also target orderings. The average of this percentage over all problems in the testing dataset represents the prediction accuracy. Similarly, the computing time for such methods was assessed as the average computing time over all predicted orderings, and it is this that is summed up for all problems in the testing dataset.

4 Results

We compare the four ML models on the percentage of problems where they selected the optimum ordering, and the total computation time (in seconds) for solving all the problems with their chosen orderings. We also compare the ML models with the two human-made heuristics (with the adaptations outlined in Sect. 3.7) and finally the outcome of a random choice between the 6 orderings. The results are presented in Table 3. We might expect a random choice to be correct one sixth of the time for this data set (16.6%). The actual accuracy is a little higher because the dataset is not uniform, and for some problem instances there were multiple variable orderings with equally fast timings.

Table 3. The comparative performance of DT, KNN, MLP, SVM, and the Brown and sotd heuristics on the testing dataset.

	DT	KNN	MLP	SVM	Brown	sotd	random
Accuracy	62.6%	63.3%	61.6%	58.8%	51%	49.5%	22.7%
Computation time (s)	9, 994	10, 105	9, 822	10, 725	10, 951	11, 938	30, 235

Moreover, we evaluate the distribution of the computation time for the ML methods and the heuristics. The differences between the computation time of each method and the minimum computation time, given as a percentage of the minimum time, are depicted in Fig. 1.

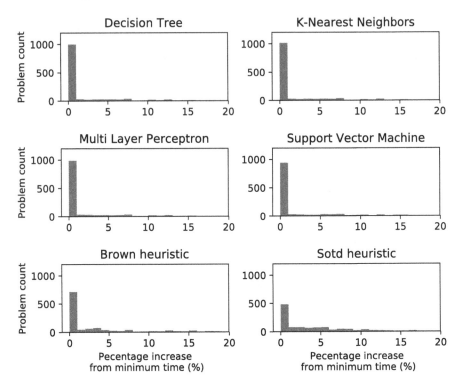

Fig. 1. The histograms of the percentage increase in computation time relative to the minimum computation time for each method, calculated for a bin size of 1%.

4.1 Range of Possible Outcomes

We note that the minimum total computing time achieved by selecting an optimal variable ordering for every problem would be 8, 623 s. Choosing at random would take 30, 235 s, almost 4 times as much. The maximum total computing time, determined by selecting the variable ordering with the longest computing time, is 64, 534 s. The choices with the quickest time among the methods considered were achieved by the Decision Tree model: 9, 994 s, which is 16% more than the minimal possible. So there are clearly great time savings to be made by taking this choice into account.

4.2 Human-Made Heuristics

Of the two human-made heuristics, Brown performed the best, as it did in [37]. As was noted there this is surprising since the sotd heuristic has access to additional information (not just the input polynomials but also their projections). Unlike the ML models and the Brown heuristic, obtaining an ordering for a problem instance with sotd is not instantaneous. Generating an ordering with sotd for all problems in the testing dataset took over 30 min.

Brown could solve all problems in 10,951 s, 27% more than the minimum. While sotd is only 0.7% less accurate than Brown in identifying the best ordering, it is much slower at 11,938 s or 38% more than the minimum. This shows that while Brown is not much better at identifying the best ordering, it does a much better job at discarding the worst!

4.3   ML Choices

The results show that all ML approaches outperform the human-made heuristics in terms of both accuracy and timings. Figure 1 shows that the human-made heuristics result in computing times that are often significantly larger than 1% of the corresponding minimum time for each problem. The ML methods, on the other hand, all result in almost 1000 problems ($\sim$75% of the testing dataset) within 1% of the minimum time.

The key finding of the present paper is that there are significantly better models to use for the problem than SVM: each of the other three had 10% higher accuracy and much lower timings. It is interesting to note that the MLP model leads to a lower accuracy than DT and KNN, but achieves the lowest overall computing time. This suggests that on this dataset, the MLP model is best at leaving out variable orderings that lead to long computing times, even if it has a slightly higher chance of missing the target variable ordering.

4.4   Conclusion

For a casual user of computer algebra the key consideration is probably that their computation does not hang, and that it finishes reasonably fast on the widest variety of questions. Hence of the tested models we may recommend the MLP for use going forward. However, all the models show promise and we emphasise that this conclusion applies only for the present dataset and we need wider experimentation to see if this finding is replicated.

5   Final Thoughts

The experiment shows a clear advance on the prior state of the art: both in terms of accuracy of predictions for CAD variable ordering; and in understanding which models are the best suited for this problem. But we acknowledge that there is much more to do and emphasise that this is only the initial findings of the project. The following extensions will be undertaken shortly:

- Extending the experiment to include problems with more variables from the dataset. Unlike some CAD implementations the one used does not change algorithm when $n > 3$; however, like all CAD implementation the time required will increase exponentially.
- Using the trained classifiers to test on CAD problems from outside the dataset, in particular, those which are not fully existentially quantified (SAT problems). In such cases the algorithms can change (terminate early) and it is not clear if models trained for the SAT case can be applied there.

– Using the trained classifiers to test on CAD implementations other than the one in the MAPLE `RegularChains` Library. For example, can the classifiers also usually pick variable orderings for QEPCAD-B, [13], or REDLOG [24].
– Examining how best to derive additional features to use for the training, and the use of feature selections tools to find an optimal subset.
– Test a dynamical selection of the variable ordering, where ML only picks the first variable for a problem, the polynomials are projected along that variable, and then the process repeats iteratively.

Finally, we note the wide variety of additional problems in computer algebra systems open to study with machine learning [25].

Acknowledgments. The authors are supported by EPSRC Project EP/R019622/1: *Embedding Machine Learning within Quantifier Elimination Procedures.*

Research Data Statement. Data supporting the research in this paper is available at: http://doi.org/10.5281/zenodo.2658626.

References

1. Ábrahám, E., et al.: SC^2: satisfiability checking meets symbolic computation. In: Kohlhase, M., Johansson, M., Miller, B., de de Moura, L., Tompa, F. (eds.) CICM 2016. LNCS (LNAI), vol. 9791, pp. 28–43. Springer, Cham (2016). https://doi.org/10.1007/978-3-319-42547-4_3
2. Alemi, A., Chollet, F., Een, N., Irving, G., Szegedy, C., Urban, J.: DeepMath-deep sequence models for premise selection. In: Proceedings of the 30th International Conference on Neural Information Processing Systems, NIPS 2016, pp. 2243–2251, Curran Associates Inc. (2016). https://papers.nips.cc/paper/6280-deepmath-deep-sequence-models-for-premise-selection.pdf
3. Arnon, D., Collins, G., McCallum, S.: Cylindrical algebraic decomposition I: the basic algorithm. SIAM J. Comput. **13**, 865–877 (1984). https://doi.org/10.1137/0213054
4. Barrett, C., Sebastiani, R., Seshia, S., Tinelli, C.: Satisfiability modulo theories. In: Biere, A., Heule, M., van Maaren, H., Walsh, T. (eds.) Handbook of Satisfiability. Frontiers in Artificial Intelligence and Applications, Chap. 26, vol. 185 pp. 825–885. IOS Press (2009)
5. Bishop, C.: Pattern Recognition and Machine Learning. Springer, New York (2006)
6. Bradford, R., Chen, C., Davenport, J.H., England, M., Moreno Maza, M., Wilson, D.: Truth table invariant cylindrical algebraic decomposition by regular chains. In: Gerdt, V.P., Koepf, W., Seiler, W.M., Vorozhtsov, E.V. (eds.) CASC 2014. LNCS, vol. 8660, pp. 44–58. Springer, Cham (2014). https://doi.org/10.1007/978-3-319-10515-4_4
7. Bradford, R., et al.: A case study on the parametric occurrence of multiple steady states. In: Proceedings of the 42nd International Symposium on Symbolic and Algebraic Computation, ISSAC 2017, pp. 45–52. ACM (2017). https://doi.org/10.1145/3087604.3087622
8. Bradford, R., Davenport, J., England, M., McCallum, S., Wilson, D.: Cylindrical algebraic decompositions for Boolean combinations. In: Proceedings of the 38th International Symposium on Symbolic and Algebraic Computation, ISSAC 2013, pp. 125–132. ACM (2013). https://doi.org/10.1145/2465506.2465516

9. Bradford, R., Davenport, J., England, M., McCallum, S., Wilson, D.: Truth table invariant cylindrical algebraic decomposition. J. Symb. Comput. **76**, 1–35 (2016). https://doi.org/10.1016/j.jsc.2015.11.002

10. Bradford, R., Davenport, J.H., England, M., Wilson, D.: Optimising problem formulation for cylindrical algebraic decomposition. In: Carette, J., Aspinall, D., Lange, C., Sojka, P., Windsteiger, W. (eds.) CICM 2013. LNCS (LNAI), vol. 7961, pp. 19–34. Springer, Heidelberg (2013). https://doi.org/10.1007/978-3-642-39320-4_2

11. Bridge, J., Holden, S., Paulson, L.: Machine learning for first-order theorem proving. J. Autom. Reason. **53**, 141–172 (2014). 10.1007/s10817-014-9301-5

12. Brown, C.: Improved projection for cylindrical algebraic decomposition. J. Symb. Comput. **32**(5), 447–465 (2001). https://doi.org/10.1006/jsco.2001.0463

13. Brown, C.: QEPCAD B: a program for computing with semi-algebraic sets using CADs. ACM SIGSAM Bull. **37**(4), 97–108 (2003). https://doi.org/10.1145/968708.968710

14. Brown, C., Davenport, J.: The complexity of quantifier elimination and cylindrical algebraic decomposition. In: Proceedings of the 32nd International Symposium on Symbolic and Algebraic Computation, ISSAC 2007, pp. 54–60. ACM (2007). https://doi.org/10.1145/1277548.1277557

15. Brown, C., Kosta, M.: Constructing a single cell in cylindrical algebraic decomposition. J. Symb. Comput. **70**, 14–48 (2015). https://doi.org/10.1016/j.jsc.2014.09.024

16. Caviness, B., Johnson, J.: Quantifier Elimination and Cylindrical Algebraic Decomposition. TEXTSMONOGR. Springer, Vienna (1998). https://doi.org/10.1007/978-3-7091-9459-1

17. Chen, C., Moreno Maza, M.: An incremental algorithm for computing cylindrical algebraic decompositions. In: Feng, R., Lee, W., Sato, Y. (eds.) Computer Mathematics. LNCS (LNAI), pp. 199–221. Springer, Heidelberg (2014). https://doi.org/10.1007/978-3-662-43799-5_17

18. Chen, C., Moreno Maza, M., Xia, B., Yang, L.: Computing cylindrical algebraic decomposition via triangular decomposition. In: Proceedings of the 34th International Symposium on Symbolic and Algebraic Computation, ISSAC 2009, pp. 95–102. ACM (2009). https://doi.org/10.1145/1576702.1576718

19. Collins, G.E.: Quantifier elimination for real closed fields by cylindrical algebraic decompostion. In: Brakhage, H. (ed.) GI-Fachtagung 1975. LNCS, vol. 33, pp. 134–183. Springer, Heidelberg (1975). https://doi.org/10.1007/3-540-07407-4_17

20. Collins, G., Hong, H.: Partial cylindrical algebraic decomposition for quantifier elimination. J. Symb. Comput. **12**, 299–328 (1991). https://doi.org/10.1016/S0747-7171(08)80152-6

21. Davenport, J., Bradford, R., England, M., Wilson, D.: Program verification in the presence of complex numbers, functions with branch cuts etc. In: 14th International Symposium on Symbolic and Numeric Algorithms for Scientific Computing, SYNASC 2012, pp. 83–88. IEEE (2012). https://doi.org/10.1109/SYNASC.2012.68

22. Davenport, J., Heintz, J.: Real quantifier elimination is doubly exponential. J. Symb. Comput. **5**(1–2), 29–35 (1988). https://doi.org/10.1016/S0747-7171(88)80004-X

23. Dolzmann, A., Seidl, A., Sturm, T.: Efficient projection orders for CAD. In: Proceedings of the 29th International Symposium on Symbolic and Algebraic Computation, ISSAC 2004, pp. 111–118. ACM (2004). https://doi.org/10.1145/1005285.1005303

24. Dolzmann, A., Sturm, T.: REDLOG: computer algebra meets computer logic. SIGSAM Bull. **31**(2), 2–9 (1997). https://doi.org/10.1145/261320.261324

25. England, M.: Machine learning for mathematical software. In: Davenport, J.H., Kauers, M., Labahn, G., Urban, J. (eds.) ICMS 2018. LNCS, vol. 10931, pp. 165–174. Springer, Cham (2018). https://doi.org/10.1007/978-3-319-96418-8_20

26. England, M., Bradford, R., Chen, C., Davenport, J.H., Maza, M.M., Wilson, D.: Problem formulation for truth-table invariant cylindrical algebraic decomposition by incremental triangular decomposition. In: Watt, S.M., Davenport, J.H., Sexton, A.P., Sojka, P., Urban, J. (eds.) CICM 2014. LNCS (LNAI), vol. 8543, pp. 45–60. Springer, Cham (2014). https://doi.org/10.1007/978-3-319-08434-3_5

27. England, M., Bradford, R., Davenport, J.: Improving the use of equational constraints in cylindrical algebraic decomposition. In: Proceedings of the 40th International Symposium on Symbolic and Algebraic Computation, ISSAC 2015, pp. 165–172. ACM (2015). https://doi.org/10.1145/2755996.2756678

28. England, M., Bradford, R., Davenport, J.H., Wilson, D.: Choosing a variable ordering for truth-table invariant cylindrical algebraic decomposition by incremental triangular decomposition. In: Hong, H., Yap, C. (eds.) ICMS 2014. LNCS, vol. 8592, pp. 450–457. Springer, Heidelberg (2014). https://doi.org/10.1007/978-3-662-44199-2_68

29. England, M., Errami, H., Grigoriev, D., Radulescu, O., Sturm, T., Weber, A.: Symbolic versus numerical computation and visualization of parameter regions for multistationarity of biological networks. In: Gerdt, V.P., Koepf, W., Seiler, W.M., Vorozhtsov, E.V. (eds.) CASC 2017. LNCS, vol. 10490, pp. 93–108. Springer, Cham (2017). https://doi.org/10.1007/978-3-319-66320-3_8

30. England, M., Wilson, D., Bradford, R., Davenport, J.H.: Using the regular chains library to build cylindrical algebraic decompositions by projecting and lifting. In: Hong, H., Yap, C. (eds.) ICMS 2014. LNCS, vol. 8592, pp. 458–465. Springer, Heidelberg (2014). https://doi.org/10.1007/978-3-662-44199-2_69

31. Erascu, M., Hong, H.: Real quantifier elimination for the synthesis of optimal numerical algorithms (case study: square root computation). J. Symb. Comput. **75**, 110–126 (2016). https://doi.org/10.1016/j.jsc.2015.11.010

32. Graebe, H., Nareike, A., Johanning, S.: The SymbolicData project: towards a computer algebra social network. In: England, M., et al. (eds.) Joint Proceedings of the MathUI, OpenMath and ThEdu Workshops and Work in Progress track at CICM. CEUR Workshop Proceedings, vol. 1186 (2014). http://ceur-ws.org/Vol-1186/#paper-21

33. Heinle, A., Levandovskyy, V.: The SDEval benchmarking toolkit. ACM Commun. Comput. Algebra **49**(1), 1–9 (2015). https://doi.org/10.1145/2768577.2768578

34. Hong, H.: An improvement of the projection operator in cylindrical algebraic decomposition. In: Proceedings of the 15th International Symposium on Symbolic and Algebraic Computation, ISSAC 1990, pp. 261–264. ACM (1990), https://doi.org/10.1145/96877.96943

35. Huang, Z., England, M., Davenport, J., Paulson, L.: Using machine learning to decide when to precondition cylindrical algebraic decomposition with Groebner bases. In: 18th International Symposium on Symbolic and Numeric Algorithms for Scientific Computing (SYNASC 2016), pp. 45–52. IEEE (2016). https://doi.org/10.1109/SYNASC.2016.020

36. Huang, Z., England, M., Wilson, D., Bridge, J., Davenport, J.H., Paulson, L.: Using machine learning to improve cylindrical algebraic decomposition. Math. Comput. Sci. (2019). https://doi.org/10.1007/s11786-019-00394-8

37. Huang, Z., England, M., Wilson, D., Davenport, J.H., Paulson, L.C., Bridge, J.: Applying machine learning to the problem of choosing a heuristic to select the variable ordering for cylindrical algebraic decomposition. In: Watt, S.M., Davenport, J.H., Sexton, A.P., Sojka, P., Urban, J. (eds.) CICM 2014. LNCS (LNAI), vol. 8543, pp. 92–107. Springer, Cham (2014). https://doi.org/10.1007/978-3-319-08434-3_8

38. Iwane, H., Yanami, H., Anai, H., Yokoyama, K.: An effective implementation of a symbolic-numeric cylindrical algebraic decomposition for quantifier elimination. In: Proceedings of the 2009 Conference on Symbolic Numeric Computation, SNC 2009, pp. 55–64 (2009). https://doi.org/10.1145/1577190.1577203

39. Jovanović, D., de Moura, L.: Solving non-linear arithmetic. In: Gramlich, B., Miller, D., Sattler, U. (eds.) IJCAR 2012. LNCS (LNAI), vol. 7364, pp. 339–354. Springer, Heidelberg (2012). https://doi.org/10.1007/978-3-642-31365-3_27

40. Kobayashi, M., Iwane, H., Matsuzaki, T., Anai, H.: Efficient subformula orders for real quantifier elimination of non-prenex formulas. In: Kotsireas, I.S., Rump, S.M., Yap, C.K. (eds.) MACIS 2015. LNCS, vol. 9582, pp. 236–251. Springer, Cham (2016). https://doi.org/10.1007/978-3-319-32859-1_21

41. Kühlwein, D., Blanchette, J.C., Kaliszyk, C., Urban, J.: MaSh: machine learning for sledgehammer. In: Blazy, S., Paulin-Mohring, C., Pichardie, D. (eds.) ITP 2013. LNCS, vol. 7998, pp. 35–50. Springer, Heidelberg (2013). https://doi.org/10.1007/978-3-642-39634-2_6

42. Liang, J.H., Hari Govind, V.K., Poupart, P., Czarnecki, K., Ganesh, V.: An empirical study of branching heuristics through the lens of global learning rate. In: Gaspers, S., Walsh, T. (eds.) SAT 2017. LNCS, vol. 10491, pp. 119–135. Springer, Cham (2017). https://doi.org/10.1007/978-3-319-66263-3_8

43. McCallum, S.: An improved projection operation for cylindrical algebraic decomposition. In: Caviness, B.F., Johnson, J.R. (eds.) Quantifier Elimination and Cylindrical Algebraic Decomposition. TEXTSMONOGR, pp. 242–268. Springer, Vienna (1998). https://doi.org/10.1007/978-3-7091-9459-1_12

44. McCallum, S., Parusiñiski, A., Paunescu, L.: Validity proof of Lazard's method for CAD construction. J. Symb. Comput. **92**, 52–69 (2019). https://doi.org/10.1016/j.jsc.2017.12.002

45. Mulligan, C., Bradford, R., Davenport, J., England, M., Tonks, Z.: Non-linear real arithmetic benchmarks derived from automated reasoning in economics. In: Bigatti, A., Brain, M. (eds.) Proceedings of the 3rd Workshop on Satisfiability Checking and Symbolic Computation (SC^2 2018). CEUR Workshop Proceedings, vol. 2189, pp. 48–60 (2018). http://ceur-ws.org/Vol-2189/

46. Mulligan, C.B., Davenport, J.H., England, M.: TheoryGuru: a mathematica package to apply quantifier elimination technology to economics. In: Davenport, J.H., Kauers, M., Labahn, G., Urban, J. (eds.) ICMS 2018. LNCS, vol. 10931, pp. 369–378. Springer, Cham (2018). https://doi.org/10.1007/978-3-319-96418-8_44

47. Paulson, L.C.: MetiTarski: past and future. In: Beringer, L., Felty, A. (eds.) ITP 2012. LNCS, vol. 7406, pp. 1–10. Springer, Heidelberg (2012). https://doi.org/10.1007/978-3-642-32347-8_1

48. Pedregosa, F., et al.: Scikit-learn: machine learning in Python. J. Mach. Learn. Res. **12**, 2825–2830 (2011). http://www.jmlr.org/papers/v12/pedregosa11a.html

49. Platzer, A., Quesel, J.-D., Rümmer, P.: Real world verification. In: Schmidt, R.A. (ed.) CADE 2009. LNCS (LNAI), vol. 5663, pp. 485–501. Springer, Heidelberg (2009). https://doi.org/10.1007/978-3-642-02959-2_35

50. Strzeboński, A.: Cylindrical algebraic decomposition using validated numerics. J. Symb. Comput. **41**(9), 1021–1038 (2006). https://doi.org/10.1016/j.jsc.2006.06.004

51. Strzeboński, A.: Cylindrical algebraic decomposition using local projections. J. Symb. Comput. **76**, 36–64 (2016). https://doi.org/10.1016/j.jsc.2015.11.018

52. Sturm, T.: New domains for applied quantifier elimination. In: Ganzha, V.G., Mayr, E.W., Vorozhtsov, E.V. (eds.) CASC 2006. LNCS, vol. 4194, pp. 295–301. Springer, Heidelberg (2006). https://doi.org/10.1007/11870814_25

53. Tarski, A.: A decision method for elementary algebra and geometry. RAND Corporation, Santa Monica, CA (reprinted in the collection [16]) (1948)

54. Urban, J.: MaLARea: a metasystem for automated reasoning in large theories. In: Empirically Successful Automated Reasoning in Large Theories (ESARLT 2007). CEUR Workshop Proceedings, vol. 257, p. 14 (2007). http://ceur-ws.org/Vol-257/

55. Wilson, D., Bradford, R., Davenport, J., England, M.: Cylindrical algebraic sub-decompositions. Math. Comput. Sci. **8**, 263–288 (2014). https://doi.org/10.1007/s11786-014-0191-z

56. Wilson, D., Davenport, J., England, M., Bradford, R.: A "piano movers" problem reformulated. In: 15th International Symposium on Symbolic and Numeric Algorithms for Scientific Computing, SYNASC 2013, pp. 53–60. IEEE (2013). https://doi.org/10.1109/SYNASC.2013.14

57. Wilson, D., England, M., Davenport, J., Bradford, R.: Using the distribution of cells by dimension in a cylindrical algebraic decomposition. In: 16th International Symposium on Symbolic and Numeric Algorithms for Scientific Computing, SYNASC 2014, pp. 53–60. IEEE (2014). https://doi.org/10.1109/SYNASC.2014.15

58. Wilson, D., Bradford, R., Davenport, J.: A repository for CAD examples. ACM Commun. Comput. Algebra **46**(3), 67–69 (2012). https://doi.org/10.1145/2429135.2429137

59. Xu, L., Hutter, F., Hoos, H., Leyton-Brown, K.: SATzilla: portfolio-based algorithm selection for SAT. J. Artif. Intell. Res. **32**, 565–606 (2008). https://doi.org/10.1613/jair.2490

Towards Specifying Symbolic Computation

Jacques Carette and William M. Farmer[✉]

Computing and Software, McMaster University, Hamilton, Canada
{carette,wmfarmer}@mcmaster.ca
http://www.cas.mcmaster.ca/~carette
http://imps.mcmaster.ca/wmfarmer

Abstract. Many interesting and useful symbolic computation algorithms manipulate mathematical expressions in mathematically meaningful ways. Although these algorithms are commonplace in computer algebra systems, they can be surprisingly difficult to specify in a formal logic since they involve an interplay of syntax and semantics. In this paper we discuss several examples of syntax-based mathematical algorithms, and we show how to specify them in a formal logic with undefinedness, quotation, and evaluation.

1 Introduction

Many mathematical tasks are performed by executing an algorithm that manipulates expressions (syntax) in a "meaningful" way. For instance, children learn to perform arithmetic by executing algorithms that manipulate strings of digits that represent numbers. A *syntax-based mathematical algorithm (SBMA)* is such an algorithm, that performs a mathematical task by manipulating the syntactic structure of certain expressions. SBMAs are commonplace in mathematics, and so it is no surprise that they are standard components of computer algebra systems.

SBMAs involve an interplay of syntax and semantics. The *computational behavior* of an SBMA is the relationship between its input and output expressions, while the *mathematical meaning* of an SBMA is the relationship between the *meaning*[1] of its input and output expressions. Understanding what a SBMA does requires understanding how its computational behavior is related to its mathematical meaning.

A complete specification of an SBMA is often much more complex than one might expect. This is because (1) manipulating syntax is complex in itself, (2) the interplay of syntax and semantics can be difficult to disentangle, and (3) seemingly benign syntactic manipulations can generate undefined expressions. An SBMA specification has both a syntactic component and a semantic component,

---

[1] I.e., denotation.

This research is supported by NSERC.

C. Kaliszyk et al. (Eds.): CICM 2019, LNAI 11617, pp. 109–124, 2019.
https://doi.org/10.1007/978-3-030-23250-4_8

but these components can be intertwined. Usually the more they are separated, the easier it is to understand the specification.

This inherent complexity of SBMA specifications makes SBMAs tricky to implement correctly. Dealing with the semantic component is usually the bigger challenge for computer algebra systems as they excel in the realm of computation but have weak reasoning facilities, while the syntactic component is usually the bigger obstacle for proof assistants, often due to partiality issues.

In this paper, we examine four representative examples of SBMAs, present their specifications, and show how their specifications can be written in $\mathrm{CTT_{uqe}}$ [12], a formal logic designed to make expressing the interplay of syntax and semantics easier than in traditional logics. The paper is organized as follows. Section 2 presents background information about semantic notions and $\mathrm{CTT_{uqe}}$. Section 3 discusses the issues concerning SBMAs for factoring integers. Normalizing rational expressions and functions is examined in Sect. 4. Symbolic differentiation algorithms are considered in Sect. 5. Section 6 gives a brief overview of related work. And the paper ends with a short conclusion in Sect. 7.

The principal contribution of this paper, in the author's opinion, is not the specifications themselves, but rather bringing to the fore the subtle details of SBMAs themselves, along with the fact that traditional logics are ill-suited to the specification of SBMAs. While here we use $\mathrm{CTT_{uqe}}$ for this purpose, the most important aspect is the ability to deal with two levels at once, syntax and semantics. The examples are chosen because they represent what are traditionally understood as fairly simple, even straightforward, symbolic algorithms, and yet they are nevertheless rather difficult to formalize properly.

2   Background

To be able to formally display the issues involved, it is convenient to first be specific about definedness, equality, quasi-equality, and logics that can deal with syntax and semantics directly.

2.1   Definedness, Equality, and Quasi-equality

Let e be an expression and D be a domain of values. We say e *is defined in* D if e denotes a member of D. When e is defined in D, the *value of e in D* is the element in D that e denotes. When e is undefined in D (i.e., e does not denote a member of D), the value of e in D is undefined. Two expressions e and e' are *equal in* D, written $e =_D e'$, if they are both defined in D and they have the same values in D and are *quasi-equal in* D, written $e \simeq_D e'$, if either $e =_D e'$ or e and e' are both undefined in D. When D is a domain of interest to mathematicians, we will call e a *mathematical expression*.

2.2 $\mathrm{CTT_{qe}}$ and $\mathrm{CTT_{uqe}}$

$\mathrm{CTT_{qe}}$ [13] is a version of Church's type theory with a built-in *global reflection infrastructure* with global quotation and evaluation operators geared towards reasoning about the interplay of syntax and semantics and, in particular, for specifying, defining, applying, and reasoning about SBMAs. The syntax and semantics of CTT_{qe} is presented in [13]. A proof system for CTT_{qe} that is sound for all formulas and complete for eval-free formulas is also presented in [13]. (An expression is *eval-free* if it does not contain the evaluation operator.) By modifying HOL Light [14], we have produced a rudimentary implementation of CTT_{qe} called HOL Light QE [5].

CTT_{uqe} [12] is a variant of CTT_{qe} that has built-in support for partial functions and undefinedness based on the traditional approach to undefinedness [10]. It is well-suited for specifying SBMAs that manipulate expressions that may be undefined. Its syntax and semantics are presented in [12]. A proof system for CTT_{uqe} is not given there, but can be straightforwardly derived by merging those for CTT_{qe} [13] and $\mathcal{Q}_0^{\text{u}}$ [11].

The global reflection infrastructure of CTT_{uqe} (and CTT_{qe}) consists of three components. The first is an inductive type ϵ of *syntactic values*: these typically represent the syntax tree of an eval-free expression of CTT_{uqe}. Each expression of type ϵ denotes a syntactic value. Thus reasoning about the syntactic structure of expressions can be performed by reasoning about syntactic values via the expressions of type ϵ. The second component is a *quotation operator* $\ulcorner \cdot \urcorner$ such that, if $\mathbf{A}_\alpha$ is an eval-free expression (of some type α), then $\ulcorner \mathbf{A}_\alpha \urcorner$ is an expression of type ϵ that denotes the syntactic value that represents the syntax tree of $\mathbf{A}_\alpha$. Finally, the third component is an *evaluation operator* $[\![\cdot]\!]_\alpha$ such that, if $\mathbf{E}_\epsilon$ is an expression of type ϵ, then $[\![\mathbf{E}_\epsilon]\!]_\alpha$ denotes the value of type α denoted by the expression $\mathbf{B}$ represented by $\mathbf{E}_\epsilon$ (provided the type of $\mathbf{B}$ is α). In particular the *law of disquotation* $[\![\ulcorner \mathbf{A}_\alpha \urcorner]\!]_\alpha = \mathbf{A}_\alpha$ holds in CTT_{uqe} (and CTT_{qe}).

The reflection infrastructure is *global* since it can be used to reason about the entire set of eval-free expressions of CTT_{uqe}. This is in contrast to *local reflection* which constructs an inductive type of syntactic values only for the expressions of the logic that are relevant to a particular problem. See [13] for discussion about the difference between local and global reflection infrastructures and the design challenges that stand in the way of developing a global reflection infrastructure within a logic.

The type ϵ includes syntax values for all eval-free expressions of all types as well as syntax values for ill-formed expressions like $(\mathbf{x}_\alpha \, \mathbf{x}_\alpha)$ in which the types are mismatched. Convenient subtypes of ϵ can be represented via predicates of type $\epsilon \to o$. (o is the type of boolean values.) In particular, CTT_{uqe} contains a predicate is-expr$^\alpha_{\epsilon \to o}$ for every type α that represents the subtype of syntax values for expressions of type α.

Unlike CTT_{qe}, CTT_{uqe} admits undefined expressions and partial functions. The formulas $\mathbf{A}_\alpha \downarrow$ and $\mathbf{A}_\alpha \uparrow$ assert that the expression $\mathbf{A}_\alpha$ is defined and undefined, respectively. Formulas (i.e., expressions of type o) are always defined. Evaluations may be undefined. For example, $[\![\ulcorner \mathbf{A}_\alpha \urcorner]\!]_\beta$ is undefined when $\alpha \neq \beta$. See [11,12] for further details.

3   Factoring Integers

3.1   Task

Here is a seemingly simple mathematical task: Factor (over $\mathbb{N}$) the number 12. One might expect the answer $12 = 2^2 * 3$—but this is not actually the answer one gets in many systems! The reason is, that in any system with built-in beta-reduction (including all computer algebra systems as well as theorem provers based on dependent type theory), the answer is immediately evaluated to $12 = 12$, which is certainly not very informative.

3.2   Problem

So why is $2^2 * 3$ not an answer? Because it involves a mixture of *syntax* and *semantics*. A better answer would be $\ulcorner 2^2 * 3 \urcorner$ (the quotation of $2^2 * 3$) that would make it clear that $*$ *represents* multiplication rather than *being* multiplication. In other words, this is about intension and extension: we want to be able to both represent operations and perform operations. In Maple, one talks about inert forms, while in Mathematica, there are various related concepts such as Hold, Inactive and Unevaluated. They both capture the same fundamental dichotomy about passive representations and active computations.

3.3   Solution

Coming back to integer factorization, interestingly both Maple and Mathematica choose a fairly similar option to represent the answer—a list of pairs, with the first component being a prime of the factorization and the second being the multiplicity of the prime (i.e., the exponent). Maple furthermore gives a leading unit (-1 or 1), so that one can also factor negative numbers. In other words, in Maple, the result of ifactors(12) is

$$[1, [2, 2], [3, 1]]$$

where lists are used (rather than proper pairs) as the host system is untyped. Mathematica does something similar.

3.4   Specification in Maple

Given the following Maple routine[2]

```
remult := proc(l :: [{-1,1}, list([prime,posint])])
  local f := proc(x, y) (x[1] ^ x[2]) * y end proc;
  l[1] * foldr(f, 1, op(l[2]))
end proc;
```

---

[2] There are nonessential Maple-isms in this routine: because of how foldr is defined, op is needed to transform a list to an expression sequence; in other languages, this is unnecessary. Note however that it is possible to express the type extremely precisely.

then the specification for ifactors is that, for all $n \in \mathbb{Z}$, (A) ifactors(n) represents a signed prime decomposition and

$$\text{(B) remult (ifactors } (n)) = n.$$

(A) is the syntactic component of the specification and (B) is the semantic component.

3.5   Specification in CTT$_{\text{uqe}}$

We specify the factorization of integers in a theory T of CTT$_{\text{uqe}}$ using CTT$_{\text{uqe}}$'s reflection infrastructure. We start by defining a theory $T_0 = (L_0, \Gamma_0)$ of integer arithmetic. L_0 contains a base type i and the constants $0_i, 1_i, 2_i, \ldots, -_{i \to i}$, $+_{i \to i \to i}, *_{i \to i \to i}$, and $\wedge_{i \to i \to i}$. Γ_0 contains the usual axioms of integer arithmetic.
    Next we extend T_0 to a theory $T_1 = (L_1, \Gamma_1)$ by defining the following two constants using the machinery of T_0:

1. Numeral$_{\epsilon \to o}$ is a predicate representing the subtype of ϵ that denotes the subset $\{0_i, 1_i, 2_i, \ldots\}$ of expressions of type i. Thus, Numeral$_{\epsilon \to o}$ is the subtype of numerals and, for example, Numeral$_{\epsilon \to o}$ $\ulcorner 2_i \urcorner$ is valid in T_1.
2. PrimeDecomp$_{\epsilon \to o}$ is a predicate representing the subtype of ϵ that denotes the subset of expressions of type i of the form 0_i or

$$\pm 1 * p_0^{e_0} * \cdots * p_k^{e_k}$$

where parentheses and types have been dropped, the p_i are numerals denoting unique prime numbers in increasing order, the e_i are also numerals, and $k \geq 0$. Thus PrimeDecomp$_{\epsilon \to o}$ is a subtype of signed prime decompositions and, for example, PrimeDecomp$_{\epsilon \to o}$ $\ulcorner 1 * 2^2 * 3^1 \urcorner$ (where again parentheses and types have been dropped) is valid in T_2.

Finally, we can extend T_1 to a theory $T = (L, \Gamma)$ in which L contains the constant factor$_{\epsilon \to \epsilon}$ and Γ contains the following axiom specFactor$_o$:

$\forall u_\epsilon.$
    if (Numeral$_{\epsilon \to o} u_\epsilon$)
        (PrimeDecomp$_{\epsilon \to \epsilon}$(factor$_{\epsilon \to \epsilon} u_\epsilon$) $\wedge$ $[\![u_\epsilon]\!]_i = [\![$factor$_{\epsilon \to \epsilon} u_\epsilon]\!]_i$)
        (factor$_{\epsilon \to \epsilon} u_\epsilon$) $\uparrow$

specFactor$_o$ says that factor$_{\epsilon \to \epsilon}$ is only defined on numerals and, when u_ϵ is a numeral, factor$_{\epsilon \to \epsilon} u_\epsilon$ is a signed prime decomposition (the syntactic component) and denotes the same integer as u_ϵ (the semantic component). Notice that specFactor$_o$ does not look terribly complex on the surface, but there is a significant amount of complexity embodied in the definitions of Numeral$_{\epsilon \to o}$ and PrimeDecomp$_{\epsilon \to \epsilon}$.

3.6 Discussion

Why do neither of Maple or Mathematica use their own means of representing intensional information? History! In both cases, the integer factorization routines predates the intensional features by more than *two decades*. And backward compatibility definitely prevents them from making that change.

Furthermore, factoring as an operation produces output in a very predictable *shape*: $s * p_0^{e_0} * p_1^{e_1} * \cdots * p_k^{e_k}$. To parse such a term's syntax to extract the information is tedious and error prone, at least in an untyped system. Such a shape could easily be coded up in a typed system using a very simple algebraic data type that would obviate the problem. But computer algebra systems are very good at manipulating lists[3], and thus this output *composes* well with other system features.

It is worth noting that none of the reasons for the *correctness* of this representation is clearly visible: once the integers are partitioned into negative, zero and positive, and only positive natural numbers are subject to "prime factorization", their structure as a *free commutative monoid* on infinitely many generators (the primes) comes out. And so it is natural that *multisets* (also called *bags*) are the natural representation. The list-with-multiplicities makes that clear, while in some sense the more human-friendly syntactic representation $s * p_0^{e_0} * p_1^{e_1} * \cdots * p_k^{e_k}$ obscures that.

Nevertheless, the main lesson is that a simple mathematical task, such as factoring the number 12, which seems like a question about simple integer arithmetic, is not. It is a question that can only be properly answered in a context with a significantly richer term language that includes either lists or pairs, or an inductive type of syntactic values, or access to the expressions of the term language as syntactic objects.

All the issues we have seen with the factorization of integers appear again with the factorization of polynomials.

4   Normalizing Rational Expressions and Functions

Let $\mathbb{Q}$ be the field of rational numbers, $\mathbb{Q}[x]$ be the ring of polynomials in x over $\mathbb{Q}$, and $\mathbb{Q}(x)$ be the field of fractions of $\mathbb{Q}[x]$. We may assume that $\mathbb{Q} \subseteq \mathbb{Q}[x] \subseteq \mathbb{Q}(x)$.

The language $\mathcal{L}_{\mathrm{re}}$ of $\mathbb{Q}(x)$ is the set of expressions built from the symbols $x, 0, 1, +, *, -, {}^{-1}$, elements of $\mathbb{Q}$, and parentheses (as necessary). For greater readability, we will take the liberty of using fractional notation for ${}^{-1}$ and the exponential notation x^n for $x * \cdots * x$ (n times). A member of $\mathcal{L}_{\mathrm{re}}$ can be something simple like $\frac{x^4-1}{x^2-1}$ or something more complicated like

$$\frac{\frac{1-x}{3/2x^{18}+x+17}}{\frac{1}{9834*x^{19393874}-1/5}} + 3 * x - \frac{12}{x}.$$

---

[3] This is unsurprising given that the builders of both Maple and Mathematica were well acquainted with Macsyma which was implemented in Lisp.

The members of $\mathcal{L}_{\mathrm{re}}$ are called *rational expressions (in x over $\mathbb{Q}$)*. They denote elements in $\mathbb{Q}(x)$. Of course, a rational expression like $x/0$ is undefined in $\mathbb{Q}(x)$.

Let $\mathcal{L}_{\mathrm{rf}}$ be the set of expressions of the form $(\lambda x : \mathbb{Q}\,.\,r)$ where $r \in \mathcal{L}_{\mathrm{re}}$. The members of $\mathcal{L}_{\mathrm{rf}}$ are called *rational functions (in x over $\mathbb{Q}$)*. That is, a rational function is a lambda expression whose body is a rational expression. Rational functions denote functions from $\mathbb{Q}$ to $\mathbb{Q}$. Even though rational expressions and rational functions look similar, they have very different meanings due to the role of x. The x in a rational expression is an *indeterminant* that does not denote a value, while the x in a rational function is a *variable* ranging over values in $\mathbb{Q}$.

4.1   Task 1: Normalizing Rational Expressions

Normalizing a rational expression is a useful task. We are taught that, like for members of $\mathbb{Q}$ (such as $5/15$), there is a *normal form* for rational expressions. This is typically defined to be a rational expression p/q for two polynomials $p, q \in \mathbb{Q}[x]$ such that p and q are themselves in polynomial normal form and $\mathsf{gcd}(p, q) = 1$. The motivation for the latter property is that we usually want to write the rational expression $\frac{x^4-1}{x^2-1}$ as x^2+1 just as we usually want to write $5/15$ as $1/3$. Thus, the normal forms of $\frac{x^4-1}{x^2-1}$ and $\frac{x}{x}$ are $x^2 + 1$ and 1, respectively. This definition of normal form is based on the characteristic that the elements of the field of fractions of a integral domain D can be written as quotients r/s of elements of D where $r_0/s_0 = r_1/s_1$ if and only if $r_0 * s_1 = r_1 * s_0$ in D.

We would like to normalize a rational expression by putting it into normal form. Let normRatExpr be the SBMA that takes $r \in \mathcal{L}_{\mathrm{re}}$ as input and returns the $r' \in \mathcal{L}_{\mathrm{re}}$ as output such that r' is the normal form of r. How should normRatExpr be specified?

4.2   Problem 1

normRatExpr must normalize rational expressions as expressions that denote members of $\mathbb{Q}(x)$, not members of $\mathbb{Q}$. Hence normRatExpr(x/x) and normRatExpr$(1/x - 1/x)$ should be 1 and 0, respectively, even though x/x and $1/x - 1/x$ are undefined when the value of x is 0.

4.3   Solution 1

The hard part of specifying normRatExpr is defining exactly what rational expressions are normal forms and then proving that two normal forms denote the same member of $\mathbb{Q}(x)$ only if the two normal forms are identical. Assuming we have adequately defined the notion of a normal form, the specification of normRatExpr is that, for all $r \in \mathcal{L}_{\mathrm{re}}$, (A) normRatExpr$(r)$ is a normal form and (B) $r \simeq_{\mathbb{Q}(x)}$ normRatExpr(r). (A) is the syntactic component of the specification, and (B) is the semantic component. Notice that (B) implies that, if r is undefined in $\mathbb{Q}(x)$, then normRatExpr(r) is also undefined in $\mathbb{Q}(x)$. For example, since $r = \frac{1}{x-x}$ is undefined in $\mathbb{Q}(x)$, normRatExpr(r) should be the (unique) undefined normal form (which, for example, could be the rational expression $1/0$).

4.4   Task 2: Normalizing Rational Functions

Normalizing a rational function is another useful task. Let $f = (\lambda x : \mathbb{Q} . r)$ be a rational function. We would like to normalize f by putting its body r in normal form of some appropriate kind. Let normRatFun be the SBMA that takes $f \in \mathcal{L}_{\mathrm{rf}}$ as input and returns a $f' \in \mathcal{L}_{\mathrm{rf}}$ as output such that f' is the normal form of f. How should normRatFun be specified?

4.5   Problem 2

If $f_i = (\lambda x : \mathbb{Q} . r_i)$ are rational functions for $i = 1, 2$, one might think that $f_1 =_{\mathbb{Q} \to \mathbb{Q}} f_2$ if $r_1 =_{\mathbb{Q}(x)} r_2$. But this is not the case. For example, the rational functions $(\lambda x : \mathbb{Q} . x/x)$ and $(\lambda x : \mathbb{Q} . 1)$ are not equal as functions over $\mathbb{Q}$ since $(\lambda x : \mathbb{Q} . x/x)$ is undefined at 0 while $(\lambda x : \mathbb{Q} . 1)$ is defined everywhere. But $x/x =_{\mathbb{Q}(x)} 1$! Similarly, $(\lambda x : \mathbb{Q} . (1/x - 1/x)) \neq_{\mathbb{Q} \to \mathbb{Q}} (\lambda x : \mathbb{Q} . 0)$ and $(1/x - 1/x) =_{\mathbb{Q}(x)} 0$. (Note that, in some contexts, we might want to say that $(\lambda x : \mathbb{Q} . x/x)$ and $(\lambda x : \mathbb{Q} . 1)$ do indeed denote the same function by invoking the concept of *removable singularities*).

4.6   Solution 2

As we have just seen, we cannot normalize a rational function by normalizing its body, but we can normalize rational functions if we are careful not to remove points of undefinedness. Let a *quasinormal form* be a rational expression p/q for two polynomials $p, q \in \mathbb{Q}[x]$ such that p and q are themselves in polynomial normal form and there is no irreducible polynomial $s \in \mathbb{Q}[x]$ of degree ≥ 2 that divides both p and q. One should note that this definition of quasinormal form depends on the field $\mathbb{Q}$ because, for example, the polynomial $x^2 - 2$ is irreducible in $\mathbb{Q}$ but not in $\overline{\mathbb{Q}}$ (the algebraic closure of $\mathbb{Q}$) or $\mathbb{R}$ (since $x^2 - 2 =_{\mathbb{R}[x]} (x - \sqrt{2})(x + \sqrt{2})$).

We can then normalize a rational function by quasinormalizing its body. So the specification of normRatFun is that, for all $(\lambda x : \mathbb{Q} . r) \in \mathcal{L}_{\mathrm{rf}}$, (A) normRatFun$(\lambda x : \mathbb{Q} . r) = (\lambda x : \mathbb{Q} . r')$ where r' is a quasinormal form and (B) $(\lambda x : \mathbb{Q} . r) \simeq_{\mathbb{Q} \to \mathbb{Q}}$ normRatFun$(\lambda x : \mathbb{Q} . r)$. (A) is the syntactic component of its specification, and (B) is the semantic component.

4.7   Specification in CTT$_{\mathrm{uqe}}$

We specify normRatExpr and normRatFun in a theory of CTT$_{\mathrm{uqe}}$ again using CTT$_{\mathrm{uqe}}$'s reflection infrastructure. A complete development of T would be long and tedious, thus we only sketch it.

The first step is to define a theory $T_0 = (L_0, \Gamma_0)$ that axiomatizes the field $\mathbb{Q}$; L_0 contains a base type q and constants 0_q, 1_q, $+_{q \to q \to q}$, $*_{q \to q \to q}$, $-_{q \to q}$, and $-1_{q \to q}$ representing the standard elements and operators of a field. Γ_0 contains axioms that say the type q is the field of rational numbers.

The second step is to extend T_0 to a theory $T_1 = (L_1, \Gamma_1)$ that axiomatizes $\mathbb{Q}(x)$, the field of fractions of the ring $\mathbb{Q}[x]$. L_1 contains a base type f; constants $0_f, 1_f, +_{f \to f \to f}, *_{f \to f \to f}, -_{f \to f}$, and $-1_{f \to f}$ representing the standard elements and operators of a field; and a constant X_f representing the indeterminant of $\mathbb{Q}(x)$. Γ_1 contains axioms that say the type f is the field of fractions of $\mathbb{Q}[x]$. Notice that the types q and f are completely separate from each other since $\mathrm{CTT}_{\mathrm{uqe}}$ does not admit subtypes as in [9].

The third step is to extend T_1 to a theory $T_2 = (L_2, \Gamma_2)$ that is equipped to express ideas about the expressions of type q and $q \to q$ that have the form of rational expressions and rational functions, respectively. T_2 is obtain by defining the following constants using the machinery of T_1:

1. $\mathsf{RatExpr}_{\epsilon \to o}$ is the predicate representing the subtype of ϵ that denotes the set of expressions of type q that have the form of rational expressions in x_q (i.e., the expressions of type q built from the variable x_q and the constants representing the field elements and operators for q). So, for example, $\mathsf{RatExpr}_{\epsilon \to o} \ulcorner x_q / x_q \urcorner$ is valid in T_2.
2. $\mathsf{RatFun}_{\epsilon \to o}$ is the predicate representing the subtype of ϵ that denotes the set of expressions of type $q \to q$ that are rational functions in x_q (i.e., the expressions of the form $(\lambda\, x_q \,.\, \mathbf{R}_q)$ where $\mathbf{R}_q$ has the form of a rational expression in x_q). For example $\mathsf{RatFun}_{\epsilon \to o} \ulcorner \lambda\, x_q \,.\, x_q / x_q \urcorner$ is valid in T_2.
3. $\mathsf{val\text{-}in\text{-}}f_{\epsilon \to f}$ is a partial function that maps each member of the subtype $\mathsf{RatExpr}_{\epsilon \to o}$ to its denotation in f. So, for example,

$$\mathsf{val\text{-}in\text{-}}f_{\epsilon \to f} \ulcorner x_q +_{q \to q \to q} 1_q \urcorner = X_f +_{f \to f \to f} 1_f$$

and $(\mathsf{val\text{-}in\text{-}}f_{\epsilon \to f} \ulcorner 1_q / 0_q \urcorner) {\uparrow}$ are valid in T_2. $\mathsf{val\text{-}in\text{-}}f_{\epsilon \to f}$ is partial on is domain since an expression like $1_q / 0_q$ does not denote a member of f.
4. $\mathsf{Norm}_{\epsilon \to o}$ is the predicate representing the subtype of ϵ that denotes the subset of the subtype $\mathsf{RatExpr}_{\epsilon \to o}$ whose members are normal forms. So, for example, $\neg(\mathsf{Norm}_{\epsilon \to o} \ulcorner x_q / x_q \urcorner)$ and $\mathsf{Norm}_{\epsilon \to o} \ulcorner 1_q \urcorner$ are valid in T_2.
5. $\mathsf{Quasinorm}_{\epsilon \to o}$ is the predicate representing the subtype of ϵ that denotes the subset of the subtype $\mathsf{RatExpr}_{\epsilon \to o}$ whose members are quasinormal forms. So, for example, $\mathsf{Quasinorm}_{\epsilon \to o} \ulcorner x_q / x_q \urcorner$ and $\neg(\mathsf{Quasinorm}_{\epsilon \to o} \ulcorner \mathbf{A}_q / \mathbf{A}_q \urcorner)$, where $\mathbf{A}_q$ is $x_q^2 +_{q \to q \to q} 1_q$, are valid in T_2.
6. $\mathsf{body}_{\epsilon \to \epsilon}$ is a partial function that maps each member of ϵ denoting an expression of the form $(\lambda\, x_\alpha \,.\, \mathbf{B}_\beta)$ to the member of ϵ that denotes $\ulcorner \mathbf{B}_\beta \urcorner$ and is undefined on the rest of ϵ. Note that there is no *scope extrusion* here as, in syntactic expressions, the x_α is visible.

The final step is to extend T_2 to a theory $T = (L, \Gamma)$ in which L has two additional constants $\mathsf{normRatExpr}_{\epsilon \to \epsilon}$ and $\mathsf{normRatFun}_{\epsilon \to \epsilon}$ and Γ has two additional axioms $\mathsf{specNormRatExpr}_o$ and $\mathsf{specNormRatFun}_o$ that specify them. $\mathsf{specNormRatExpr}_o$ is the formula

$$\forall u_\epsilon . \tag{1}$$
$$\text{if } (\mathsf{RatExpr}_{\epsilon \to o} u_\epsilon) \tag{2}$$
$$(\mathsf{Norm}_{\epsilon \to \epsilon}(\mathsf{normRatExpr}_{\epsilon \to \epsilon} u_\epsilon) \wedge \tag{3}$$
$$\text{val-in-} f_{\epsilon \to f} u_\epsilon \simeq \text{val-in-} f_{\epsilon \to f}(\mathsf{normRatExpr}_{\epsilon \to \epsilon} u_\epsilon)) \tag{4}$$
$$(\mathsf{normRatExpr}_{\epsilon \to \epsilon} u_\epsilon) \uparrow \tag{5}$$

(3) says that, if the input to $\mathsf{RatExpr}_{\epsilon \to o}$ represents a rational expression in x_q, then the output represents a rational expression in x_q in normal form (the syntactic component). (4) says that, if the input represents a rational expression in x_q, then either the input and output denote the same member of f or they both do not denote any member of f (the semantic component). And (5) says that, if the input does not represent a rational expression in x_q, then the output is undefined.

specNormRatFun$_o$ is the formula

$$\forall u_\epsilon . \tag{1}$$
$$\text{if } (\mathsf{RatFun}_{\epsilon \to o} u_\epsilon) \tag{2}$$
$$(\mathsf{RatFun}_{\epsilon \to o} (\mathsf{normRatFun}_{\epsilon \to \epsilon} u_\epsilon) \wedge \tag{3}$$
$$\mathsf{Quasinorm}_{\epsilon \to \epsilon}(\mathsf{body}_{\epsilon \to \epsilon}(\mathsf{normRatExpr}_{\epsilon \to \epsilon} u_\epsilon)) \wedge \tag{4}$$
$$[\![u_\epsilon]\!]_{q \to q} = [\![\mathsf{normRatExpr}_{\epsilon \to o} u_\epsilon]\!]_{q \to q}) \tag{5}$$
$$(\mathsf{normRatFun}_{\epsilon \to \epsilon} u_\epsilon) \uparrow \tag{6}$$

(3–4) say that, if the input to $\mathsf{RatFun}_{\epsilon \to o}$ represents a rational function in x_q, then the output represents a rational function in x_q whose body is in quasinormal form (the syntactic component). (5) says that, if the input represents a rational function in x_q, then input and output denote the same (possibly partial) function on the rational numbers (the semantic component). And (6) says that, if the input does not represent a rational function in x_q, then the output is undefined.

Not only is it possible to specify the algorithms normRatExpr and normRatFun in $\mathrm{CTT_{uqe}}$, it is also possible to define the functions that these algorithms implement. Then applications of these functions can be evaluated in $\mathrm{CTT_{uqe}}$ using a proof system for $\mathrm{CTT_{uqe}}$.

4.8   Discussion

So why are we concerned about rational expressions and rational functions? Every computer algebra system implements functions that normalize rational expressions in several indeterminants over various fields guaranteeing that the normal form will be 0 if the rational expression equals 0 in the corresponding field of fractions. However, computer algebra systems make little distinction between a rational expression interpreted as a member of a field of fractions and a rational expression interpreted as a rational function.

For example, one can always *evaluate* an expression by assigning values to its free variables or even convert it to a function. In Maple[4], these are done respectively via `eval(e, x = 0)` and `unapply(e, x)`. This means that, if we normalize the rational expression $\frac{x^4-1}{x^2-1}$ to x^2+1 and then evaluate the result at $x=1$, we get the value 2. But, if we evaluate $\frac{x^4-1}{x^2-1}$ at $x=1$ without normalizing it, we get an error message due to division by 0. Hence, if a rational expression r is interpreted as a function, then it is not valid to normalize it, but a computer algebra system lets the user do exactly that since there is no distinction made between r as a rational expression and r as representing a rational function, as we have already mentioned.

The real problem here is that the normalization of a rational expression and the evaluation of an expression at a value are not compatible with each other. Indeed the function $g_q : \mathbb{Q}(x) \to \mathbb{Q}$ where $q \in \mathbb{Q}$ that maps a rational expression r to the rational number obtained by replacing each occurrence of x in r with q is not a homomorphism! In particular, x/x is defined in $\mathbb{Q}(x)$, but $g_0(x/x)$ is undefined in $\mathbb{Q}$.

To avoid unsound applications of normRatExpr, normRatFun, and other SBMAs in mathematical systems, we need to carefully, if not formally, specify what these algorithms are intended to do. This is not a straightforward task to do in a traditional logic since SBMAs involve an interplay of syntax and semantics and algorithms like normRatExpr and normRatFun can be sensitive to definedness considerations. We can, however, specify these algorithm, as we have shown, in a logic like $\mathrm{CTT}_{\mathrm{qe}}$.

5 Symbolically Differentiating Functions

5.1 Task

A basic task of calculus is to find the derivative of a function. Every student who studies calculus quickly learns that computing the derivative of $f : \mathbb{R} \to \mathbb{R}$ is very difficult to do using only the definition of a derivative. It is a great deal easier to compute derivatives using an algorithm that repeatedly applies symbolic differentiation rules. For example,

$$\frac{d}{dx}\mathsf{sin}(x^2 + x) = (2x + 1)\mathsf{cos}(x^2 + x)$$

by applying the chain, sine, sum, power, and variable differentiation rules, and so the derivative of

$$\lambda\, x : \mathbb{R}\,.\,\mathsf{sin}(x^2 + x)$$

is

$$\lambda\, x : \mathbb{R}\,.\,(2x + 1)\mathsf{cos}(x^2 + x).$$

---

[4] Mathematica has similar commands.

Notice that the symbolic differentiation algorithm is applied to expressions (e.g., $\sin(x^2 + x)$) that have a designated free variable (e.g., x) and not to the function $\lambda x : \mathbb{R} . \sin(x^2 + x)$ the expression represents.

5.2   Problem

Let $f = \lambda x : \mathbb{R} . \ln(x^2 - 1)$ and f' be the derivative of f. Then

$$\frac{d}{dx} \ln(x^2 - 1) = \frac{2x}{x^2 - 1}$$

by standard symbolic differentiation rules. But

$$g = \lambda x : \mathbb{R} . \frac{2x}{x^2 - 1}$$

is not f'! The domain of f is $D_f = \{x \in \mathbb{R} \mid x < -1 \text{ or } x > 1\}$ since the natural log function $\ln$ is undefined on the nonpositive real numbers. Since f' is undefined wherever f is undefined, the domain $D_{f'}$ of f' must be a subset of D_f. But the domain of g is $D_g = \{x \in \mathbb{R} \mid x \neq -1 \text{ and } x \neq 1\}$ which is clearly a superset of D_f. Over $\mathbb{C}$ there are even more egregious examples where infinitely many singularities are "forgotten". Hence symbolic differentiation does not reliably produce derivatives.

5.3   A Solution

Let $\mathcal{L}$ be the language of expressions of type $\mathbb{R}$ built from x, the rational numbers, and operators for the following functions: $+$, $*$, $-$, $^{-1}$, the power function, the natural exponential and logarithm functions, and the trigonometric functions. Let diff be the SBMA that takes $e \in \mathcal{L}$ as input and returns the $e' \in \mathcal{L}$ by repeatedly applying standard symbolic differentiation rules in some appropriate manner. The specification of diff is that, for all $e \in \mathcal{L}$, (A) diff$(e) \in \mathcal{L}$ and (B), for $a \in \mathbb{R}$, if $f = \lambda x : \mathbb{R} . e$ is differentiable at a, then the derivative of f at a is $(\lambda x : \mathbb{R} . \text{diff}(e))(a)$. (A) is the syntactic component and (B) is the semantic component.

5.4   Specification in CTT$_{\text{uqe}}$

We specify diff in a theory T of CTT$_{\text{uqe}}$ once again using CTT$_{\text{uqe}}$'s reflection infrastructure. Let $T_0 = (L_0, \Gamma_0)$ be a theory of real numbers (formalized as the theory of a complete ordered field) that contains a base type r representing the real numbers and the usual individual and function constants.

We extend T_0 to a theory $T_1 = (L_1, \Gamma_1)$ by defining the following two constants using the machinery of T_0:

1. DiffExpr$_{\epsilon \to o}$ is a predicate representing the subtype of ϵ that denotes the subset of expressions of type r built from x_r, constants representing the rational

numbers, and the constants representing $+$, $*$, $-$, $^{-1}$, the power function, the natural exponential and logarithm functions, and the trigonometric functions. Thus, $\mathsf{DiffExpr}_{\epsilon \to o}$ is the subtype of expressions that can be symbolically differentiated and, for example, $\mathsf{DiffExpr}_{\epsilon \to o}$ $\ulcorner \ln(x_r^2 - 1) \urcorner$ (where parentheses and types have been dropped) is valid in T_1.

2. $\mathsf{deriv}_{(r \to r) \to r \to r}$ is a function such that, if f and a are expressions of type $r \to r$ and r, respectively, then $\mathsf{deriv}_{(r \to r) \to r \to r} f a$ is the derivative of f at a if f is differentiable at a and is undefined otherwise.

Finally, we can extend T_1 to a theory $T = (L, \Gamma)$ in which L contains the constant $\mathsf{diff}_{\epsilon \to \epsilon}$ and Γ contains the following axiom $\mathsf{specDiff}_o$:

$$\forall u_\epsilon . \tag{1}$$
$$\text{if } (\mathsf{DiffExpr}_{\epsilon \to o}\, u_\epsilon) \tag{2}$$
$$(\mathsf{DiffExpr}_{\epsilon \to \epsilon}(\mathsf{diff}_{\epsilon \to \epsilon}\, u_\epsilon) \wedge \tag{3}$$
$$\forall a_r . \tag{4}$$
$$(\mathsf{deriv}_{(r \to r) \to r \to r} (\lambda x_r . [\![u_e]\!]_r)\, a_r) \downarrow \supset \tag{5}$$
$$\mathsf{deriv}_{(r \to r) \to r \to r} (\lambda x_r . [\![u_e]\!]_r)\, a_r = (\lambda x_r . [\![\mathsf{diff}_{\epsilon \to \epsilon}\, u_e]\!]_r)\, a_r \tag{6}$$
$$(\mathsf{diff}_{\epsilon \to \epsilon}\, u_\epsilon) \uparrow \tag{7}$$

(3) says that, if the input u_e to $\mathsf{specDiff}_o$ is a member of the subtype $\mathsf{DiffExpr}_{\epsilon \to o}$, then the output is also a member of $\mathsf{DiffExpr}_{\epsilon \to o}$ (the syntactic component). (4–6) say that, if the input is a member of $\mathsf{DiffExpr}_{\epsilon \to o}$ and, for all real numbers a, if the function f represented by u_e is differentiable at a, then the derivative of f at a equals the function represented by $\mathsf{diff}_{\epsilon \to \epsilon}\, u_e$ at a (the semantic component). And (7) says that, if the input is not a member of $\mathsf{DiffExpr}_{\epsilon \to o}$, then the output is undefined.

5.5   Discussion

Merely applying the rules of symbolic differentiation does not always produce the derivative of function. The problem is that symbolic differentiation does not actually analyze the regions of differentiability of a function. A specification of differentiation as a symbolic algorithm, to merit the name of *differentiation*, must not just perform rewrite rules on the syntactic expression, but also compute the corresponding validity region. This is a mistake common to essentially all symbolic differentiation engines that we have been able to find.

A better solution then is to have syntactic representations of functions have an explicit syntactic component marking their *domain of definition*, so that a symbolic differentiation algorithm would be forced to produce such a domain on output as well.

In other words, we should regard the "specification" $f = \lambda x : \mathbb{R} . \ln(x^2 - 1)$ itself as incorrect, and replace it instead with $f = \lambda x : \{y \in \mathbb{R} \mid y < -1 \text{ or } y > 1\} . \ln(x^2 - 1)$.

6   Related Work

The literature on the formal specification of symbolic computation algorithms is fairly modest; it includes the papers [7, 17–19]. One of the first systems to implement SBMAs in a formal setting is MATHPERT [2] (later called MathXpert), the mathematics education system developed by Michael Beeson. Another system in which SBMAs are formally implemented is the computer algebra system built on top of HOL Light [14] by Cezary Kaliszyk and Freek Wiedijk [16]. Both systems deal in a careful way with the interplay of syntax and semantics that characterize SBMAs. Kaliszyk addresses in [15] the problem of simplifying the kind of mathematical expressions that arise in computer algebra system resulting from the application of partial functions in a proof assistant in which all functions are total. Stephen Watt distinguishes in [22] between *symbolic computation* and *computer algebra* which is very similar to the distinction between syntax-based and semantics-based mathematical algorithms.

There is an extensive review in [13] of the literature on metaprogramming, metareasoning, reflection, quotation, theories of truth, reasoning in lambda calculus about syntax, and undefinedness related to CTT_{qe} and CTT_{uqe}. For work on developing infrastructures in proof assistants for global reflection, see [1, 3, 4, 6, 8, 20, 21], which covers, amongst others, the recent work in Agda, Coq, Idris, and Lean in this direction. Note that this infrastructure is all quite recent, and has not yet been used to deal with the kinds of examples in this paper—thus we do not yet know how *adequate* these features are for the task.

7   Conclusion

Commonplace in mathematics, SBMAs are interesting and useful algorithms that manipulate the syntactic structure of mathematical expressions to achieve a mathematical task. Specifications of SBMAs are often complex because manipulating syntax is complex by its own nature, the algorithms involve an interplay of syntax and semantics, and undefined expressions are often generated from the syntactic manipulations. SBMAs can be tricky to implement in mathematical software systems that do not provide good support for the interplay of syntax and semantics that is inherent in these algorithms. For the same reason, they are challenging to specify in a traditional formal logic that provides little built-in support for reasoning about syntax.

In this paper, we have examined representative SBMAs that fulfill basic mathematical tasks. We have shown the problems that arise if they are not implemented carefully and we have delineated their specifications. We have also sketched how their specifications can be written in CTT_{uqe} [12], a version of Church's type that is well suited for expressing the interplay of syntax and semantics by virtue of its global reflection infrastructure.

We would like to continue this work first by writing complete specifications of SBMAs in CTT_{uqe} [12], CTT_{qe} [13], and other logics. Second by formally defining SBMAs in CTT_{uqe} and CTT_{qe}. Third by formally proving in CTT_{uqe} [12] and

CTT$_{qe}$ [13] the mathematical meanings of SBMAs from their formal definitions. And fourth by further developing HOL Light QE [5] so that these SBMA definitions and the proofs of their mathematical meanings can be performed and machine checked in HOL Light QE. As a small startup example, we have defined a symbolic differentiation algorithm for polynomials and proved its mathematical meaning from its definition in [13, subsections 4.4 and 9.3].

Acknowledgments. This research was supported by NSERC. The authors would like to thank the referees for their comments and suggestions.

References

1. Anand, A., Boulier, S., Cohen, C., Sozeau, M., Tabareau, N.: Towards certified meta-programming with typed TEMPLATE-COQ. In: Avigad, J., Mahboubi, A. (eds.) ITP 2018. LNCS, vol. 10895, pp. 20–39. Springer, Cham (2018). https://doi.org/10.1007/978-3-319-94821-8_2

2. Beeson, M.: Logic and computation in MATHPERT: an expert system for learning mathematics. In: Kaltofen, E., Watt, S. (eds.) Computers and Mathematics, pp. 202–214. Springer, New York (1989). https://doi.org/10.1007/978-1-4613-9647-5_25

3. Boyer, R., Moore, J.: Metafunctions: proving them correct and using them efficiently as new proof procedures. In: Boyer, R., Moore, J. (eds.) The Correctness Problem in Computer Science, pp. 103–185. Academic Press, Cambridge (1981)

4. Buchberger, B., et al.: Theorema: towards computer-aided mathematical theory exploration. J. Appl. Log. **4**, 470–504 (2006)

5. Carette, J., Farmer, W.M., Laskowski, P.: HOL light QE. In: Avigad, J., Mahboubi, A. (eds.) ITP 2018. LNCS, vol. 10895, pp. 215–234. Springer, Cham (2018). https://doi.org/10.1007/978-3-319-94821-8_13

6. Christiansen, D.R.: Type-directed elaboration of quasiquotations: a high-level syntax for low-level reflection. In: Proceedings of the 26th 2014 International Symposium on Implementation and Application of Functional Languages, IFL 2014, pp. 1:1–1:9. ACM, New York (2014). https://doi.org/10.1145/2746325.2746326

7. Dunstan, M., Kelsey, T., Linton, S., Martin, U.: Lightweight formal methods for computer algebra systems. In: Weispfenning, V., Trager, B.M. (eds.) Proceedings of the 1998 International Symposium on Symbolic and Algebraic Computation, pp. 80–87. ACM (1998)

8. Ebner, G., Ullrich, S., Roesch, J., Avigad, J., de Moura, L.: A metaprogramming framework for formal verification. Proc. ACM Program. Lang. **1**(ICFP), 34 (2017)

9. Farmer, W.M.: A simple type theory with partial functions and subtypes. Ann. Pure Appl. Log. **64**, 211–240 (1993)

10. Farmer, W.M.: Formalizing undefinedness arising in calculus. In: Basin, D., Rusinowitch, M. (eds.) IJCAR 2004. LNCS (LNAI), vol. 3097, pp. 475–489. Springer, Heidelberg (2004). https://doi.org/10.1007/978-3-540-25984-8_35

11. Farmer, W.M.: Andrews' type system with undefinedness. In: Benzmüller, C., Brown, C., Siekmann, J., Statman, R. (eds.) Reasoning in Simple Type Theory: Festschrift in Honor of Peter B. Andrews on his 70th Birthday, pp. 223–242. Studies in Logic, College Publications (2008)

12. Farmer, W.M.: Theory morphisms in Church's type theory with quotation and evaluation. In: Geuvers, H., England, M., Hasan, O., Rabe, F., Teschke, O. (eds.) CICM 2017. LNCS (LNAI), vol. 10383, pp. 147–162. Springer, Cham (2017). https://doi.org/10.1007/978-3-319-62075-6_11

13. Farmer, W.M.: Incorporating quotation and evaluation into Church's type theory. Inf. Comput. **260**, 9–50 (2018)

14. Harrison, J.: HOL light: an overview. In: Berghofer, S., Nipkow, T., Urban, C., Wenzel, M. (eds.) TPHOLs 2009. LNCS, vol. 5674, pp. 60–66. Springer, Heidelberg (2009). https://doi.org/10.1007/978-3-642-03359-9_4

15. Kaliszyk, C.: Automating side conditions in formalized partial functions. In: Autexier, S., Campbell, J., Rubio, J., Sorge, V., Suzuki, M., Wiedijk, F. (eds.) CICM 2008. LNCS (LNAI), vol. 5144, pp. 300–314. Springer, Heidelberg (2008). https://doi.org/10.1007/978-3-540-85110-3_26

16. Kaliszyk, C., Wiedijk, F.: Certified Computer Algebra on Top of an Interactive Theorem Prover. In: Kauers, M., Kerber, M., Miner, R., Windsteiger, W. (eds.) Calculemus/MKM -2007. LNCS (LNAI), vol. 4573, pp. 94–105. Springer, Heidelberg (2007). https://doi.org/10.1007/978-3-540-73086-6_8

17. Khan, M.T.: Formal specification and verification of computer algebra software. Ph.D. thesis, RISC, Johannes Kepler Universität Linz (2014)

18. Khan, M.T., Schreiner, W.: Towards the formal specification and verification of maple programs. In: Jeuring, J., et al. (eds.) CICM 2012. LNCS (LNAI), vol. 7362, pp. 231–247. Springer, Heidelberg (2012). https://doi.org/10.1007/978-3-642-31374-5_16

19. Limongelli, C., Temperini, M.: Abstract specification of structures and methods in symbolic mathematical computation. Theor. Comput. Sci. **104**, 89–107 (1992)

20. Melham, T., Cohn, R., Childs, I.: On the semantics of ReFLect as a basis for a reflective theorem prover. Computing Research Repository (CoRR) abs/1309.5742 (2013). arxiv:1309.5742

21. van der Walt, P., Swierstra, W.: Engineering proof by reflection in agda. In: Hinze, R. (ed.) IFL 2012. LNCS, vol. 8241, pp. 157–173. Springer, Heidelberg (2013). https://doi.org/10.1007/978-3-642-41582-1_10

22. Watt, S.M.: Making computer algebra more symbolic. In: Proceedings of Transgressive Computing 2006, Granada, Spain, pp. 43–49 (2006)

Lemma Discovery for Induction
A Survey

Moa Johansson[(✉)]

Department of Computer Science and Engineering,
Chalmers University of Technology, Gothenburg, Sweden
moa.johansson@chalmers.se

Abstract. Automating proofs by induction can be challenging, not least because proofs might need auxiliary lemmas, which themselves need to be proved by induction. In this paper we survey various techniques for automating the discovery of such lemmas, including both top-down techniques attempting to generate a lemma from an ongoing proof attempt, as well as bottom-up theory exploration techniques trying to construct interesting lemmas about available functions and datatypes, thus constructing a richer background theory.

1 Introduction

Induction is a proof method often needed to reason about repetition, for instance about recursive datatypes and functions in computer programs. However, automating proofs by induction in a theorem prover can be challenging as inductive proofs often need auxiliary lemmas, including both generalisations of the conjecture at hand as well as discovery of completely new lemmas. The lemmas themselves may also need induction to prove. On a theoretical level, this is captured by the *cut rule* of inference:

$$\frac{\Gamma, \psi \vdash \phi \quad \Gamma \vdash \psi}{\Gamma \vdash \phi}$$

Reasoning backwards, this rule states we can prove the goal ϕ, given Γ, if it is possible to: (1) prove the goal ϕ from Γ with the extra assistance of a lemma ψ, and (2) lemma ψ can be proved from Γ. Note that this potentially introduces an infinite branching point in the search space, as ψ can be any formula. Furthermore, there is a risk that ψ cannot be proved from Γ, if it turns out to be an over-generalisation or otherwise invalid lemma. In some logics, the cut rule is redundant: we say that the logic allows *cut-elimination*. If so, there is no need to worry about having to introduce auxiliary lemmas. However, in logics allowing e.g. structural induction over recursive datatypes, cut-elimination is in general not possible. For these reasons, most major proof assistants such as Isabelle/HOL [37], ACL2 [29] and others, treat induction interactively, the human user takes the main responsibility for how to apply induction as well as

© Springer Nature Switzerland AG 2019
C. Kaliszyk et al. (Eds.): CICM 2019, LNAI 11617, pp. 125–139, 2019.
https://doi.org/10.1007/978-3-030-23250-4_9

inventing and proving any extra lemmas that might be needed. There are however several methods for automating lemma discovery in the context of inductive proofs, which we survey in this paper. For a more general history of the automation of mathematical induction, and a survey of some historical systems that have implemented a variety of methods for induction we refer to [35].

Various techniques for discovering lemmas have been explored since the early days of automating induction in the influential Boyer-Moore prover in the 1970's [3]. Initially, lemma discovery methods focused on generalisations of the conjecture at hand, guided by heuristics [2], while later methods also attempted to construct lemmas of other shapes, using information from failed proofs, introduction of meta-variables and higher-order unification [22]. These methods have in common that they work top-down, trying to derive a lemma from the conjecture we are trying to prove. The search space for top-down methods can be large, especially when more complex lemmas are required. A different approach is to instead proceed by generating lemmas bottom-up, using techniques for *theory exploration*. Here, candidate lemmas are constructed more freely given a set of functions and datatypes, with the intention of creating a richer background theory in which to prove subsequent theorems. This method has been successful in current state-of-the-art automated inductive provers [10].

The remainder of the paper is structured as follows: In Sect. 2 we survey some standard techniques for lemma discovery by generalisation which have been adapted and implemented in many provers since the early days of automated induction. In Sect. 3 we discuss primarily *proof critics*, techniques used to analyse failed proof attempts in various ways to come up with elaborate lemmas while avoiding over-generalisations. In Sect. 4 we then survey several systems for theory exploration, and their performance for automating inductive proofs. Lemma discovery by analysis of large mathematical libraries and machine learning is yet a relatively under-explored area, which we address in Sect. 5. Recently, there has also been work on integrating induction in first-order and SMT-solvers, which we discuss in Sect. 6.

Notation. In subsequent examples we will use the notation $x::xs$ for the list cons-operator and the symbol @ to denote list append. We use $t \mapsto s$ to denote simplification of a term t to s.

2 Lemma Discovery by Generalisation

The Boyer-Moore prover was one of the first systems to attempt to automate proofs by induction [3]. The prover was structured according to a *waterfall model* centred around a pool of open subgoals (see Fig. 1). First a simplification procedure was applied, and if that did not prove the subgoal additional methods were attempted, e.g. trying to prove the goal using an assumption (such as applying an induction hypothesis) or attempting to generalise the goal. The last step of the waterfall was to apply a new induction, after which the resulting base-case(s) and step case(s) re-entered the waterfall from the beginning. This waterfall structure is still used by the decedents of the original Boyer-Moore prover, such as present day ACL2 [29], and has also been re-implemented in HOL Light [38].

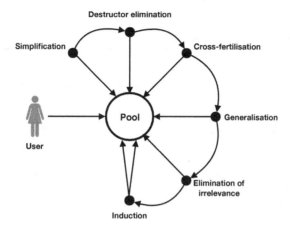

Fig. 1. The Boyer-Moore waterfall model. *Destructor elimination* is a heuristic used to remove so called destructor functions, making implied term structures explicit by replacing variables with terms. *Cross-fertilisation* is concerned with the application of an equational assumption (often an inductive hypothesis) as a rewrite rule. The *Generalisation* step will try to replace sub-terms by variables. The *Elimination of irrelevance* step is also a kind of generalisation which attempts to discard an unnecessary hypothesis

The generalisation step in the waterfall may suggest candidate lemmas that could be useful for proving the original conjecture using several heuristics for replacement of some sub-term(s) with fresh variables. The main heuristic would pick the minimal non-variable common sub-term, i.e. occurring more than once, for generalisation. Generalisations which introduced a new variable in a position to which induction could potentially be applied were preferred, as such lemmas more likely would be provable by induction. However, deciding which sub-term(s) to generalise can be non-trivial. If the wrong one is picked the result might be an over-generalisation, producing a non-theorem. An overview of generalisation methods for induction can be found in [2], where it is also pointed out that generalisation methods are safest considered in conjunction with counter-example checking, to avoid wasting time proving non-theorems.

Example 1. Consider a small functional program implementing *insertionSort*:

```
sorted [] = True
sorted [x] = True
sorted (x::y::ys) = x <= y /\ sorted(y::ys)

insert x [] = [x]
insert x (y::ys) = if x <= y then (x::y::ys) else y::(insert x ys)

insertionSort [] = []
insertionSort (x::xs) = insert x (insertionSort xs)
```

Suppose we want to prove that it produces a sorted list: *sorted(insertionSort xs)*. Applying structural induction on *xs* results in:

$$\text{Base Case: } sorted(insertionSort\ []) \mapsto sorted([]) \mapsto True$$

$$\text{Step Case: } \underbrace{sorted(insertionSort\ xs)}_{ind.\ hyp.} \implies \underbrace{sorted(insertionSort(x :: xs))}_{ind.\ concl.}$$

Applying one step of rewriting to the induction conclusion, using the definition of *insertionSort*, results in the new subgoal:

$$sorted(\mathbf{insertionSort\ xs}) \implies sorted(insert\ x\ (\mathbf{insertionSort\ xs}))$$

Now, note that the sub-term **insertionSort xs** appear in both the induction hypothesis and in the conclusion. The Boyer-Moore generalisation heuristic would replace this sub-term with a fresh variable, producing the key lemma for proving our original conjecture:

$$sorted\ ys \implies sorted(insert\ x\ ys)$$

However, it was observed that the lemma generation heuristics too often produced useless or false conjectures and the Boyer-Moore family of provers instead moved towards becoming interactive, where the user provides the appropriate lemmas. ACL2 still uses the waterfall model from Fig. 1 including generalisation techniques, but rely on the user to steer the prover away from unproductive parts of the search space, such as trying to prove an over-generalisation.

Sophisticated generalisation methods have also been implemented in many other systems supporting proofs by induction, such as the INKA system [21]. These include replacement of common sub-terms with new variables as well as replacement of independent sub-terms. Aderhold further enhanced these methods in the VeriFun system [1], an interactive verification system for functional programs. These methods include common sub-term generalisation where induction is applicable to the new variable, a method for renaming variables apart, removing conditions and as well as techniques specific to systems applying destructor-style induction. Moreover, he includes a counter-example checker to filter out any over-generalisations. These methods were demonstrated to be useful in for instance the verification proofs of several sorting algorithms.

Zeno [42] is an automated inductive prover for proving properties about a subset of Haskell programs. It can generate lemmas by the common sub-term technique shown in Example 1, and applies a counter-example finder to avoid over-generalisations.

To summarise, lemma discovery by generalisation can work very well, as we saw in Example 1, but can also be expensive, as it will increase the size of the search space of the prover and may over-generalise and produce false statements. To avoid the prover wasting time trying to prove false conjectures, it can be beneficial to combine generalisation with counter-example checking. For these reasons, it is not always obvious when generalisation should be applied. In [31], experimental evaluation suggested that generalisation was difficult to control and often produced over-generalisations if attempted before applying induction. Better results were obtained if generalisation was deferred until induction had been tried and failed to complete the proof. In the next section, we will survey techniques for lemma discovery which are applied only when no other options remain. We will also consider the discovery of lemmas that cannot be found by the generalisation methods described so far, such as the following:

Example 2. In this example, we consider a proof requiring a lemma with some "extra" term structure introduced, which could not be found just by sub-term generalisation.

```
len []  = 0
len (x::xs)  = Suc(len xs)

rotate 0 xs = xs
rotate (Suc n) []  = []
rotate (Suc n) (x::xs)  = rotate n (xs @ [x])
```

Consider proving that rotating a list around its length results in the same list as you started with: *rotate (len xs) xs = xs*. Applying structural induction on *xs* results in:

$$\text{Base Case: } rotate \ (len \ [])\ [] = [] \mapsto [] = [] \mapsto \textit{True}$$

$$\text{Step Case: } \underbrace{rotate \ (len \ xs) \ xs = xs}_{ind.hyp.} \Longrightarrow \underbrace{rotate \ (len \ (x :: xs))\ (x :: xs) = (x :: xs)}_{ind.concl.}$$

Rewriting to the induction conclusion using the definitions of rotate and len results in:

$$rotate \ (len \ xs)\ (xs \ @\ [x]) = (x :: xs)$$

At this point, common sub-term generalisation will not help us find the missing lemma. What is required is a lemma which both has an extra variable, as well as some additional term-structure compared to our original conjecture:

$$rotate \ (len \ ys)\ (ys \ @\ zs) = zs \ @\ ys$$

Our conjecture is a special case of this lemma, with *zs* happening to be the empty list. Figuring out what the structure of this lemma is a difficult task, and we discuss methods for doing so in Sects. 3 and 4.

3   Lemma Discovery from Failed Proofs

Proof-planning was introduced by Bundy [6], and motivated by the need to control proof search for inductive proofs in the NuPRL system [13]. The heuristics of the Boyer-Moore prover were used as inspiration. It was observed that the Boyer-Moore prover could prove a large number of theorems by induction using the same heuristics, but it was never made explicit exactly how and in which order these heuristics had been applied in a particular proof. A proof-plan was thus suggested as an explicit description of a *strategy* to solve a particular family of proofs, such as proofs by induction. Proof-plans could then be composed by *methods*, each a declarative wrapper for a *tactic*[1] including explicit heuristic information about under what condition the tactic should be applied, what effects it would have if successful and so on. Other motivations for proof-plans were the desire to produce human readable proof descriptions and, importantly, to deal with failure of methods by attempting to recover and patch the proof. The idea of *proof-planning critics* was introduced to handle such failures [22]. *Rippling* became an important method in proof planning for guiding rewriting in step-cases of inductive proofs towards being able to apply the inductive hypothesis [7]. Rippling uses annotations (called *wave-fronts*) on the rewrite rules and sub-goals to keep track of which parts match the inductive hypothesis and which ones do not, and steers rewriting towards minimising these differences. The rippling method fails if some crucial lemma is missing. Depending on the which one of the pre-conditions of the rippling method had failed (see Chap. 3 of [7] for details), one of several lemma discovery critics would be triggered:

Lemma Calculation. If an inductive proof failed after the inductive hypothesis had been applied, this critic would apply common sub-term generalisation (similar to what was described in Sect. 2) to the remaining goal, and attempt to prove the resulting conjecture as a lemma. This simple critic often worked well in practice.

Generalisation. The generalisation techniques described in Sect. 2 could not deal with more complicated generalisations, such as Example 2. Rippling would in these cases fail, as its heuristics would realise that it would not be possible to apply the inductive hypothesis without introducing a generalisation of the conjecture, containing some extra new universally quantified variable (a *sink* in rippling terminology). To figure out where and how such a new variable should be introduced, a schematic lemma, containing some higher-order meta-variables would be constructed. The system would then apply *middle-out reasoning* [20], trying to prove the schematic lemma by induction and expecting to instantiate the meta-variables by subsequent rewrites and the eventual application of the inductive hypothesis. The lemma from Example 2 can be found in this manner, although it requires that some lemmas about the append-functions are already present (see [7], Sect. 3.7.2).

Lemma Speculation. If rippling got stuck before the inductive hypothesis could be applied, the lemma speculation critic would be triggered. Similarly to the generalisation critic, an underspecified lemma would be constructed and applied to the goal: the right-hand side chosen to match some suitable sub-term to rewrite, and the left-hand side consisting of a higher-order meta-variable expected to be instantiated by middle-out reasoning as before. Note that there might be several possible such schematic lemmas, and that higher-

---

[1] A small program executing one or several proof steps automatically.

order unification is required to complete the instantiation of the lemma which may require a fair bit of search.

These proof-planning critics for rippling were implemented in the OYSTER-CLAM system [8, 22]. The original paper on proof critics in CLAM also contained a set of benchmarks of theorems needing inductive proofs and lemmas (including Examples 1 and 2). These were later digitalised and made available to developers of inductive theorem provers in the TIP benchmark library [11], and are commonly used to evaluate inductive theorem provers.

An advantage of proof-planning was to clarify exactly when a critic should be triggered, minimising the risk of producing over-generalisations and allowing for more complex lemmas to be automatically synthesised by using middle-out reasoning and higher-order unification. A similar lemma discovery method, based on the instantiation of meta-variables in schematic lemmas was also proposed for the RRL system [28]. Here, the instantiation of the schematic lemma was guided by constraints and not rippling. The lemma calculation and lemma speculation critics were also later implemented in IsaPlanner system [15, 16]. However, experimental evaluation of lemma speculation in IsaPlanner was largely negative, the critic was found to be rarely applicable, and the complexities of the many options of how and where to introduce meta-variables could lead to a large search space for higher-order unification [24].

In the context of lemma speculation, we also mention the work by Sonnex on the Elea system [43]. This system takes quite a different approach to automating induction inspired by ideas from functional programming and supercompilation. Elea supports lemma discovery when otherwise stuck by introducing meta-variables and attempting to synthesise functions of a special shape, so called fold-functions, which restricts the search space.

Nagashima and Parsert presented a conjecture generation method for Isabelle/HOL based on generalisation and mutation of stuck subgoals [36]. Here, existing rewrite rules are used to suggest mutations of the goal, and counterexample checking filters out non-theorems. However, no evaluation was provided comparing it to other lemma discovery techniques.

4 Bottom-Up Lemma Discovery: Theory Exploration

The lemma discovery techniques covered so far have all tried to somehow construct a missing lemma from an ongoing proof attempt of a given conjecture. A different approach is that of *theory exploration*: starting from the bottom up in a new theory given the set of available symbols (such as functions and datatypes) what are the basic, interesting lemmas? In the context of automating induction, the system should try to find and prove as many useful lemmas as possible, and then try to tackle harder proofs in this richer theory, hoping that the key lemmas have already been discovered. The term theory exploration was first coined by Buchberger [4] to describe the workflow of a human mathematician starting a new theory, and how it differs from that of an automated theorem prover, which proves theorems in isolation. Instead, he argues, mathematical software should support an exploratory workflow, by which new concepts are introduced and their relationship to existing concepts explored before proofs of complex theorems are attempted. This is largely how interactive theorem provers are used, and motivated the design of the Theorema system by Buchberger's group [5]. Theorema introduced the concept of *knowledge schemas* representing some interesting mathematical knowledge, and which could be instantiated in new theories, but did not automate the process.

In the following sections we survey theory exploration systems that have been applied to inductive theories. All system have in common that they first generate terms and/or equations followed by some form of evaluation on concrete values, or counter-example checking. Finally, they attempt automated inductive proofs, using previously discovered and proved lemmas if needed. However, they differ in heuristics for how they generate the conjectures, how to evaluated them, and how to judge their interestingness.

4.1 MATHsAiD

MATHsAiD [33], was primarily designed for theory exploration in algebra, but has also been applied to simple inductive theories about natural numbers [32]. MATHsAiD first heuristically constructs a set of potential left-hand sides, called *terms of interest* starting with smaller terms and using some heuristics such as specifically looking for common properties like associativity, commutativity and distributivity. Next, MATHsAiD selects a variable in each term of interest, and instantiates it with some concrete value "TWO" (e.g. for natural numbers, this would be $suc(suc\ 0)$, for lists a list of two elements). It then applies (bounded) forward reasoning from each potential left-hand side term, using function definitions as rewrite rules, until arriving at a different term, also containing an instance of "TWO". At this point, a candidate equation can be constructed by replacing "TWO" by a variable again. MATHsAiD successfully discovered and proved basic lemmas about addition and multiplication in Peano arithmetic, but its wider application to inductive theories was not explored.

4.2 IsaCoSy

IsaCoSy was the first theory exploration system designed specifically for discovering basic inductive lemmas that would be useful in more difficult subsequent proofs [25]. As the name suggests, it was built on top of the Isabelle/HOL proof assistant [37], and used IsaPlanner [15], to prove discovered candidate conjectures. The key idea to restrict the search-space of possible conjectures was to only generate new terms that were irreducible, i.e. terms not possible to reduce further by rewriting using any equations proved so far. IsaCoSy would generate equational terms starting from the minimal size of left- and right-hand sides (single constants, variables) and generate all possible irreducible type-correct terms of that size. Next, the equations would be filtered through a counter-example finder and those surviving passed on to IsaPlanner for proof. IsaCosy then generated constraints from any theorems found to avoid generating any reducible terms in the next iteration when the term size was increased (up to a maximum size given by the user). IsaCosy demonstrated high recall on theories of lists and natural numbers from Isabelle's library. Although precision was lower, one could argue that the lemmas suggested would be reasonable additions to the library. IsaCoSy also performed better at finding lemmas required by difficult inductive proofs than IsaPlanner's lemma speculation critic [24]. On the downside, the runtimes could be very long, primarily due to the non-optimised implementation and the many calls to Isabelle's counter-example finder.

4.3   IsaScheme

IsaScheme was another theory exploration system for Isabelle/HOL [34], using the above-mentioned idea of user-defined schemas from Theorema [5], to generate conjectures and functions, but automating the process of instantiating them. Conjecture schemas would typically capture common patterns such as associativity, distributivity etc. After the instantiation of a schema, IsaScheme would check that the resulting conjecture did not follow trivially from known facts (similar to IsaCoSy's irreducibility heuristic), then pass it on to a counter-example checker and finally for proof using IsaPlanner. IsaScheme furthermore included a Knuth-Bendix completion pass, as lemmas could be discovered in the "wrong" order - a new conjecture might be a generalisation of a previous one (which then was discarded) and which also ensured that the lemmas discovered formed a terminating set of rewrite rules.

4.4   QuickSpec and HipSpec/Hipster

QuickSpec [12,41] was originally designed to be a system for automatically inventing and testing equational specifications of Haskell programs. While QuickSpec itself does not perform any proofs, it is considerably faster at generating conjectures compared to other systems like e.g. IsaCoSy and IsaScheme. QuickSpec does not generate whole equations at once, but rather just terms which would make candidate left- and right hand sides, up to a given maximum size. All terms are initially placed in a single equivalence class. Next, QuickSpec calls Haskell's testing tool QuickCheck [9], to generate random values for all variables in terms (variables were assumed to be shared), followed by evaluation and splitting of the equivalence class(es) accordingly. After many rounds of testing when equivalence classes have stabilised, equations can be extracted. This way, it is never necessary to counter-example check individual equalities, testing and equation-generation is integrated.

The HipSpec system [10], integrated QuickSpec in an inductive theorem prover, and successfully proved most of the difficult theorems from the CLAM-critics benchmark set available in the TIP library [11,22]. HipSpec itself was a rather lightweight prover, it simply applied induction to conjectures and passed the resulting proof obligations to an external automated prover (first-order or SMT-solver). It did however achieve state-of-the-art results by first letting QuickSpec come up with a set of candidate lemmas about the functions occurring in the problem, proving these, and then tackling the main conjectures. This included a fully automatic proof of the rotate-length lemma from Example 2, with all required lemmas found by theory exploration.

Hipster [23, 26] is a sister-system to HipSpec, which also use QuickSpec for conjecture generation but conducts formally checked proofs in Isabelle/HOL. As QuickSpec treats the program as a black box, it might re-discover equations representing e.g. function definitions or equations already present in Isabelle's library, which are unnecessary to present to an Isabelle user (but might be interesting if exploring a program for which the source code is not available). To judge which conjectures are likely interesting to a human user, Hipster is therefore parametrised by two tactics: one for *routine reasoning* and one for *hard reasoning*. The idea is that lemmas that are proved by the routine tactic, are somewhat trivial and therefore discarded and not displayed to the user, while lemmas requiring the hard reasoning tactic are judged interesting and returned. Common configurations are to use Isabelle's simplifier (rewriting) or Sledgehammer (a method for calling external first-order automated provers [39]) as routine tactics, and some form of induction as the hard reasoning tactic, but any tactics could be used. Hipster is under ongoing development, and is currently employing the most recent version of QuickSpec [41]. Hipster has added capabilities for conditional lemma discovery which were lacking from HipSpec, as well as support for co-induction [17]. Hipster can thus discover and prove the required lemmas from both Example 1 (insertion sort) and Example 2 (rotate-length).

5   Machine Learning and Lemmas by Analogy

Many proof assistants have large libraries with already formalised mathematics, including many common lemmas. Heras et al. [19] demonstrated a small prototype system for ACL2 where machine learning was used for identifying similarities between a new conjecture and existing ones in the library. From such a similar library fact, one could examine its proof and, if any lemmas had been used, extract a lemma schema from it. Next, a restricted form of theory exploration searched for new lemmas appropriate for the current case. This worked well for examples of the kind of lemmas needed in inductive proofs of the equivalence between recursive functions and their tail-recursive counterparts, but has not been more widely applied or evaluated.

Gauthier et al. also experiment with conjecturing lemmas based on statistical analysis and machine learning from the Mizar mathematical library [18], although they do not consider lemmas for inductive theories and proofs.

Exploring the use of machine learning seems a promising direction for further work. In particular, it could potentially help reducing the search space for theory exploration to specifically target a sub-space where we are more likely to find a lemma which is useful for a particular proof attempt at hand. The theory exploration systems described in Sect. 4 typically search broadly for lemmas, meaning that they typically also discover and prove a lot of extra things, which might be undesirable if speed is an issue, or if the term size of the lemma required is large.

6   Induction in First-Order Provers and SMT Solvers

More recently, there has been work in integrating induction also in automated superposition based first-order provers [14,44], and SMT-solvers [30,40].

The induction method implemented in the SMT-solver CVC4 employs local theory exploration integrated in the DPLL(T) engine to generate extra lemmas during a proof attempt [40]. The lemma generation module enumerates terms, similarly to QuickSpec, up to a given maximum size. It then heuristically chooses a subset of these candidates (typically around 3) depending on the current context, which will enter the proof search. These heuristic filters include removing reducible terms, similarly to the heuristics used in IsaCoSy, as well as generating ground instances of terms (similar to how QuickSpec used QuickCheck) to detect if any such assignment in the current context falsifies any speculated equations. The performance of CVC4 is comparable to that of other inductive provers mentioned, but it does not quite reach the numbers proved by HipSpec on the proof-critics benchmarks from the TIP library [11,22], which require slightly more difficult lemmas.

Wand developed an extension to superposition calculus to include a type system and induction over datatypes for his PhD thesis [44], which was implemented in the Pirate system. Pirate supports several generalisation techniques for conjecturing lemmas from stuck subgoals, and thus belong to the category of top-down lemma discovery methods. Pirate is reported to perform similarly to HipSpec on the TIP-benchmarks.

Cruanes extended the superposition prover Zipperposition with support for induction [14]. The prover uses an architecture supporting interleaving several inductive proof attempts simultaneously, in the same saturation loop, anticipating that proving lemmas will be needed in many inductive proofs. Once a lemma has been proved, it can be used automatically as a normal axiom. While this system itself only supports some simpler generalisations as a lemma discovery method, it is argued that it could easily be integrated with other techniques such as theory exploration. The capability for interleaving several proof attempts seems as if it could be very useful for theory exploration, where the system often gets a list of conjectures to prove, where some will need others as lemmas.

7   Summary

Lemma discovery is crucial in all but the simplest inductive proofs, and many methods have been implemented. They fall primarily into three groups: Generalisations, proof critics and theory exploration. Variants of generalisation techniques have proved useful in many contexts, in particular those based on replacing (common) sub-terms with new variables, which are easy to implement and often work well. However, there is a risk of over-generalisation so these techniques are safest employed in conjunction with counter-example checking or user interaction. The rippling-based proof critics discussed in Sect. 3 are today largely obsolete, as most modern inductive provers have abandoned rippling in favour of more general automated rewriting techniques, which do a good enough job without requiring quite as many annotations and heuristics as rippling. Furthermore, theory exploration based techniques can find also the more difficult lemmas which were previously requiring advanced proof critics. Theory exploration has many advantages, it is not dependent on any particular proof technique or prover and it can be run once when a new theory is initiated to provide basic lemmas, after which many harder conjectures from standard benchmark suites are provable. One potential downside is that to find very large lemmas, the search space might also grow rapidly. Theory exploration is also not very good at finding complex conditional lemmas, as it is difficult to generate random ground values which satisfies arbitrary conditions automatically. Furthermore, it can be time consuming to explore functions that have high computational complexity, as evaluation of ground instances then takes a long time. As mentioned in Sect. 5, one possibility is to exploit existing libraries and machine learning for guiding and restricting lemma discovery.

Strengths and weaknesses:
Generalisation

  + Can quickly and effectively find the right lemma, if correct generalisation found (see Example 1).
  - Might over-generalise and produce non-theorems unless coupled with a good counter-example finder, or included in an interactive environment where a human can catch such cases.
  - Not always clear when to apply generalisation. Should it be applied before or after attempting induction, and if so, should one defer until after the induction hypothesis has been applied (lemma calculation) or allow more eager generalisation, such as the Boyer-Moore provers?

Proof Critics

  + Clear under which conditions the critic is supposed to be applied.
  + Reduces risk of generating over-generalisations.
  + Can find (some) lemmas that are not generalisations of terms (see Example 2).
  - Relies heavily on rippling heuristic, might need work to transfer to other context.
  - Some critics rely on middle-out reasoning and higher-order unification which may lead to a rather large search space.

Theory Exploration

  + Bottom-up, can explores theory to find lemmas up-front, not (only) after failed proof attempt. Automatically finds and proves both lemmas required for Examples 1 and 2.
  + Not reliant on any particular proof-technique.
  +/- Relies on evaluation of random ground values for variables in terms. Often fast, but can be computationally heavy if highly complex functions given to the system.

- So far limited to simple conditional lemmas, as automated generation of random values satisfying arbitrary conditions is a non-trivial
  problem.
- Scalability. Can be difficult to search for very large lemmas featuring
  many different functions as the search space then increase a lot. Term
  sizes up to 7–9 on each side of an equality is usually OK though.

Finally, we note that automated lemma discovery seems to fit in nicely as
a complement to the recent success of *hammers* in interactive theorem proving
systems. Such systems, e.g. Sledgehammer [39] for Isabelle and HOLyHammer
for HOL Light [27], use machine learning to select a subset of all the available
facts in the provers library, and sends them to an external and powerful first-
order prover or SMT-solver. If a proof is found, the external prover reports back
which lemmas it used and the interactive theorem prover reconstructs it using
its internal trusted tactics, without having to re-do all the search. However,
in a new theory, the key facts might not yet be there, why lemma discovery
techniques could be helpful, especially if the hammer had access to a first-order
prover supporting induction, as discussed in Sect. 6.

References

1. Aderhold, M.: Improvements in formula generalization. In: Pfenning, F. (ed.)
   CADE 2007. LNCS (LNAI), vol. 4603, pp. 231–246. Springer, Heidelberg (2007).
   https://doi.org/10.1007/978-3-540-73595-3_16
2. Aubin, R.: Mechanizing structural induction. Ph.D. thesis, University of Edinburgh
   (1976)
3. Boyer, R.S., Moore, J.S.: A Computational Logic. ACM Monographs in Computer
   Science (1979)
4. Buchberger, B.: Theory exploration with Theorema. Analele Universitatii Din
   Timisoara ser. Mat.-Informatica **38**(2), 9–32 (2000)
5. Buchberger, B., et al.: Theorema: towards computer-aided mathematical theory
   exploration. J. Appl. Log. **4**(4), 470–504 (2006). Towards Computer Aided Mathematics
6. Bundy, A.: The use of explicit plans to guide inductive proofs. In: Lusk, E., Over-
   beek, R. (eds.) CADE 1988. LNCS, vol. 310, pp. 111–120. Springer, Heidelberg
   (1988). https://doi.org/10.1007/BFb0012826
7. Bundy, A., Basin, D., Hutter, D., Ireland, A.: Rippling: Meta-Level Guidance for
   Mathematical Reasoning. Cambridge University Press, Cambridge (2005)
8. Bundy, A., van Harmelen, F., Horn, C., Smaill, A.: The O^YS^TER-CL^AM system.
   In: Stickel, M.E. (ed.) CADE 1990. LNCS, vol. 449, pp. 647–648. Springer, Heidelberg (1990). https://doi.org/10.1007/3-540-52885-7_123
9. Claessen, K., Hughes, J.: QuickCheck: a lightweight tool for random testing of
   Haskell programs. In: Proceedings of ICFP, pp. 268–279 (2000)
10. Claessen, K., Johansson, M., Rosén, D., Smallbone, N.: Automating inductive
    proofs using theory exploration. In: Bonacina, M.P. (ed.) CADE 2013. LNCS
    (LNAI), vol. 7898, pp. 392–406. Springer, Heidelberg (2013). https://doi.org/10.
    1007/978-3-642-38574-2_27

11. Claessen, K., Johansson, M., Rosén, D., Smallbone, N.: TIP: tons of inductive problems. In: Kerber, M., Carette, J., Kaliszyk, C., Rabe, F., Sorge, V. (eds.) CICM 2015. LNCS (LNAI), vol. 9150, pp. 333–337. Springer, Cham (2015). https://doi.org/10.1007/978-3-319-20615-8_23

12. Claessen, K., Smallbone, N., Hughes, J.: QuickSpec: guessing formal specifications using testing. In: Fraser, G., Gargantini, A. (eds.) TAP 2010. LNCS, vol. 6143, pp. 6–21. Springer, Heidelberg (2010). https://doi.org/10.1007/978-3-642-13977-2_3

13. Constable, R.L., Allen, S.F., Bromley, H.M.: Implementing Mathematics with the nuPRL Development System. Prentice Hall, Upper Saddle River (1986)

14. Cruanes, S.: Superposition with structural induction. In: Dixon, C., Finger, M. (eds.) FroCoS 2017. LNCS (LNAI), vol. 10483, pp. 172–188. Springer, Cham (2017). https://doi.org/10.1007/978-3-319-66167-4_10

15. Dixon, L., Fleuriot, J.: Higher order rippling in IsaPlanner. In: Slind, K., Bunker, A., Gopalakrishnan, G. (eds.) TPHOLs 2004. LNCS, vol. 3223, pp. 83–98. Springer, Heidelberg (2004). https://doi.org/10.1007/978-3-540-30142-4_7

16. Dixon, L., Johansson, M.: IsaPlanner 2: a proof planner in Isabelle. DReaM Technical report (System description) (2007)

17. Einarsdóttir, S.H., Johansson, M., Åman Pohjola, J.: Into the infinite - theory exploration for coinduction. In: Fleuriot, J., Wang, D., Calmet, J. (eds.) AISC 2018. LNCS (LNAI), vol. 11110, pp. 70–86. Springer, Cham (2018). https://doi.org/10.1007/978-3-319-99957-9_5

18. Gauthier, T., Kaliszyk, C., Urban, J.: Initial experiments with statistical conjecturing over large formal corpora. In: Joint Proceedings of the FM4M, MathUI, and ThEdu Workshops, Doctoral Program, and Work in Progress at the Conference on Intelligent Computer Mathematics 2016 (CICM-WiP 2016). CEUR, vol. 1785, pp. 219–228. CEUR-WS.org (2016)

19. Heras, J., Komendantskaya, E., Johansson, M., Maclean, E.: Proof-pattern recognition and lemma discovery in ACL2. In: McMillan, K., Middeldorp, A., Voronkov, A. (eds.) LPAR 2013. LNCS, vol. 8312, pp. 389–406. Springer, Heidelberg (2013). https://doi.org/10.1007/978-3-642-45221-5_27

20. Hesketh, J.: Using middle out reasoning to guide inductive theorem proving. Ph.D. thesis, University of Edinburgh (1992)

21. Hummel, B.: An investigation of formula generalization heuristics for inductive proofs. Interner Bericht Nr, 6/87, Universität Karlsruhe (1987)

22. Ireland, A., Bundy, A.: Productive use of failure in inductive proof. J. Autom. Reasoning **16**, 79–111 (1996)

23. Johansson, M.: Automated theory exploration for interactive theorem proving: an introduction to the hipster system. In: Ayala-Rincón, M., Muñoz, C.A. (eds.) ITP 2017. LNCS, vol. 10499, pp. 1–11. Springer, Cham (2017). https://doi.org/10.1007/978-3-319-66107-0_1

24. Johansson, M., Dixon, L., Bundy, A.: Dynamic rippling, middle-out reasoning and lemma discovery. In: Siegler, S., Wasser, N. (eds.) Verification, Induction, Termination Analysis. LNCS (LNAI), vol. 6463, pp. 102–116. Springer, Heidelberg (2010). https://doi.org/10.1007/978-3-642-17172-7_6

25. Johansson, M., Dixon, L., Bundy, A.: Conjecture synthesis for inductive theories. J. Autom. Reasoning **47**(3), 251–289 (2011)

26. Johansson, M., Rosén, D., Smallbone, N., Claessen, K.: Hipster: integrating theory exploration in a proof assistant. In: Watt, S.M., Davenport, J.H., Sexton, A.P., Sojka, P., Urban, J. (eds.) CICM 2014. LNCS (LNAI), vol. 8543, pp. 108–122. Springer, Cham (2014). https://doi.org/10.1007/978-3-319-08434-3_9

27. Kaliszyk, C., Urban, J.: Learning-assisted automated reasoning with flyspeck. J. Autom. Reasoning **53**(2), 173–213 (2014)

28. Kapur, D., Subramaniam, M.: Lemma discovery in automating induction. In: McRobbie, M.A., Slaney, J.K. (eds.) CADE 1996. LNCS, vol. 1104, pp. 538–552. Springer, Heidelberg (1996). https://doi.org/10.1007/3-540-61511-3_112

29. Kaufmann, M., Panagiotis, M., Moore, J.S.: Computer-Aided Reasoning: An Approach. Kluwer Academic Publishers, Boston (2000)

30. Leino, K.R.M.: Automating induction with an SMT solver. In: Kuncak, V., Rybalchenko, A. (eds.) VMCAI 2012. LNCS, vol. 7148, pp. 315–331. Springer, Heidelberg (2012). https://doi.org/10.1007/978-3-642-27940-9_21

31. Maclean, E.: Generalisation as a critic. Master's thesis, University of Edinburgh (1999)

32. McCasland, R., Bundy, A., Autexier, S.: Automated discovery of inductive theorems. In: Matuszewski, R., Rudnicki, P. (eds.) From Insight to Proof: Festschrift in Honor of A. Trybulec (2007)

33. McCasland, R., Bundy, A., Smith, P.: MATHsAiD: automated mathematical theory exploration. Appl. Intell. **47**(3), 585–606 (2017)

34. Montano-Rivas, O., McCasland, R., Dixon, L., Bundy, A.: Scheme-based theorem discovery and concept invention. Expert Syst. Appl. **39**(2), 1637–1646 (2012)

35. Moore, J.S., Wirth, C.-P.: Automation of mathematical induction as part of the history of logic. IfCoLog J. Log. Their Appl. **4**(5), 1505–1634 (2014). SEKI-Report SR-2013-02

36. Nagashima, Y., Parsert, J.: Goal-oriented conjecturing for Isabelle/HOL. In: Rabe, F., Farmer, W.M., Passmore, G.O., Youssef, A. (eds.) CICM 2018. LNCS (LNAI), vol. 11006, pp. 225–231. Springer, Cham (2018). https://doi.org/10.1007/978-3-319-96812-4_19

37. Nipkow, T., Paulson, L.C., Wenzel, M.: Isabelle/HOL – A Proof Assistant for Higher-Order Logic. LNCS, vol. 2283. Springer, Heidelberg (2002). https://doi.org/10.1007/3-540-45949-9

38. Papapanagiotou, P., Fleuriot, J.: The Boyer-Moore waterfall model revisited (2011). https://arxiv.org/pdf/1808.03810.pdf

39. Paulson, L.C., Blanchette, J.C.: Three years of experience with Sledgehammer, a practical link between automatic and interactive theorem provers. In: IWIL-2010 (2010)

40. Reynolds, A., Kuncak, V.: Induction for SMT solvers. In: D'Souza, D., Lal, A., Larsen, K.G. (eds.) VMCAI 2015. LNCS, vol. 8931, pp. 80–98. Springer, Heidelberg (2015). https://doi.org/10.1007/978-3-662-46081-8_5

41. Smallbone, N., Johansson, M., Claessen, K., Algehed, M.: Quick specifications for the busy programmer. J. Funct. Program. **27**, e18 (2017)

42. Sonnex, W., Drossopoulou, S., Eisenbach, S.: Zeno: an automated prover for properties of recursive data structures. In: Flanagan, C., König, B. (eds.) TACAS 2012. LNCS, vol. 7214, pp. 407–421. Springer, Heidelberg (2012). https://doi.org/10.1007/978-3-642-28756-5_28

43. Sonnex, W.: Fixed point promotion: taking the induction out of automated induction. Technical report UCAM-CL-TR-905, University of Cambridge, Computer Laboratory, March 2017

44. Wand, D.: Superposition: types and induction. Ph.D. thesis, Saarland University (2017)

Experiments on Automatic Inclusion of Some Non-degeneracy Conditions Among the Hypotheses in Locus Equation Computations

Zoltán Kovács[1]([✉])[iD] and Pavel Pech[2]

[1] The Private University College of Education of the Diocese of Linz,
Salesianumweg 3, 4020 Linz, Austria
`zoltan@geogebra.org`
[2] Faculty of Education, University of South Bohemia,
Jeronýmova 10, 370 01 České Budějovice, Czech Republic
`pech@pf.jcu.cz`

Abstract. In automated reasoning in geometry, in particular in computing locus equations, degenerate components usually play an important role. Although degeneracy may have multiple meanings by considering different mathematical traditions, avoiding degenerate components is useful from the geometrical point of view.

Computation of locus equations is usually based on elimination of variables. In most cases the graphical output is checked *after* the computations and then the degenerate components will be removed manually. In our experiments we prescribe non-degeneracy *before* starting any computations and expect disappearing of the degenerate components automatically.

In this paper we investigate if such assumptions may be automatized, and if they can help in improving the output by getting the degenerate components automatically removed, and whether the calculation is still feasible due to the higher amount of computations. Our experiments have already been tried in an implementation of our algorithm in GeoGebra 5.0.524.0.

Keywords: Automated reasoning in geometry ·
Non-degeneracy conditions · Locus equation · GeoGebra

1 Introduction

Automated deduction in geometry (ADG) has its roots in logic, geometry, algebraic geometry and computer science. A boost on its research can be identified after Chou's revolutionary book [1] that showed evidence that effective algorithms can prove several non-trivial planar geometry problems very quickly.

In this paper we focus on locus equation computation that is a part of ADG and proven to be popular also in educational uses. (See Fig. 1 for a LEGO model

© Springer Nature Switzerland AG 2019
C. Kaliszyk et al. (Eds.): CICM 2019, LNAI 11617, pp. 140–154, 2019.
https://doi.org/10.1007/978-3-030-23250-4_10

of Watt's linkage [2] that can produce a motion that corresponds to a sextic polynomial curve.) The first appearances of the possibility of computing the equation of a geometric locus include *GDI-Locus* [3] and *FeliX* [4], two software applications, but recently also a large amount of development was committed to the open source dynamic mathematics software *GeoGebra*.

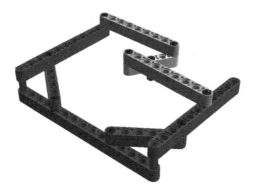

Fig. 1. A LEGO model that produces a motion that can be described by a sextic polynomial curve, namely, Watt's curve, a lemniscate

GeoGebra, like some other systems, uses elimination of variables to compute locus equations. That is, the geometric construction is translated first into an algebraic setup. The obtained equation system, roughly speaking, contains several variables that describe the coordinates of the geometric drawing. A locus equation is technically an equation in two variables, usually denoted by x and y, that describes the curve of the movement of a point, at least in most cases.

Geometrically we can distinguish between *explicit* and *implicit* loci.

The geometric notion of *explicit locus* is the following [5]:

Consider an input point $\mathcal{I}$ on a path $\mathcal{P}$, some construction steps, and an output point $\mathcal{O}$. The task is to determine the equation $\mathcal{E}$ of the locus of $\mathcal{O}$ while $\mathcal{I}$ is moving on $\mathcal{P}$, and then plot $\mathcal{E}$. Point $\mathcal{I}$ is usually called *mover*, $\mathcal{O}$ is the *tracer*. $\mathcal{E}$ is called the *locus equation*, and its graphical visualization is the *locus*.

The geometric notion of *implicit locus* is as follows:

Consider a given input point $\mathcal{I}$, either as a free point, or on a path $\mathcal{P}$. Moreover, assume some construction steps are also given. The user claims a Boolean condition $\mathcal{C}$ holds on some objects of the construction. The task is to determine an equation $\mathcal{E}$ such that for all points $\mathcal{I}'$ of it, if $\mathcal{I} = \mathcal{I}'$, then $\mathcal{C}$ holds. Again, $\mathcal{E}$ is called locus equation, and its graphical representation is the locus.

An example of an explicit locus can be found in Figs. 2 and 3. More precisely, to obtain the sextic polynomial shown in Fig. 3 GeoGebra computed

$$\left\langle x - \frac{m+f}{2}, y - \frac{n+g}{2}, (m-(-7))^2 + (n-2)^2 - 8^2, \right.$$
$$\left. (f-7)^2 + (g-(-2))^2 - 8^2, (m-f)^2 + (n-g)^2 - 4^2 \right\rangle \cap \mathbb{Q}[x,y]$$

by using an internal computer algebra command for performing elimination via Gröbner bases. The graphical output in Fig. 3 was obtained with the command LocusEquation($\mathcal{O}, \mathcal{I}$) after all preliminary points of the figure were properly constructed (see https://www.geogebra.org/m/DpPyzRdx for a similar GeoGebra applet).

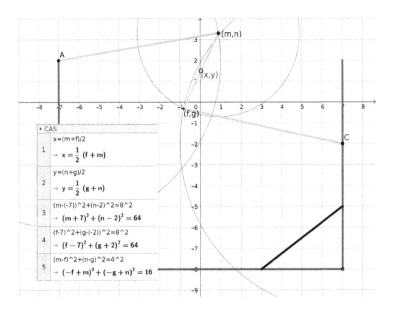

Fig. 2. Graphical representation of Watt's linkage and the equation system according to it, constructed in GeoGebra

For a simple example of implicit locus we can think of a definition of the perpendicular bisector of a segment whose points are equally distant from the end points of the segment—here we do not explicitly describe how to construct the bisector but just a property is given that uniquely defines it.

The method we use to obtain locus equations is very helpful to compute *envelopes* as well, because with just minor modifications we get remarkable curves in a feasible time. More precisely [5]:

Given an input point $\mathcal{I}$ on a path $\mathcal{P}$, some construction steps, and an output path $\mathcal{O}$, either a line or a circle, the task is to determine the equation

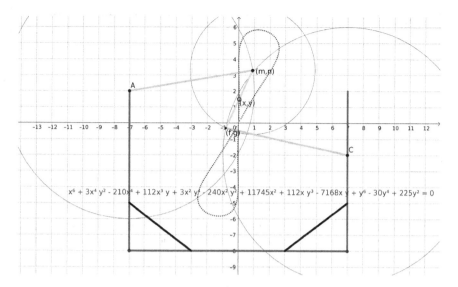

Fig. 3. A projection of the equation system on the variables x and y with automated elimination, by using GeoGebra's `LocusEquation` command, and plotting the graph of the locus equation as an implicit curve

$\mathcal{E}$ of a curve $\mathcal{C}$ which is tangent to $\mathcal{O}$, while $\mathcal{I}$ is moving on $\mathcal{P}$. Then finally plot $\mathcal{E}$. $\mathcal{I}$ is called the mover. $\mathcal{E}$ is called the *envelope equation*, and its graphical visualization is the *envelope*.

A simple example of an envelope is the following: Consider a circle with a fixed radius whose center moves on a line, here the envelope of this family of circles is two parallel lines that designate the track of movement of the circle.

In this paper we focus on explicit locus equations, but many concepts can be transferred to implicit locus and envelope equations as well. Also, our benchmarks will effect all three types of computations (see Table 2).

In many cases, the workflow of obtaining the explicit locus equation can be described by a simple algorithm (see Algorithm 1). We remark here that the algorithm will return an error if I is generated by more the one polynomial— in this case some further steps are required to describe the output suitable for graphical presentation.

Also, sometimes the algorithm output P may contain algebraic components that do not have any geometrical meaning. In such cases P must be interpreted manually and its extraneous components must be removed by hand. Some examples of this unwanted behavior are listed in [6] and [5, p. 39, Fig. 7]—here we recall an example of the latter paper in Fig. 4.

A possible approach to work around such problems is to do some more sophisticated computations than given in Algorithm 1, for example, to define degenerate points and components in a rigorous way [7]. As an application of this kind of taxonomy, it is possible to use the Gröbner Cover algorithm to get a detailed

---

Algorithm 1. A simple algorithm to obtain an explicit locus equation

---

1: **procedure** LocusEquation($\mathcal{C}$)
2:     $H \leftarrow$ algebraic translation of $\mathcal{C}$
3:     $I \leftarrow$ eliminate all variables from H except x and y
4:     **if** I is generated by the polynomial $p(x, y)$ **then**
5:         $P \leftarrow$ SquarefreeFactorization(p)
6:         **return** P
7:     **else**
8:         **return** error

---

classification of the output components fully automated [8]. Roughly speaking, the Gröbner Cover of a parametric ideal $I \subset K[\mathbf{a}][\mathbf{x}]$ consists of a set of pairs (S_i, B_i), where the S_i are disjoint locally closed segments of the parameter space, and the B_i are the reduced Gröbner bases of the ideal on every point of S_i. In fact, GeoGebra also provides a way to establish direct connection to the computer algebra system *Singular* that implements the Gröbner Cover algorithm [9]. But it turns out that this approach is sometimes too slow: [10] shows a comparison that in 52 test cases out of 152 the Gröbner Cover was not able to give the correct answer within a timeout of 60 s, even if it removes some unwanted components in 9 cases perfectly, unlike Algorithm 1.

In this contribution we consider another approach. We *prescribe* non-degeneracy conditions by extending the set of hypotheses H through the Rabinowitsch trick [11]. In other words, we add some extra hypotheses to the problem setting that may help avoid degenerate geometrical situations—for example, to avoid degenerate triangles to appear.

It will be important to keep the extension as small as possible because each non-degeneracy condition will increase the number of variables by 1, and in worst case elimination can be doubly exponential in the number of variables [12]. That is, such an extension can slow the computations down in an extreme way. As a result we get a modified algorithm (see Algorithm 2) that is explained in detail in the next section.

Algorithm 2. A modified algorithm to obtain an explicit locus equation

---

1: **procedure** LocusEquation($\mathcal{C}$)
2:     $H \leftarrow$ algebraic translation of $\mathcal{C}$
3:     Extend H by some prescribed non-degeneracy conditions
4:     $I \leftarrow$ eliminate all variables from H except x and y
5:     **if** I is generated by the polynomial $p(x, y)$ **then**
6:         $P \leftarrow$ SquarefreeFactorization(p)
7:         **return** P
8:     **else**
9:         **return** error

---

2 Prescribing Non-degeneracy Conditions

By elimination of variables we often obtain an algebraic equation which may not represent the locus. We have to discard extra points due to Zariski closed sets, or sometimes we encounter the case, where together with the locus also some extraneous components occur [7]. In our experience we will remove the degenerate components as geometrically irrelevant: they usually correspond to degenerate instances of a construction, such as two coincident points defining a line, for example. Since we often do not get *one-to-one correspondence between the mover and the tracer* and instead of a point we get an infinite set of points— an extra component. Here we refer to [7] that provides a precise definition for a possible notion of degenerate components.

In the following examples we meet such extra components and propose how to get rid of them. The first example presents the case when the locus is a strophoid plus a line as an extra component, see [6].

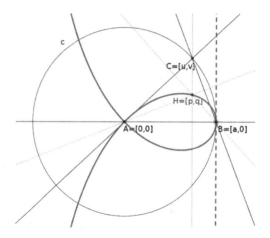

Fig. 4. The strophoid and the line

Example 1. Let ABC be a triangle with a side AB and a vertex C on a circle c centered at A and radius $|AB|$. Determine the locus of the orthocenter H of ABC when C moves along c.

Solution: Let us introduce a rectangular system of coordinates such that $A = [0,0]$, $B = [a,0]$, $C = [u,v]$ and $H = [p,q]$. Then:

$$HC \perp AB \Leftrightarrow h_1 : p - u = 0,$$

$$HA \perp BC \Leftrightarrow h_2 : p(u - a) + qv = 0,$$

$C \in c \Leftrightarrow h_3 : u^2 + v^2 - a^2 = 0.$

Elimination of u, v in the ideal $I = (h_1, h_2, h_3)$, using graded reverse lexico-graphical order of variables a, p, q, u, v, gives the elimination ideal consisting of the polynomial of the *fourth* degree which decomposes into the strophoid and the line

$$(p^3 - ap^2 + aq^2 + pq^2)(p - a) = 0, \tag{1}$$

see Fig. 4. Why does the line (shown dashed) appear in the locus?

The problem arises when C arrives at B, i.e. when $u = a, v = 0$, and the line BC is not defined. Then the system $h_1 = 0$, $h_2 = 0$, $h_3 = 0$ transforms into the only equation

$$p - a = 0$$

representing the line.

To avoid this "unwanted" component, we add the condition $B \neq C$, that is, that points B and C are different, or equivalently $((u-a)^2 + v^2)t - 1 = 0$, where t is a slack variable, into the ideal above (see [11] on explaining this idea). Then we get the only equation of the strophoid

$$\kappa : p^3 - ap^2 + aq^2 + pq^2 = 0.$$

Similarly we proceed in the next example.

Example 2. Given a circle c and a point A on it. Let t be a tangent of c at a touch point M. Determine the locus of the foot P of the perpendicular from A to the tangent t when M moves along the circle c.

Solution: Let c be a circle centered at $B = [a, 0]$, a point $A = [0, 0]$ on the circle c and an arbitrary point $M \in c$, the point of contact of the tangent t.

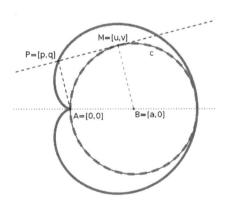

Fig. 5. Cardioid and the circle c

Denote $M = [u, v]$, $P = [p, q]$, then:

$M \in c \Leftrightarrow h_1 := (u - a)^2 + v^2 - a^2 = 0$,

$AP \perp MP \Leftrightarrow h_2 := p(p - u) + q(q - v) = 0$,

$MP \perp BM \Leftrightarrow h_3 := (p - u)(u - a) + (q - v)v = 0$,

Elimination of u, v in the system of equations $h_1 = 0, h_2 = 0, h_3 = 0$ gives the equation

$$(p^2 + q^2 - 2ap)((p^2 + q^2 - ap)^2 - a^2(p^2 + q^2)) = 0,$$

see Fig. 5.

The result is an algebraic curve of the 6th degree which decomposes into the circle c (shown dashed)

$$p^2 + q^2 - 2ap = 0,$$

and a cardioid

$$(p^2 + q^2 - ap)^2 - a^2(p^2 + q^2) = 0. \tag{2}$$

The circle c appears when the points P and M coincide and the line PM is not defined. Namely, if $u = p$ and $v = q$ then $h_1 = 0$ is the equation of c, whereas $h_2 = 0$ and $h_3 = 0$ vanish.

Suppose that $P \neq M$, i.e. $((p - u)^2 + (q - v)^2)t - 1$. Then we get directly the equation (2) of a cardioid.

Remark: If we keep $h_1 = 0, h_3 = 0$ and instead of $h_2 = 0$ we take

$PA \parallel MB \Leftrightarrow h_4 := pv - q(u - a) = 0$,

we get directly the equation of a cardioid (here "$\parallel$" denotes parallelism). We see that the change of the formulation of a problem can lead to a simpler solution without extra components.

In the previous examples, the presence of extra components, a line and a circle, occur. Their solutions could help us learn how to discard such extra components *before* computing the locus equation. We need to ensure that all lines which occur in the formulation of a problem are uniquely defined.

In the first example we suppose the conjunction

$$A \neq B \wedge H \neq A \wedge H \neq C \wedge B \neq C.$$

We can algebraically express each condition separately. This requires more slack variables, or we can put all the conditions into one in the form of a product

$$a(p^2 + q^2)((p - u)^2 + (q - v)^2)((u - a)^2 + v^2)t - 1 = 0,$$

where t is a slack variable. Adding this condition immediately leads to the correct locus.

In the second example we suppose

$$A \neq P \wedge B \neq M \wedge M \neq P$$

or equivalently

$$(p^2 + q^2)((u - a)^2 + v^2)((p - u)^2 + (q - v)^2)t - 1) = 0.$$

We immediately get the correct locus.

3   Technical Considerations

In the previous section we considered two examples that describe the problem and also possible solutions were sketched. In general, we also have the following questions:

1. Is it possible to automatically generate a set of the desirable conditions by a machine, without any human interaction?
2. Can we optimize the added set automatically? Here optimization can be, for example:
   (a) Minimization of the number of introduced new slack variables.
   (b) Minimization of the maximum degree of introduced new polynomials.
   (c) Minimization of the sum of the degree of introduced new polynomials.

First of all, we note that these are on-going research questions and are subject of further study. In fact, optimization is very important because fast computation of the locus equation curve can be crucial in real-time visualizations in dynamic geometry applications (see [10] for more details).

The main issue in optimization is that it is difficult to tell in advance which additions will take effect in the speed of computation. The elimination process, despite it contains simple operations, works usually like a black box that may require billions of more steps even if the input changes just in one or two constants. Therefore there is room to develop simple methods that work "frequently enough" as well as to design more complicated algorithms that may use big databases of previously processed data. Also, machine learning techniques could be exploited. (See also [13] for a similar approach, but directly for automated *proofs.*)

In this paper we look for a simple algorithm that *seems* to work well in many cases. For a comparison we will use the benchmark from [10].

From now on we will consider GeoGebra and its `LocusEquation` command that is a freely available implementation of Algorithm 1 (prior version 5.0.524.0). The `LocusEquation` command always outputs a certain implicit curve $p(x, y) \in \mathbb{Q}[x, y]$. It considers fixed inputs for all free points, except for those that are "involved in the motion". That is, in the first example A and B are considered fixed, C is free (with the constraint that it must lie on the circle c) and H is dependent. Also, in the second example A and B are fixed, M is free (with the constraint that it must lie on the circle c) and P is dependent.

For this case in both examples, the precondition $A \neq B$ is superfluous, since the user sets this preliminary assumption already when the construction is drawn. Of course, later it is possible to move A over B (or vice versa), but this does not make sense for the geometrical experiment.

In fact, in the first example the precondition $B \neq C$ was alone satisfactory to get the correct geometric locus, and in the second one, the precondition $M \neq P$ was sufficient. Both preconditions help avoiding to refer a non-existing object: in the first example a secant of the circle, and in the second example the point P cannot be defined unless the precondition holds.

For explicit loci we can create a dependency graph of the objects that appear in the construction (Fig. 6). An arrow connects object a and b if a is a parent of b, that is, if a is required in the construction steps of b.

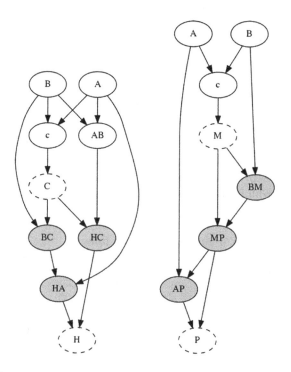

Fig. 6. Dependency graph of the objects in both examples

In the first graph we consider the lines that appear between the mover C and tracer H, namely HC, BC and HA. All of these objects are controlled by the input C, and only they have influence on the degeneracy of the output H. On the other hand, in the second graph the lines between the mover M and tracer P are BM, MP and AP—all of these objects are controlled by the input and only they have influence on the output.

It is however not straightforward geometrically, why the assumption $B \neq C$ alone yields the correct locus, but, on the other hand, why the assumption $M \neq P$ alone is sufficient but $A \neq P$ alone not. (In fact, geometrically the assumptions $M \neq P$ and $A \neq P$ seem to be equivalent.) Unfortunately, not every geometrical equivalence can be translated into to the algebraic representation. That is, an automated selection of elements for a set of sufficient assumptions does not seem to be managable from a pure geometric point of view.

On the other hand, according to the above considerations, introducing any subset of assumptions cannot be harmful (that is, we cannot introduce new unwanted components, but we may just remove some of them), unless the computation time increases unacceptably. Hence we can focus on finding good heuristics on creating selection algorithms for the possible subsets.

4   Benchmark

We had two experiments on creating the subset of assumptions in GeoGebra's source code. The first approach ("2a") was to use Algorithm 2 with the following extension (for step 3):

> If the mover point is M, then for each free point F, the inequality $F \neq M$ is added.

This first approach worked in many cases, but significant slowdown appeared sometimes. An output of the benchmark can be found at https://prover-test. geogebra.org/job/GeoGebra-art-plottertest/627/artifact/test/scripts/benchmark/art-plotter/html/all.html, and it can be compared to the output of Algorithm 1 at https://prover-test.geogebra.org/job/GeoGebra-art-plottertest/624/artifact/test/scripts/benchmark/art-plotter/html/all.html (note that benchmark numbers 627 and 624 appear in the web links).

There were hardly any tests that no longer worked after using the first approach. We could classify the problematic cases into these ones (see also Table 2 for a summary later):

1. We expect a different output. There are two such cases with Ptolemy's theorem (`Ptolemy-1` and `Ptolemy-5`) and one with the Chebyshev linkage (`linkage-Chebyshev-puzzle`). These tests are using the possibility that one of the free points may be the same as the mover point. In the Ptolemy tests an empty locus is returned, but for the Chebyshev file we get some visible loci which do not contain one important point.
2. Several tests are significantly slower than before. The slowdown is because of the more complicated Gröbner basis computations, but this is not significant in the simpler tests. Interestingly enough, there is no slowdown in the Euler inequality tests (they are usually very time consuming). Moreover, they became faster. A few tests became, however, too slow, for example, Surynkova's kinematic tests were mostly too heavy after the first approach.
3. Several tests gave simpler and more accurate results than before. Almost all problematic tests, including Agnesi's witch, the Euler inequality, Steiner's deltoid, Russell's linkage, Hašek's parabola, a caustic of the circle, and the string art envelope did not contain extra components or just less amount of extra components (a caustic of the circle has still one extra component, but not two).

Keeping in mind the considerations of the previous sections, however, this first approach is very naive and incomplete—even if the results were surprisingly positive. The second approach ("2b") was to use Algorithm 2 with the following extension (again for step 3):

1. Initialize $\mathcal{D} = \emptyset$. (It will contain the direct dependencies of the mover point M.)
2. If M is defined as an element of a linear path AB, then $\mathcal{D} := \mathcal{D} \cup \{A, B\}$.
3. If M is defined as an element of a circular path c, then for each point Q in the construction, if MQ is a line in the construction, then $\mathcal{D} := \mathcal{D} \cup \{Q\}$.
4. For all points $D \in \mathcal{D}$ the hypothesis $M \neq D$ will be added to H.

This second approach is used since GeoGebra 5.0.524 (as of 7 February 2019) and produces the results listed at https://prover-test.geogebra.org/job/GeoGebra-art-plottertest/761/artifact/test/scripts/benchmark/art-plotter/html/all.html. Some remarkable slowdown was occured in tests `Botana-ladder-Lissajous` 2 and 3 (11 FPS[1] instead of 15 and 20 FPS, respectively), `Surynkova-kinematic-2` (0.08 FPS instead of 1.11 FPS) and `mirror-tangents-ellipse-hyperbola1` (11 FPS instead of 17 FPS), otherwise still 150 tests work properly and quickly enough (out of 152): the total speed score for the new approach was 14272 (instead of 14438), see Table 1 for an explanation on scoring for each test. All tests were run in the desktop version of GeoGebra.

Table 1. Scoring based on FPS results

Classification	FPS	Score
Extremely fast	Over 50 FPS	100
Very fast	Between 20 and 50 FPS	99
Fast	Between 12 and 20 FPS	98
Moderate	Between 5 and 12 FPS	97
Jerky (slow)	Between 1 and 5 FPS	95
Heavy (very slow)	Between 0.2 and 1 FPS	70
Extremely heavy	Below 0.2 FPS	20
Wrong answer, no answer or timeout	–	0

Table 2 shows the differences among Algorithms 1, 2a, 2b, and the Gröbner Cover. We admit that the *expected* result may be different when we have a different understanding of "geometric" locus. See [14] for an explanation on some possible cultural differences as well.

---

[1] Frame per second.

Table 2. Comparison of degree of outputs for some tests that produce different output components. The expected output is shown in green and bold, "–" means timeout or no answer, and X means that the output is not acceptable because some geometrical components are missing. Type can be "el" (explicit locus), "il" (implicit locus) or "e" (envelope)

Test	Type	Reference	Alg. 1	Alg. 2a	Alg. 2b	Gröbner Cover
Agnesi-witch	el	[15]	4	**3**	**3**	4
Arbeo-B02	el	[16]	3	**1**	3	3
*limacon	el	[16]	6	**4**	**4**	**4**
Euler-ineq-*	il	[17]	18	**16**	18	18
Hasek-Apollonius-converse	el	[18]	3	**2**	**2**	**2**
linkage-Russell	el	[2]	3	**1**	**1**	3
linkage-Chebyshev-puzzle	el	[2]	6	X	**6**	**6**
nephroid-parallel	e	[15]	8	**7**	8	–
Ptolemy-1	il	[19]	4	X	**4**	**4**
Ptolemy-5	il	[19]	6	X	**6**	**6**
Steiner-deltoid	e	[20]	5	**4**	5	–
string-art	e	[15]	5	**4**	**4**	–
strophoid	el	[6]	4	**3**	**3**	**3**

5   Related Work

Removing meaningless components from the geometric output is a well-known topic in algebraic geometry, and discussed, among others, in [7, 21–23]—the investigations are not limited to explicit loci only, but, for instance, envelopes are included.

In fact, non-degeneracy plays an important role in ADG in general (see [1, Chapter 3.3.3.2] and [24, Chapter 6, §4] for more details). Prescribing non-degeneracy conditions before performing the heavy computations is, however, not widely discussed yet. A remarkable contribution is [25] that expresses the importance of the order of introducing non-degeneracy by adding new variables and then performing elimination before or after the algebraic computations, concerning the statement truth.

Also, a "before"-type approach has already been used in GeoGebra for automated theorem proving tasks, to avoid further investigation of the result (see [26, Chapter 2.3.6.2]). However, this approach was recently removed in version 5.0.519.0 because of some speed related and technical considerations (see [27]).

6   Conclusion

In spite of the promising results these experiments are still a work in progress. First of all, the currently used algorithm 2b in GeoGebra 5.0.524.0 ignores the dependency graph of the objects in the construction—instead of it, some basic heuristics are used. But clearly, for future improvements, it should be considered.

In this paper we concentrated on one type of degeneracy, namely, on coincidence of two points that implies that the line which is given by these two points is not defined. Avoiding other types of degeneracy, for instance, *three collinear vertices of a triangle or a quadrilateral*, may also be useful. On the other hand, considering to avoid *zero radius of a circle*, can be fruitful, however we do not yet have appropriate examples where these assumptions really help. Therefore, developing more sophisticated algorithms that work on a wider range of input is subject for future work.

Also, a deeper, more theoretical comparison of the geometrical assumptions and the algebraic considerations is planned for a subsequent project of the authors and some other researchers. In particular, an extensive study is to be performed on a set of sophisticated algorithms and the Gröbner Cover.

Acknowledgments. We are thankful to Tomás Recio for his numerous suggestions on improving this paper. The first author was partially supported by a grant MTM2017-88796-P from the Spanish MINECO (Ministerio de Economia y Competitividad) and the ERDF (European Regional Development Fund).

References

1. Chou, S.C.: Mechanical Geometry Theorem Proving. Springer, Heidelberg (1987)
2. Kovács, Z., Recio, T., Vélez, M.P.: Reasoning about linkages with dynamic geometry. J. Symb. Comput. (2019). https://www.sciencedirect.com/science/article/abs/pii/S0747717118301299
3. Botana, F., Valcarce, J.: A software tool for the investigation of plane loci. Math. Comput. Simul. **61**, 139–152 (2003)
4. Oldenburg, R.: FeliX - mit Algebra Geometrie machen. Computeralgebra Rundbrief, Sonderheft zum Jahr der Mathematik (2008)
5. Kovács, Z., Recio, T., Vélez, M.P.: Using automated reasoning tools in GeoGebra in the teaching and learning of proving in geometry. Int. J. Technol. Math. Educ. **25**, 33–50 (2018)
6. Blažek, J., Pech, P.: Locus computation in dynamic geometry environment. Math. Comput. Sci. **2018**, 1–10 (2018)
7. Abánades, M., Botana, F., Montes, A., Recio, T.: An algebraic taxonomy for locus computation in dynamic geometry. Comput. Aided Des. **56**, 22–33 (2014)
8. Abánades, M.A., Botana, F., Montes, A., Recio, T.: Software using the GRÖBNER COVER for geometrical loci computation and classification. In: Hong, H., Yap, C. (eds.) ICMS 2014. LNCS, vol. 8592, pp. 492–499. Springer, Heidelberg (2014). https://doi.org/10.1007/978-3-662-44199-2_74
9. Montes, A.: The Gröbner Cover. Springer, Heidelberg (2019)
10. Kovács, Z.: Achievements and challenges in automatic locus and envelope animations in dynamic geometry. Math. Comput. Sci. **2018**, 1–11 (2018)
11. Kapur, D.: Using Gröbner bases to reason about geometry problems. J. Symb. Comput. **2**, 399–408 (1986)
12. Mayr, E., Meyer, A.: The complexity of the word problem for commutative semigroups and polynomial ideals. Adv. Math. **46**, 305–329 (1982)
13. Nikolić, M., Marinković, V., Kovács, Z., Janičić, P.: Portfolio theorem proving and prover runtime prediction for geometry. Ann. Math. Artif. Intell. **85**(2–4), 119–146 (2019). https://doi.org/10.1007/s10472-018-9598-6

14. Botana, F., Recio, T.: On the envelope of a family of ellipses. (A propósito de la envolvente de una familia de elipses.). Boletín. Sociedad "Puig Adam" de Profesores de Matemáticas **95**, 15–30 (2013). https://www.ucm.es/data/cont/media/www/pag-81677/Indice%20del%20Boletin%2095.pdf

15. Botana, F., Kovács, Z.: New tools in GeoGebra offering novel opportunities to teach loci and envelopes. CoRR abs/1605.09153 (2016)

16. Arbeo, S.: From locus construction to polynomials. GeoGebra developer wiki (2010). https://dev.geogebra.org/trac/wiki/LocusLineEquation/Examples/Locus_2_polynomials

17. Kovács, Z., Vajda, R.: A note about Euler's inequality and automated reasoning with dynamic geometry. CoRR abs/1708.02993v2 (2017)

18. Hašek, R.: Dynamic geometry software supplemented with a computer algebra system as a proving tool. Math. Comput. Sci. (2018). https://doi.org/10.1007/s11786-018-0369-x

19. Kovács, Z., Recio, T., Sólyom-Gecse, C.: Rewriting input expressions in complex algebraic geometry provers. Ann. Math. Artif. Intell. **85**, 73–87 (2019)

20. Lockwood, E.H.: A Book of Curves. Cambridge University Press, Cambridge (1961)

21. Botana, F., Recio, T.: A proposal for the automatic computation of envelopes of families of plane curves. J. Syst. Sci. Complex. **32**, 150–157 (2019)

22. Botana, F., Recio, T.: Some issues on the automatic computation of plane envelopes in interactive environments. Math. Comput. Simul. **125**, 115–125 (2016)

23. Botana, F., Recio, T.: Computing envelopes in dynamic geometry environments. Ann. Math. Artif. Intell. **80**, 3–20 (2017)

24. Cox, D., Little, J., O'Shea, D.: Ideals, Varieties, and Algorithms. Springer, New York (2007). https://doi.org/10.1007/978-0-387-35651-8

25. Ladra, M., Páez-Guillán, P., Recio, T.: Two ways of using Rabinowitsch trick for imposing non-degeneracy conditions. In: Narboux, J., Schreck, P., Streinu, I. (eds.) ADG 2016, Eleventh International Workshop on Automated Deduction in Geometry, pp. 144–151. University of Strasbourg, Strasbourg (2016)

26. Kovács, Z.: Computer based conjectures and proofs in teaching Euclidean geometry. Ph.D. thesis, Johannes Kepler University, Linz (2015)

27. Kovács, Z.: Unifying the prover in GeoGebra–and speeding it up (2019). https://kovz0l.blogspot.com/2019/01/unifying-prover-in-geogebraand-speeding.html

Formalization of Dubé's Degree Bounds for Gröbner Bases in Isabelle/HOL

Alexander Maletzky$^{(\boxtimes)}$ (iD)

RISC, Johannes Kepler University Linz, Linz, Austria
alexander.maletzky@risc.jku.at

Abstract. We present an Isabelle/HOL formalization of certain upper bounds on the degrees of Gröbner bases in multivariate polynomial rings over fields, due to Dubé. These bounds are not only of theoretical interest, but can also be used for computing Gröbner bases by row-reducing Macaulay matrices.

The formalization covers the whole theory developed by Dubé for obtaining the bounds, building upon an extensive existing library of multivariate polynomials and Gröbner bases in Isabelle/HOL. To the best of our knowledge, this is the first thorough formalization of degree bounds for Gröbner bases in any proof assistant.

1 Introduction

Gröbner bases [1,3] are one of the most powerful and most widely used tools in modern computer algebra, as they allow to effectively solve many problems related to ideals of multivariate polynomial rings. More precisely, Gröbner bases are generating sets of ideals with certain additional properties; Buchberger, in his doctoral thesis [3], proved that every ideal has a finite Gröbner basis and even provided an algorithm for computing one. Later, Dubé in [4] derived general upper bounds on the degrees of polynomials in Gröbner bases, which only depend on the number of indeterminates and the maximum degree of the polynomials in *some* generating set on the ideal under consideration.

Upper bounds for the degrees of Gröbner bases are not only of theoretical interest, but also have practical relevance. For instance, Wiesinger-Widi in [14] shows that Gröbner bases can be computed by row-reducing a certain *Macaulay matrix* corresponding to the input set. The Macaulay matrix of a set of polynomials is just a huge matrix whose entries are the coefficients of the given polynomials. The caveat of this approach is, however, that upper bounds on the degrees of the resulting Gröbner bases must be known a-priori – and thanks to Dubé such bounds can be easily computed for every input set.

In this paper we describe a recent formalization of Dubé's bounds in the Isabelle/HOL proof assistant [11,13]; to the best of our knowledge, it is the first-ever formal treatment of said bounds in *any* proof assistant. In a nutshell,

---

The research was funded by the Austrian Science Fund (FWF): P 29498-N31.

C. Kaliszyk et al. (Eds.): CICM 2019, LNAI 11617, pp. 155–170, 2019.
https://doi.org/10.1007/978-3-030-23250-4_11

the formalization introduces the constant $\text{Dube}_{n,d}$ depending on $n, d \in \mathbb{N}_0$ such that, for every finite set F of multivariate polynomials in n indeterminates having maximum degree d, there exists a Gröbner basis G of F the degrees of whose elements are at most $\text{Dube}_{n+1,d}$ (cf. Corollary 2). Although this statement might look innocent, the machinery needed to prove it is fairly extensive: one needs to define so-called *cone decompositions* of the polynomial ring, establish their relationship to the *Hilbert function*, and finally do a series of algebraic manipulations and estimations involving sums over generalized binomial coefficients. In the upcoming sections we not only show the formalized definitions and theorems in Isabelle/HOL, but also present their informal counterparts and therefore try to make the paper as self-contained as possible; still, due to the lack of space, we cannot include all the details (let alone proofs), so the interested reader is referred to [4] instead.

The formalization is freely available online as a GitHub repository [8, theory 'Dube_Bound'] and is compatible with the development versions of Isabelle[1] and the Archive of Formal Proofs[2]. We plan to submit it to the Archive of Formal Proofs eventually.

The remainder of this paper is organized as follows: In Sect. 2 we briefly recall the necessary mathematical background of multivariate polynomials and Gröbner bases, and also present the foundations in Isabelle/HOL our formalization builds upon. Section 3 is all about cone decompositions, the key tool to obtaining Dubé's bounds. Section 4, then, briefly sketches how the final bounds can eventually be obtained and also lists the main theorems. Section 5 concludes the paper.

2 Preliminaries

2.1 Mathematical Background

We briefly review the most important mathematical concepts appearing in our formalization. Clearly, since our main goal is to prove degree bounds on Gröbner bases, we have to begin by explaining the rough idea behind Gröbner bases.

First of all, we fix a field K and a finite set of indeterminates $X = \{x_1, \ldots, x_n\}$; $K[X]$, then, denotes the multivariate polynomial ring over K, i.e. the set of all finite sums of the form $c_1 t_1 + \ldots + c_m t_m$, where the c_i are non-zero coefficients in K and the t_i are *power-products* of the form $x_1^{e_1} \cdots x_n^{e_n}$ ($e_j \in \mathbb{N}_0$). The set of all power-products appearing in a polynomial p with non-zero coefficient is called the *support* of p, denoted by $\text{supp}(p)$. The set of *all* power-products over X will be denoted by $[X]$.

We now fix an *admissible order relation* $\preceq$ on $[X]$, that is, $\preceq$ is a well-order on $[X]$ additionally satisfying (i) $1 \preceq t$ for all $t \in [X]$, and (ii) $s \preceq t \Rightarrow us \preceq ut$ for all $s, t, u \in [X]$. Note that there are infinitely many such admissible order relations if $n > 1$.

---

[1] http://isabelle.in.tum.de/repos/isabelle.
[2] http://devel.isa-afp.org/.

With respect to $\preceq$, every polynomial $p \neq 0$ possesses a *leading power-product* lpp(p): this is the unique largest (w. r. t. $\preceq$) power-product in supp(p).

Finally, we recall the definition of an *ideal*: in a commutative ring R with unit, and ideal is a subset of R that is closed under addition and under multiplication by arbitrary elements of R. The ideal generated by a set $B \subseteq R$, denoted by $\langle B \rangle$, is the (unique) smallest ideal containing B.

Now, we have all the ingredients for defining Gröbner bases [1,3]: a *Gröbner basis* $G \subseteq K[X]\backslash\{0\}$ is a *finite* set of polynomials such that, for all $p \in \langle G \rangle\backslash\{0\}$, there exists a $g \in G$ such that lpp(g) | lpp(p) (where '|' is the usual divisibility relation on $[X]$). Gröbner bases have a lot of interesting properties, of which we summarize the most important ones here:

- Every ideal in $K[X]$ has Gröbner basis, i. e. for every $F \subseteq K[X]$ there exists some $G \subseteq K[X]$ that is a Gröbner basis and satisfies $\langle G \rangle = \langle F \rangle$. For the sake of simplicity, G is also called a Gröbner basis of F (not just $\langle F \rangle$).
- By imposing additional constraints on Gröbner bases, one can even make them unique for every ideal. This leads to the concept of *reduced Gröbner bases*: every ideal in $K[X]$ has a unique reduced Gröbner basis.[3]
- If G is a Gröbner basis, then for every $p \in K[X]$ there exists a *unique* $q \in K[X]$ such that (i) lpp(g) $\nmid t$ for all $t \in$ supp(q) and $g \in G$, and (ii) $p-q \in \langle G \rangle$. Hence, if $F \subseteq K[X]$ is arbitrary, we can define the *normal form* (w. r. t. F) of any polynomial p to be the unique q satisfying the above two properties for the reduced Gröbner basis of F. We will denote the normal form of p w. r. t. F by nf$_F$(p). Note that nf$_F$(p) = 0 if, and only if, $p \in \langle F \rangle$.
- (Reduced) Gröbner bases and normal forms are effectively computable, but the details are not so important here.

Besides Gröbner bases, we need a couple of other notions related to polynomials which we briefly introduce/recall:

- For $F \subseteq K[X]$, the set $N_F \subseteq K[X]$ contains precisely the polynomials that are in normal form w. r. t. F, i. e. those p satisfying nf$_F$(p) = p. Apparently $\langle F \rangle \cap N_F = \{0\}$.
- For $z \in \mathbb{N}_0$ and $p \in K[X]$, the *homogeneous component* of p at z is the subpolynomial of p all of whose power-products have degree z. Hence, p can be written as $p = \sum_{z=0}^{\infty} p_z$. If $T \subseteq K[X]$, then T_z is the set of the homogeneous components of the elements of T at z.
- A polynomial is *homogeneous* if, and only if, it has at most one non-zero homogeneous component, i. e. all power-products in its support have the same degree. A set $T \subseteq K[X]$ is called homogeneous if it is a K-vector space and, for every $p \in T$ and $z \in \mathbb{N}_0$, $p_z \in T$ as well. Obviously, if T is homogeneous, then T_z constitutes a K-vector space for all z. Also, it is well-known that an ideal is homogeneous if, and only if, it can be generated by a set of homogeneous polynomials. N_F is always homogeneous.

---

[3] Reduced Gröbner bases are unique for every admissible order relation, but different orders may yield different reduced Gröbner bases for the same ideal.

– If $T \subseteq K[X]$ is homogeneous, then the *Hilbert function* of T, denoted by $\varphi_T(z)$, maps every $z \in \mathbb{N}_0$ to the dimension of T_z as a K-vector space.

– Let $T \subseteq K[X]$ and $S_1, \ldots, S_m \subseteq T$. Then the S_i form a *direct decomposition* of T, written $T = S_1 \oplus \cdots \oplus S_m$, if every $p \in T$ can be *uniquely* expressed as a sum of the form $p = \sum_{i=1}^m s_i$ with $s_i \in S_i$ for all $1 \le i \le m$. If furthermore each of the S_i is homogeneous, then $\varphi_T(z) = \sum_{i=1}^m \varphi_{S_i}(z)$. Also, it is easy to see that $K[X] = \langle F \rangle \oplus \mathrm{N}_F$ for all $F \subseteq K[X]$, hence

$$\binom{z+n-1}{n-1} = \varphi_{K[X]}(z) = \varphi_{\langle F \rangle}(z) + \varphi_{\mathrm{N}_F}(z) \tag{1}$$

if F contains only homogeneous polynomials.

2.2   Isabelle/HOL

Due to space limitations we have to presuppose from the reader basic knowledge of the (mostly self-explanatory) syntax of Isabelle/HOL. We only slightly deviate from the usual Isabelle/HOL syntax in that the image of a set A under a function f will be denoted by $f \bullet A$ here, to ease readability. So, for instance $(*)$ $x \bullet A$ is a compact representation of the set $\{x * a \mid a \in A\}$.

Multivariate polynomials and Gröbner bases have already been formalized in Isabelle/HOL in [6,12]. We only recall the most important aspects of these formalizations here, to make the paper as self-contained as possible. The fundamental concept underlying polynomials are so-called *polynomial mappings*, which are functions from some type α to some other type $\beta :: \mathtt{zero}$, such that only finitely many arguments are mapped to non-zero values. The type of such polynomial mappings is $\alpha \Rightarrow_0 \beta$. So, a multivariate polynomial with indeterminates of type χ and coefficients of type α is simply a term of type $(\chi \Rightarrow_0 \mathtt{nat}) \Rightarrow_0 \alpha$: $\chi \Rightarrow_0 \mathtt{nat}$ is the type of power-products, where every indeterminate is mapped to some exponent, and in terms of type $(\chi \Rightarrow_0 \mathtt{nat}) \Rightarrow_0 \alpha$ every power-product is mapped to some coefficient. Throughout the paper, the type $\chi \Rightarrow_0 \mathtt{nat}$ is abbreviated by χ pp, the type χ pp $\Rightarrow_0 \alpha$ is abbreviated by (χ, α) poly, the type variable χ always represents the type of indeterminates, and α always represents the type of coefficients (usually tacitly assumed to belong to sort field).

For a set X of indeterminates of type χ, .$[X]$ is the formalization of the set of power-products in X (i.e. $[X]$, but in the formal sources we had to add a dot to distinguish it from a singleton list), and $\mathsf{P}[X]$ is the formalization of the set of polynomials with power-products in .$[X]$ (roughly corresponds to $K[X]$, but we chose the letter 'P' because 'K' would suggest the coefficients be in a field, whereas $\mathsf{P}[X]$ does not impose any restrictions on the coefficients). $\mathsf{P}[X]$ and .$[X]$ are needed, because often we have to consider subsets of the whole types (χ, α) poly and χ pp, respectively, where only indeterminates in X occur.

The following are the formalizations of the basic concepts related to polynomials and Gröbner bases that are mentioned in Sect. 2.1: $\mathtt{reduced\_GB}$ F is the reduced Gröbner basis of F (w.r.t. the admissible order relation $\preceq$ which is implicitly fixed in a locale); $\mathtt{ideal}$ F corresponds to $\langle F \rangle$; $\mathtt{normal\_form}$ F p corresponds to $\mathrm{nf}_F(p)$, and hence $\mathtt{normal\_form}$ $F \bullet \mathtt{UNIV}$ corresponds to N_F (if the indeterminates shall be restricted to X it is normal_form $F \bullet$ P$[X]$); deg_pm t and poly_deg p refer to the degree of a power-product and of a polynomial, respectively[4]; homogeneous p expresses that p is a homogeneous polynomial; direct_decomp T ss states that the list of sets ss constitutes a direct decomposition of the set T; and Hilbert_fun T z, finally, is the Hilbert function of T. Since there is nothing interesting about the formal definitions of these concepts in Isabelle/HOL, we omit them here, but interested readers might want to have a look at [9].

Remark 1. This remark is only relevant for readers intending to look at the actual Isabelle sources of the formalization. There, power-products are written *additively* rather than multiplicatively, for technical reasons. This means that 0 is used in the place of 1 and + in the place of $\cdot$. In this paper we use the standard multiplicative notation for the sake of clarity, though.

3 Cone Decompositions

3.1 Basics

The key to obtaining Dubé's degree bounds is decomposing the ring $K[X]$ into so-called *cones*, which are subsets of $K[X]$ whose Hilbert functions can be described easily.

Definition 1. *Let $h \in K[X]\backslash\{0\}$, and let $U \subseteq X$. Then the* cone *of h and U, denoted by* cone(h, U), *is the set $\{gh \mid g \in K[U]\}$.*

A cone decomposition *of a set $T \subseteq K[X]$ is a finite set $\{(h_1, U_1), \ldots, (h_r, U_r)\}$ of pairs such that $T = $ cone$(h_1, U_1) \oplus \cdots \oplus$ cone(h_r, U_r). If the h_i are homogeneous, we call the cone decomposition* homogeneous, *and if the h_i are monic monomials we call the cone decomposition a* monomial *cone decomposition.*

To gain some intuition about cones, the interested reader is referred to [4]. Roughly, a cone cone(h, U) corresponds to a principal ideal, where multiplication is only allowed by polynomials in $K[U]$ rather than $K[X]$, though. Note, however, that h is still a polynomial in $K[X]$, and may therefore contain indeterminates in $X\backslash U$.

Definition 2. *Let P be a cone decomposition of some set T and $k \in \mathbb{N}_0$. P is called k-standard if, and only if, for all $(h, U) \in P$ with $U \neq \emptyset$ it holds that (i) $\deg(h) \geq k$, and (ii) for every $k \leq d \leq \deg(h)$ there exists $(g, V) \in P$ with $\deg(g) = d$ and $|V| \geq |U|$.*

Formalizing the above definitions in Isabelle/HOL is absolutely straightforward, building upon the library of multivariate polynomials sketched in Sect. 2.2. Before, however, we fix a finite set X of indeterminates (of type χ) in a local theory context:

---

[4] poly_deg 0 is defined to be 0.

```
context
  fixes X :: "χ set"
  assumes "finite X"
begin
```

So, all subsequent definitions and lemmas are implicitly parameterized over the finite set X. The reason for fixing X in this way is that the type χ is not necessarily finite; indeed, it is very convenient to be able to instantiate χ by type nat if one wishes to have an infinite supply of indeterminates. However, most results we are going to formalize are only valid in polynomial rings with *finitely* many indeterminates, meaning that very often we have to add explicit assumptions of the form $p \in \mathsf{P}[X]$ or $F \subseteq \mathsf{P}[X]$, as will be seen below.

These are now the definitions of cones and cone decompositions, respectively:

```
definition cone :: "(((χ, α) poly × χ set) ⇒ ((χ, α) poly) set"
  where "cone hU = (*) (fst hU) • P[snd hU]"

definition cone_decomp :: "((χ, α) poly) set ⇒
                  ((χ, α) poly × χ set) list ⇒ bool"
  where "cone_decomp T ps = direct_decomp T (map cone ps)"
```

There are a few things to note:

- In the formalization, constant cone is defined for pairs of arguments rather than two individual arguments, i.e. it is uncurried. This turned out more convenient for our purpose.
- Also, cone (h, U) does not check whether $h \in K[X] \setminus \{0\}$ and whether $U \subseteq X$. Instead, we introduced the predicate valid_decomp which, for a given cone decomposition, performs that check on all pairs in it explicitly.
- Cone decompositions are defined for lists of pairs rather than sets of pairs. This is mainly because direct_decomp is also defined for lists, and it also allows us to avoid many explicit finiteness checks we would have to make otherwise (which would be feasible but inconvenient).

Besides cone, cone_decomp and valid_decomp there are also hom_decomp ps, monomial_decomp ps and standard_decomp k ps, which express that ps is a homogeneous, monomial or k-standard cone decomposition, respectively.

Here comes the first important property of k-standard cone decompositions:

```
lemma standard_decomp_geE:
  assumes "valid_decomp X ps" "cone_decomp T ps" "standard_decomp k ps" "k ≤ d"
  obtains qs where "valid_decomp X qs" "cone_decomp T qs" "standard_decomp d qs"
    "monomial_decomp ps ⟹ monomial_decomp qs" "hom_decomp ps ⟹ hom_decomp qs"
```

This lemma states that for any k-standard cone decomposition P of T, and for all $d \geq k$, there exists a d-standard cone decomposition Q of T; furthermore, if P is a homogeneous or monomial cone decomposition, then so is Q. The proof of *standard-decomp-geE* is based on the fact that for any $h \in K[X]\backslash\{0\}$ and $U = \{x_{i_1}, \ldots, x_{i_m}\} \subseteq X$, the set

$$\{(h, \emptyset)\} \cup \{(x_{i_j} h, \{x_{i_j}, \ldots, x_{i_m}\}) \mid 1 \leq j \leq m\}$$

constitutes a $(\deg(h) + 1)$-standard cone decomposition of $\mathrm{cone}(h, U)$.

Remark 2. Apparently, Lemma *standard-decomp-geE* only asserts the *existence* of the desired d-standard cone decomposition Q, but does not provide an algorithm for actually *computing* it – despite the fact that its proof is actually constructive. This reveals a general principle we adhered to throughout the formalization: many lemmas only stipulate the *existence* of certain cone decompositions, without showing how to construct them. The reason for this inconstructive approach is simple: cone decompositions merely constitute a theoretical artifact needed for obtaining the desired degree bounds, but they do not appear in these bounds at all. The final degree bounds *are* effectively computable, of course.

3.2   Cone Decompositions of $\langle F \rangle$ and N_F

Our next goal is to construct cone decompositions with certain special properties of both $\langle F \rangle$ and N_F, where $F \subseteq K[X]$. More precisely, we formally prove the following two theorems:

Theorem 1 (Theorem 4.11. in [4]). *Let $F \subseteq K[X]$. Then there exists a 0-standard cone decomposition Q of N_F. Moreover, if the polynomials in F are homogeneous, then $\deg(g) \leq d$ for all g in the reduced Gröbner basis of F, where $d = 1 + \max\{\deg(h) \mid (h, U) \in Q\}$.*

Theorem 2 (Corollary 5.2. in [4]). *Let $F \subseteq K[X]$ be finite, let $f \in F$, and assume that f has maximal degree among all polynomials in F. Then there exist $T \subseteq K[X]$ and a $\deg(f)$-standard cone decomposition P of T such that $\langle F \rangle = \langle f \rangle \oplus T$. Moreover, if the polynomials in F are homogeneous, then P is a homogeneous cone decomposition.*

As can be seen, Theorem 1 already provides some sort of degree bound for the reduced Gröbner basis of a set F, depending, however, on a cone decomposition of N_F. How it is possible to get rid of that cone decomposition, and what Theorem 2 is needed for, will be illustrated in Sects. 3.3 and 4. But first let us have a look at the formalizations of the two theorems in Isabelle/HOL.

As a starting point, we need to introduce the following auxiliary concept:

```
definition splits_wrt ::
        "(((χ, α) poly × χ set) list × ((χ, α) poly × χ set) list) ⇒
        (χ, α) poly set ⇒ (χ, α) poly set ⇒ bool"
    where "splits_wrt pqs T F = (let ps = fst pqs; qs = snd pqs in
                cone_decomp T (ps @ qs) ∧
                (∀hU∈set ps. cone hU ⊆ ideal F) ∧
                (∀(h, U)∈set qs. cone (h, U) ∩ ideal F = {0}))"
```

Informally, `splits_wrt` (P, Q) T F asserts that (i) $P \cup Q$ is a cone decomposition of T, (ii) $\text{cone}(h, U) \subseteq \langle F \rangle$ for all $(h, U) \in P$, and (iii) $\text{cone}(h, U) \cap \langle F \rangle = \{0\}$ for all $(h, U) \in Q$.[5]

One can prove that, under the assumption `splits_wrt` (P, Q) T F, P and Q are cone decompositions of certain sets:

```
lemma splits_wrt_cone_decomp_1:
  assumes "splits_wrt (ps, qs) T F" "monomial_decomp qs" "is_monomial_set F"
  shows "cone_decomp (T ∩ ideal F) ps"

lemma splits_wrt_cone_decomp_2:
  assumes "splits_wrt (ps, qs) T F" "monomial_decomp qs" "is_monomial_set F"
      "F ⊆ P[X]"
  shows "cone_decomp (T ∩ normal_form F • P[X]) qs"
```

This already looks promising, because if T is sufficiently large (e. g. the whole ring $K[X]$), these two lemmas assert that P and Q are cone decompositions of $\langle F \rangle$ and N_F, respectively – at least if F only consists of monomials. So, it would be great if we could prove that (under some restrictions on T and F) there always exist P and Q satisfying `splits_wrt` (P, Q) T F. And indeed, such P and Q do exist, because they can be constructed by the recursive function `split`:

```
function split :: "χ pp ⇒ χ set ⇒ χ pp set ⇒
          (((χ, α) poly × (χ set)) list) × (((χ, α) poly × (χ set)) list))"
  where
    "split t U S =
      (if 1 ∈ S then
        ([[(monomial 1 t, U)]], [])
      else if S ∩ .[U] = {} then
        ([], [(monomial 1 t, U)])
      else
        let x = (SOME x'. x' ∈ U - (max_subset U (λV. S ∩ .[V] = {})));
            (ps0, qs0) = split t (U - {x}) S;
            (ps1, qs1) = split (single x 1 * t) U ((λs. s / single x 1) • S) in
        (ps0 @ ps1, qs0 @ qs1))"
```

Some remarks on the above Isabelle/HOL code are in place:

- `split` t U S consists of three branches: the first two branches correspond to the base cases without any recursive calls, where ps and qs (i. e. P and Q) can be determined readily. In the third branch, `split` is applied recursively twice, producing ps_0, qs_0, ps_1 and qs_1, whose concatenations are eventually returned.
- `max_subset` U $(\lambda V.\ S \cap .[V] = \{\})$ returns a maximal $V \subseteq U$ satisfying $S \cap [V] = \emptyset$. x is then chosen as some element in $U \backslash V$, which is not empty by case assumption.
- `monomial 1 t` represents the monomial whose coefficient is 1 and whose sole power-product is t; likewise, `single x 1` represents the power-product in which the exponent of x is 1 and all other exponents are 0.

---

[5] Of course, `splits_wrt` is defined for *lists* ps, qs instead of sets P, Q, but informally it is easier to think of sets.

- Termination of `split` is not entirely obvious, but under some mild assumptions on its input the function does indeed terminate.
- We did not take the effort to make function `split` executable, because of the arguments put forward in Remark 2. In principle, this would be possible, though.

The fact that the result returned by function `split` really splits a set w. r. t. another set, as claimed above, is stated in the next lemma:

```
lemma split_splits_wrt:
  assumes "U ⊆ X" "finite S" "t ∈ .[X]" "ideal F ÷ t = ideal (monomial 1 ∙ S)"
  shows "splits_wrt (split t U S) (cone (monomial 1 t, U)) F"
```

So, the set T that is split w. r. t. F is actually the cone $\text{cone}(t, U)$. This suffices for our purpose, because for $t = 1$ and $U = X$ we apparently have $\text{cone}(t, U) = K[X]$, and therefore the output of `split 1 X F` really constitutes a cone decomposition of $\langle F \rangle$ and N_F, respectively, just as desired. In the assumption of Lemma *split-splits-wrt*, $\langle F \rangle \div t$ denotes the *quotient ideal* of $\langle F \rangle$ w. r. t. t, i. e. the ideal $\{p \in K[X] \mid t\,p \in \langle F \rangle\}$. So, that assumption basically demands that $\langle F \rangle \div t$ be generated by a finite set S of monomials.

Before we can prove Theorem 1, we need another crucial property of function `split` that guarantees the existence of cones of a certain shape in its second return value:

```
lemma lem_4_8:
  assumes "finite S" "S ⊆ .[X]" "1 ∉ S" "g ∈ reduced_GB (monomial 1 ∙ S)"
  obtains t U where "U ⊆ X" "(monomial 1 t, U) ∈ set (snd (split 1 X S))"
    "poly_deg g = deg_pm t + 1"
```

Together with Lemma *split-splits-wrt*, *lem-4-8* is the key to proving Theorem 1, because the desired cone decomposition Q can be shown to be precisely the second return value of `split` when applied to the appropriate input. The formalization of Theorem 1, hence, looks like this:

```
theorem standard_cone_decomp_snd_split:
  assumes "F ⊆ P[X]"
  defines "qs = snd (split 1 X (lpp ∙ reduced_GB F))"
  defines "d = 1 + Max (poly_deg ∙ fst ∙ set qs)"
  shows "standard_decomp 0 qs" "cone_decomp (normal_form F ∙ P[X]) qs"
    "(∀f∈F. homogeneous f) ⟹ g ∈ reduced_GB F ⟹ poly_deg g ≤ d"
```

This theorem connects the second return value of function `split` to a cone decomposition of N_F, and as the attentive reader can probably guess, the first return value of `split` can be utilized to obtain the desired direct decomposition $\langle F \rangle = \langle f \rangle \oplus T$, where T has a $\deg(f)$-standard cone decomposition P. Unfortunately, however, the first return value of `split` cannot be directly used for that purpose, but has to be slightly adjusted (especially for making it $\deg(f)$-standard). The details are a bit technical and can be found in [4, Sect. 5]; here, we only show the final formal statement of Theorem 2:

```
theorem ideal_decompE:
  assumes "finite F" "F ⊆ P[X]" "f ∈ F" "∀f'∈F. poly_deg f' ≤ poly_deg f"
  obtains T ps where "valid_decomp ps" "standard_decomp (poly_deg f) ps"
    "cone_decomp T ps" "direct_decomp (ideal F ∩ P[X]) [ideal {f} ∩ P[X], T]"
    "(∀f'∈F. homogeneous f') ⟹ hom_decomp ps"
```

Please note that we cannot simply write ideal F and ideal $\{f\}$, but we explicitly have to restrict these sets to polynomials in $P[X]$, since the ideal operator allows multiplication by polynomials in arbitrary indeterminates of type χ.

3.3   Exact Cone Decompositions

We begin by summarizing the main definitions and results of this subsection informally:

Definition 3. *Let Q be a cone decomposition. Q is called exact if, and only if, for all pairs $(h, U), (g, V) \in Q$, if $U \neq \emptyset$, $V \neq \emptyset$ and $\deg(h) = \deg(g)$, then $(h, U) = (g, V)$.*

Definition 4. *Let Q be a cone decomposition. Then $\mathfrak{a}_Q$ is the smallest $k \in \mathbb{N}_0$ such that Q is k-standard, or 0 if Q is not k-standard for any k.*
Also, the sequence $\mathfrak{b}_{Q,i}$ for $i \in \mathbb{N}_0$ is defined as

$$\mathfrak{b}_{Q,i} := \min\{d \geq \mathfrak{a}_Q \mid \forall (h, U) \in Q : |U| \geq i \Longrightarrow \deg(h) < d\}.$$

Similar to the previous section, the main result of this section ensures the existence of certain cone decompositions, in this case exact ones:

Theorem 3 (Lemma 6.3. in [4]). *Let Q be a k-standard cone decomposition of some set T. Then there also exists an exact k-standard cone decomposition Q' of T such that $\max\{\deg(h) \mid (h, U) \in Q\} \leq \max\{\deg(h) \mid (h, U) \in Q'\}$. Furthermore, if Q is a homogeneous or monomial decomposition, then so is Q'.*

Theorems 1 and 3, together with the definition of $\mathfrak{b}$, immediately imply the following:

Corollary 1. *Let $F \subseteq K[X]$. Then there exists an exact 0-standard monomial cone decomposition Q of $\mathbb{N}_F$. Moreover, if the polynomials in F are homogeneous, then $\deg(g) \leq \mathfrak{b}_{Q,0}$ for all g in the reduced Gröbner basis of F.*

The importance of exact cone decompositions stems from the fact that the Hilbert function of sets with an exact cone decomposition Q can be easily described in terms of the constants $\mathfrak{b}_{Q,i}$, for $1 \leq i \leq n+1$. This in turn enables us to obtain an upper bound for $\mathfrak{b}_{Q,0}$, which, by virtue of Corollary 1, is also an upper bound for the degrees of reduced Gröbner bases. Details follow in Sect. 4.

There is nothing special about the formal definitions of exact cone decompositions (constant exact_decomp), $\mathfrak{a}$ or $\mathfrak{b}$, hence we omit them here. Instead, we list some simple facts about $\mathfrak{b}$:

lemma b_decreasing: "i ≤ j ⟹ b qs j ≤ b qs i"

lemma b_zero: "qs ≠ [] ⟹ Max (poly_deg • fst • set qs) < b qs 0"

lemma b_card_X: "card X < i ⟹ b qs i = a qs"

The first lemma,b- *decreasing*, states that the sequence $(b_{Q,i})_{i \geq 0}$ is decreasing, b-*zero* states that $b_{Q,0}$ is an upper bound for the degrees of the tips h of pairs $(h, U) \in Q$, and b-*card-X* states that $b_{Q,i}$ stabilizes to a_Q for sufficiently large i.

With respect to the proof of Theorem 3, the situation here parallels Sect. 3.2: there is an algorithm for transforming an arbitrary k-standard cone decomposition into an exact one, and this algorithm is implemented in function **exact** in the formalization. However, since the implementation of **exact** is more complicated than the one of **split** shown in Sect. 3.2, we omit it here. Using **exact**, the formal statement of Theorem 3 is distributed across several lemmas:

lemma exact:
  assumes "valid_decomp qs" "standard_decomp k qs"
  shows "valid_decomp (exact k qs)" "standard_decomp k (exact k qs)"
    "exact_decomp (exact k qs)"

lemma cone_decomp_exact:
  assumes "valid_decomp qs" "standard_decomp k qs" "cone_decomp T qs"
  shows "cone_decomp T (exact k qs)"

lemma Max_exact_ge:
  assumes "valid_decomp qs" **and** "standard_decomp k qs"
  shows "Max (poly_deg • fst • set qs) ≤ Max (poly_deg • fst • set (exact k qs))"

Note that **exact** not only takes a cone decomposition Q as input, but also a k for which Q is k-standard; if Q is not k-standard, nothing can be said about the cone decomposition returned by **exact**.

Finally, Corollary 1 is formalized as:

lemma normal_form_exact_decompE:
  assumes "F ⊆ P[X]"
  obtains qs **where** "valid_decomp qs" "standard_decomp 0 qs" "monomial_decomp qs"
    "cone_decomp (normal_form F • P[X]) qs" "exact_decomp qs"
    "⋀g. (∀f∈F. homogeneous f) ⟹ g ∈ reduced_GB F ⟹ poly_deg g ≤ b qs 0"

4   Obtaining the Degree Bound

We have almost all prerequisites to obtain the final degree bound. But still, we need one more definition:

Definition 5. *Let* $b = (b_1, \ldots, b_{n+1})$ *be a tuple of natural numbers, where as usual* $n = |X|$. *Then the* Hilbert polynomial *in* b, *denoted by* $\overline{\varphi}_b(z)$, *is defined as*

$$\overline{\varphi}_b(z) := \binom{z - b_{n+1} + n}{n} - 1 - \sum_{i=1}^{n} \binom{z - b_i + i - 1}{i}.$$

Since the upper entries of the binomial coefficients can be arbitrary numbers, the binomial coefficients are generalized bin. coeffs.: $\binom{a}{n} := \frac{a(a-1)(a-2)...(a-(n-1))}{n!}$.

Abusing notation, we will abbreviate $\overline{\varphi}_{\flat_P}(z)$ *simply by* $\overline{\varphi}_P(z)$ *if P is a cone decomposition.*

Theorem 4 (see Sect. 7 in [4]). *Let P be an exact k-standard homogeneous cone decomposition of T. Then, if* $z \geq \flat_{P,0}$, *the Hilbert function of T equals the Hilbert polynomial of P, i. e.* $\varphi_T(z) = \overline{\varphi}_P(z)$.

The proof of Theorem 4 is based on the fact that the Hilbert function of T is just the sum of the Hilbert functions of the cones in a homogeneous cone decomposition P of T, and that this sum can be fully characterized by the $\flat_{P,i}$ if P is exact and k-standard. The rest is mere rewriting of (sums of) binomial coefficients by well-known binomial identities.

Now, let $F \subseteq K[X]$ be a finite set of homogeneous polynomials, and let $f \in F$ whose degree d is maximal among the degrees of the polynomials in F. Let Q be the exact 0-standard monomial cone decomposition of N_F whose existence is guaranteed by Corollary 1; since Q is 0-standard, we also know $\flat_{Q,n+1} = \mathfrak{a}_Q = 0$. Let $T \subseteq K[X]$ and P be an exact d-standard homogeneous cone decomposition of T such that $\langle F \rangle = \langle f \rangle \oplus T$, whose existence is guaranteed by Theorem 2 (strictly speaking, the cone decomposition from that theorem still has to be made exact using Theorem 3); similarly to $\flat_{Q,n+1}$, we know $\flat_{P,n+1} = d$. So, by Theorem 4 we obtain the following two identities for sufficiently large z:

$$\varphi_{N_F}(z) = \overline{\varphi}_Q(z) = \binom{z+n}{n} - 1 - \sum_{i=1}^{n} \binom{z - \flat_{Q,i} + i - 1}{i}, \tag{2}$$

$$\varphi_{\langle F \rangle}(z) = \overline{\varphi}_{\{(f,X)\}}(z) + \overline{\varphi}_P(z)$$
$$= \binom{z - d + n - 1}{n - 1} + \binom{z + d - n}{n} - 1 - \sum_{i=1}^{n} \binom{z - \flat_{P,i} + i - 1}{i}. \tag{3}$$

Together with (1) from Sect. 2.1 we therefore obtain the key identity

$$\binom{z+n-1}{n-1} = \binom{z-d+n-1}{n-1} + \binom{z-d+n}{n} + \binom{z+n}{n} - 2$$
$$- \sum_{i=1}^{n} \left(\binom{z - \flat_{P,i} + i - 1}{i} + \binom{z - \flat_{Q,i} + i - 1}{i} \right) \tag{4}$$

which holds for all sufficiently large z; but, since both sides of the equality are polynomials in z, and two polynomials agree everywhere if they agree on infinitely many arguments, we can conclude that the above identity actually holds for *all* z.

After a lengthy chain of simplifications and estimations of (4), which are in detail explained in [4], one can prove that $\flat_{P,j}$ and $\flat_{Q,j}$ satisfy $\flat_{P,j} + \flat_{Q,j} \leq$

$\mathrm{Dube}_{n,d}(j)$ for $0 < j \le n-1$, where $\mathrm{Dube}_{n,d}(j)$ is defined recursively as

$$\mathrm{Dube}_{n,d}(n-1) = 2d \tag{5}$$

$$\mathrm{Dube}_{n,d}(n-2) = d^2 + 2d \tag{6}$$

$$\mathrm{Dube}_{n,d}(j) = 2 + \binom{\mathrm{Dube}_{n,d}(j+1)}{2} + \sum_{i=j+3}^{n-1} \binom{\mathrm{Dube}_{n,d}(i)}{i-j+1}. \tag{7}$$

Note that $\mathrm{Dube}_{n,d}(j)$ is defined in terms of $\mathrm{Dube}_{n,d}(k)$ for *larger* k. In particular, $\mathfrak{b}_{P,1} + \mathfrak{b}_{Q,1} \le \mathrm{Dube}_{n,d}(1) =: \mathrm{Dube}_{n,d}$, and since also $\mathfrak{b}_{Q,0} \le \max\{\mathfrak{b}_{P,1}, \mathfrak{b}_{Q,1}\}$ can be proved, $\mathrm{Dube}_{n,d}$ is an upper bound for $\mathfrak{b}_{Q,0}$, too. Therefore, thanks to Corollary 1, $\mathrm{Dube}_{n,d}$ is the desired upper bound for the degrees of the polynomials in the reduced Gröbner basis of F.

Theorem 5 (Variant of Theorem 8.2. in [4]). *Let $F \subseteq K[X]$ be a finite set of homogeneous polynomials, and let d be the maximum degree of the polynomials in F. Then every g in the reduced Gröbner basis of F satisfies $\deg(g) \le \mathrm{Dube}_{n,d}$.*

Remark 3. Some of the steps in the derivation above only hold if $d > 0$ and $n > 1$. The remaining cases of $d = 0$ and $n \le 1$ can easily be handled separately, though: it is easy to see that d is a valid degree bound in these cases.

But even if the ideal under consideration is not homogeneous a result similar to Theorem 5 holds; in fact, it is even stronger, because it gives a bound on the *representation* of the Gröbner basis elements in terms of the polynomials in F:

Corollary 2 (Variant of Corollary 5.4. in [2]). *Let $F \subseteq K[X]$ be finite and let d be the maximum degree of the polynomials in F. Then there exists a Gröbner basis G of F such that every $g \in G$ can be written as $g = \sum_{f \in F} q_f f$ for some polynomials q_f, such that $\deg(q_f f) \le \mathrm{Dube}_{n+1,d}$ for all $f \in F$. In particular, g also satisfies $\deg(g) \le \mathrm{Dube}_{n+1,d}$.*

This corollary can be obtained easily from Theorem 5 by first *homogenizing* F, then computing the reduced Gröbner basis of the homogenized set, and eventually *dehomogenizing* this Gröbner basis. Only note that in the bound we get $n+1$ instead of n, and that the bound holds for *some* Gröbner basis of F, not necessarily the reduced one.

Let us now turn to the formalization of the concepts and results presented above, starting with the Hilbert polynomial:

```
definition Hilbert_poly :: "(nat ⇒ nat) ⇒ int ⇒ int"
  where "Hilbert_poly b z = (let n = card X in
                    ((z - b (n + 1) + n) gchoose n) - 1 -
                    (∑i=1..n. (z - b i + i - 1) gchoose i))"
```

Note that `Hilbert_poly` is defined for, and returns, integers. Working with integers proved tremendously more convenient in the upcoming derivation than working with natural numbers. The infix operator `gchoose`, contained in the standard library of Isabelle/HOL, represents generalized binomial coefficients.

Note that in a term like $z - b\ (n + 1) + n$, where z has type int and the other summands have type nat, the other summands are automatically coerced to type int by Isabelle/HOL.

So, in the formal development Theorem 4 corresponds to:

```
theorem Hilbert_fun_eq_Hilbert_poly:
  assumes "X ≠ {}" "valid_decomp ps" "hom_decomp ps" "cone_decomp T ps"
      "standard_decomp k ps" "exact_decomp ps" "b ps 0 ≤ z"
  shows "int (Hilbert_fun T z) = Hilbert_poly (b ps) z"
```

We spare the reader the formalization of the lengthy derivation of the degree bound, and only show the formal definition of $Dube_{n,d}$ and the ultimate theorems:

```
function Dube_aux :: "nat ⇒ nat ⇒ nat ⇒ nat" where
  "Dube_aux n d j = (if j + 2 < n then
                     2 + ((Dube_aux n d (j + 1)) choose 2) +
                       (∑i=j+3..n-1. (Dube_aux n d i) choose (i - j + 1))
              else if j + 2 = n then
                d² + 2 * d
              else 2 * d)"
```

```
definition Dube :: "nat ⇒ nat ⇒ nat"
  where "Dube n d = (if n ≤ 1 ∨ d = 0 then d else Dube_aux n d 1)"
```

```
theorem Dube:
  assumes "finite F" "F ⊆ P[X]" "∀f∈F. homogeneous f" "g ∈ reduced_GB F"
  shows "poly_deg g ≤ Dube (card X) (maxdeg F)"
```

```
corollary Dube_is_GB_cofactor_bound_explicit:
  assumes "finite F" "F ⊆ P[X]"
  obtains G where "is_Groebner_basis G" "ideal G = ideal F" "G ⊆ P[X]"
    "⋀g. g ∈ G ⟹ ∃q. g = (∑f∈F. q f * f) ∧
                (∀f. poly_deg (q f * f) ≤ Dube (card X + 1) (maxdeg F))"
```

As can be seen, the statement of the formal Theorems *Dube* and *Dube-is-GB-cofactor-bound-explicit* correspond exactly to the statements of Theorem 5 and Corollary 2, respectively. Also, functions Dube and Dube_aux are effectively computable by means of Isabelle's code generator [5], meaning that for a concrete set F of polynomials one can compute an upper bound for the maximum degree of a Gröbner basis of F by a formally verified algorithm.

5   Conclusion

In the preceding sections we presented our Isabelle/HOL formalization of a degree bound for reduced Gröbner bases of homogeneous ideals, closely following [4]. In fact, the only substantial deviation from [4] is that there the constant $Dube_{n,d}$ is further bounded from above by a nice closed form:

$$Dube_{n,d} \leq 2\left(\frac{d^2}{2} + d\right)^{2^{n-2}}$$

for all $n \geq 2$. However, the proof of this inequality ([4, Lemma 8.1.]) contains two little mistakes: first, the recursive description of $\mathrm{Dube}_{n,d}(j)$ (cf. (7)) lacks the summand 2, and second, the author wrongly assumes that the sum $\sum_{i=j+3}^{n-1} \frac{2^{i-j}}{(i-j+1)!}$ is never greater than $1/2$; this is not true, e.g., for $n = 7$, $d = 2$ and $j = 1$, where that sum is $23/45$. To the best of our knowledge, these mistakes have remained unnoticed until now. Nevertheless, experiments indicate that the closed form *is* a valid upper bound, typically even *much* larger than the value of $\mathrm{Dube}_{n,d}$ for concrete n and d,[6] but a rigorous proof of this claim must be left as future work. For our purpose the recursively defined function $\mathrm{Dube}_{n,d}$ is absolutely sufficient anyway: it is (easily) computable and, as said before, typically gives much better bounds.

Formalizing the results presented in this paper was not entirely trivial, despite the fact that Dubé's original paper is written very well and explains every step of the proof in detail. The reason is that during the formalization process we had to backtrack a design choice we made at the beginning: at first, we wanted to simplify matters and therefore did not base the development on polynomials and their leading power-products, but on power-products directly; this is reflected, for instance, in function `split`, which only takes power-products as input and originally returned power-products rather than polynomials, too. Later it turned out, however, that some theorems simply cannot be proved without any reference to polynomials and ideals thereof, not even after adjusting their statements to fit into the 'power-products-only' framework; Theorem 2 serves as a good example. Fortunately the wrong design choice could be corrected with only moderate effort and did not cost too much time in the end. This also owes to the large arsenal of sophisticated proof methods offered by the underlying Isabelle system, which enabled us to construct rather abstract proofs that remained valid even after replacing power-products by polynomials (think of `auto`, for instance). In general, it was not necessary to develop any new proof methods or other tools for completing the formalization.

The total number of lines of proof of the formalization is more than 11000, which is quite significant. Note that [8] also contains other material this paper is not concerned with and which is therefore not counted in the lines of proof; in particular, it contains a formalization of the Macaulay-matrix-based approach to Gröbner bases mentioned in the introduction (theory 'Groebner_Macaulay'), described in [7]. Formalizing the theory took roughly 270 working hours.

Having settled the general case of arbitrary input sets F, one could now try to look at special cases that admit tighter degree bounds. For instance, Wiesinger-Widi in [14] restricts herself to sets F consisting only of two binomials and derives significantly better bounds there. Formalizing her results is a challenging task, though, especially since her proofs make use of fairly different techniques than Dubé's proof presented here.

Acknowledgments. I thank the anonymous referees for their valuable comments.

---

[6] Although asymptotically $\mathrm{Dube}_{n,d}$ also has to grow double exponentially in n, as shown in [10].

References

1. Adams, W.W., Loustaunau, P.: An Introduction to Gröbner Bases, Graduate Studies in Mathematics, vol. 3. AMS, Providence (1994)
2. Aschenbrenner, M., Leykin, A.: Degree bounds for Gröbner bases in algebras of solvable type. J. Pure Appl. Algebra **213**, 1578–1605 (2009). https://doi.org/10.1016/j.jpaa.2008.11.022
3. Buchberger, B.: Ein Algorithmus zum Auffinden der Basiselemente des Restklassenrings nach einem nulldimensionalen Polynomideal. Ph.D. thesis, Mathematisches Institut, Universität Innsbruck, Austria (1965). English translation in J. Symb. Comput. **41**(3–4), 475–511 (2006)
4. Dubé, T.W.: The structure of polynomial ideals and Gröbner bases. SIAM J. Comput. **19**(4), 750–773 (1990). https://doi.org/10.1137/0219053
5. Haftmann, F.: Code Generation from Isabelle/HOL Theories. http://isabelle.in.tum.de/dist/Isabelle2018/doc/codegen.pdf. Part of the Isabelle documentation
6. Immler, F., Maletzky, A.: Gröbner Bases Theory. Archive of Formal Proofs (2016). http://isa-afp.org/entries/Groebner_Bases.html. Formal proof development
7. Maletzky, A.: Gröbner bases and Macaulay matrices in Isabelle/HOL. Technical report, RISC, Johannes Kepler University Linz, Austria (2018). http://www.risc.jku.at/publications/download/risc_5814/Paper.pdf
8. Maletzky, A.: Isabelle/HOL formalization of advanced Gröbner bases material (2019). https://github.com/amaletzk/Isabelle-Groebner/
9. Maletzky, A., Immler, F.: Gröbner bases of modules and Faugère's F_4 algorithm in Isabelle/HOL. In: Rabe, F., Farmer, W.M., Passmore, G.O., Youssef, A. (eds.) CICM 2018. LNCS (LNAI), vol. 11006, pp. 178–193. Springer, Cham (2018). https://doi.org/10.1007/978-3-319-96812-4_16
10. Mayr, E.W., Meyer, A.R.: The complexity of the word problems for commutative semigroups and polynomial ideals. Adv. Math. **46**(3), 305–329 (1982). https://doi.org/10.1016/0001-8708(82)90048-2
11. Nipkow, T., Wenzel, M., Paulson, L.C. (eds.): Isabelle/HOL. LNCS, vol. 2283. Springer, Heidelberg (2002). https://doi.org/10.1007/3-540-45949-9
12. Sternagel, C., Thiemann, R., Maletzky, A., Immler, F.: Executable multivariate polynomials. Archive of Formal Proofs (2010). http://isa-afp.org/entries/Polynomials.html. Formal proof development
13. Wenzel, M.: The Isabelle/ISAR Reference Manual (2018). https://isabelle.in.tum.de/dist/Isabelle2018/doc/isar-ref.pdf. Part of the Isabelle documentation
14. Wiesinger-Widi, M.: Gröbner bases and generalized sylvester matrices. Ph.D. thesis, RISC, Johannes Kepler University Linz, Austria (2015). http://epub.jku.at/obvulihs/content/titleinfo/776913

The Coq Library as a Theory Graph

Dennis Müller[1,2,3(✉)], Florian Rabe[1,2,3(✉)], and Claudio Sacerdoti Coen[3(✉)]

[1] University Erlangen-Nuremberg, Erlangen, Germany
{dennis.mueller,florian.rabe}@fau.de
[2] LRI, Université Paris Sud, Orsay, France
[3] University of Bologna, Bologna, Italy
sacerdot@cs.unibo.it

Abstract. Representing proof assistant libraries in a way that allows further processing in other systems is becoming increasingly important. It is a critical missing link for integrating proof assistants both with each other or with peripheral tools such as IDEs or proof checkers. Such representations cannot be generated from library source files because they lack semantic enrichment (inferred types, etc.) and only the original proof assistant is able to process them. But even when using the proof assistant's internal data structures, the complexities of logic, implementation, and library still make this very difficult.

We describe one such representation, namely for the library of Coq, using OMDoc theory graphs as the target format. Coq is arguably the most formidable of all proof assistant libraries to tackle, and our work makes a significant step forward.

On the theoretical side, our main contribution is a translation of the Coq module system into theory graphs. This greatly reduces the complexity of the library as the more arcane module system features are eliminated while preserving most of the structure. On the practical side, our main contribution is an implementation of this translation. It takes the entire Coq library, which is split over hundreds of decentralized repositories, and produces easily-reusable OMDoc files as output.

1 Introduction and Related Work

Motivation. A critical bottleneck in interactive theorem proving is data sharing, both between proof assistants and between proof assistants and related tools. The general situation is in starch contrast to the global push for FAIR data practices [oFD18], i.e., findable, accessible, interoperable, and reusable sharing of data. Currently, for example, any reuse of a library must go through the respective proof assistant. Thus, any novel idea is typically limited to the implementation framework and data flows provided by the proof assistant; and out-of-the-box experiments that by-pass the proof assistant are expensive, often prohibitively so. This limitation is particularly relevant as proof assistants are becoming more mature and many challenges are shifting from prover design to library management tasks like refactoring, reuse, search, and user interfaces.

© Springer Nature Switzerland AG 2019
C. Kaliszyk et al. (Eds.): CICM 2019, LNAI 11617, pp. 171–186, 2019.
https://doi.org/10.1007/978-3-030-23250-4_12

For multiple reasons, Coq is the most formidable target for library sharing among all proof assistants: Firstly, the logic of Coq is arguably the most complex among all major proof assistants. This applies not only to the core logic, but also to the processing pipeline from user-visible source to kernel representation and the library-building features of module system, sections, etc. Secondly, the code base of the Coq system has grown to a point where it is very hard for outsiders to navigate it. Thirdly, Coq has been so successful that its library is now so vast that it is non-trivial to even understand its extent—it is now split over several hundred repositories with non-uniform build processes.

Contribution. Our overall goal is making the Coq library easier to access, search, interoperate with, and reuse. Even though we make a substantial first step, comprehensive progress on this front will take years. Concretely, in this paper, we translate the high-level structure of the Coq library that is visible to the Coq kernel (including modules and sections but not records or type classes) into the MMT language [RK13] for theory graphs. Theory graphs are an attractive target format because they allow preserving most of the library structure while being significantly simpler. Besides being designed to maintain theory graphs, MMT also provides a flexible logical framework that allows us to define the logical syntax of Coq. Thus, our MMT theories include all information in the Coq kernel including universes, inductive types, proof terms, and termination of recursive functions.

We translate all 49 Coq packages that are distributed via opam (a package manager originally designed for ocaml software) and that compile with the latest version of Coq (8.9.0). These comprise more than 383,500 logical declarations, making ours one of the largest proof assistant library translations ever and the largest for Coq.

Related Work. Multiple ad hoc exports between different proof assistant libraries have been achieved. The general design of instrumenting the proof assistant kernel to export the library as a trace of checking it was first applied in [OS06]. This has proved to be the only feasible design, and all major later exports including ours employed variants of it. For example, Coq was the target format in [KW10].

Exports specifically into MMT were achieved for Mizar in [IKRU13], HOL Light in [KR14], PVS in [KMOR17], and very recently for Isabelle in not-yet published work. This overall line of research was presented in [KR16].

Similarly, to the MMT research, proof assistant libraries have been exported into Dedukti [BCH12]. Coqine is the tool used for translating Coq to Dedukti, and while MMT exports focus on preserving the original structure, Coqine focuses on reverifying proofs. Unlike our logic definition, Coqine includes a formalization of the typing rules in order to type check the export. In order to make this feasible, this translation eliminates several features of the Coq logic so that the typing rules become simpler. Our export, on the contrary, makes the dual trade-off, covering the entire logic at the expense of representing the typing rules. Concretely, the original version [BB12] covered most of the small standard library, using simplifications like collapsing the universe hierarchy. A later reimplementation [Ass15] used a more faithful representation of the logic. But it still omitted several language features such as modules, functors and universe polymorphism and therefore could not translate a significant part of the library.

[CK18] develops a translation of Coq into first-order logic in order to apply automated provers as hammers. Like Coqine, it only covers a subset of the language. It can in principle be used to translate the entire library, but that would have very limited use: Indeed, due to the nature of this application, it is actually *beneficial* to ignore all modular structure and even to not care about soundness, for example to collapse all universes.

Overview. The structure of our paper follows the three major parts of building a library: the core logical language, the language for library building, and the library itself. Section 3 describes the representation of the Coq logics (As we will see, Coq technically provides a few slightly different logics.) in MMT. This results in a few manually written MMT theories. Section 4 specifies how the library language features of Coq can be mapped to MMT theories and morphisms. And Sect. 5 describes the implementation that translates the Coq library into MMT. We recap the relevant preliminaries about Coq and MMT in Sect. 2, and we discuss limitations and future work in Sect. 6.

2   Preliminaries

2.1   Coq

We give only an extremely dense explanation of the Coq language and refer to Appendix A[1] and [Coq15] for details. We use a **grammar** for the *abstract* syntax seen by the Coq kernel (Fig. 1) because that is the one that our translation works with. Even though we do not have space to describe all aspects of the translation in detail, we give an almost entire grammar here in order to document most of the language features we translate. A slightly more comprehensive grammar is presented in the companion paper [Sac19]: the omitted features do not pose additional problems to the translation to MMT and are omitted to simplify the presentation.

The Coq library is organized hierarchically into (from high to low) packages, nested directories, files, nested modules, and nested sections, where "nested" means that multiple levels of the same kind may be nested. Modules and sections are optional, i.e., logical declarations can occur in files, modules, or sections. When forming base logic expressions E, universes U, module expressions M, and module type expressions T, declarations can be referred to by **qualified identifiers** e, u, m, resp. t formed from

1. The root identifier that is defined by the Coq package. Typically, but not necessarily, every package introduces a single unique root identifier.
2. One identifier each for every directory or file that leads from the package root to the respective Coq source file.

---

[1] Available online at https://kwarc.info/people/dmueller/pubs/CoqImport.pdf.

decl   ::= — *base logic declarations*
                $\underline{e}@\{y^*\} : E[:= E]$
             | **Universe** $\underline{u}$
             | **Constraint** $u(< | \le | =)u$
             | (**Inductive** | **CoInductive**) $(\underline{e}@\{y^*\} : E := (\underline{e}@\{y^*\} : E)^*)^*$
             — *section declarations and variables in sections*
             | **Section** $\underline{s}$:= decl*
             | **Variable** $x : E$
             | **Polymorphic Universe** y
             | **Polymorphic Constraint** $(u | y)(< | \le | =)(u | y)$
             — *module (type) declarations*
             | **Module Type** $\underline{m}\ (\underline{m} : T)^* <: T^* := (T | \mathrm{decl}^*)$
             | **Module** $\underline{t}\ (\underline{m} : T)^*\ [: T]\ <: T^*\ [:= (M | \mathrm{decl}^*)]$

E ::= — *base logic expressions*
             $e@\{U^*\} | x | \mathbf{Prop} | \mathbf{Set} | \mathbf{Type}@\{U\} | \Pi x : E.E | \lambda x : E.E | E\ E$
             | $\mathbf{Match}\,e\,E\,E^* | (\mathbf{Fix} | \mathbf{CoFix})\,\mathbb{N}\,(\underline{e} : E := E)^* | \mathbf{let}\ x : E := E\ \mathbf{in}\ E$
             | $E.\mathbb{N} | (E : E)$

U ::= — *universes*
             $u | y | \max U\,U | \mathrm{succ}\,U$

T ::= — *module type expressions*
             $[!]\ t\ m^* | T\ \mathbf{with}\ e' := E | T\ \mathbf{with}\ m' := M$

M ::= — *module expressions*
             $[!]\ m\ m^*$

x, y ::= variables for term, universe respectively
e, u, m, t, s ::= qualified identifiers of expressions, universes, modules, module types, sections
e', m' ::= relative qualified identifiers of expressions, modules
$\underline{e}, \underline{u}, \underline{m}, \underline{t}, \underline{s}$ ::= fresh (unqualified) identifiers

Fig. 1. Coq kernel grammar

3. One identifier each (possibly none) for every nested module (type) inside that source file that contains the declarations.
4. The unqualified name $\underline{e}$, $\underline{u}$, $\underline{m}$, resp. $\underline{t}$.

Note that section identifiers do not contribute to qualified names: the declarations inside a section are indistinguishable from the ones declared outside the section. Relative qualified names are always relative to a module type, i.e. they are missing the root identifiers and the directory identifiers.

Expressions are the usual λ-calculus expressions with dependent products $\Pi x : term.term$ (used to type λ-abstractions), let binder, let...in, sorts Prop, Set, Type@{U} (used to type types), casts $(E : E)$, (co)inductive types with primitive pattern-matching, (co)fixpoints definitions (i.e. terminating recursive functions) and record projections $(E.\mathbb{N})$. Notably, Coq maintains a partially ordered **universe hierachy** (a directed acyclic graph) with consistency constraints of the form $U(< | \le)U'$.

Module types and modules are the main mechanism for grouping base logic declarations. Public identifiers introduced in modules are available outside the module via qualified identifiers, whereas module types only serve to specify what declarations are public in a module. We say that a module M *conforms* to the module type T if

- M declares every constant name that is declared in T and does so with the same type,
- M declares every module name $\underline{m}$ that is declared in T and does so with a module type that conforms to the module type (= the set of public declarations) of $\underline{m}$ in T,
- if any such name has a definiens in T, it has the same definiens in M.

Conformation of a module *type* to a module type is defined accordingly.

Both modules and module types may be defined in two different ways: *algebraically* as an abbreviation for a module (type) expression (the definiens), or *interactively* as a new module (type) given by a list of declarations (the body). Every module (type) expression can be elaborated into a list of declarations so that algebraic module (type) declarations can be seen as abbreviations of interactive ones. A module may also be abstract, i.e., have neither body nor definiens. The <: and : operators may be used to attach conformation conditions to a module (type), and we will explain their semantics in Sect. 4.2.

Module (type)s can be abstracted over a list of module bindings $\underline{m} : T$, which may be used in the definiens/body. When the list is not empty the module (type) is called a *functor* (type). A functor must be typed with a functor type that has the same list of module bindings. Conformation induces a notion of subtyping between module and functor types. Coq treats functor types contravariantly and allows for higher-order functors. However, from our experiments, it seems that this feature is never used in any of the libraries we exported from Coq.

Module (type) expressions can be obtained by functor application, whose semantics is defined by β-reduction in the usual way, unless "!" annotations are used. According to complex rules that we will ignore in the rest of the paper for lack of space, the "!" annotations performs β-reduction and then triggers the replacement of constants defined in the actual functor argument with their definiens. Finally, the with operator adds a definition to an abstract field in a module type.

Sections may be used to subdivide files and module (type)s. These are similar to module functors except that they abstract over base logic declarations, which are interspersed in the body and marked by the **Variable** and **Polymorphic** keywords. The section itself has no semantics: outside the section, all normal declarations are $\lambda\Pi$-abstracted over all **Variable**/**Polymorphic** declarations.

2.2 MMT

MMT aims at being a universal representation language for formal systems. Its syntax was designed carefully to combine simplicity and expressivity. Figure 2 gives the fragment needed for Coq, and we refer to [RK13, Rab17] for details.

$$decl ::= \textbf{Theory } l =^{[E]} \textbf{decl}^*$$
$$| \quad \textbf{Morph } l : E \to E =^{[E]} \textbf{decl}^*$$
$$| \quad \textbf{include } E$$
$$| \quad l[: E][= E]$$
$$| \quad \textbf{Rule } \text{Scala object}$$
$$E \quad ::= g \mid g?l \mid x \mid g?l((x[: E][= E])^*, E^*)$$
$$g \quad ::= URI?l \mid g/l$$
$$l \quad ::= \text{local identifiers}$$

Fig. 2. MMT grammar

An expression **Theory** $l =^{[E]} B$ introduces a named **theory** l with body B and (optional) meta-theory E. In the simplest case, nested theories create a tree of declarations, whose leafs are **constant** declarations $l : E_1 = E_2$ introducing a local identifier l with optional type E_1 and definiens E_2.

Named theories have global identifiers g of the form $g = NS?l_1/\ldots/l_n$ where NS is the namespace URI assigned by the containing source file, and the l_i are the local identifier of the nested theories (i.e. l_n is the local identifier of the theory itself, l_{n-1} is the local identifier of the containing theory etc.).

Every constant has a unique URI of the form $g?l$ where g is the global identifier of the containing theory and l is the local identifier of the constant. In an expression E, every theory or constant is always referenced via its global identifier.

Every theory g induces a set of **expressions** E formed from identifiers, bound variables x, and composed expressions $g?l(C, E_1, \ldots, E_n)$, where C is a (possibly empty) list of variables $x[(: E')][(= E'')]$ considered bound in the subexpressions E_i. The semantics of expressions is signaled by the chosen constructor $g?l$, which is usually a constant declared in the meta-theory.

Meta-theories yield the language-independence of MMT: The meta-theory L of a theory t defines the language in which t is written. For example, the diagram on the right indicates the form of the theory graph we built in this paper: all theories in the Coq library will be translated to MMT theories with meta-theory Coq, which in turn has meta-theory **LFX**. LFX is an extension of the logical framework LF [HHP93] that is strong enough to define the Coq

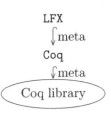

logic in a theory Coq. The semantics of **LFX** itself is obtained by declaring **rules**: these are Scala objects that are injected dynamically into the MMT kernel. We refer to [Rab18] for the general mechanism and the definition of LF. Most importantly, **LFX** declares

1. 5 constants for forming the composed expressions type, $A \to B$, $\Pi x : A.B$, $\lambda x : A.t$ and function applications $f(a_1, \ldots, a_n)$;
2. syntax rules that render the composed expression LFX?lambda$(x : A, t)$ as $\lambda x : A.t$; and
3. about 10 typing rules for the LF type system.

The MMT theory graphs arise from adding **morphisms** $m : s \rightarrow t =^M B$. Here m is a morphism that maps the meta-theory of s to t, and the body B must contain a defined constant $g?c = E$ for every s-constant $g?c$ and some t-expression E. Then the homomorphic extension of m maps any s-expression to a t-expression in a way that, critically, preserves all judgments, e.g., if $\vdash_s e : E'$, then $\vdash_t m(e) : m(E')$. Such morphisms have theorem-flavor and are used to represent language translations and refinement or interpretation theorems. Alternatively, include declarations **include** s in a theory t are used to create morphisms $s \rightarrow t$ that hold by definition: their semantics is that all s-constants are also visible to t, which implies that the identity map of constants is a theory morphism. Include morphisms are used to represent inheritance and extension relations between theories and are depicted in diagrams as $s \hookrightarrow t$. Expressions over a theory t can use all constants declared in t, in the meta-theory of t, a parent theory of t, or in theories included into t.

3   Defining the Coq Base Logics in a Logical Framework

We define an MMT theory Coq that defines the base logic of Coq. This theory will occur as the meta-theory of all MMT theories generated from files in the Coq library (except when flags are used, see below). The theory Coq is available at https://gl.mathhub.info/Coq/foundation/blob/master/source/Coq.mmt. We briefly describe it in the sequel and refer to Appendix B[2] for details.

Expressions. Due to lack of space, we only present the encoding of the PTS fragment of Coq, i.e. we omit let...in, projections, inductive types, pattern matching and (co)fixpoints. The encoding is quite straightforward.

Theory Coq $=^{\text{LFX}}$
univ : type   max : univ $\rightarrow$ univ $\rightarrow$ univ   succ : univ $\rightarrow$ univ
expr : type   Prop : expr   Set : expr   Type : univ $\rightarrow$ expr
Π : expr $\rightarrow$ (expr $\rightarrow$ expr) $\rightarrow$ expr λ : expr $\rightarrow$ (expr $\rightarrow$ expr) $\rightarrow$ expr
app : expr $\rightarrow$ expr $\rightarrow$ expr
hastype : expr $\rightarrow$ expr $\rightarrow$ type
exprOfType : expr $\rightarrow$ type $= \lambda e : \text{expr}.\{x : \text{expr} | \text{hastype}\, x\, e\}$

Our representation of the syntax is a Curry-style encoding, in which all expressions have the same LF type and the binary typing judgment between expressions is formalized by separate judgment **hastype**. We do not give any typing rules here, but they could now be added in a straightforward way (except of course that Coq's typing rules are very complex and doing so is correspondingly time consuming). There are alternative Church-style encodings, where a Coq expression of type E is represented as an LF-expression of type exprOfType E for an operator exprOfType : expr $\rightarrow$ type. These would be preferable because they

---

[2] Available online at https://kwarc.info/people/dmueller/pubs/CoqImport.pdf.

allow declaring Coq identifiers as, e.g., `zero : exprOfType Nat` instead of erasing their type by using a declaration `zero : expr`. This is also why they are used in Coqine [BB12, Ass15] to formalize the calculus of constructions in Dedukti. However, Church encodings introduce so much representational overhead that they would make the translation of the entire Coq library infeasible. To gain the best of both worlds, we use predicate subtyping to define the `exprOfType E` as the subtype of `expr` containing those x for which the judgment `hastype x E` holds.

With these declarations in place, we can for example translate the definition of a universe-polymorphic identity function

$$\texttt{id}@\{y\} : \Pi A : \texttt{Type}@\{y\}.A \to A := \lambda A : \texttt{Type}@\{y\}.\lambda x : A.x$$

of Coq to the following MMT definition over the theory `Coq`

$$\texttt{id} : \Pi y : \texttt{univ. exprOfType}\left(\Pi\left(\texttt{Type}\, y\right)\left(\lambda A.A \to A\right)\right)$$
$$= \lambda y.\, \lambda\left(\texttt{Type}\, y\right)\left(\lambda A.\lambda A\left(\lambda x.x\right)\right)$$

This captures all relevant information of the Coq definition with minimal representational overhead. Note how Coq's Π and λ-binding are represented using LF higher-order abstract syntax, whereas universe polymorphism is represented directly using LF's binders.

Logic Variants. Maybe surprisingly, Coq does not actually use a single logic: it offers flags that allow choosing variants of the type theory. Two flags are of particular importance as they are required by some of the libraries:

- `-impredicative-set` changes the typing rule of the dependent function space Π so that the type of functions that takes in input an inhabitant of a large universe and return a set is still a (small) set instead of being a larger type; the flag is inconsistent when assumed together with any axiom of choice and classical logic
- `-type-in-type` squashes all universe except `Prop` and `Set` into the single universe `Type`. The resulting inconsistency `Type : Type` is acceptable and useful in some applications, e.g., those that focus on computation rather than deduction and need the possibility to write non terminating functions.

All variants can be formalized similarly using slightly different typing rules. As we omit the typing rules anyway, we simply create theories `Coq`, `ImpredicativeCoq`, and `InconsistentCoq`, all of which include `CoqSyntax` and then contain placeholder comments for the typing rules. When extracting the library from Coq, we record the flags used to compile each Coq file. Depending on that information, we choose one of the above three theories as the meta-theory of the MMT-theory that is the translation of that file.

4 Representing the Coq Structuring Language in MMT

4.1 Overview

Figure 3 gives an overview of our translation. Above the file level, our translation preserves the structure of Coq exactly: every directory or file in a Coq package is translated to a corresponding directory resp. file in an MMT archive. Therefore, all Coq directories result in MMT namespace URIs.

Coq	MMT
package	namespace
directory	namespace
file	file that declares a theory
module type	theory
module	theory
visibility of a module m to p	inclusion morphism $m \hookrightarrow p$
module typing $M : T$	morphism $T \to M$
module conformation $M <: T$	morphism $T \to M$
module type conformation $T <: T'$	morphism $T' \to T$
section	theory
variable in a section	constant
any base logic declaration	constant

Fig. 3. Overview of the translation

A **qualified identifier** consisting of root r, directories $d_1, \ldots, d_r$, file name f with extension v, modules (types) $m_1, \ldots, m_s$, and name n is translated to the MMT URI coq $:/r/d_1/\ldots/d_r?f/m_1/\ldots/m_s?n$. Note that the MMT URI makes clear, which parts of the qualified identifier are directory, file, or module (type) names without having to dereference any part of the URI.

The only subtlety here is that we translate every Coq source file to a theory. Effectively, we treat every Coq file f.v in directory D like the body of a module of name f; and we translate it to an OMDoc file f.omdoc containing exactly one MMT theory with URI $D?f$.

If we translated files to namespaces instead of theories, the above MMT URI would be coq $: /r/d_1/\ldots/d_r/f?/m_1/\ldots/m_s?n$. We would have preferred this, but it is not possible: In Coq, base logic declarations may occur directly in files whereas MMT constants may only occur inside theories. Thus, we have to wrap every Coq source file into an MMT theory. This is inconsequential except that we have to add corresponding include declarations in MMT: for every file f' that is referenced in a file f, the resulting MMT theory must include the MMT theory of f'. Fortunately, this information is anyway stored by Coq so that this is no problem.

In the sequel, we write $\bar{i}$ for the MMT translation of the Coq item i except that, if i is a Coq identifier, we write i in MMT as well if no confusion is possible.

We omit the translation of base logic expressions and refer to Appendix C[3] for the translation of sections.

4.2   Modules and Module Types

We translate all files and module (type)s to MMT theories. Thus, the parent p of every module (type), which is either a file or a module (type), is always translated to an MMT theory; and every module (type) with parent p is translated to an MMT theory nested into $\bar{p}$. Overall, Coq's tree of nested module (type) and constant declarations is translated to an isomorphic tree of nested MMT theories and constants, augmented with the theory morphisms induced by module type conformation (explained below).

We first consider the non-functor case and generalize to functors in Sect. 4.3. An algebraic module (type) is translated by first computing its explicit representation as an interactive one, according to the meta-theory of Coq. In this way we only have to consider the interactive case and we lift from the user the burden of understanding the intricacies of algebraic module (type) resolution (e.g. the complex semantics given by "!" annotations, or the issue of generativity for functors application).

Module and Module Types as Theories. So let us consider an interactive module type **Module Type** $t <: T_1 \ldots T_n := B$. We translate it to an MMT theory $\bar{t}$ whose body arises by declaration-wise translation of the declarations in B. However, we have to treat universes specially because Coq maintains them globally: all universes and constraint declared in B are not part of $\bar{t}$ and instead treated as if they had been declared at the beginning of the containing source file. We discuss the treatment of <: attributions below.

A module is translated in exactly the same way as a module type. The semantic difference between modules and module types is that a module m, once closed, exports all declarations in its body to its parent p. We capture this difference in MMT exactly by additionally generating an include declaration **include** $\overline{m}$ after the theory $\overline{m}$, which makes $\overline{m}$ available to $\bar{p}$.

It may be tempting to alternatively translate module types t to theories $\bar{t}$ and a module $m : t$ to a theory morphism $\overline{m} : \bar{t} \to \bar{p}$. This would elegantly capture how every module is an implementation of the module type by providing definitions for the abstract declarations in t. But that is not possible because Coq allows abstract fields even in modules, and such modules would not induce MMT theory morphisms. A maybe surprisingly example is the following, which is well-typed in Coq:

> **Module Type** $s := e : \mathsf{False}$
> **Module** $m : s := e' : \mathsf{False},\ e : \mathsf{False} := e'$
> $x : \mathsf{False} := m.e$

Here the abstract declaration of e' in the module m is allowed even though it is used to implement the interface s of m.

---

[3] Available online at https://kwarc.info/people/dmueller/pubs/CoqImport.pdf.

Conformation as a Theory Morphism. Now we translate the attributions $<: T_i$ on a module (type) and the attributions $: T$ on a module. Our translation does not distinguish modules and module types, and if multiple attributions $<: T_i$ are present, they are translated individually. Thus, we only need to consider the cases $m <: T$ and $m : T$. In both cases, our translation consists of a morphism $\overline{m}^*$ from $\overline{T}$ to $\overline{m}$ that witnesses that m conforms to T.

Inspecting the grammar, we see that T has normal form $(t\, m_1 \ldots m_r)\, \texttt{with}\, k_1 := K_1 \ldots \texttt{with}\, k_s := K_s$, where $k := K$ unifies the cases of constant and module instantiations. As we will see below, if t is a module type functor (i.e., if $r! = 0$), its module parameters $x_1 : T_1, \ldots, x_r : T_r$ are translated as if t were not functorial and the $x_i : T_i$ were abstract modules in the body of t. Accordingly, we treat T in the same way as $t\, \texttt{with}\, x_1 := m_1 \ldots \texttt{with}\, x_r := m_r\, \texttt{with}\, k_1 := K_1 \ldots \texttt{with}\, k_s := K_s$, and therefore we can restrict attention to the case $r = 0$.

We know that t is translated to a theory $\bar{t}$, and if T is well-typed, recursively translating the K_i already yields a partial theory morphism φ from t to $\overline{p}$. Because $\overline{m}$ is a theory nested into $\overline{p}$, φ is also a morphism into $\overline{m}$. It remains to extend φ with assignments for the remaining declarations of $\bar{t}$. Now we observe that if m conforms to T in Coq, we obtain a well-typed MMT theory morphism $\overline{m}^*$ by extending φ with assignments $\bar{t}?k := \overline{m}?k$ for every such name k. (The converse is also true if we add typing rules to Coq that adequately capture the typing relation of base logic expressions.)

For $<:$ attributions, this is all we have to do. But an attribution $m : T$ is stronger than an attribution $m <: T$. It additionally restricts the interface of m to what is declared in T. Therefore, we have to do a little bit more in the case $m : T$ as shown on the right:

$$\bar{t} \xrightarrow{\overline{m}^*} \overline{m} \xrightarrow{r} \overline{m.\texttt{impl}}$$

1. We rename the theory $\overline{m}$ to $\overline{m.\texttt{impl}}$.
2. We create a second theory $\overline{m}$ that is a copy of $\bar{t}$ where all qualified names use m in place of t.
3. We create a morphism $r : \overline{m} \to \overline{m.\texttt{impl}}$ that maps every name of $\overline{m}$ to itself.
4. We create the renaming morphism $\overline{m}^*$ with codomain m in the same way as for the case $m <: T$. The morphism just performs the renaming since $\overline{m}$ and $\bar{t}$ only differs on names.

The $:$ attributions of Coq are peculiar because $\overline{m.\texttt{impl}}$ can never be referenced again—the morphism r can be seen as a dead end of the theory graph. In fact, trying to understand this part of the translation made us realize the following curiosity about the Coq module system. Consider the well-typed example on the right, where we use indentation for scoping. The attribution $m : s$ in the module type t hides the definition of the field f in the module m. Because that definition is never considered again, the module n can supply a different definition for f later on.

Module Type $s := f : \texttt{Nat}$
Module Type $t :=$
    Module $m : s := f : \texttt{Nat} := 0$
Module $n : t :=$
    Module $m \quad := f : \texttt{Nat} := 1$

Indeed, the Coq kernel imperatively throws away $\overline{m.\texttt{impl}}$ after checking it. When f declares a logical axiom instead of a type like **Nat**, the behaviour is somewhat more intuitive: if we only care that a definition (i.e., proof) exists, it is fine to give two different ones in different places. But this treatment is markedly different from analogous features of other languages: In object-oriented programming, n would not be allowed to redefine m because the definition of f is still inherited even if remains inaccessible. Similarly, in theory graphs with hiding [MAH06, CHK+12], the model n of t would be required to implement e in a way that is consistent with the hidden definition in t.

4.3   Functors

Declaring Functors. In many ways the parameters of an interactive module (type) can be treated in the same way as the declarations in its body B. Indeed, the declaration **Module** (**Type**) $t(x_1 : T_1, \ldots, m_r : T_r) := B$ is well-typed iff **Module** (**Type**) $t :=$ **Module** $x_1 : T_1, \ldots,$ **Module** $m_r : T_r, B$ is.

This motivates what we call the *covariant* translation of functors, which we employ: parameters of interactive modules or module types are translated as if they occurred as abstract module declarations at the beginning of the body. Thus, the two variants of t above are translated to the exact same MMT theory. The resulting diagram is shown on the right.

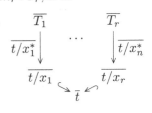

Note that the theories $\overline{t/x_i}$ are nested into $\overline{t}$ and additionally included into $\overline{t}$. We also add metadata to the declarations of the $\overline{t/x_i}$ to record the fact that they used to be functor parameters. Algebraic module (type) functors and <: and : attributions are handled in the same way as in Sect. 4.2.

Technically, only a *contra*variant translation that translates functors to theory-valued functions would capture the semantics of functors adequately. For example, the covariant translation of **Module** $m(x_1 : T_1, \ldots, m_r : T_r) := B$ results in the same diagram as above with an additional inclusion morphism from $\overline{m}$ into the parent p of m. Thus, the theories $\overline{t/x_i}$ become falsely included into $\overline{p}$. More formally:

1. the covariant translation preserves well-typedness only if the library does not rely on Coq's contravariant rule for functor type subtyping, which is the case for all the libraries exported so far.
2. the covariant translation does not reflect well-typedness.

However, considering that the Coq library is already well-typed and that the covariant translation is so much simpler, that is sufficient for many practical applications.

Applying Functors. Coq functor application may be partial and curried. Thus, it is sufficient to restrict attention to $r = 1$. So consider a module type declaration **Module Type** $t(x : T) := B$ and a module $m : T$. We have to define the translation of the module type $t(m)$, whose semantics is determined in Coq by substituting m for x in B. We want the translation to be compositional, i.e., defined in terms of the theory $\bar{t}$ arising from the translation of t and the morphism $\overline{m}^* : \bar{t} \to \overline{m}$ arising from the translation of m, as in the diagram on the right. As defined above, the functor t is translated to a theory $\bar{t}$ with a nested theory $\overline{t/x}$ that conforms to $\overline{T}$ as well as an include of $\overline{t/x}$. Let p be the Coq file or module (type) in which $t(m)$ is well-typed; thus, $\bar{p}$ is a theory that includes $\overline{m}$.

This situation is well-known in MMT theory graphs: to translate $t(m)$, we have to create a new theory nested into $\bar{p}$ such that the diagram is a pushout. The canonical choice of a pushout [Rab17, CMR16] amounts to copying over all declarations in $\bar{t}$ except for replacing all occurrences of x by the homomorphic translation along $\overline{m}^*$. This yields the same theory as translating the flattening of $t(m)$.

5   Translating the Coq Library

Our translation is implemented in two steps. Firstly, Coq is instrumented via kernel hooks to export the internal kernel data structures into Coq-near gzipped XML files. This part of the translation is described in detail in [Sac19]. Secondly, we read these XML files into MMT and translate them to MMT data structure, which we then write out to disk as OMDoc files. (Actually, we use xz-compressed OMDoc files because the uncompressed files would be too large.)

This separation into a Coq-export and an MMT-import may seem inefficient. But this design has proved very successful in the past [IKRU13, KR14, KMOR17]. Moreover, it allows separating the formidable practical task of exporting anything from the theoretical task of specifying the translation.

Notably, the whole export of the 49 opam packages for Coq libraries that currently compile with Coq 8.9.0 (recently released) comprises about 1.3 million XML files totaling 224.7 GB (interestingly, merely counting the number and sizes of XML files takes around 15 min). More packages will be translated in the future as soon as they are ported from previous Coq versions. Translating to MMT only the Coq standard library takes about 22 h on a standard laptop, converting 15.4 GB of (uncompressed) XML into 28.9 MB of (compressed) OMDoc. This reduction is not only due to a high compressibility of the OMDoc, but also reflects the fact that every declaration in Coq corresponds to multiple XML files with partially redundant information.

6 Conclusion

Evaluation. Our translation covers entirely the syntax of the Coq language and it preserves typing and soundness, with the exception of higher order functors, functor declarations and contravariant functor subtyping. The latter three features do not seem to occur in the 49 libraries that have an opam package which is up-to-date with the last Coq release. As more libraries become available, we will have to verify that our covariant functor translation is still adequate.

Moreover, we are confident that, if and when future work yields a complete formalization of the Coq typing rules in an LF-like logical framework, our translation will be in a format suitable for rechecking the entire library—with the obvious caveat that such a rechecking would face even more serious scalability issues than we had to overcome so far.

An obvious way to verify that the exported information is sound and complete for type-checking would be to implement an importer for Coq itself or, in alternative, for an independent verifier for the logic of Coq, like the one implemented in Dedukti or the one developed in the HELM/MoWGLI projects [APS+03] and later incorporated into Matita 0.5.x series [ARCT11]. In both cases one would need to develop a translation from MMT theories to the modular constructs of the language, which requires more research. For example, no translation of MMT theories and theory morphisms into modules, module types and functors is currently known.

We would also like to stress that independent verification is not the aim of our effort: the main point of exporting the library of Coq to MMT is to allow independent services over them, like queries, discovery of alignments with libraries of other tools or training machine learning advisers that can drive hammers. Most of these services can be implemented even if the typing information is incomplete or even unsound (e.g. if all unvierses are squashed to a single universe, making the logic inconsistent).

Limitations and Future Work. Our translation starts with the Coq kernel data structures and is thus inherently limited to the structure seen by the kernel. Therefore, record types and type classes are presented just as inductive types, that is the way they are elaborated before passing them to the kernel. This is unfortunate as recent Coq developments, most importantly the Mathematical Components project [GGMR09], have made heavy use of records to represent theory graph–like structuring and an unelaborated representation would be more informative to the user and to reasoning tools.

In fact, even sections are not visible to the kernel, and we were able to include them because we were able to reconstruct the section structure during our translation. We expect that similar efforts may allow for including record types and canonical structures in the theory graph in the future and we plan to start working on that next.

Many libraries avoid module and functors and achieve modularity using other more recent features of Coq that are invisible at the kernel level, like type classes.

Moreover type classes, canonical structures, coercions, etc. are necessary information to extend a library because they explain how the various mathematical notions are meant to be used. While the already cited services that we plan to provide do not depend on them, importing the library in another system to build on top of it surely does. Therefore a future challenge will be to find system independent generalizations and representations of such constructs, which will be necessary to incorporate them into a logic and system independent tool like MMT.

Our formal representation of Coq declarations includes the types of all constants and variables, but we use a single type in the logical framework for all Coq expressions. As we explain in Sect. 3, we consider a typed representation of expressions infeasible at this point. Our representation does not include the typing rules for the expression, but this is not due to a principal limitation: it is possible to add these rules to let MMT type-check the library. But formalizing the rules of the Coq type system is in itself a major challenge, and representing the details of, e.g., Coq's treatment of pattern matching or sort polymorphism may even require innovations in logical framework design.

Acknowledgments. The authors were supported by DFG grant RA-18723-1 OAF and EU grant Horizon 2020 ERI 676541 OpenDreamKit. Tom Wiesing helped with scripting for automatically creating the necessary mathhub.info repositories and pushing to them.

References

[APS+03] Asperti, A., Padovani, L., Sacerdoti Coen, C., Guidi, F., Schena, I.: Mathematical knowledge management in HELM. Ann. Math. Artif. Intell. **38**(1–3), 27–46 (2003)

[ARCT11] Asperti, A., Ricciotti, W., Sacerdoti Coen, C., Tassi, E.: The matita interactive theorem prover. In: Bjørner, N., Sofronie-Stokkermans, V. (eds.) CADE 2011. LNCS (LNAI), vol. 6803, pp. 64–69. Springer, Heidelberg (2011). https://doi.org/10.1007/978-3-642-22438-6_7

[Ass15] Assaf, A.: A framework for defining computational higher-order logics. Ph.D. thesis, École Polytechnique (2015)

[BB12] Boespflug, M., Burel, G.: CoqInE: translating the calculus of inductive constructions into the lambda pi-calculus modulo. In: Pichardie, D., Weber, T. (eds.) Proof Exchange for Theorem Proving (2012)

[BCH12] Boespflug, M., Carbonneaux, Q., Hermant, O.: The λΠ-calculus modulo as a universal proof language. In: Pichardie, D., Weber, T. (eds.) Proceedings of PxTP2012: Proof Exchange for Theorem Proving, pp. 28–43 (2012)

[CHK+12] Codescu, M., Horozal, F., Kohlhase, M., Mossakowski, T., Rabe, F.: A proof theoretic interpretation of model theoretic hiding. In: Mossakowski, T., Kreowski, H.-J. (eds.) WADT 2010. LNCS, vol. 7137, pp. 118–138. Springer, Heidelberg (2012). https://doi.org/10.1007/978-3-642-28412-0_9

[CK18] Czajka, L., Kaliszyk, C.: Hammer for Coq: automation for dependent type theory. J. Autom. Reason. **61**(1–4), 423–453 (2018)

[CMR16] Codescu, M., Mossakowski, T., Rabe, F.: Selecting colimits for parameterisation and networks of specifications. In: Roggenbach, M., James, P. (eds.) Workshop on Algebraic Development Techniques (2016)

[Coq15] Coq Development Team: The Coq proof assistant: reference manual. Technical report, INRIA (2015)

[GGMR09] Garillot, F., Gonthier, G., Mahboubi, A., Rideau, L.: Packaging mathematical structures. In: Berghofer, S., Nipkow, T., Urban, C., Wenzel, M. (eds.) TPHOLs 2009. LNCS, vol. 5674, pp. 327–342. Springer, Heidelberg (2009). https://doi.org/10.1007/978-3-642-03359-9_23

[HHP93] Harper, R., Honsell, F., Plotkin, G.: A framework for defining logics. J. Assoc. Comput. Mach. **40**(1), 143–184 (1993)

[IKRU13] Iancu, M., Kohlhase, M., Rabe, F., Urban, J.: The Mizar mathematical library in OMDoc: translation and applications. J. Autom. Reason. **50**(2), 191–202 (2013)

[KMOR17] Kohlhase, M., Müller, D., Owre, S., Rabe, F.: Making PVS accessible to generic services by interpretation in a universal format. In: Ayala-Rincón, M., Muñoz, C.A. (eds.) ITP 2017. LNCS, vol. 10499, pp. 319–335. Springer, Cham (2017). https://doi.org/10.1007/978-3-319-66107-0_21

[KR14] Kaliszyk, C., Rabe, F.: Towards knowledge management for HOL light. In: Watt, S.M., Davenport, J.H., Sexton, A.P., Sojka, P., Urban, J. (eds.) CICM 2014. LNCS (LNAI), vol. 8543, pp. 357–372. Springer, Cham (2014). https://doi.org/10.1007/978-3-319-08434-3_26

[KR16] Kohlhase, M., Rabe, F.: QED reloaded: towards a pluralistic formal library of mathematical knowledge. J. Formaliz. Reason. **9**(1), 201–234 (2016)

[KW10] Keller, C., Werner, B.: Importing HOL light into Coq. In: Kaufmann, M., Paulson, L.C. (eds.) ITP 2010. LNCS, vol. 6172, pp. 307–322. Springer, Heidelberg (2010). https://doi.org/10.1007/978-3-642-14052-5_22

[MAH06] Mossakowski, T., Autexier, S., Hutter, D.: Development graphs - proof management for structured specifications. J. Log. Algebr. Program. **67**(1–2), 114–145 (2006)

[oFD18] European Commission Expert Group on FAIR Data: Turning fair into reality (2018). https://doi.org/10.2777/1524

[OS06] Obua, S., Skalberg, S.: Importing HOL into Isabelle/HOL. In: Furbach, U., Shankar, N. (eds.) IJCAR 2006. LNCS (LNAI), vol. 4130, pp. 298–302. Springer, Heidelberg (2006). https://doi.org/10.1007/11814771_27

[Rab17] Rabe, F.: How to identify, translate, and combine logics? J. Logic Comput. **27**(6), 1753–1798 (2017)

[Rab18] Rabe, F.: A modular type reconstruction algorithm. ACM Trans. Comput. Logic **19**(4), 1–43 (2018)

[RK13] Rabe, F., Kohlhase, M.: A scalable module system. Inf. Comput. **230**(1), 1–54 (2013)

[Sac19] Sacerdoti Coen, S.: A plugin to export Coq libraries to XML. In: 12th International Conference on Intelligent Computer Mathematics, CICM 2019. Lecture Notes in Artificial Intelligence (2019)

BNF-Style Notation as It Is Actually Used

Dee Quinlan, Joe B. Wells, and Fairouz Kamareddine$^{(\boxtimes)}$

Heriot-Watt University, Edinburgh, UK
fairouzcedar@gmail.com

Abstract. The famous BNF grammar notation, as introduced and used in the Algol 60 report, was subsequently followed by numerous notational variants (EBNF, ABNF, RBNF, etc.), and later by a new formal "grammars" metalanguage used for discussing structured objects in Computer Science and Mathematical Logic. We refer to this latter offspring of BNF as *MBNF* (Math-BNF), and to aspects common to MBNF, BNF, and its notational variants as *BNF-style*. MBNF is sometimes called "abstract syntax", but we avoid that name because MBNF is in fact a concrete form and there is a more abstract form. What all BNF-style notations share is the use of production rules like (P) below which state that "every instance of $\circ_i$ for $i \in \{1, ..., n\}$ is also an instance of $\bullet$".

$$\bullet ::= \circ_1 \mid \cdots \mid \circ_n \qquad\qquad (P)$$

However, MBNF is distinct from all variants of BNF in the entities and operations it allows. Instead of strings, MBNF builds arrangements of symbols that we call math-text and allows "syntax" to be built by interleaving MBNF production rules and other mathematical definitions that can contain chunks of math-text. The differences between BNF (or its variant forms) and MBNF have not been clearly presented before. (There is also no clear definition of MBNF anywhere but this is beyond the scope of this paper.)

This paper reviews BNF and some of its variant forms as well as MBNF, highlighting the differences between BNF (including its variant forms) and MBNF. We show via a series of detailed examples that MBNF, while superficially similar to BNF, differs substantially from BNF and its variants in how it is written, the operations it allows, and the sets of entities it defines. We also argue that the entities MBNF handles may extend far outside the scope of rewriting relations on strings and syntax trees derived from such rewriting sequences, which are often used to express the meaning of BNF and its notational variants.

1 Introduction

In this paper we discuss a form of BNF-style notation which is sometimes called abstract syntax, but which we term Math-BNF (hereafter MBNF), because MBNF is

© Springer Nature Switzerland AG 2019
C. Kaliszyk et al. (Eds.): CICM 2019, LNAI 11617, pp. 187–204, 2019.
https://doi.org/10.1007/978-3-030-23250-4_13

in fact a concrete form and there is a more abstract form.[1] MBNF is important for interpreting papers in theoretical computer science. Out of the 30 papers in the ESOP 2012 proceedings [30], 19 used MBNF and none used BNF.[2] Section 2 covers existing definitions for BNF as well as some formally defined standards which extend it into BNF variants. It also covers some limitations of BNF and its notational variants, which drive computer scientists to use what we term MBNF, despite the fact that MBNF lacks a formal definition. Section 3 discusses how MBNF differs from BNF and its variants.

First we introduce some notational conventions. Since the text of other documents' meta-levels is part of the object level of this one, we introduce the following notation. We use "boxes" for both inline and block text.

> " Text placed in a quotebox (aside from this one) is quoted directly from another document. "

Text placed in an undecorated box (aside from this one) is intended to imitate the text of other documents which we may look to deal with, and is usually derived from things written elsewhere, but it is not a direct quote.

2   BNF and Its Variants

We give a brief overview of BNF and its more popular variants which remain broad enough to cover how BNF variants normally work, the kinds of entity they work with and the kinds of operations they usually allow. According to Zaytev [35]:

"The grammarware technological space is commonly perceived as mature and drained of any scientific challenge, but provides many unsolved problems for researchers who are active in that field."

While we agree with Zaytev that there are still numerous reasons for a deeper comparison of these relatives to BNF, which might touch on more obscure examples and order them in terms of how quickly they may be used to build syntax or their expressive

---

[1] For example, consider an abstract syntax tree (AST) representing $\lambda x.e$. An AST is a tree where each branch goes to a syntactic evaluation of a metavariable and each node is either a metavariable assignment which contains no further evaluations or a function taking metavariables, which represents an evaluation. In an AST for $\lambda x.e$, we would not be interested that the x and the e are arranged with a dot between them and a λ in front of them. Rather, $(\lambda\square.\square)$ would just be a name for a particular function taking two arguments of an appropriate type.

[2] We chose ESOP 2012, but we could equally pick any other conferences. Because the first book we picked contained an abundance of challenging instances of MBNF, our wider searching has mainly been to find even more challenging examples. We will be happy to receive pointers to additional interesting cases. We also checked the POPL 2017 proceedings [11] and found that out of 46 papers using BNF-style notation, not one used notation exactly corresponding to the EBNF [20], ABNF [6] or RBNF [10] standards and only one [16] could possibly be thought of as EBNF or ABNF with variant syntax. Out of the other 45 POPL 2017 papers featuring BNF-style notation, 44 use what we call MBNF.

power, this is not what we aim to provide here. The main purpose of this section is as a preliminary to our examination of MBNF. The idea we intend readers to take away from this section is that, while the notations examined here allow for a great deal of variation between them, they are still more like one another than they are like MBNF.

2.1 How BNF Works

BNF can be thought of as a game: you start with a non-terminal and are then given rules for what you can replace this with. The value of the non-terminal defined by the BNF grammar is just the set of all things you can produce by applying these rules to each non-terminal provided you reach a string entirely composed of terminal symbols after a finite number of steps.

The rules are called production rules, and normally look like this:

$$\bullet ::= \circ_1 \mid \cdots \mid \circ_n$$

A production rule simply states that the symbol on the left-hand side of the ::= must be replaced by one of the alternatives on the right hand side. For example the non-terminal $\langle a \rangle$ in $\boxed{\langle a \rangle ::= \langle b \rangle \mid \langle b \rangle \langle a \rangle}$ would range over things of the form $\langle b \rangle$, $\langle b \rangle \langle b \rangle$, $\langle b \rangle \langle b \rangle \langle b \rangle$ etc. If we were also given $\boxed{\langle b \rangle ::= cd}$, then it would range over cd, $cdcd$, etc. The alternatives are separated by |. Alternatives usually consist of "non-terminals" and "terminals". Terminals are simply pieces of the final string that are not "non-terminals". They are called terminals because there are no production rules for them: they terminate the production process. We can write a tree (sometimes called an abstract syntax tree) to show how BNF style notation produces syntax as an instance of a non-terminal (where each child node is an instance of its parent). Here is how we would write $cdcd$ as an instance of a given the rules $\boxed{\langle a \rangle ::= \langle b \rangle \mid \langle b \rangle \langle a \rangle}$ and $\boxed{\langle b \rangle ::= cd}$:

Non-terminals are distinguished from terminals either by placing them in triangular brackets or by surrounding terminals by quotes and using either a comma or a space to separate both non-terminals and terminals. The language of $\bullet$ is the set of all things of the form $\circ_i$ for $1 < i < n$. In the example where $\boxed{a ::= b \mid ba}$ and $\boxed{b ::= cd}$ the language of a would be $\{(cd)^n \mid n \in \mathbb{N} \wedge n > 0\}$ where $\mathbb{N}$ is the set of natural numbers and $(cd)^n$ denotes something of the form cd concatenated with itself n times.

2.2 Backus and Naur

To illustrate what the original BNF looked like we present an example of BNF as it was used by Backus and BNF as it was used by Naur.

Backus. [1, p. 129] used ":≡" to symbolise a production and "$\overline{or}$" to separate production rules. He picked out non-terminals by surrounding them with angle brackets.

"
$$\langle digit \rangle := 0 \, \overline{or} \, 1 \, \overline{or} \, 2 \, \overline{or} \, 3 \, \overline{or} \, 4 \, \overline{or} \, 5 \, \overline{or} \, 6 \, \overline{or}$$
$$7 \, \overline{or} \, 8 \, \overline{or} \, 9$$
$$\langle integer \rangle := \langle digit \rangle \, \overline{or} \, \langle integer \rangle \langle digit \rangle$$
"

Here, $\langle digit \rangle$ ranges over the set of symbols {"0", "1", "2", "3", "4", "5", "6", "7", "8", "9"}. $\langle integer \rangle$ ranges over the set of strings one would use to write the non-negative integers using digits 0 to 9.

Naur. [2, p. 3,5] used ":: =" instead of ":≡" and "|" instead of "$\overline{or}$". Other than that the grammar is the same.

"
$$\langle digit \rangle :: = 0 \mid 1 \mid 2 \mid 3 \mid 4 \mid 5 \mid 6 \mid 7 \mid 8 \mid 9$$
$$\langle unsigned\ integer \rangle :: = \langle digit \rangle \mid \langle unsigned\ integer \rangle \langle digit \rangle$$
"

Here $\langle digit \rangle$ ranges over the same set $\langle digit \rangle$ ranged over in the previous example and $\langle unsigned\ integer \rangle$ ranges over the same set $\langle integer \rangle$ did.

2.3 Extensions to BNF

The following are extensions to BNF, which, unlike MBNF have a formal definition.

EBNF. (Extended Backus-Naur Form) adds facilities for dealing with repetition of syntactic rules (braces around repeated text), special sequences (Two ?s around names of special characters), optional choice of syntactic rules (square brackets around optional text) and exceptions to syntactic rules (written $R - E$ where R is a rule and E an exception). Instead of having non-terminal symbols surrounded by angle brackets, terminal symbols are surrounded by single quotes and all symbols are separated by commas. Each line is ended in a semicolon. A full copy of the syntax for EBNF is found in [20].

In EBNF, the terminating decimals *DI* can be written as:

$$DI ::= [`-`], D, \{D\}, [`.`, D, \{D\}];$$
$$D ::= `0` \mid `1` \mid `2` \mid `3` \mid `4` \mid `5` \mid `6` \mid `7` \mid `8` \mid `9`;$$

We read the rule $\boxed{DI ::= [`-`], D, \{D\}, [`.`, D, \{D\}];}$ as giving the following instructions for producing something of the form *DI*: First, begin with an optional minus, $\boxed{[`-`]}$, followed by a choice of D, $\boxed{D}$, followed by any number of choices of D, $\boxed{\{D\}}$, followed by an optional choice of a member of a group, $\boxed{[`.`, D, \{D\}]}$. This group consists of things produced with the following instructions: begin with a dot, $\boxed{`.`}$, followed by a choice of D, $\boxed{D}$, followed by any number of choices of D, $\boxed{\{D\}}$.

EBNF without exceptions to syntactic rules is not more powerful than BNF in terms of what sets of strings it can generate, but it is more convenient and the parse trees it generates may look different. The above example is more cumbersome in BNF:

$$\langle DI \rangle ::= \langle PD \rangle \mid -\langle PD \rangle \mid \langle PD \rangle.\langle PD \rangle \mid -\langle PD \rangle.\langle PD \rangle$$
$$\langle PD \rangle ::= \langle D \rangle \mid \langle PD \rangle \langle D \rangle$$
$$D ::= 0 \mid 1 \mid 2 \mid 3 \mid 4 \mid 5 \mid 6 \mid 7 \mid 8 \mid 9$$

Lemma 1. *Repetition and choice can be written into equivalent BNF productions.*

Proof. Let ε stands for the empty string. We outline the process:

- Convert every repetition { E } to a fresh non-terminal X and add $X = \varepsilon \mid X\,E$.
- Convert every option [E] to a fresh non-terminal X and add $X = \varepsilon \mid E$.
  (We can convert X = A [E] B. to X = A E B | A B.)
- Convert every group (E) to a fresh non-terminal X and add X = E.

○

Exceptions to syntactic rules mean EBNF is not context-free.

Lemma 2. *Production rules of the form R − E have no BNF equivalent.*

Proof. Let ε stands for the empty string. First consider intersection

1. The language of $L_1 = \{a^n b^n a^m \mid n, m \geq 0\}$ is generated by:
   $$\langle L_1 \rangle:: = \langle X \rangle \langle A \rangle \quad \langle X \rangle:: = \langle X \rangle b \mid \varepsilon \quad \langle A \rangle:: = \langle A \rangle a \mid \varepsilon$$
2. The language of $L_2 = \{a^n b^m a^m \mid n, m \geq 0\}$ is generated by: $\langle L_2 \rangle ::= \langle A \rangle \langle X \rangle$
3. $L_1 \cap L_2 = \{a^n b^n a^n \mid n \geq 0\}$ is not context free by the pumping lemma [3, p. 110] since, for a given $p \geq 1$ we can choose $n > p$ such that $s = a^n b^n a^n$ is in our language and we cannot pick any substring q of s such that q is of length p, $s = xqy$ for some strings x and y, and $xq^n y \in L_1 \cap L_2$ (since q would have to take in at least one a and should take in the same number of as on the left as on the right).

It follows easily that rules of the form $R - E$ cannot be modelled in BNF, since BNF only generates the context free grammars and $\{a^n b^n a^n \mid n \geq 0\} = L_1 - (L_1 - L_2)$

○

Lemma 2 shows that some things represented in EBNF cannot be represented in BNF.

P.E.G.s. (Parsing Expression Grammars) [12] have many of the same facilities as EBNF, but contain an ordered choice operator which indicates parsing preference between options. For example, the EBNF rules $A = a, b \mid a$ and $A = a \mid a, b$ are equivalent, but the P.E.G. rules $A \leftarrow a\,b \mid a$ and $A \leftarrow a \mid a\,b$ are different. The second alternative in the latter P.E.G. rule will never succeed because the first choice is always taken if the input string to be recognized begins with 'a'. P.E.G. rules also add and, '&', and not, '!', syntactic predicates which match a pattern only if a certain context is present. The expression '&e' attempts to match pattern e, then unconditionally backtracks to the starting point, preserving only the knowledge of whether *e* succeeded or failed to match. Conversely, the expression '!*e*' fails if *e* succeeds, but succeeds if *e* fails. E.g. !EndOfLine . matches any single character so long as the nonterminal End-OfLine does not match starting at the same position. P.E.G. provides us with slightly more power than EBNF. However, understanding P.E.G. rules rests on the user's intuitive understanding of parsing and string recognition - the body of literature for which is very large. In addition there is not a particularly close correspondence between the extra operators provided by P.E.G. and anything in the syntax of MBNF.

ABNF. (Augmented Backus-Naur Form) [6] contains no facilities not also included in ENBF (which ISO gives as the standard for BNF itself at the time of writing). We include it here only for completeness.

RBNF. (Routing Backus-Naur Form) [10] Contains most of the facilities of EBNF aside from the ability to write exceptions to syntactic rules. RBNF can generate the same syntax as BNF. We include it here only for completeness.

LBNF. (Labelled BNF) [13] extends EBNF with functionality for dealing with polymorphic lists of rules. It also provides a few pre-defined sets such as characters, integers, strings, and identifiers. It also provides labels which deal with higher order abstract syntax [26], however this is not intended to be used in LBNF grammars written by hand, but in ones generated from the grammar formalism GF (Grammatical Framework) [28].

Again there is no clear mathematical model of this functionality to aid human understanding; analysing the given functions requires understanding the programs used to compile expressions in the grammar. In addition there is not a particularly close correspondence between the labels provided by LBNF and anything in the syntax of MBNF.

TBNF. (Translational Backus-Naur Form) [24] Puts non terminals in the place of internal nodes and terminals in place of external nodes on a tree (which we call an abstract syntax tree or AST). When the resulting syntax is parsed, the AST it creates is traversed. It adds to EBNF additional production arrows as follows:

[~>]   Reverse Production Arrow. An arrow preceding the right side of a rule for which you want the nodes to be arranged in reverse order.

[=>]   Call A Function. This means to call a function when a rule in the grammar has been recognized. A rule in the grammar may have multiple function calls.

[+>]   Make A Node. This means to make a node corresponding to this rule in the grammar. During AST traversal this node will be processed with a built-in default node processing function.

[*>]   Make A Node and during AST traversal, call a function with the same name as this node, instead of calling the default node-processing function. This allows customization of the code-generation process.

[$1]   Parse Stack Position. This refers to the symbol in parse stack position # 1, the first symbol in the right side of the rule. $n refers to the *n*th position.

[..*]   Node Traversal Indicator. Indicates when processing for this node should occur, at top-down, pass-over, or bottom-up time, respectively. *.. indicates top-down only. ..* indicates bottom-up only. *.* indicates top-down and bottom-up.

[(...)]   The Arguments. Arguments are used for function calls (=>) and node processing (+>). For node processing the arguments apply to the relative '*' in the Node Traversal Indicator. *-* would require two string arguments.

[& 0]   Counter Indicator. When the AST processor enters a node, it increments a counter for the node and puts in on a stack. The '& 0' indicates the current count for the node taken from the stack. A '& 1' means the counter for the parent node on the stack and '& 2' means the counter of the grandparent. This provides a unique number for labels.

TBNF provides a very rich extension to EBNF which is particularly well suited for relating expressions to their abstract syntax trees. However a clear mathematical model of the trees generated by TBNF is not provided alongside its syntax (again these are created in a compiler rather than presented in a form intuitive to human beings). In addition while it covers some of the functionality authors expect when they use MBNF it does not particularly resemble the way in which it is written.

2.4   Limitations of BNF and Its Variants

When deciding if a BNF-like syntax can be readily converted into BNF, it is important to note that BNF is a language for building sets of strings and the only notion of equality it deals with easily is string equality. It is possible to derive a notion of tree equality from the parse trees generated by an EBNF grammar, but there is no guarantee that parse trees will be unambiguous. Unless an author writes their grammar with a parser in mind, inferring a sensible parse tree from a set of productions is non-trivial.

BNF can describe exactly the context-free grammars in Chomsky's hierarchy [5]. Non-context-free grammars cannot be written without extending BNF in some way.

3   MBNF

In this section, we highlight ways in which the notation we call MBNF differs from BNF and its variants. We show that MBNF is non-trivially different from existing extensions of BNF and does not deal with the same kinds of entities as these extensions.

3.1   Where BNF and Its Variants Use Strings, MBNF Uses Math-Text

Parentheses for disambiguation are not needed in MBNF grammars and when an MBNF grammar specifies such parentheses they can often be omitted without any need to explain. E.g. writing $\boxed{(\lambda x.xx)\lambda y.y}$ instead of $\boxed{((\lambda x.(xx))(\lambda y.y))}$. When possible, MBNF takes advantage of the tree-like structure implicit in the layout of symbols on the page when features like superscripting and overbarring are used. E.g. in $\boxed{f_x^{n+1} + \overline{y \cdot fj}}$.

Instead of non-terminal symbols, MBNF uses *metavariables*[3], which appear in what we call *math-text* and obey the conventions of mathematical variables. Metavariables are not distinguished from other symbols by annotating them as BNF and its notational variants do, but by math-text features such as font, spacing, or merely tradition.

In addition to arranging symbols from left to right on the page, math-text allows subscripting, superscripting, pre-subscripting, pre-superscripting and placing text above or below other text. It also allows for marking whole segments of text, for example with an overbar (a vinculum). Readers can find more detailed information on how math-text can be laid out in The TeXbook [22], or the Presentation MathML [19] and OpenDocument [21] standards. Here is a nonsense piece of Math-text to show how it may be laid out:

$$^c\!\!\downarrow a' = \check{p}\langle v''_x \odot a^{2+1}\rangle - \overline{f^n_x + \overline{y \cdot f j}} + \sum_{i=0}^{\infty} s_{i\in 1...n} \xrightarrow{a,b,c} b\hat{a}$$

3.2 MBNF Is Aimed Exclusively at Human Readers

MBNF can be used to write all of the grammars BNF and its variants can produce, but it also defines grammars BNF does not. However, unlike BNF, MBNF is meant to be interpreted by humans, not computers, as it has not been adequately formalised yet. Authors may define an MBNF grammar in an article for humans and a separate grammar for use with a parser generator to build a corresponding implementation. MBNF defines entities not intended or expected to be serialized or parsed. Dolan and Mycroft provide a typical example in [7, pp. 61–65]

> " e ::= $x \mid \lambda x.e \mid e_1 e_2 \mid \{\ell_1 = e_1, ..., \ell_n = e_n\} \mid e.\ell \mid true \mid false \mid if\ e_1\ then\ e_2\ else\ e_3$
> $\quad\quad \mid \hat{\mathbf{x}} \mid let\ \hat{\mathbf{x}} = e_1\ in\ e_2$
> Γ ::= $\epsilon \mid \Gamma, x : \tau \mid \Gamma, \hat{\mathbf{x}} : \forall \alpha.\tau$
> τ ::= $bool \mid \tau_1 \to \tau_2 \mid \{\ell_1 : \tau_1, ..., \ell_n : \tau_n\} \mid \alpha \mid \top \mid \bot \mid \tau \sqcup \tau \mid \tau \sqcap \tau$
> Δ ::= $\epsilon \mid \Delta, x : \tau$
> Π ::= $\epsilon \mid \Pi, \hat{\mathbf{x}} : [\Delta]\tau$ "

In this example Γ, Δ and Π are never intended to be serialised. The authors provide an implementation in OCaml which looks very little like the above syntax.[4]

Most MBNF grammars are missing features needed to disambiguate complex terms (e.g. notation for separating metavariables from concrete syntax and from other kinds of evaluated syntax (like $\langle$ and $\rangle$ do in BNF), bracketing (as covered in Sect. 3.1) and notation for declaring operator precedence (for the example above [7], no rules are given for the order in which patterns should be matched). Papers often put complicated uses of the mathematical metalanguage inside MBNF notation (examples of this can be found throughout this section).

---

[3] Here a metavariable is a variable at the meta-level which denotes something at an object-level.
[4] www.cl.cam.ac.uk/~sd601/mlsub/.

3.3   MBNF Allows Powerful Operators Like Context Hole Filling (a.k.a Tree Splicing)

Chang and Felleisen [4, p 134] present an MBNF grammar defining the λ-term contexts with one hole where the spine[5] is a balanced segment[6] ending in a hole. For explanatory purposes, we write $e@e$ instead of $e\,e$ and add parentheses. Concrete syntax and BNF-style notation are green. Metavariables are blue. Tree-splicing operators are red.

$$e ::= x \mid (\lambda x.e) \mid (e@e)$$
$$A ::= [\,] \mid (A[(\lambda x.A)]@e)$$

One can think of the context hole filling operation ($[\,]$ in $(A[(\lambda x.A)]@e)$) as performing tree splicing operations within the syntax. Here are trees illustrating steps in building syntax trees for A (the operation $\bullet@\bullet$ is higher up the tree than $\bullet[\,\bullet\,]$ because of parsing precedence inherited from math):

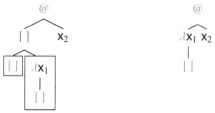

These trees show the result of the second rule where each A is $[\,]$ and e is a variable. The tree on the left is the tree corresponding to $A[\lambda x.A]@e$ before the hole filling operation is performed, where the first A is assigned $[\,]$. The tree on the right represents an unparsing of the typical syntax tree for $((\lambda x_1.[\,])@x_2)$. x_1 and x_2 are disambiguated instances of x. A metavariable assigned a value won't appear in the final tree. If it's not a terminal node, $[\,]$ tells us to fill in the leaf in the frame on the left with the tree in the frame on the right. Once performed, $[\,]$ disappears.

We can show that unlike BNF, the "language" of the metavariable/non-terminal A (the set of strings derived from A using roughly the rules of BNF plus hole filling) is not context-free and so MBNF certainly isn't.

For this section we use ToStr informally to mean a function which takes an object that an MBNF metavariable may range over, provided it can be written as a chunk of math-text whose only operation is concatenation and whose only equivalence is syntactic equivalence, and takes them to the fully parenthesised string one might use to refer to them. For example if $O = (\lambda a.[\,])@b$ declares the object O, then ToStr(O) = "$((\lambda a.[\,])@b)$" where "$((\lambda a.[\,])@b)$" is the symbol "(" concatenated with another "(" concatenated with "λ" etc. and O is the data structure $(\lambda a.[\,])@b$ represents. In order

---

[5] The root node is on the spine. If A is applied to B by an application on the spine, the root node of A is on the spine and the root node of B is not. If a node on the spine is an abstraction each of its children is on the spine (i.e., every node appearing on the furthest left hand side of the tree is on the spine).

[6] A balanced segment is one where each application has a matching abstraction and where each application/abstraction pair contains a balanced segment.

to show that MBNF is not context free this we make use of the pumping lemma for context-free languages [3, p. 110].

Lemma 3. Hole Filling is Not "Context-free" *For A given by the MBNF above, the language given by* $\{\, x \in \mathsf{String} \mid x = \mathsf{ToStr}(A) \,\}$ *is not context-free.*

Proof Sketch. We need to show that for any given $p \geq 1$ we can produce an $s = \mathsf{ToStr}(A)$ such that no substring of s can be "pumped" (some non-empty part of one or both of its outermost substrings repeated) to give another string in the language $\{\, x \in \mathsf{String} \mid x = \mathsf{ToStr}(A) \,\}$.

Since each A has a balanced segment along the spine we must be expected to keep count of both abstractions and applications. Parentheses must also be balanced. Getting the desired result is as simple as picking an $s = \mathsf{ToStr}(A)$ such that the abstraction at the bottom of the spine of A is more than p abstractions away from the application closest to the bottom of the spine of A and such that A contains no e long enough to be pumped. Since parentheses are balanced, the only possible section we might pick to "pump" is around the hole and since there are p abstractions before we reach an application, there is no way that "pumping" this could give us a balanced segment.

◯

BNF itself is context free. EBNF [20], ABNF [6] and RBNF [10] don't use tree-splicing or context hole filling.

3.4   MBNF Mixes Mathematical Language with BNF-Style Notation

Germane and Might [14, p. 20] mix BNF-style notation freely with mathematical notation in such a way that the resulting grammar relies upon both sets produced with set theory notation and MBNF production rules which use metavariables defined using mathematical notation:

$$
\begin{aligned}
\text{``} \qquad u \in UVar &= \text{a set of identifiers} & ccall \in CCall &::= (q\,e^*)_\gamma \\
k \in CVar &= \text{a set of identifiers} & e, f \in UExp &= UVar + ULam \\
lam \in Lam &= ULam + CLam & q \in CExp &= CVar + CLam \\
ulam \in ULam &::= (\lambda e(u^* k)call) & \ell \in ULab &= \text{a set of labels} \\
clam \in CLam &::= (\lambda_\gamma (u^*)call) & \gamma \in CLab &= \text{a set of labels} \\
call \in Call &= UCall + CCall & ucall \in UCall &::= (f e^* q)_\ell \qquad \text{''}
\end{aligned}
$$

The results of math computations are interleaved with MBNF production rules, not just applied after the results of the production rules have been obtained. This grammar uses $\bullet_1 \in \bullet_2$ to mean "$\bullet_2$ is the language of $\bullet_1$" (this is the case in both the MBNF production rules (:: =) and the math itself (=)).

In the MBNF above + is used as union and we have the additional requirement that there must exist some procedure for choosing sets fulfilling these constraints such that, if, for some terms X and Y, $X + Y$ appears in the grammar, then X and Y do not intersect. Here, the requirement is most likely fulfilled by the author following the convention that any arbitrary sets declared separately are disjoint (i.e., $CVar \cap UVar = \emptyset$). However, in order to check that grammars like the one above are correct, we would still need a general procedure for checking that $ULam$ and $CLam$ don't overlap if such a convention is chosen.

BNF, EBNF, ABNF and RBNF don't have a concept of disjoint union and don't allow one to interleave set theoretic operations on the language of a non-terminal with ordinary BNF definitions.

3.5   MBNF Has at Least the Power of Indexed Grammars

Inoe and Taha [18, p. 361] use this MBNF:

$$\text{``}\qquad \mathcal{E}^{\ell,m} \in ECtx_n^{\ell,m} ::= \cdots \mid \langle \mathcal{E}^{\ell+1,m} \rangle \mid \cdots \qquad \text{''}$$

This suggests that MBNF deals with the family of indexed grammars [17, p 389-390], which is yet another reason it's not context-free. The $\ell + 1$ is a calculation that is not intended to be part of the syntax. The production rule above defines an infinite set of metavariables ranging over different sets.

BNF, EBNF, ABNF and RBNF don't allow for indexing.

3.6   MBNF Has a Native Concept of Binding

In Germane and Might [14, p. 20] we found the following:

$$pr \in Pr = \{ulam : ulam \in Ulam, \text{closed}(ulam)\}$$

In order to perform this evaluation of the set $Ulam$ we must recognise which variables are bound.

In addition we need a notion of binding to deal with some of the issues surrounding α-equivalence that often arise when authors start working with the grammar they define as part of a reduction system. Chang and Felleisen [4, p 134] give the following axiom:

$$\hat{A}[A_1[\lambda x.\check{A}[E[x]]]A_2[v]] = \hat{A}[A_1[A_2[\check{A}[E[x]]x := v]]]\qquad\qquad \text{where } \hat{A}[\check{A}] \in A$$

Here we are meant to recognise an implicit convention, known as the Barendregt convention, on the terms we are β-reducing over. In this case the Barendregt convention would require that we pick terms from the α-equivalence class of $\hat{A}[A_1[\lambda x.\check{A}[E[x]]]A_2[v]]$ such that no bound variable of $A_1[\lambda x.\check{A}[E[x]]]$ is a free variable in $A_2[v]$ and none of the bound variables in $A_2[v]$ are free variables in $\check{A}[E[x]]$.[7] Since Chang and Felleisen also expect the Church-Rosser property to hold of their reduction relations, terms are identified up to α-equivalence again after performing the reduction and filling the holes.

A notion of binding is not native to BNF, EBNF, ABNF, RBNF or TBNF but must be defined after the grammar.

---

[7] Actually a slightly weaker condition than the one we give here is probably sufficient for the Barendregt convention to hold, but it would be more complicated to state.

3.7   MBNF Allows "Arbitrary" Side Conditions on Production Rules

An example of a production rule with a side condition can be found in Chang and Felleisen [4, p 134]:

$$\text{``} \quad E = [\,] \mid Ee \mid A[E] \mid \hat{A}[A[\lambda x.\check{A}[E[x]]]E] \qquad \text{where } \hat{A}[\check{A}] \in A \quad \text{''}$$

It is possible to make side conditions that prevent MBNF rules from having a solution. A definition for MBNF can help in finding conditions on side conditions that ensure MBNF rules actually define something.

Potential Contradictions When Dealing with Side Conditions. Side conditions may cause problems in making sure an MBNF is well defined. We offer a set of assumptions about what one may be allowed to do in an MBNF which are separately plausible and unproblematic, but which allow us to create a grammar which is obviously undefined if we use all of them unrestrictedly.

Where we are allowed to use $\in$ we are usually allowed to use $\notin$. The side condition of the MBNF for E has a metavariable that is created by filling a hole in a member of $\hat{A}$ with a member of $\check{A}$. This suggests that we may be allowed to use mathematical productions similar to those used in the production rules themselves to create the metavariables featuring in the side conditions of the production rules. We may conclude that, provided we have a production rule for B, we can have $\lambda x.B$ in one of our side conditions. MBNF also allows us to have production rules that reference themselves, either directly or indirectly. By allowing all these assumptions, we can produce an MBNF which defines a non existent language.

$$
\begin{aligned}
A &::= x \mid \lambda x.A \mid B \qquad\qquad \text{Where } \lambda x.B \notin C \\
B &::= x \mid A \mid \pi x.B \\
C &::= A \mid B
\end{aligned}
$$

There exists $b \in B$ such that b is of the form $\pi x.B$, consider one such b. Suppose that $\lambda x.b \notin C$. Then $b \in A$ and since, for all $a \in A$, $\lambda x.a \in A$ we would have that $\lambda x.b \in A$ and, since $C ::= A \mid B$, $\lambda x.b \in C$. Suppose instead that $\lambda x.b \in C$, then either $\lambda x.b \in A$ or $\lambda x.b \in B$. Every statement in B is either an x, or else it begins with π, or else it is also in A, so $\lambda x.b \in A$. $\lambda x.y \in A$ if and only if $y \in A$, so $b \in A$. Since b is not of the form x or $\lambda x.A$, then b can only be produced by the production rule B, in which case $\lambda x.b \notin C$. So we have that, if $\lambda x.b \in C$ then $\lambda x.b \notin C$ and if $\lambda x.b \notin C$ then $\lambda x.b \in C$.

So there is no set of statements we can produce that satisfies the rules of the grammar. We can't isolate any particular production rule which causes the problem, each rule alone may be fine within the context of a slightly different grammar.

We believe that authors often have some heuristic in mind which allows them to avoid cross reference of the sort in our fictitious example, but do not know of a definition which explicitly says what's allowed.

Neither BNF nor its variants allow arbitrary side conditions on production rules.

3.8   MBNF Can Contain Very Large Infinite Sets as Part of the "Syntax"

Toronto and McCarthy [34, p 297] write:

> "
> $$e:: = \cdots \mid \langle t_{set}, \{e^{*\kappa}\} \rangle$$
> Here $\{e^{*\kappa}\}$ means sets of no more than κ terms from the language of e.
> "

> " ...The language of $v:: = \langle t_{set}, \{v^{*\kappa}\} \rangle$ consists of the encodings of all the hereditarily accessible sets.
> "

The author does not state what κ is, but elsewhere in the paper it is an inaccessible cardinal. It seems as though κ is also intended to be an inaccessible cardinal here.

BNF and its notational variants, by contrast, only deal with strings of finite length.

3.9   MBNF Allows Infinitary Operators

Díaz and Núñez [23, p. 539] write an MBNF with an infinitary operator:

> "
> $$P:: = \cdots \mid \prod_{i \in I} P_i \mid \cdots$$
> ...But, for instance in our language we have the term
> $$\prod_{n \in \mathbb{N}} P_n$$
> where each P_n is born at time n, and so P is born at time $\omega + 1$.
> ...So, to fully formalize the set of valid expressions, we begin by bounding the size of the possible sets of indices I, and that of the set of actions Act by some infinite cardinal κ. The functional governing the right hand side of the equation is clearly monotone, but it is not so obvious whether it has any fixpoint. Fortunately it has. Besides, it is guaranteed that it is reached after (at most) λ iterations, where λ is the smallest regular cardinal bigger than κ. Then, the principle of structural induction is valid and corresponds to the principle of transfinite induction.
> "

We may think of infinitary operators as defining trees of infinite breadth (i.e., trees whose internal nodes may have infinitely many direct children), where BNF and its notational variants deal with finite data structures (usually strings).

3.10   MBNF Allows Co-inductive Definitions

Eberhart, Hirschowitz and Seiller [8, p 94] write:

❝ We consider processes to be infinite terms as generated by the grammar:

$$P, Q ::= \Sigma_{i \in n} G_i \mid (P|Q) \qquad G ::= \overline{a}\langle b\rangle.P \mid a(b).P \mid va.P \mid \tau.P \mid \heartsuit.P$$

up to renaming of bound variables as usual. Such a coinductive definition... ❞

We may think of co-inductive definitions as allowing us to define trees of infinite depth (i.e. trees in which paths may pass through infinitely many nodes), where BNF and its notational variants deal with finite data structures.

3.11 MBNF May Be Considered up to "Arbitrary" Equivalences

As well as α-equivalence and binding, the objects created by a piece of MBNF may be considered up to various other equivalences, e.g., associativity and composition with a 0 element (as in the π-calculus [25]), equivalence up to the exchanging of labels (as in the λ-calculus with records [27, p. 129]), equivalence up to repetition of elements (as with set-like syntactic objects), and additional equivalences which may be defined by the author. Tobisawa [33, p. 386] defines equivalences $\simeq_s$ & $\simeq_t$:

❝
$$id\langle v, d\rangle := v^d[id],$$
$$(^w{\downarrow}\,(M) \cdot \sigma)\langle v, d\rangle := \begin{cases} M & \text{If } v = w \text{ and } d = 0, \\ \sigma\langle v, d - \delta_{vw}\rangle & \text{otherwise,} \end{cases}$$
$$({\uparrow}_w \cdot \sigma)\langle v, d\rangle := \sigma\langle v, d + \delta_{vw}\rangle$$
❞

where δ_{vw} is the integer defined by

❝
$$\delta_{vw} := \begin{cases} 1 & \text{If } v = w \\ 0 & \text{otherwise.} \end{cases}$$
❞

Then $\simeq_s$ and $\simeq_t$ are defined inductively.

❝
$$id \simeq_s id$$
$$\sigma \simeq_s \tau \qquad \text{if } \sigma\langle v, d\rangle \simeq_t \tau\langle v, d\rangle \text{ for any } v, d$$
$$v^d[\sigma] \simeq_t v^d[\tau] \qquad \text{if } \sigma \simeq_s \tau$$
$$\lambda v.M \simeq_t \lambda v.N \qquad \text{if } M \simeq_t N$$
$$M_1 @_\ell M_2 \simeq_t N_1 @_\ell N_2 \text{ if } M_1 \simeq_t N_1 \text{ and } M_2 \simeq_t N_2$$
❞

However in order to work modulo these equivalences, he must also be working modulo arithmetic equivalence on some computations. He must also be working with the implicit assumption that := is a bijective transformation, that maps syntax to syntax preserving equivalence. Let $f : A \mapsto B$ be a function from some subset of the terms defined by the BNF, A, to some other set of terms, B, which are possibly meant to be definable with a different BNF (with side conditions and arithmetic computations), such that $\forall a \in A$; $a := f(a)$ and if $a := b$, then $b = f(a)$. The author wishes us to use a convention where, two terms $a, b \in A$ are equivalent in the paper if and only if $f(a), f(b) \in B$ are equivalent.

A sufficiently general notion of equivalence is not native to BNF and its notational variants but must be defined after the grammar.

4 Related Work

There has already been some work done in the area of defining MBNF, however, to our knowledge, no other authors have highlighted all the issues we have, or presented it as a significant departure from BNF and its notational variants. In fact, MBNF is rarely even given a name to distinguish it from similar notations, on the few occasions authors do refer to it they call it "abstract syntax," which is misleading. We have had to coin the term MBNF to make it clear what we are talking about.

We take a look at some of the existing work related to the definition of MBNF and talk about why this paper exposes important issues which existing work does not address. Since MBNF has not yet been properly recognised as a notation distinct from BNF and its extensions, which is in need of a definition, we have chosen papers dealing with a broad set of different problems. Some of this work deals with syntactic structures which are in some way related to the syntactic structures used by MBNF. Some of this work focusses on comparison of BNF-style notations (which may or may not include MBNF), but does not focus on the issues we do. One of the pieces we cite evaluates non-MBNF syntax, but allows some functionality more commonly associated with MBNF and produces something like MBNF as output.

Ott [31] provides a formal language for writing specifications like those written in MBNF. The process of moving from an Ott specification to an MBNF can be performed automatically. However, Ott does not offer support for interpreting MBNF without requiring it to be specified in a theorem-prover friendly format. Ott focuses on translating to Coq 8.3, HOL 4 and Isabelle directly, but offers less support for those seeking a general mathematical intuition. Ott only allows contexts with a single hole, does not allow for hole-filling operations to appear in the clause of a production rule and currently does not support rules being used coinductively. Ott also does not handle the common practice of using mathematical text outside of the MBNF grammar as part of its definition.

Steele [32] covers many of the notational variants of BNF, and some MBNF. However, he is primarily interested in making an initial attempt at documenting computer science meta-notation. He focuses on the differences between CSM and earlier versions, such as BNF, only insofar as they help this goal, and remind us of alternative choices that might have been better than the ones we ended up with. He does not discuss how the underlying mathematical structure of MBNF differs wildly from BNF and its variants.

Grewe et al. [15] discuss the exploration of language specifications with first-order theorem provers. However, they still require the reader to be able to intuitively translate language specifications to a sufficiently formal language first.

Reynolds [29, p. 1-51] has the best attempt at a definition of MBNF which we could find after looking through the books in our collection, which he calls "abstract syntax"[8]. However, he only deals with context-free grammars and usually proceeds by example.

Farmer [9] deals with syntax featuring evaluation and quotation. This resembles the kinds of entity MBNF works with. However, he is more concerned with syntax evaluation as it stands for some algorithmic operations than syntax standing for itself modulo some equivalence and he does not go into how syntax featuring evaluation and quotation is meant to be combined with BNF-style notation.

Zaytsev [35] provides a comprehensive review of BNF variants and a tool for studying mappings between them. He does not deal with MBNF at all nor does he claim to, but his work highlights in detail the similarities between BNF and its extensions touched upon in Sect. 2 as well as other variants we did not have space to cover. A comparison of MBNF to the grammars examined in his work undelines that MBNF is not an extension of BNF with some transformation applied to its syntax.

None of the above authors deal with MBNF grammars with very large infinite things in them or with mixing math and MBNF. They do not even discuss this as a permissible practice, nor the need to treat MBNF as a notation distinct from BNF and its extensions.

5   Conclusions

While MBNF bears a superficial resemblance to BNF and its variants, we have demonstrated that it is different in the entities it works with and the operations it allows. We conclude neither BNF nor any or its variants are suitable to express the range of modern Computer Science and Mathematical Logic, since MBNF is used frequently in these fields and differs from BNF and its variants on a deep conceptual level. In particular, BNF and its variants deal with strings and the trees detailing string building operations, both of which are finite with a natural ordering. MBNF, on the other hand, deals with the richer syntactic structures used in writing mathematics, which may be infinite rather than finite and which are defined modulo some notion of equivalence, where it is largely irrelevant to understanding the syntax whether or not members of that equivalence class have a canonical order. The operations allowed in BNF and its variants are defined as standard alongside its production rules and belong to the class of string building operations. Rather than define operations in this way, MBNF adds the concept of syntax to the broader category of mathematical entities and the concept of the production rule to a broader class of mathematical operators. These concepts may then be used alongside any concept the author needs from the field of mathematics.

While some work exists which might address some aspects of MBNF, none provides a full definition. We are not aware of another work that highlights all the differences we have here, or that recognises MBNF as a significant departure from BNF, as opposed to merely a syntactic variant, so this is unsurprising. We offer this paper as a reference point for the main issues which authors aiming to define this notation need to overcome.

---

[8] As previously noted we avoid that name, because MBNF is a concrete form.

References

1. Backus, J.W.: The syntax and semantics of the proposed international algebraic language of the Zurich ACM-GAMM conference. In: IFIP Congress (1959). https://dblp.uni-trier.de/db/conf/ifip/ifip1959.html
2. Backus, J.W., et al.: Revised report on the algorithm language ALGOL 60. Commun. ACM **6**(1), 1–17 (1963)
3. Berstel, J., Lauve, A., Reutenauer, C., Saliola, F.V.: Combinatorics on Words. Christoffel Words and Repetitions in Words. American Mathematical Society (AMS), Providence (2009)
4. Chang, S., Felleisen, M.: The call-by-need lambda calculus, revisited. In: Seidl [30]
5. Chomsky, N.: Three models for the description of language. IRE Trans. Inf. Theory **2**(3), 113–124 (1956)
6. Crocker, D., Overell, P. (ed.): Augmented BNF for syntax specifications: ABNF. Internet Requests for Comments (2008). http://www.rfc-editor.org/info/rfc5234
7. Dolan, S., Mycroft, A.: Polymorphism, subtyping, and type inference in MLsub. In: Fluet [11]
8. Eberhart, C., Hirschowitz, T., Seiller, T.: An intensionally fully-abstract sheaf model for π^*. In: Moss, L.S., Sobocinski, P., (eds.) 6th Conference on Algebra and Coalgebra in Computer Science (CALCO 2015), vol. 35 of Leibniz International Proceedings in Informatics (LIPIcs), Dagstuhl, Germany (2015). Schloss Dagstuhl-Leibniz-Zentrum fuer Informatik
9. Farmer, W.M.: The formalization of syntax-based mathematical algorithms using quotation and evaluation. CoRR, abs/1305.6052 (2013). http://arxiv.org/abs/1305.6052
10. Farrel, A.: Routing Backus-Naur form (RBNF): A syntax used to form encoding rules in various routing protocol specifications. RFC 5511, RFC Editor (2009). https://tools.ietf.org/html/rfc5511
11. Fluet, M., (ed.): POPL 2017: Proceedings of the 44th ACM SIGPLAN Symposium on Principles of Programming Languages. ACM, New York (2017)
12. Ford, B.: Parsing expression grammars: a recognition-based syntactic foundation. In Proceedings of the 31st ACM SIGPLAN-SIGACT Symposium on Principles of Programming Languages, POPL 2004, ACM, New York (2004). http://doi.acm.org/10.1145/964001.964011
13. Forsberg, M., Ranta, A.: The labelled BNF grammar formalism (2005)
14. Germane, K., Might, M.: A posteriori environment analysis with pushdown delta CFA. In: Fluet [11]
15. Grewe, S., Erdweg, S., Pacak, A., Raulf, M., Mezini, M.: Exploration of language specifications by compilation to first-order logic. Sci. Comput. Program. **155**, 146–172 (2018)
16. Grigore, R.: Java generics are turing complete. In: Fluet [11]
17. Hopcroft, J.E., Motwani, R., Ullman, J.D.: Introduction to Automata Theory, Languages, and Computation, 3rd edn. Addison-Wesley Longman Publishing Co., Inc., Boston (2006)
18. Inoue, J., Taha, W.: Reasoning about multi-stage programs. In: Seidl [30]
19. Ion, P.D.F., Poppelier, N., Carlisle, D., Miner, R.R.: Mathematical markup language (MathML) version 2.0. W3C recommendation, W3C (2001). https://www.w3.org/TR/MathML2/chapter3.html
20. ISO: Information technology - Syntactic metalanguage - Extended BNF. Standard, International Organization for Standardization, Geneva, CH (1996)
21. ISO: Information technology - Open Document Format for Office Applications (OpenDocument) v1.2 - Part 1: OpenDocument Schema. Standard, International Organization for Standardization, Geneva, CH (2015)
22. Knuth, D.E.: The TeXbook. Addison-Wesley Professional, Boston (1986)

23. Llana Díaz, L.F., Núñez, M.: Testing semantics for unbounded nondeterminism. In: Lengauer, C., Griebl, M., Gorlatch, S. (eds.) Euro-Par 1997. LNCS, vol. 1300, pp. 538–545. Springer, Heidelberg (1997). https://doi.org/10.1007/BFb0002780

24. Mann, P.B.: A translational BNF grammar notation (TBNF). SIGPLAN Not. **41**(4), 16–23 (2006)

25. Milner, R., Parrow, J., Walker, D.: A calculus of mobile processes, i. Inf. Comput. **100**(1), 1–40 (1992). https://doi.org/10.1016/0890-5401(92)90008-4

26. Pfenning, F., Elliott, C.: Higher-order abstract syntax. In: Proceedings of the ACM SIG-PLAN 1988 Conference on Programming Language Design and Implementation, PLDI 1988. ACM, New York (1988) https://doi.org/10.1145/53990.54010

27. Pierce, B.C.: Types and Programming Languages, 1st edn. The MIT Press, Cambridge (2002)

28. Ranta, A.: Grammatical framework. J. Funct. Program. **14**(2), 145–189 (2004). https://doi.org/10.1017/S0956796803004738

29. Reynolds, J.C.: Theories of Programming Languages, 1st edn. Cambridge University Press, New York (2009)

30. Seidl, H. (ed.): Programming Languages and Systems. Springer, Heidelberg (2012)

31. Sewell, P., et al.: Ott: effective tool support for the working semanticist. SIGPLAN Not. **42**(9), 1–12 (2007)

32. Steele Jr., G.L.: It's time for a new old language. In: Proceedings of the 22nd ACM SIGPLAN Symposium on Principles and Practice of Parallel Programming, PPoPP 2017. ACM, New York (2017)

33. Tobisawa, K.: A meta lambda calculus with cross-level computation. In: POPL 2015 (2015)

34. Toronto, N., McCarthy, J.: Computing in Cantor's paradise with λ_{ZFC}. In: Schrijvers, T., Thiemann, P. (eds.) FLOPS 2012. LNCS, vol. 7294, pp. 290–306. Springer, Heidelberg (2012). https://doi.org/10.1007/978-3-642-29822-6_23

35. Zaytsev, V.: The grammar hammer of 2012. CoRR, abs/1212.4446 (2012). https://arxiv.org/abs/1212.4446

MMTTeX: Connecting Content and Narration-Oriented Document Formats

Florian Rabe[1,2(✉)] (iD)

[1] LRI, Université Paris Sud, Orsay, France
florian.rabe@gmail.com
[2] Erlangen-Nuremberg, Erlangen, Germany

Abstract. Narrative, presentation-oriented assistant systems for mathematics such as LaTeX on the one hand and formal, content-oriented ones such as proof assistants and computer algebra systems on the other hand have so far been developed and used largely independently. The former excel at communicating mathematical knowledge and the latter at certifying its correctness.

MMTTeX aims at combining the advantages of the two paradigms. Concretely, we use LaTeX for the narrative and MMT for the content-oriented representation. Formal objects may be written in MMT and imported into LaTeX documents or written in the LaTeX document directly. In the latter case, MMT parses and checks the formal content during LaTeX compilation and substitutes it with LaTeX presentation macros.

Besides checking the formal objects, this allows generating higher-quality LaTeX than could easily be produced by hand, e.g., by inserting hyperlinks and tooltips into formulas. Moreover, it allows reusing formalizations across narrative documents as well as between formal and narrative ones. As a case study, the present document was already written with MMTTeX.

1 Introduction

A major open problem in mathematical document authoring is to elegantly combine formal and informal mathematical knowledge. Multiple proof assistants and controlled natural language systems have developed custom formats for that purpose, e.g., [Wen11, TB85, WAB07, CFK+09]. Other languages L allow for integrating LaTeX into L-source files in a literate programming style (e.g., lhs2tex[1] for Haskell) or for integrating L-source chunks into LaTeX files (e.g., SageTeX[2] for SageMath). The design of MMTTeX is close to the latter, i.e., to combine MMT and LaTeX sources.

---

[1] https://www.andres-loeh.de/lhs2tex/.
[2] https://github.com/sagemath/sagetex.

© Springer Nature Switzerland AG 2019
C. Kaliszyk et al. (Eds.): CICM 2019, LNAI 11617, pp. 205–210, 2019.
https://doi.org/10.1007/978-3-030-23250-4_14

The goal of MMTTeX is very similar to sTeX [Koh08], where authors add content markup that allows converting a LaTeX to an OMDoc document. MMT-TeX differs in several ways: authors write *fully formal* content in MMT syntax [RK13] directly in the LaTeX source, either in addition to or instead of informal text; and MMT is used to type-check the formal parts during LaTeX compilation workflow. This enables several advanced features: Formal content in LaTeX sources can use or be used by MMT content written elsewhere; in particular, background knowledge formalized elsewhere can be used inside the LaTeX document. And formulas written in MMT syntax are not only type-checked but result in high-quality pdf by, e.g., displaying inferred types as tooltips or adding hyperlinks to operator occurrences.

Online Resources. All resources are available as a part of the MMT repository[3]. These resources include the MMT and LaTeX side of the implementation, the system documentation, and the sources of this paper, which is itself written with MMTTeX.

2   Design and Behavior

2.1   Overview

MMTTeX consists of two components:

- an MMT plugin `latex-mmt` that converts MMT theories to LaTeX packages,
- a small LaTeX package `mmttex.sty` (about 100 loc with only standard dependencies), which allows for embedding MMT content.

The two components are tied together in bibtex-style, i.e.,

1. While running LaTeX on `doc.tex`, `mmttex.sty` produces an additional output file `doc.tex.mmt`, which is a regular MMT file. `doc.tex.mmt` contains all formal content that was embedded in the `tex` document.
2. `latex-mmt` is run on `doc.tex.mmt` and produces `doc.tex.mmt.sty`. This type-checks the embedded formal content and generates macro definitions for rendering it in the following step.
3. When running LaTeX the next time, the package `doc.tex.mmt.sty` is included at the beginning. Now all embedded formal content is rendered using the macro definitions from the previous step. If the formal content changed, `doc.tex.mmt` also changes.

Note that `latex-mmt` only needs to be re-run if the formal content document changed. That is important for sharing documents with colleagues or publishers who want to or can only run plain LaTeX: by simply supplying `doc.tex.mmt.sty` along with `doc.tex`, running plain LaTeX is sufficient to build `doc.pdf`.

---

[3] https://github.com/UniFormal/MMT/tree/devel/src/latex-mmt.

2.2   Formal Content in LaTeX Documents

`mmttex.sty` provides presentation-*irrelevant* and presentation-*relevant* macros for embedding formal content in addition to resp. instead of informal text.

Presentation-irrelevant macros only affect `doc.tex.mmt` and do not produce anything that is visible in the pdf document. These macros can be used to embed a (partial) formalization of the informal text. The formalization can occur as a single big chunk, be interspersed with the LaTeX source akin to parallel markup, or be anything in between. Importantly, if split into multiple chunks, one formal chunk may introduce names that are referred to in other formal chunks, and LaTeX environments are used to build nested scopes for these names.

At the lowest level, this is implemented by a single macro that takes a string and appends it to `doc.tex.mmt`. On top, we provide a suite of syntactic sugar that mimics the structure of the MMT language.

As a simple example, we will now define the theory of groups informally and embed its parallel MMT formalization into this paper. Of course, the embedded formalization is invisible in the pdf. Therefore, we added listings in gray that show the presentation-irrelevant macros that occur in the LaTeX sources of this paper and that embed the formalization. If this is confusing, readers may want to inspect the source code of this paper at the URL given above.

Our example will refer to the theory SFOLEQ, which formalizes sorted first-order logic with equality and is defined in the `examples` archive of MMT.[4] To refer to it conveniently, we will import its namespace under the abbreviation ex.

```
\mmtimport{ex}{http://cds.omdoc.org/examples}
\begin{mmttheory}{Group}{ex:?SFOLEQ}
```

A group consists of

- a set U,
  ```
  \mmtconstant{U}{sort}{}{}
  ```
- an operation $U \to U \to U$, written as infix $*$,
  ```
  \mmtconstant{operation}{tm U --> tm U --> tm U}{}
                                              {1 * 2 prec 50}
  ```
- an element e of U called the unit
  ```
  \mmtconstant{unit}{tm U}{}{e}
  ```
- an inverse element function $U \to U$, written as postfix $'$ and with higher precedence than $*$.
  ```
  \mmtconstant{inv}{tm U --> tm U}{}{1 ' prec 60}
  ```

We omit the axioms.
```
\end{mmttheory}
```

Here the environment mmttheory wraps around the theory. It takes two arguments: the name and the meta-theory, i.e., the logic in which the theory is written.

The macro mmtconstant introduces a constant declaration inside a theory. It takes 4 arguments: the name, type, definiens, and notation. All but the name may be empty.

---

[4] See https://gl.mathhub.info/MMT/examples/blob/master/source/logic/sfol.mmt.

We can also use the MMT module system, e.g., the following creates a theory that extends Group with a definition of division (where square brackets are the notation for λ-abstraction employed by SFOLEQ):

```
\begin{mmttheory}{Division}{ex:?SFOLEQ}
\mmtinclude{?Group}
\mmtconstant{division}
    {tm U --> tm U --> tm U}{[x,y] x*y'}{1 / 2 prec 50}
```

Note that we have not closed the theory yet, i.e., future formal objects will be processed in the scope of Division.

Presentation-relevant macros result in changes to the pdf document. The most important such macro provided by `mmttex.sty` is one that takes a math formula in MMT syntax and parses, type-checks, and renders it. For this macro, we provide special syntax that allows using quotes instead of dollars to have formulas processed by MMT: if we write "F" (including the quotes) instead of F, then F is considered to be a math formula in MMT syntax and processed by MMT. For example, the formula "forall [x] x/x = e" is parsed by MMT relative to the current theory, i.e., Division; then MMT type-checks it and substitutes it with LATEX commands. In the previous sentence, the LATEX source of the quoted formula is additionally wrapped into a verbatim macro to avoid processing by MMT; if we remove that wrapper, the quoted formula is rendered into pdf as $\forall[x]\frac{x}{x}\doteq e$.

Type checking the above formula infers the type tm U of the bound variable x. This is shown as a tooltip when hovering over the binding location of x. (Tooltip display is supported by many but not all pdf viewers. Unfortunately, pdf tooltips are limited to strings so that we cannot show tooltips containing LATEX or MathML renderings even though we could generate them easily.) Similarly, the sort argument of equality is inferred. Moreover, every operator carries a hyperlink to the point of its declaration. Currently, these links point to the MMT server, which is assumed to run locally.

This is implemented as follows:

1. An MMT formula "F" simply produces a macro call \mmt@X for for a running counter X. If that macro is undefined, a placeholder is shown and the user is warned that a second compilation is needed. Additionally, a definition mmt@X = F in MMT syntax is placed into `doc.tex.mmt`.
2. When `latex-mmt` processes that definition, it additionally generates a macro definition \newcommand{\mmt@X}{$\overline{F}$} in `doc.tex.mmt.sty`, where $\overline{F}$ is the intended LATEX representation of F.
3. During the next compilation, MMT @X produces the rendering of $\overline{F}$. If F did not type-check, additional a LATEX error is produced with the error message.

Before we continue, we close the current theory:
```
\end{mmttheory}
```

2.3   Converting MMT Content to LaTeX

We run `latex-mmt` on every theory T that is part of the background knowledge, e.g., SFOLEQ, and on all theories that are part of `doc.tex.mmt`, resulting in one LaTeX package (sty file) each. This package contains one RequirePackage macro for every dependency and one `\newcommand` macro for every constant declaration. `doc.tex.mmt.sty` is automatically included at the beginning of the document and thus brings all necessary generated LaTeX packages into scope.

The generated `\newcommand` macros use (only) the notation of the constant. For example, for the constant named operator from above, the generated command is essentially. `\newcommand{\operator}[2]{#1*#2}`. Technically, however, the macro definition is much more complex: Firstly, instead of `#1*#2`, we produce a macro definition that generates the right tooltips, hyperreferences, etc. Secondly, instead of `\operator,,` we use the fully qualified MMT URI as the LaTeX macro name to avoid ambiguity when multiple theories define constants of the same local name.

The latter is an important technical difference between MMTTeX and sTeX [Koh08]: sTeX intentionally generates short human-friendly macro names because they are meant to be called by humans. That requires relatively complex scope management and dynamic loading of macro definitions to avoid ambiguity. But that is inessential in our case because our macros are called by generated LaTeX commands (namely those in the definiens of `\mmt@X`). Nonetheless, it would be easy to add macros to `mmttex.sty` for creating aliases with human-friendly names.

The conversion from MMT to LaTeX can be easily run in batch mode so that any content available in MMT can be easily used as background knowledge in LaTeX documents.

3   Conclusion

We have presented a system that allows embedding formal MMT content inside LaTeX documents. The formal content is type-checked in a way that does not affect any existing LaTeX work flows and results in higher quality LaTeX than could be easily produced manually. Moreover, the formal content may use and be used by any MMT content formalized elsewhere, which allows interlinking across document formats.

Of course, we are not able to verify the informal parts of a document this way—only those formulas that are written in MMT syntax are checked. But our design supports both gradual formalization and parallel formal-informal representations.

It is intriguing to apply the same technology to formal proofs. This is already possible for formal proof terms, but those often bear little resemblance to informal proofs. Once MMT supports a language for structured proofs, that could be used to write formal proofs in MMTTeX. Morever, future work could apply

MMT as a middleware between LaTeX and other tools, e.g., MMT could run a computation through a computer algebra system to verify a computation in LaTeX.

Acknowledgments. Both this paper and the MMTTeX implementation were redone from scratch by the author. But that work benefited substantially from two unpublished prototypes that were previously developed in collaboration with Deyan Ginev, Mihnea Iancu, and Michael Kohlhase. The author was supported by DFG grant RA-18723-1 OAF and EU grant Horizon 2020 ERI 676541 OpenDreamKit.

References

[CFK+09] Cramer, M., Fisseni, B., Koepke, P., Kühlwein, D., Schröder, B., Veldman, J.: The naproche project controlled natural language proof checking of mathematical texts. In: Fuchs, N.E. (ed.) CNL 2009. LNCS (LNAI), vol. 5972, pp. 170–186. Springer, Heidelberg (2010). https://doi.org/10.1007/978-3-642-14418-9_11

[Koh08] Kohlhase, M.: Using LaTeX as a semantic markup format. Math. Comput. Sci. **2**(2), 279–304 (2008)

[RK13] Rabe, F., Kohlhase, M.: A scalable module system. Inf. Comput. **230**(1), 1–54 (2013)

[TB85] Trybulec, A., Blair, H.: Computer assisted reasoning with MIZAR. In: Joshi, A. (ed.) Proceedings of the 9th International Joint Conference on Artificial Intelligence, pp. 26–28. Morgan Kaufmann (1985)

[WAB07] Wagner, M., Autexier, S., Benzmüller, C.: PLATO: a mediator between text-editors and proof assistance systems. In: Autexier, S., Benzmüller, C. (eds.) 7th Workshop on User Interfaces for Theorem Provers (UITP 2006), pp. 87–107. Elsevier (2007)

[Wen11] Wenzel, M.: Isabelle as document-oriented proof assistant. In: Davenport, J.H., Farmer, W.M., Urban, J., Rabe, F. (eds.) CICM 2011. LNCS (LNAI), vol. 6824, pp. 244–259. Springer, Heidelberg (2011). https://doi.org/10.1007/978-3-642-22673-1_17

Diagram Combinators in MMT

Florian Rabe[1,2] and Yasmine Sharoda[3(✉)]

[1] Computer Science, FAU Erlangen-Nürnberg, Erlangen, Germany
florian.rabe@fau.de
[2] LRI, Université Paris Sud, Orsay, France
[3] Computing and Software, McMaster University, Hamilton, Canada
sharodym@mcmaster.ca

Abstract. Formal libraries, especially large ones, usually employ modularity to build and maintain large theories efficiently. Although the techniques used to achieve modularity vary between systems, most of them can be understood as operations in the category of theories and theory morphisms. This yields a representation of libraries as diagrams in this category, with all theory-forming operations extending the diagram.

However, as libraries grow even bigger, it is starting to become important to build these diagrams modularly as well, i.e., we need languages and tools that support computing entire diagrams at once. A simple example would be to systematically apply the same operation to all theories in a diagram and return both the new diagram and the morphisms that relate the old one to the new one.

In this work, we introduce such diagram combinators as an extension to the MMT language and tool. We provide many important combinators, and our extension allows library developers to define arbitrary new ones. We evaluate our framework by building a library of algebraic theories in an extremely compact way.

1 Introduction and Related Work

Motivation. Throughout the development of formal mathematical languages, we can see how when the size of formalizations reached new scales, novel concepts and language features became necessary. In particular, as libraries grow bigger and require extensive maintenance, the elimination of redundancy becomes even more critical.

Originally, only basic declarations such as operators, and axioms were used. Over time *theories* were made explicit in order to name groups of basic declarations. Then calculi were introduced to build larger theories from smaller ones. Using the language of category theory proved particularly useful: *theory morphisms* could be used to relate theories, and operators like *colimits* could be used to compose them. Structured theories [1,14] introduced, among other

---

The authors were supported by DFG grant RA-18723-1 OAF and EU grant Horizon 2020 ERI 676541 OpenDreamKit.

C. Kaliszyk et al. (Eds.): CICM 2019, LNAI 11617, pp. 211–226, 2019.
https://doi.org/10.1007/978-3-030-23250-4_15

operations, unions and translations of theories. Systems like OBJ [7] and most comprehensively CASL [4] further developed these ideas.

Today many major systems support some language features for theory formation such as Isabelle's locale expressions [8] or Coq's module system. Specware [15] is notable for introducing colimits on arbitrary diagrams early on. For maximizing reuse, it is advisable to apply the little theories approach [6] that formalizes the mathematical principle of making every statement in the smallest theory that supports it—even if that means retroactively splitting theories up into smaller ones. This leads to an organization of formal libraries as large diagrams of theories and theory morphisms, in which results can be moved between theories along morphisms.

We believe that one next step in this development will be *diagram operations* that operate not just on individual theories but on entire diagrams. They will allow building structured diagrams by reusing diagram-level structure systematically. For example, one might build a diagram with > 100 theories for the algebraic hierarchy (containing the theories of groups, rings, etc.) and then, in a single operation, systematically duplicate it and add the axiom of finiteness to each theory.

Contribution. We develop a formal language for named diagrams of theories and operations on such diagrams. To our knowledge, this is the first time such a language has been developed systematically.

We work in the context of the MMT system [13], which is practical for us because it already provides a logic-independent language for structured theories and morphisms. Moreover, because its kernel is designed to be extensible [12], even disruptively new concepts like ours can be added with relative ease. However, our ideas are not tied to MMT and can be transferred easily to any formalism for diagram of theories.

Our solution is extensible in the sense that users can add new diagram operators, beside the initial suite that we provide.

Related Work. Our work is inspired by and generalizes two recent results. Firstly, the DOL language [5] and its implementation in Hets [9] uses named diagrams together with operations for building larger diagrams by merging or removing elements from smaller ones. It operates on names only, i.e., diagrams are formed by listing the names of subdiagrams, theories, and morphisms that should be included or excluded. DOL is developed in the context of ontology languages, but the ideas are logic-independent.

Secondly, the MathScheme project revisited theory combinators in [2]. This work recognized that many theory-formation operators can actually be better understood as operators returning diagrams, e.g., the pushout operator return not only a theory but also three morphisms. It does not use diagrams as input yet, and we believe our generalization brings out its ideas much more clearly.

Overview. The structure of the paper is very simple. In Sect. 2, we recap mmt theories and morphisms. Moreover, we introduce MMT diagrams, a new definition that adapts the standard notion of diagrams from category theory for our purposes. In Sect. 3, we specify our initial library of diagram operators. Some of these operators are closely related to existing ones, while others are new. Finally in Sect. 4, we describe how diagrams and diagram operators are implemented in MMT.

2 Diagrams

2.1 Theories and Morphisms

The main building blocks of diagrams are theories and morphisms, and we briefly introduce MMT's definitions for them. We refer to [11,12] for details.

Definition 1 (Theory). *A **theory** is a pair of an optional theory M—the **meta-theory**—and a list of declarations.*

*A **declaration** is of the form $c\,[: A]\,[= t]\,[\#N]$ where*

- *c is a fresh identifier—the **name**,*
- *A is an optional expression—the **type**,*
- *t is an optional expression—the **definiens**,*
- *N is an optional **notation** (which we only need in this paper to make examples legible).*

*Every theory T induces a set of T-**expressions**. The details of how expressions are formed are not essential for our purposes except that they are syntax trees formed from (among other things) references to constants declared in T or its meta-theory M.*

The role of the meta-theory is to make MMT logic-independent. Individual logics L are formalized as theories as well, which declare the logic's primitive operators and typing rules and are then used as the meta-theory of L-theories.

Example 1. The following is an MMT theory declaration that introduces the theory Magma with typed first-order logic as the meta-theory:

```
theory Magma : SFOL =
    U : type
    op : U → U → U # 1 ∘ 2
```

The theory Semigroup arises by extending Magma with the axiom

$$\text{associativity} \ : \ \forall\,[x,y,z]\ (x \circ y) \circ z \doteq x \circ (y \circ z)$$

Definition 2 (Morphism). *Given two theories S and T a **morphism** $S \to T$ consists of an optional meta-morphism and a list of assignments.*

*An **assignment** is of the form $c := t$ for an S-constant c and a T-expressions t, and there must be exactly one assignment for every S-constant.*

*Every morphism $m : S \to T$ induces the **homomorphic extension** $m(-)$ that maps S-expressions to T-expressions. The details depend on the (omitted) definition of expressions, and we only say that $m(E)$ arises by replacing every reference to an S-constant c with the expression t provided by the corresponding assignment in m.*

The role of the meta-morphism is to translate the meta-theory of S (if any) to the meta-theory of T. For our purposes, it is sufficient to assume that we work with a fixed meta-theory and all meta-morphisms are the identity.

We omit the typing conditions on assignments and only mention that t must be such that the homomorphic extension preserves all judgments, e.g., if $\vdash_S t : A$ then $\vdash_T m(t) : m(A)$. This preservation theorem is critical to move definitions and theorems between theories along morphisms in a way that preserves theoremhood.

Example 2. The inclusion morphism from `Magma` to `Semigroup` can be spelled out explicit as

```
Magma2Semigroup : Magma → Semigroup =id_SFOL
   U  := U
   op := op
```

Let `AdditiveMagma` be the variant of `Magma` with the operator `op` renamed to `+`. Then the following defines the morphism that performs the renaming:

```
Additive : Magma → AdditiveMagma =id_SFOL
   U  := U
   op := +
```

Both morphisms are trivial because they are just renamings. The following morphism, whips flips the arguments of the magma operation is more complex:

```
Flip : Magma → Magma =id_SFOL
   U  := U
   op := λ x,y.y ∘ x
```

2.2 Diagrams

Using the straightforward definitions of identity and composition, MMT theories and morphisms form a category `THY`. Category theory defines *diagrams* over `THY` as pairs of a (usually finite) category G and a functor $D : G \to$ `THY`. Here G only defines the graph structure of the diagram, and the actual G-objects are only relevant as distinct labels for the nodes and edges of the diagram. D assigns to each node or edge a theory resp. morphism.

However, for an implementation in a formal system, this abstract definition is not optimal, and we adapt it slightly. Moreover, we allow each diagram to have a *distinguished* node, and we allow morphisms to be *implicit*. These are novel variations of how diagrams are usually defined that will be very helpful later on:

Definition 3 (Diagrams). *A **diagram** D consists of*

- *a list of **nodes**, each written as* $\mathrm{Node}(l, D(l))$ *where*
  - l *is an identifier—the **label***
  - $D(l)$ *is a theory*

- a list of **edges**, each written as $\mathrm{Edge}(l, d \overset{i}{\to} c, D(l))$ where
  - l is an identifier—the **label**
  - d and c are labels of nodes—the **domain** and **codomain**
  - $D(l)$ is a morphism $D(d) \to D(c)$
  - i is a boolean flag that may or may not be present—indicating whether the edge is **implicit**
- an optional label $D^{\mathtt{dist}}$ of a node—the **distinguished** node

The labels of nodes and edges must be unique, and we write (as already used above) $D(l)$ for the theory/morphism with label l.

Every node may be the codomain of at most one implicit edge, and we write $f \overset{\vec{e}}{\to} t$ if e is the list of implicit edges forming the path from node f to node t. Here $\vec{e}$ is uniquely determined if it exists.

Remark 1 (Distinguished Nodes). In practice, diagram operations are often used to define a specific theory. The pushout, as we show in Example 3, can be seen as a map between diagrams. But often we want to identify the resulting diagram with the new theory it contains. This is the purpose of using a distinguished node: if the pushout operator marks the new node as distinguished, we can later refer to the diagram as a whole when we mean that node.

Remark 2 (Implicit Edges). Implicit MMT morphisms were introduced in [10] as a generalization of inclusion morphisms. The main idea is that the collection of all implicit morphisms forms a commutative sub-diagram of the (not necessarily commutative) diagram of all theories and morphisms named in a user's development. Identity and inclusions morphisms are always implicit, and so is the composition of implicit morphisms. This has the effect that for any two theories S and T there may be at most one implicit morphism $S \to T$, which MMT can infer automatically. MMT uses for a number of implicit coercions that simplify concrete syntax, e.g., to allow S-expressions in T-contexts.

When implementing diagram operators, it will be particularly useful to conveniently refer to the implicit morphisms into the distinguished node.

In general, the same theory/morphism may occur at multiple nodes/edges of the same diagram with different labels. However, very often we have the following situation: a node/edge refers simply to a previously named theory/morphism, which only occurs once in the diagram. If a theory/morphism has not been previously named or occurs multiple times, we have to generate labels for them.

Example 3 (Diagram). The morphism `Magma2Semigroup` from Example 2 can be seen as a diagram D_1 with

- $\mathrm{Node}(\texttt{Magma}, (\mathrm{SFOL}, U : \ldots, \mathrm{op} : \ldots))$
- $\mathrm{Node}(\texttt{Semigroup}, \mathrm{SFOL}, U : \ldots, \mathrm{op} : \ldots, \mathtt{associative} : \ldots)$
- $\mathrm{Edge}(\texttt{Magma2Semigroup}, \texttt{Magma} \overset{i}{\to} \texttt{Semigroup}, id_{\mathrm{SFOL}}, U := U, op := op)$

where we have omitted the types for brevity. We made this edge implicit because we want it to be inferred whenever a morphism `Magma` → `Semigroup` is needed so that we do not have to write `Magma2Semigroup` explicitly.

Let D_2 be the corresponding diagram for `AdditiveMagma`. We can now already indicate the usefulness of diagram operators: if we had a diagram operator to glue D_1 and D_2 together into a span, and another diagram operator to build the pushout of a span, we could simply define `AdditiveSemigroup` as the resulting pushout diagram:

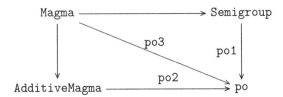

Here, we draw only labels for each node/edge. The labels `po`, `po1`, `po2`, and `po3` refer to nodes/edges added by the pushout operator.

Of course, we want `AdditiveSemigroup` to be the theory at node `po`, not the entire diagram. Therefore, the pushout operator should return a diagram in which `po` is the distinguished node. That way, if we use `AdditiveSemigroup` as a theory, the system can infer which theory is meant. Similarly, we mark the morphism `po3` as the implicit edge of the morphism, so whenever we use `AdditiveSemigroup` as a morphism, the system infers `po3`. Above and in the sequel, we follow the convention of drawing distinguished nodes and implicit arrows in blue.

3   Operations on Diagrams

There is a wide range of possible operations on diagrams. Our realization in MMT is extensible: as we describe in Sect. 4, we built a general framework in which users can implement new operators. In this section, we specify the individual operators that we are implementing within this framework. In Sect. 3.1, we introduce operators based on formation combinators like extend or pushout. In Sect. 3.2, we introduce basic operators for building diagrams by simply aggregating previously defined theories and morphisms. This includes operators for set-theoretic operations like unions. In Sect. 3.3, we combine the previous operators to introduce many theories at once.

All of the above operators can be defined for an arbitrary meta-theory. In Sect. 3.4, we give an example of an advanced, meta-theory-specific operator. To simplify the presentation, from now on, we assume that unless mentioned otherwise all theories have the same fixed meta-theory so that we can omit it from the notation.

3.1   Theory Formation Operators

Extension. Consider the definition of Semigroup in Example 1. We can define
Semigroup more easily using a theory operator for extension:

$$\texttt{Semigroup} := \texttt{Magma\,EXTEND}\,\{\,\texttt{associativity} : \cdots\}$$

The central idea of [2] is that the combinator should create not just the theory
Semigroup but also the morphism Magma2Semigroup. While Magma2Semigroup
is trivial, more general combinators (in particular colimits) would introduce
more and more complex new morphisms. Notably, these morphisms are often
computed anyway when evaluating a combinator; thus, it would be wasteful to
throw them away after building the theory.

  We can capture this elegantly by defining extension as a diagram operator:
We define $D\,\texttt{EXTEND}\,\{\Sigma\}$, where D is a diagram and Σ is a list of declarations,
as the diagram consisting of the following components:

- all nodes and arrows in D.
- a new node labeled **pres** with all declarations in $D(D^{\texttt{dist}})$ and Σ.
- a new edge $\text{Edge}(\texttt{extend}, D^{\texttt{dist}} \xrightarrow{i} \texttt{pres}, id)$ where id maps every constant to
  itself,
- **pres** is the distinguished node.

Example 4. We build some extensions of Magma that we will use later on. We
also recover Magma as an extension of the theory Carrier.

```
Carrier  := Empty EXTEND {U: type}
Magma  := Carrier EXTEND
          {op : U → U → U # 1 ∘ 2}
Semigroup := Magma EXTEND
  {associative_op : ∀ [x,y,z] (x ∘ y) ∘ z ≐ x ∘ (y ∘ z)}
Commutative := Magma EXTEND
  {commutative_op : ∀ [x,y] x ∘ y ≐ y ∘ x}
Idempotent := Magma EXTEND
  {idempotent_op : ∀ [x] x ∘ x ≐ x }
```

  In the sequel, we give a few more examples how theory-forming operators
can be captured elegantly as diagram operators. Our presentation and notation
roughly follows [2] and Table 1 gives an overview.

Renaming. We define $D\,\texttt{RENAME}\,\{c \rightsquigarrow c'\}$, where D is a diagram and c and c' are
names, as the diagram consisting of the following components:

- all nodes and arrows in D,
- a new node **pres** which contains all declarations in $D(D^{\texttt{dist}})$ with every
  occurrence of c replaced by the expression c',
- a new edge $\text{Edge}(\texttt{rename}, D^{\texttt{dist}} \xrightarrow{i} \texttt{pres}, m)$ where m maps $c := c'$ and other
  constants to themselves.

Table 1. Theory-forming diagram operators

Theory Expression	Input Diagram(s)	Output Diagram
D extends Σ	$\longrightarrow D^{\text{dist}}$	$\longrightarrow D^{\text{dist}} \longrightarrow$ pres
D rename r	$\longrightarrow D^{\text{dist}}$	$\longrightarrow D^{\text{dist}} \longrightarrow$ pres
combine D_1 r_1 D_2 r_2 mixin D_1 r_1 D_2 r_2	$S \longrightarrow D_1^{\text{dist}}$ $\downarrow$ D_2^{dist}	$S \longrightarrow D_1^{\text{dist}} \longrightarrow R_1$ $\downarrow$ D_2^{dist} $\downarrow$ $R_2 \longrightarrow$ pres
D_1 ; D_2	$S \longrightarrow D_1^{\text{dist}}$ $D_1^{\text{dist}} \longrightarrow D_2^{\text{dist}}$	$S \longrightarrow D_1^{\text{dist}} \longrightarrow D_2^{\text{dist}}$

In general, input diagrams may contain arbitrary other nodes/edges, which are copied over to the output diagram. Distinguished nodes and implicit edges are shown in blue.

Example 5. We obtain additive and multiplicative variants of Magma as follows:

```
AdditiveMagma       := Magma RENAME {op ⤳ +}
MultiplicativeMagma := Magma RENAME {op ⤳ *}
```

Combine. Combine is a pushout operator for the special case where both of the inputs are embedding morphisms. Intuitively, an embedding is a composition of extensions and renames:

Definition 4 (Embedding). *An **embedding** is a morphism in which each assignment is of the form $c := c'$ for a definition-less constant c' and in which there are no two assignment with the same constant on the right-hand side.*

We say that a diagram D has an embedding $e : S \to T$ if $S \xrightarrow{\vec{e}} T$ such that each e_i is an extension or a renaming and their composition is an embedding.

The notation for combine is COMBINE D_1 r_1 D_2 r_2 where D_i are diagrams and r_i are lists of renamings like above. It is defined as follows:

– all nodes and edges in D_1 and D_2
– a new node **pres** which contains the following theory: Let $S \xrightarrow{\vec{e_i}} D_i^{\text{dist}}$ be the shortest embeddings in D_i such that the distinguished node of each D_i embeds the same node S. Let R_i be the theory that arises by applying all renamings in r_i to D_i^{dist}. **pres** is the canonical pushout (if that exists) of the two morphisms that arise by composing $\vec{e_i}$ and the renaming morphisms

$D_i^{\mathtt{dist}} \to R_i$. While the pushout always exists, the *canonical* pushout exists only if there are no name clashes, i.e., if every name of S is renamed in neither R_i or in the same way in both R_i. In that case, the pushout can reuse the names of S, R_1, and R_2.

– three new edges, $\mathtt{diag}$, $\mathtt{extend_1}$ and $\mathtt{extend_2}$ with codomain $\mathtt{pres}$ and domains S, $D_1^{\mathtt{dist}}$, resp. $D_2^{\mathtt{dist}}$.

– the new node is the distinguished node, and the edge $\mathtt{diag}$ is implicit.

Example 6. Continuing our running example, we define

```
Band := COMBINE Semigroup {} Idempotent {}
Semilattice := COMBINE Band {} Commutative {}
```

The two diagrams $\mathtt{Semigroup}$ and $\mathtt{Idempotent}$ have implicit edges that are extensions of $\mathtt{Magma}$, which becomes the common source node S. As a result of the pushout, the arrow $\mathtt{diag} : \mathtt{Magma} \to \mathtt{Band}$ is created and marked as implicit. Therefore, when defining $\mathtt{Semilattice}$ in the next step, $\mathtt{Magma}$ is again found as the common source of implicit edges into $\mathtt{Band}$ and $\mathtt{Commutative}$.

In the case of $\mathtt{Band}$ and $\mathtt{Semilattice}$, no name conflicts exist to begin with, so no renamings are needed. To show why renames are useful, consider the following:

```
AdditiveCommutative :=
    COMBINE Commutative {op ⤳ +} AdditiveMagma {}
```

Here $\mathtt{Magma}$ is again the common source, but the name *op* of $\mathtt{Magma}$ is renamed in two different way along the implicit edges into $\mathtt{Commutative}$ and $\mathtt{AdditiveMagma}$. This would preclude the existence of the canonical pushout because there is no canonical choice of which name to use. Therefore, an explicit rename is needed to remove the name conflict, and the name + is used in the pushout.

Mixin. Mixin is a special case of pushout related to combine. Whereas combine is symmetric, mixin takes one arbitrary morphism, one embedding, and two rename functions as arguments. Consider a morphism $m : S \to T$ and a diagram D with an embedding $e : S \to D^{\mathtt{dist}}$. We write $\mathtt{MIXIN}\, m\, r_1\, D\, r_2$ for the diagram consisting of:

– all nodes and edges from D,
– m and T (if not already part of D),
– a new node $\mathtt{pres}$ resulting from the pushout of m composed with $T \to R_1$ and e composed with $D^{\mathtt{dist}} \to R_2$. Similar to combine, rename functions are used to avoid name clashes.
– 3 edges similar to combine.

Example 7. Consider a theory $\mathtt{LeftNeutral}$ that extends $\mathtt{Magma}$ with a left-neutral element. The theory $\mathtt{RightNeutral}$ can be obtained by applying $\mathtt{mixin}$ to the view $\mathtt{Flip}$, from Example 2, with the diagram $\mathtt{LeftNeutral}$, as follows

```
RightNeutral := MIXIN Flip {} LeftNeutral {}
```

Composition. We write $D_1; D_2$ for the composition of two morphisms. Technically, our definition is more general because it allows arbitrary diagrams D_i as the arguments. The precise definition is that $D_1; D_2$ is defined if each D_i has an implicit edge e_i into D_i^{dist} such that the source S of e_2 is D_1^{dist}. In that case, $D_1; D_2$ contains the union of D_1 and D_2 with the distinguished node $(D_1; D_2)^{\text{dist}} = D_2^{\text{dist}}$ and a new implicit edge for the composition of e_1 and e_2.

Example 8. On our way to defining rings, we want to combine `AdditiveMagma` and `MultiplicativeMagma`. We cannot do that directly because the closest common source theory of the implicit edges in those two diagrams is still `Magma`. Thus, the pushout would not duplicate the magma operation. Instead we can use composition:

```
BiMagma  :=
  COMBINE (Magma ; AdditiveMagma) {}
          (Magma ; MultiplicativeMagma) {}
```

Because the composition diagrams have only a single implicit edge `Carrier` $\rightarrow$ `AdditiveMagma` resp. `Carrier` $\rightarrow$ `MultiplicativeMagma`, now `Carrier` is the closest common source so that we obtain the desired pushout over `Carrier`. The distinguished node of `BiMagma` now has two binary operations $+$ and $*$.

3.2   General Diagram Formation

Diagrams are essentially sets (of theories and morphisms). In particular, if all diagram components have already been defined (and thus named) previously, we can simply form diagrams by listing their names.

Diagram from Named Elements. Let $\vec{N}$ be a list of names of existing theories, morphisms, and diagrams. We write $\mathbf{diag}(N_1, \ldots, N_r)$ for the diagram consisting of

1. the listed theories and morphisms,
2. for any listed diagram, the distinguished node and all implicit edges into it
3. the domain and codomain of every morphism (if not anyway among the above)

We reuse the existing names as labels, i.e., each node/edge has label N_i.

Set-Theoretic Operations. We write $D \cup D'$ for the union of the diagrams D and D'. Here nodes/edges in D and D' are identified iff they agree on all components including their label. We define $D \cap D'$ accordingly. Note that $D \cup D'$ and $D \cap D'$ have no distinguished nodes.

Moreover, if the same label is used for different theories in the two diagrams D and D', we use qualified names to make sure the labels in the diagram $D \cup D'$ are unique.

Given a list of labels l_i of D, we write $D \setminus \vec{l}$ for the diagram that arises from D by removing

– all nodes/edges with label l_i
– all edges with domain or codomain l_i

The distinguished node of $D\backslash\vec{l}$ is the one of D if still present, and none otherwise.

Example 9. We create a diagram of the extensions of `Magma` defined in Example 4.

`MagmaExtensions := diag(Commutative, Semigroup, Idempotent)`

This diagram contains `Magma` and 3 implicit extension edges out of it.

3.3   Batch-Formation of Theories

Combining the operators from Sects. 3.1 and 3.2, we can introduce novel, very powerful operators that create many theories at once. We give two examples: batch combine and batch mixin.

Batch Combine. Consider a diagram D consisting of a set of extension arrows that all have the same source. We define **BCOMBINE** D as the diagram that applies the combine operation exhaustively to every pair of extensions.

Example 10. Continuing our running example, **BCOMBINE** `MagmaExtensions` adds the other 4 combinations of associativity, commutativity, idempotence that are not yet part of `MagmaExtensions`: The resulting diagram is

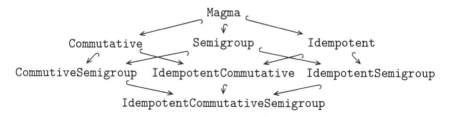

It is difficult to make sure that **BCOMBINE** generates nodes with the intended names. `Commutative`, `Semigroup`, and `Idempotent` (defined by the `extend` operator) all have a distinguished node with the same label `pres`. When applying the union operation to define `MagmaExtensions`, the resulting diagram has no distinguished node, but each node is labeled with qualified names like `Commutative_pres` etc. When performing the **BCOMBINE** operation, these labels can be used to generate reasonable names like `CommutativeSemigroup`. It is still tricky to define convenient syntax that allows the user to communicate that the name `IdempotentCommutativeSemigroup` should be preferred over `IdempotentSemigroupCommutative`, let alone that the name `Semilattice` should be used instead. We get back to that in Sect. 5.

Batch Mixin. Mixing in the morphism $m : S \rightarrow T$ is (barring some subtleties, see e.g. [3]) a functor from extensions of S to extensions T. Using the universal property of the pushout, any morphism $x : X \rightarrow Y$ between two S-extensions induces a universal morphism $m(x) : m(X) \rightarrow m(Y)$. Here we have written $m(X)$ for the theory introduced by the pushout. Consequently, we can apply mixin to an entire diagram at once.

Let D be a diagram where every node has an embedding of a fixed node S. We write **BMIXIN** $m\, D$ for the diagram that extends D with

- for every Node(l, X) with $S \xrightarrow{\vec{e}} l$,
    - a node Node$(\texttt{mixin}_l, m(e))$ where $e : S \rightarrow X$ is the morphism induced by $\vec{e}$
    - egdes that complete the pushout rectangle like for a single mixin
- for every edge Edge$(l, d \rightarrow c, x)$ an edge Edge$(\texttt{mixin}_l, \texttt{mixin}_d \rightarrow \texttt{mixin}_c, m(x))$.

Example 11. Continuing our running examples

$$\textbf{BMIXIN}\ \texttt{Additive}\ \texttt{MagmaExtensions}$$

creates the additive of every extension of `Magma`. The resulting diagram is:

Even more powerfully, we could use

$$\textbf{BMIXIN}\ \texttt{Additive}\ (\textbf{BCOMBINE}\ \texttt{MagmaExtensions})$$

3.4   Advanced Operators

Universal algebra defines a range of theory operators that apply to an arbitrary theory with meta-theory `SFOL`. Examples include homomorphisms, products, submodels, quotients models or term algebras. Like the operators from Sect. 3.1 these usually introduce some morphisms. Moreover, many of them also admit batch version. Thus, they should be seen as diagram operators.

The implementation of all these operators in MMT is still ongoing. Here we only sketch the non-batch case of the homomorphism operator as an example. Given a diagram D We write HOM D for the diagram that extends D with

- A new node `hom` whose theory is the theory of homomorphisms between two models m_1 and m_2 of D^{dist}. This theory contains two copies D^{dist} for m_1 and m_2.

– Two edges from D^{dist} to hom for the two morphisms m_1 and m_2.

Example 12. The node hom in the diagram HOM Magma contains the theory

```
theory MagmaHom : SFOL
  U1 : type
  op1: U1 → U1 → U1
  U2 : type
  op2: U2 → U2 → U2

  U  : U1 → U2
  op : ∀ [x,y:U1] (op2 (U x) (U y)) = U (op1 x y)
```

The morphism m_1 contains the assignments U:=U1, op:=op1 and accordingly for m_2.

It is easy to see the power of, e.g., chaining batch operators for combine, mixin, and homomorphism to build large diagrams with a few commands.

Note that HOM D must return an SFOL-theory even if it is applied to a theory of unsorted first-order logic FOL. Therefore, we used SFOL as the fixed logic in order to simplify our running example. But we could just as well write all Magma-extension in FOL and translate them to SFOL before applying HOM. Because FOL and SFOL are also MMT theories, this translation is just a special case of a pushout along a morphism FOL → SFOL and thus can be expressed using the mixin operation.

Finally, we sketch another operator to indicate how our diagram operators are independent of the meta-theory and can even include changes to the meta-theory:

Example 13 (Collection Types). The operator LiftToTypeFamily () maps a diagram of SFOL-theories to the corresponding diagram of polymorphic SFOL-theories: every SFOL-type declaration U : type is turned into a type operator U : type → type, and every constant is turned into a polymorphic constant that operates pointwise, e.g., op : $U \to U \to U$ becomes op : $\{a\}\, U\, a \to U\, a \to U\, a$ where $\{a\}$ binds a type variable a.

```
Singletons := LiftToTypeFamily (Carrier) EXTEND {singleton : {a} a→U a}
LiftedMagmas := LiftToTypeFamily (BCOMBINE MagmaExtensions)
```

Now combining some of the nodes in LiftedMagmas with Singletons yields many of the usual collection types. In particular, Monoid, IdempotentMonoid, and CommutativeIdempotentMonoid yield theories describing polymorphic lists, multisets, and sets, respectively. Here the lifting of the magma operation is the concatenation/union of collections and the lifting of the neutral element is the empty collection.

4   Realization in MMT

In this section we describe the realization of diagram operators in MMT.

4.1 Diagram Definitions

Previously, MMT supported only named theories and morphisms. These were introduced by toplevel declarations that supported the examples from Sect. 2.1.

We extended this syntax in two ways. First, we added a new theory Diagrams that declares three MMT constants anonymous − theory, anonymous − morphism, and anonymous − diagram along with notations and typing rules for building anonymous theories, morphism, and diagrams. This allows writing MMT expressions that represent the normal forms of theories, morphisms, resp. diagrams.

Second, we added a toplevel declaration for diagram definitions

$$\text{diagram } d : M := E$$

E is an expression that normalizes to a diagram and M is the meta-theory in which E is defined. In the simplest case, $M = $ Diagrams, but M is typically a user-declared extension of Diagrams that declares additional diagram operators (see Sect. 4.2).

The semantics of diagram definitions is that E is evaluated into a normal diagram D and then a new theory/morphism of name d_l is defined for each new node/edge with label l in D.

Example 14. For example, the MMT expression

$$\text{anoynmous} - \text{diagram(pres, Carrier : SFOL} = \{U : \text{type}\},$$
$$\text{pres : SFOL} = \{U : \text{type, op} : U \to U \to U\},$$
$$\text{extend : Carrier} \to \text{pres} = \{\ldots\})$$

is the normal form of the diagram expression $E = $ Carrier EXTEND $\{op : U \to U \to U\}$. Here the first argument pres indicates the label of the distinguished node.

The diagram definition

$$\text{diagram Magma : Diagrams} := E$$

normalizes E and finds a new node pres and a new edge extend in it. Thus, it creates a new theory named Magma_pres and a new morphism named Magma_extend of type Carrier $\to$ Magma_pres. The node Carrier is recognized as resulting from a reference to a previously defined theory and does not result in a new theory.

Because pres is the distinguished node, future references to Magma are coerced into Magma_pres if a theory is expected. Thus, users can use Magma as a theroy in the usual way. Similarly, if Magma is used where a morphism is expected, the implicit edge of the diagram (if exists) is used.

4.2 Diagram Combinators

With diagram definitions in place once and for all, we can start adding diagram combinators. Each combinator is defined by

– an MMT constant c that introduce the name and notation of the combinator,
– a rule that defines its semantics.

Here rules are user-supplied objects in MMT's underlying programming language that are injected into the MMT kernel as described in [12]. MMT automatically loads these rules at run time, and the MMT kernel always uses those rules that are visible to the current theory. Thus, users can add new combinators without rebuilding MMT, and different sets of combinators can be available in different scopes.

Example 15. We give a theory that introduces two of the combinators described in Sect. 3.1.

```
theory Combinators =
    include Diagrams
    extends # 1 EXTEND {2,...} prec −1000000
    combine # COMBINE 1 {2,...} 3 {4,...} prec −2000000
    rule rules?ComputeExtends
    rule rules?ComputeCombine
```

The constant declarations define the concrete and abstract syntax for the diagram operators. And the rules refer to the Scala objects that define their semantics.[1]

Thus, users can flexibly add new diagram operators with arbitrarily complex semantics.

5   Conclusion and Future Work

Building large digital libraries of mathematics is a challenging task that requires special kind of tool support. Diagram-level operations achieve high levels of modularity and reuse, while avoiding a lot of boilerplate.

It remains future work to assess the behavior of the combinators as the size of the library gets much larger We are currently migrating the MathScheme library to MMT, which contains over a thousand theories built modularly using the combinators in [2].

A particular problem that future work will have to address is name generation. Batch operations introduce many theories/views at once, often with unwieldy names. It is non-trivial task to provide user-friendly syntax and we expect that satisfactory options can only be determined after conducting more experiments with large case studies. For now, we have simply added a top-level declarations **alias** $n := N$ that allows users to add a nice alias for an automatically generated name.

Acknowledgment. We would like to thank Jacques Carette, William Farmer, and Michael Kohlhase for fruitful discussions.

---

[1] The Scala code is available at https://github.com/UniFormal/MMT/blob/devel/src/mmt-lf/src/info/kwarc/mmt/moduleexpressions/Combinators.scala.

References

1. Autexier, S., Hutter, D., Mantel, H., Schairer, A.: Towards an evolutionary formal software-development using CASL. In: Bert, D., Choppy, C., Mosses, P.D. (eds.) WADT 1999. LNCS, vol. 1827, pp. 73–88. Springer, Heidelberg (2000). https://doi.org/10.1007/978-3-540-44616-3_5
2. Carette, J., O'Connor, R.: Theory presentation combinators. In: Jeuring, J., et al. (eds.) CICM 2012. LNCS (LNAI), vol. 7362, pp. 202–215. Springer, Heidelberg (2012). https://doi.org/10.1007/978-3-642-31374-5_14
3. Mossakowski, T., Rabe, F., Codescu, M.: Canonical selection of colimits. In: James, P., Roggenbach, M. (eds.) WADT 2016. LNCS, vol. 10644, pp. 170–188. Springer, Cham (2017). https://doi.org/10.1007/978-3-319-72044-9_12
4. Mosses, P.D. (ed.): CASL Reference Manual. LNCS, vol. 2960. Springer, Heidelberg (2004). https://doi.org/10.1007/b96103. CoFI (The Common Framework Initiative)
5. The distributed ontology, modeling, and specification language. Technical report, Object Management Group (OMG) (2018). version 1.0
6. Farmer, W.M., Guttman, J.D., Javier Thayer, F.: Little theories. In: Kapur, D. (ed.) CADE 1992. LNCS, vol. 607, pp. 567–581. Springer, Heidelberg (1992). https://doi.org/10.1007/3-540-55602-8_192
7. Goguen, J., Winkler, T., Meseguer, J., Futatsugi, K., Jouannaud, J.: Introducing OBJ. In: Goguen, J., Coleman, D., Gallimore, R. (eds.) Applications of Algebraic Specification using OBJ, Cambridge (1993)
8. Kammüller, F., Wenzel, M., Paulson, L.C.: Locales a sectioning concept for isabelle. In: Bertot, Y., Dowek, G., Théry, L., Hirschowitz, A., Paulin, C. (eds.) TPHOLs 1999. LNCS, vol. 1690, pp. 149–165. Springer, Heidelberg (1999). https://doi.org/10.1007/3-540-48256-3_11
9. Mossakowski, T., Maeder, C., Lüttich, K.: The heterogeneous tool set, HETS. In: Grumberg, O., Huth, M. (eds.) TACAS 2007. LNCS, vol. 4424, pp. 519–522. Springer, Heidelberg (2007). https://doi.org/10.1007/978-3-540-71209-1_40
10. Müller, D., Rabe, F.: Structuring theories with implicit morphisms. In: Fiadeiro, J., Tutu, I. (eds.) Recent Trends in Algebraic Development Techniques. Springer (2019, to appear)
11. Rabe, F.: How to identify, translate, and combine logics? J. Log. Comput. **27**(6), 1753–1798 (2017)
12. Rabe, F.: A modular type reconstruction algorithm. ACM Trans. Comput. Log. **19**(4), 1–43 (2018)
13. Rabe, F., Kohlhase, M.: A scalable module system. Inf. Comput. **230**(1), 1–54 (2013)
14. Sannella, D., Wirsing, M.: A kernel language for algebraic specification and implementation extended abstract. In: Karpinski, M. (ed.) FCT 1983. LNCS, vol. 158, pp. 413–427. Springer, Heidelberg (1983). https://doi.org/10.1007/3-540-12689-9_122
15. Srinivas, Y.V., Jüllig, R.: Specware: formal support for composing software. In: Möller, B. (ed.) MPC 1995. LNCS, vol. 947, pp. 399–422. Springer, Heidelberg (1995). https://doi.org/10.1007/3-540-60117-1_22

Inspection and Selection
of Representations

Daniel Raggi[1](✉), Aaron Stockdill[1], Mateja Jamnik[1], Grecia Garcia Garcia[2],
Holly E. A. Sutherland[2], and Peter C.-H. Cheng[2]

[1] University of Cambridge, Cambridge, UK
{daniel.raggi,aaron.stockdill,mateja.jamnik}@cl.cam.ac.uk
[2] University of Sussex, Brighton, UK
{g.garcia-garcia,h.sutherland,p.c.h.cheng}@sussex.ac.uk

Abstract. We present a novel framework for inspecting representations
and encoding their formal properties. This enables us to assess and compare the informational and cognitive value of different representations
for reasoning. The purpose of our framework is to automate the process
of representation selection, taking into account the candidate representation's match to the problem at hand and to the user's specific cognitive
profile. This requires a language for talking *about* representations, and
methods for analysing their relative advantages. This foundational work
is first to devise a computational end-to-end framework where problems,
representations, and user's profiles can be described and analysed. As AI
systems become ubiquitous, it is important for them to be more compatible with human reasoning, and our framework enables just that.

Keywords: Representation in reasoning · Heterogeneous reasoning ·
Representation selection · Representational system

1   Introduction

The aim of this work is to contribute to the development of AI systems which,
similarly to human experts, can pick effective representations for the task at
hand.

The effectiveness of a representation depends on its purpose. One kind of
representation may be more useful for problem solving, while another may facilitate learning, and some may be more suitable for school children, while another
may be useful for the working professional. Thus, for a system to select representations intelligently, it needs to take into account both the *formal* (structure
and information) and *cognitive* (user and task) aspects of representations.

This is interdisciplinary foundational work bringing together artificial intelligence, computer science and cognitive science to devise a framework (the language and methods) for analysing and encoding the properties of representations. In this paper, we focus on the formal properties of representations, and

This work was supported by the EPSRC Grants EP/R030650/1 and EP/R030642/1.

C. Kaliszyk et al. (Eds.): CICM 2019, LNAI 11617, pp. 227–242, 2019.
https://doi.org/10.1007/978-3-030-23250-4_16

the analysis involved in finding a matching representation for the given *problem* amongst a variety of candidate *representational systems*. This analysis is done in a purely structural and informational manner (i.e., without taking into account the user and task). As we will argue, the formal properties are a foundational layer upon which the cognitive properties of representations depend. The details of the analysis and encoding of cognitive properties, which bring the *user* profile into the picture, are work in progress.

Furthermore, we present a proof-of-concept application of our framework, where multiple representational systems are automatically evaluated relative to a *problem*, by a measure that estimates how likely each representational system is to contain all the ingredients for finding a solution.

Automating the process of analysing and evaluating representations would lead to a new generation of interactive computer systems which adapt intelligently to the user. The automatic selection of effective representations could have applications ranging from intelligent tutoring systems, to systems that aid the working scientist, to fully automated problem-solvers.

2   The Role of Representation in Reasoning

The advantages of particular representations over others have been extensively discussed [5,6,25]. Furthermore, there are evident cognitive benefits of multiple representations over single representations [1].

Various formalisations of specific reasoning systems using a single kind of representation have been implemented, including first order [15,16], higher order [11,21], diagrammatic [13,27,28], among many others. A few heterogeneous reasoning systems that integrate multiple representations have also been built [2,26], as well as some tools for re-representing problems and knowledge across and within systems [12,19,23]. Many systems designed for numerical, algebraic, and geometric computing include tools for representing data in various ways (graphs, plots, figures, diagrams, etc.) [14,18,22,24].

Moreover, in the rapidly-advancing areas of AI (i.e., machine learning), the role that representation plays has been recognised as crucial to the effective processing of data, and *representation learning* has become a rich area of research [3]. However, the gap between the actual computations and the user's understanding seems to be increasing as the tools perform more effectively under more autonomous (and obscure) conditions. To reduce this gap, it is necessary to understand what makes representations better or worse for humans.

Some work has been done to understand the qualities of representations [4, 7]. However, to our knowledge, there is no integration of this knowledge into a framework where representational systems can be analysed, evaluated, and selected computationally, where the task and user can be taken into account. In this work we set some foundations to approach the automation of representation analysis and selection.

2.1 An Example

To illustrate the variety and efficacy of representations for reasoning, we first present a problem in probability with three example solutions.

Problem (Birds). *One quarter of all animals are birds. Two thirds of all birds can fly. Half of all flying animals are birds. Birds have feathers. If X is an animal, what is the probability that it's not a bird and it cannot fly?*

Solution (Bayesian): Let the sample space be the set of animals. Let b represent birds, f flying animals, and Pr the probability function. Then, the problem can be reformulated, in the language of conditional probability, as follows:

$$Assume: \quad \Pr(b) = \tfrac{1}{4}, \ \Pr(f|b) = \tfrac{2}{3}, \ \Pr(b|f) = \tfrac{1}{2}.$$

$$Calculate: \ \Pr(\bar{b} \cap \bar{f})$$

To solve this, we start by noting the following facts:

$$\Pr(\bar{b}) = \Pr(\bar{b} \cap \bar{f}) + \Pr(\bar{b} \cap f) \tag{1}$$

$$\Pr(f) = \Pr(b \cap f) + \Pr(\bar{b} \cap f) \tag{2}$$

$$\Pr(\bar{b} \cap f) = \Pr(\bar{b}|f)\Pr(f) = \tfrac{1}{2}\Pr(f). \tag{3}$$

From (2) and (3) we can show that $\Pr(\bar{b} \cap f) = \tfrac{1}{2}\Pr(b \cap f) + \tfrac{1}{2}\Pr(\bar{b} \cap f)$, from which we obtain

$$\Pr(\bar{b} \cap f) = \Pr(b \cap f). \tag{4}$$

Thus, we have the following:

$$
\begin{aligned}
\Pr(\bar{b} \cap \bar{f}) &= \Pr(\bar{b}) - \Pr(\bar{b} \cap f) && \text{from (1)}\\
&= \Pr(\bar{b}) - \Pr(b \cap f) && \text{from (4)}\\
&= (1 - \Pr(b)) - \Pr(f|b)\Pr(b) && \text{from probability axioms}\\
&= \tfrac{3}{4} - \left(\tfrac{2}{3}\right)\left(\tfrac{1}{4}\right) = \tfrac{7}{12}. && \text{from assumptions} \qquad \square
\end{aligned}
$$

Solution (Geometric): In the figure below, the unit square represents the set of animals. The regions representing birds and flying animals are drawn according to the assumptions.

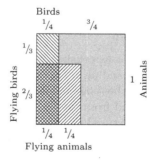

It is clear that the shaded region (non-flying, non-bird animals) has an area of $\tfrac{3}{4} - \left(\tfrac{2}{3}\right)\left(\tfrac{1}{4}\right) = \tfrac{7}{12}$. $\qquad \square$

Solution (Contingency): We start by building a table from the two relevant classes (birds and flying animals) and fill in the values that we are given. Next, the table is filled in gradually, according to simple tabular constraints.

	birds	non-birds	total
flying	$(2/3)(1/4)$	$(2/3)(1/4)$	
non-flying		$3/4 - (2/3)(1/4)$	
total	$1/4$	$3/4$	1

The rules used to fill the rest of the table are either transferred from the problem's statement (e.g., *half of all flying animals are birds* means that top cells must have the same values), or from probability theorems (e.g., *the total probability is the sum of the parts* means that the total of each column/row must be the sum of the cells in the corresponding column/row). It's worth noting that to the experienced user of contingency tables, the constraints corresponding to probability theorems do not need to be explicitly invoked from probability theory, but simply recalled as tabular/arithmetic manipulations. Thus, we reach the solution when we fill in the shaded cell.   □

Note that there may be many solutions using the same representational system (e.g., many Bayesian solutions, many Geometric solutions, etc.). In the next section we present the framework for analysing these representations.

3   Representing Representations

Representational systems are diverse, and their designs and specifications are heterogeneous. To do a comparative analysis, we need a common framework that captures the properties that make up each representation.

Our framework is based around three concepts: *representational system* (RS), *problem* (Q), and *correspondence*. In the following subsections we suggest a concrete method for inspecting and encoding their properties. The result is a set of machine-readable *tables* suitable for further analysis.

Table construction currently needs to be done by a human *analyst*, but the purpose of such tables is that they can be processed automatically to yield a representation recommendation.

3.1   Representational System

We view representational systems as consisting of two layers implemented over a medium: a *grammatical* layer, and an *inferential* layer. Broadly speaking, the grammatical layer distinguishes the sensible from the nonsensical, and the inferential layer distinguishes the valid from the invalid.

The table of an RS is a structured description of the RS. It is a collection of the most relevant *properties* of the RS. We encode these properties as pairs (k, v), where k is the property *kind* and v is the *value*. For example, if an RS table has the entry (rigorous, TRUE) this means that the RS has the property of being rigorous; and if it has (token, +) this means that the token '+' is part of the symbols used in the RS (for examples of RS tables, see Tables 1 and 2).

Grammar. The building blocks of an RS are called *tokens*. These are used to construct *expressions*. The *grammar* of an RS allows us to distinguish between admissible and inadmissible expressions. Although grammars can be constructed in various ways (e.g., by production rules [8], or by some underlying type theory [10]), our framework is agnostic to the specific *construction*, but embraces *type theory* as a generic descriptive tool. Thus, every token, and every admissible expression will be assumed to have a *type*. However, to keep our framework flexible, we make no other assumptions about the specific type theory that we use.

We encode the property of *grammatical complexity* (*g-complexity* in Tables 1 and 2) using Chomsky hierarchies, which are linked to well-known classes of computational complexity and expressiveness [9].

Inference. The medium on which an RS is implemented (e.g., a pen and paper, or a computer interface) can be manipulated by some agent. Thus, we need a concept of *state*. Broadly speaking, a state refers to the conditions of a medium at some moment in time. Manipulations are changes of state.

The *inferential* layer of an RS determines how the grammatical expressions of an RS can be manipulated *validly*. Borrowing from the field of computer-assisted theorem proving, we refer to valid manipulations as *tactics*. Moreover, tactics are often parametric on knowledge. The knowledge encoded in an RS can be represented as a collection of *facts*. These can be formulae (e.g., in Bayesian system $\Pr(x) = \Pr(x \wedge y) + \Pr(x \wedge \neg y)$), extrinsically-imposed constraints (e.g., in contingency tables the last value of a row must be the sum of the values of the row), or intrinsic constraints (e.g., the area of a region is the sum of the areas of its parts). Thus, tactics and facts are the main constituent properties of an RS.

As with grammatical complexity, inferential complexity (*i-complexity* in Tables 1 and 2) can be measured according to known standards. The partial order induced by injective embeddings of theories within one another could be a basis by which to compare systems, but a radical simplification by flattening into 5 classes turns out to be enough for a rough assessment of complexity. We propose the following levels (with a known system for reference): 1 (propositional logic), 2 (decidable fractions of arithmetic/set theory), 3 (Peano arithmetic), 4 (constructive set theory), and 5 (Zermelo-Fraenkel).

Furthermore, we include the property of *rigour* to describe whether the calculations/proofs are guaranteed to be exact/correct.

We described the most significant properties of RS tables. Our framework includes more, but it is nevertheless a fixed set of *kinds* for every RS table. This provides a template that can aid an analyst to generate tables, ensures consistency across different RSs, and is sufficient for an in-depth analysis of representations. See Tables 1 and 2 for some example RS tables.

Table 1. A section of the Bayesian RS table.

Kind	Value
types	real, event
tokens	Ω, $\emptyset$, 0, 1, $=$, $+$, $-$, $*$, $\div$, $\cup$, $\cap$, $\setminus$, $\bar{}$, Pr, $\mid$
g-complexity	type-2
facts	Bayes' theorem, law of total probability, non-negative probability, unit-measure, sigma-additivity, ...
tactics	rewrite, arithmetic calculation
i-complexity	3
rigorous	TRUE

Table 2. A section of the Geometric RS table.

Kind	Value
types	point, segment, region, real, string
tokens	$point, $segment (*the prefix $ denotes a label for an actually pictorial symbol*)
g-complexity	type-3
facts	scale-independence of ratio, non-negative area, area additivity,...
tactics	draw point, draw segment, delete, join, compare sizes
i-complexity	2
rigorous	TRUE

3.2 Problems

Abstractly, a *problem* q is a triple (O_q, G_q, C_q) where O_q is an initial condition, G_q is a goal condition, and C_q is a set of constraints on the paths leading from the states that satisfy O_q to the states that satisfy G_q [20].

This definition is difficult to square with the fact that problem specifications rarely look like such a triple. Our contention is that this is because most problems are about information recovery within a space determined by conventional information-manipulation rules.

For example, the *Birds* problem above is neither explicit about the goal condition nor about any path constraints, and we can only assume that the initial condition is whichever state things are when the problem is presented. However, a competent problem-solver will find a statement such as *what is the probability* ... informative about the *type* of the answer expected (specifically, *ratio*, *percentage*, or *real number* or any data-type usually used to encode probability values). In other words, the problem-solver is expected to perform type-inference to obtain the answer type. Moreover, the rest of the problem statement will typically provide data which, under conventional interpretations, can be manipulated to recover the answer. Thus, given a problem specification q, the information (O_q, G_q, C_q) is hidden in the specification and meant to be inferred by the problem solver.

We call the set of paths that satisfy (O_q, G_q, C_q) the *semantics* of the problem. The relation between a problem specification and its semantics is complex, because it requires, first, an understanding of how the specification relates to the triple (deemed *problem understanding* by [20]), and second, knowledge of the paths that satisfy the triple (*problem solving*).

Q Tables. Similar to RS tables, Q tables encode the properties of problems (*Q properties*) as kind–value pairs.

The presentation of a problem requires an RS. We write $q : S$ to denote 'a problem q represented under system S'. Then, a problem's properties can be encoded similar to representational systems (e.g., which types and tokens appear). The only difference is that here we qualify the properties by their semantic contribution. Thus, to build a Q table, an *analyst* is required to estimate the semantic contribution of properties. That is, they need to decide the importance of each property relative to the other properties. This means, in particular, that knowledge of individual solutions influences the content and quality of the table. Naturally, we do not assume full knowledge of the semantics, as this would require complete knowledge of solutions. We only assume partial understanding of the goal conditions, and any estimation of the relevance of different properties can help. Moreover, if the problem is presented in a system S and the analyst only knows a solution involving a different system S' where a fact α (native to S') is used, the analyst can include α in the table. This will ensure that we do not miss important knowledge of a problem/solution when building a Q table.[1]

See Table 3 for a Q table for the *Birds* problem.

Properties such as *error allowed* and *answer type* are at the top of the importance hierarchy (purple/essential) because they inform us directly about the goal condition. Specifically, *answer type* refers to the shape of the data (data-type) expected to appear in any state satisfying the goal conditions, and *error allowed* refers to the rigour expected out of the answer (i.e., how permissive is the goal condition).

Next (blue/instrumental) in the hierarchy are any tokens, types, patterns, facts, or tactics with pivotal roles in the solution(s). These properties are informative about how the paths in the state space which lead to solutions look.

One step below (green/relevant) are things which are clearly informative about the semantics of the problem, but which may also contain noise or just be informative as heuristics. This now includes tokens which may not appear in the problem specification but which may be useful along the way.

The lowest classes are either circumstances of the representation (yellow/circumstantial), or outright noise (red/noise)—that is, tokens that either appear in the specification or are evoked by it,[2] which contain no information about the

---

[1] As a consequence, Q tables may contain elements of multiple RSs. For reasons mentioned in Sect. 5, this is discouraged whenever it is avoidable.

[2] Those appearing in this example are taken from a semantic net [29].

Table 3. A Q table for the *Birds* problem with its natural language statement. The colour codes for importance relative to information content: essential (purple), instrumental (blue), relevant (green), circumstantial (yellow), noise (red).

kind	value
error allowed	0
answer type	ratio
tokens	probability, and, not
types	ratio, class
patterns	_:ratio of _:class are _:class, probability of _:class and _:class
facts	Bayes' theorem, law of total probability, unit measure, additive inverse, commutativity of + ...
tactics	deduce, calculate
tokens	one, quarter, all, animals, birds, two, thirds, can, fly, half, flying, X, animal, probability, cannot
related tokens	times, divided_by, plus, minus, equals, union, intersection, probability, zero, ...
# of tokens	67
# of distinct tokens	31
tokens	feathers
related tokens	beast, animate, creature, wing, aviate, flock, fowl, dame, carnal, being, fauna, ...

semantics. Notice, for example, that the *Birds* problem contains the statement *birds have feathers* which is not used by any solution. Thus, the token 'feathers' is classified as noise. Any tokens related to the zoological interpretation of the problem are taken as noise. Encoding these explicitly may be useful to understand potential missteps or distracting data in the specification.

Every Q table will have a fixed set of property kinds. This provides a template to generate tables—empirically, these proved sufficient for an effective analysis of candidate representations in relation to the problem.

3.3   Correspondence

We have presented a framework for encoding the properties of problems and representational systems. Now we need some method for assessing the relative value of different RS for representing a given problem. Our approach relies on the notion of *correspondence*, which is a way of relating Q properties with RS properties. It is the fundamental notion that we use for calculating the match of an RS to a problem.

Analogical Correspondences. Different RSs are linked to each other through structure-preserving transformations. For example, an *event* can be encoded as a *proposition*, or as a *set*, or as a *region* in the plane. These relations between types form the basis of more complex analogies. For example, the conjunction of two events corresponds to the intersection of two regions, and the *probability* of an event corresponds to the area of its corresponding region. Furthermore, such transformations also induce the correspondence of facts. For example, if probability corresponds to area, then the *law of total probability* corresponds to *area additivity*. It should be noted that for every property p the *reflexive* correspondence (with strength 1) is by default considered in our framework. The logic and mechanisms for reasoning through such transformations has been explored elsewhere [23]. In this work, rather than the mechanism, we are concerned with assessing the relative value that such transformations provide.

Q-Specific Correspondences. The analogical correspondences are induced by transformations between RSs (i.e., the mapping between tokens/types/facts/tactics). However, other problem-specific information may also be valuable for assessing RSs. For example, the error allowance of a problem informs us whether we need a rigorous RS or whether an imprecise one is sufficient (if there are other reasons for it to be valued, e.g., an approximate solution is sufficient for young children). Thus, correspondences such as between the Q property *error allowed = 0* and the RS property *rigorous* can be included.

Correspondence Tables. Currently, we assume that a catalogue of such transformations/analogies is known. Furthermore, we assume that we have a measure that estimates the information loss in a correspondence. We call this the correspondence *strength*.[3] For example, the injection of natural numbers into real numbers is lossless, so the strength of *type natural* to *type real* is assumed to be 1. However, any transformation from real to natural is lossy, so its strength must be less than 1 (the question of how much exactly is up for discussion). Thus, each correspondence can be encoded as a triple (p_q, p_r, s) where p_q and p_r are Q and RS properties, respectively, and s is the strength.

Each correspondence between a property of q and a property of S can be seen, roughly, as a reason why q could be represented in S. Simplistically, this could mean that adding up the values of all correspondences between q and S might give us a score of S. However, the reasons may not be independent, so adding them up may count redundant correspondences multiple times. Thus, we introduce a simple calculus for specifying correspondence in the most independent possible way (e.g., see Table 4; more details are in Sect. 4.2).

But how can Q, RS, and correspondence tables be used for representation recommendation? We present a proof-of-concept algorithm next.

4   Using the Framework

Our tables give us properties of the problem and of the candidate RSs. Correspondence tables give us explicit links between them. The task now is to exploit

---

[3] In future work, we will investigate how correspondences and their strength can be identified automatically (e.g., using machine learning).

Table 4. Some example correspondences encoded with operator OR.

Q property formula	RS property	Strength
type occurrence OR type class	type event	1
type ratio OR type percentage	type real	1
token intersection OR token and	token ∩	1
token given OR token if	token |	1
error allowed = 0	rigorous	1
error allowed = 0	NOT rigorous	−1

this information to find correspondences which match properties of both the problem and the target RS. Not all properties bear equal importance, thus we modulate the correspondence strength. Combining these assigns a real value to each potential RS indicating its relevance as a candidate RS. Algorithm 1 implements this process.

Algorithm 1. Uses properties of problems and representational systems to rank candidate RSs.

LOADTABLES()
recommendations ← [ ]
for each representation **do**
   $t \leftarrow 0$ $// \, t$ is the score
   for each correspondence **do**
      prop_q ← PROPERTIES(problem)
      prop_r ← PROPERTIES(representation)
      $(p_q, p_r, \text{strength})$ ← correspondence
      $\text{importance}_{\text{corr}}$ ← MAX(IMPORTANCE, p_q)
      if MATCH(prop_q, p_q) **and** MATCH(prop_r, p_r) **then**
         $t \leftarrow t + \text{importance}_{\text{corr}} \times \text{strength}$
      end if
   end for
   if $t > 0$ **then**
      APPEND(recommendations, $\langle t, \text{representation} \rangle$)
   end if
end for
return SORTED(recommendations)

4.1 Matching Correspondences

In our running example, we have a Q table for the *Birds* problem and four RS tables for the representational systems: Bayesian, Geometric, Contingency, Natural Language, and also an Euler RS table.[4] They are accompanied by a

---

[4] By 'Euler' we mean some implementation of Euler diagrams.

table of correspondences between properties. Algorithm 1 accesses these tables, and then iterates over the RSs to find correspondences linking the problem to the RS.

Suppose the first candidate representation for the *Birds* problem is Bayesian. Thus, we consider the Bayesian RS table and the *Birds* problem Q table. Next, we examine each correspondence: a triple (p_q, p_r, s) where p_q and p_r are properties of the problem and representation, respectively, and $s \in [-1, 1]$ is the correspondence strength. We examine if both Q table properties and RS table properties match the conditions of this correspondence. For example, the correspondence:

$$(\text{error allowed} = 0, \text{rigorous}, 1)$$

from Table 4 matches properties in the Q table in Table 3 *and* those in the RS table from Table 1. If there is no match, we disregard this correspondence. When they do match—as in this example—we take the strength s and modulate it by the importance of the matched Q property. Each importance colour band is assigned a value in the $[0, 1]$ interval, which we multiply by the strength of the correspondence s. Our example correspondence involves the property *error allowed*, which is an essential (purple) property, so is modulated by the 'essential' value 1. Altogether, this correspondence contributes $1 \times 1 = 1$ to the Bayesian RS ranking score.

4.2   Property Formulae

The p_q and p_r from the correspondence triple can be *property formulae* expressed in a simple calculus using binary connectives AND and OR, and the unary connective NOT.[5] The property calculus allows for greater expressivity and better captures the nature of correspondences between Q and RS properties. We see this in the correspondence:

$$(\text{type occurrence OR type class}, \text{type event}, 1)$$

where we require one (or both) of the properties specified in the p_q of the correspondence triple to occur in the Q table. In this situation, we do observe *type class* occurring as an instrumental (blue) property. The correspondence is matched despite the absence of *type occurrence*; notice that it was necessary to observe *type event* in the Bayesian RS table. The matched correspondence formula involved both *type class* and *type occurrence*, with the match being satisfied by an instrumental (blue) property. Thus, the correspondence strength of 1 is modulated by the 'instrumental' value[6] 0.6, increasing the Bayesian RS score to $1 \times 0.6 = 0.6$.

---

[5] AND requires that both properties appear in the property table. OR requires that at least one of the properties appears in the property table. If both properties appear in the table, the strength is only counted once. NOT requires that a specified property does not occur in the property table.

[6] The value 0.6 for 'instrumental' properties is chosen arbitrarily; the only condition is that the value-importance relation is monotonic. In future work, these parameters should be tuned with experimental data.

4.3   Making a Recommendation

Once all correspondences for a particular Q and RS are identified and modulated by importance, we combine them to a single score. This can be done in many ways: we take a simple sum. For the example of the Bayesian representation and the *Birds* problem, the correspondence analysis gives an overall score of 9.3.

Repeating the scoring process above for each candidate RS yields the following recommendation ranking:

Bayesian	9.3
Geometric	7.2
Natural Language	6.9
Contingency	5.4
Euler	1.5

We hence recommend that the *Birds* problem, initially posed in a Natural Language RS, might be better attempted in the Bayesian RS. This seems a sensible recommendation.

5   Discussion and Future Work

We showed that representation selection can be encoded in a sufficiently formal way to computationally analyse the underlying informationally-relevant structural matches across domains. This is novel and exciting. We now evaluate the quality of performance of our framework, and discuss its significance for applications and future work.

5.1   The Influence of Known Solutions

In this paper we presented an example of an RS recommendation where the input was a Q table (for the *Birds* problem), five candidate RS tables, and the associated correspondence tables. The Q table encoded the problem expressed in natural language, but it contained as *facts* some theorems from other RS, like *Bayes' theorem* in the formal Bayesian solution. We allow the Q table to be heterogeneous (e.g., consisting of properties of more than one RS), and thus include in the Q table the Bayesian facts. Clearly, such properties will boost the score of the Bayesian RS.

More generally, every property in Q table that is native to an RS will boost the score of such an RS. This implies that the RS in which the problem is stated (natural language in our example) will score points just for the fact that the problem is expressed in that RS. However, it might still not get the highest score, because it may contain foreign properties, or properties that clash with the properties of the problem (e.g., the *rigour* property of the RS may clash with the *error allowed* condition of the problem).

Thus, known solutions, regardless of their representation, can influence the recommendation if the analyst introduces their properties in the Q table. Therefore, the analyst must consider:

1. Heterogeneous tables need to be built carefully to avoid redundancy. For example, the *Law of Total Probability* is a Bayesian fact that corresponds to the Geometric fact *Additivity of Areas*. Thus, if both are added to a single Q table, they may result in unjustified boosting of the score. For this reason, the Q tables should be as homogeneous as possible.
2. Some aspects of known solutions do not affect the formal score of an RS. For example, the length of the solution is not considered because, although a shorter solution may be desirable, it is not *informationally relevant*. But it may be relevant from the cognitive point of view (e.g., in the processing cost), and thus forms part of the cognitive properties. Incorporating cognitive properties into our analysis and recommendation framework is part of our ongoing work.

5.2 Analysing the Trace

Perhaps more interesting than the resulting scores is the data that the *trace* of the algorithm execution provides. For example, it enables an analysis about how individual correspondences contribute to the total score. The high importance (essential) Q property *answer type ratio* corresponds to properties *type real* in the Bayesian, Geometric, and Contingency systems. However, in the Euler system it has no corresponding property.[7] Similarly, the token *probability* corresponds to the token Pr in Bayesian, and the tactics *compare sizes* and *compare cell values* in Geometric and Contingency, respectively, but it has no correspondence in Euler. Thus, due to the high values for the importance of the essential and instrumental properties, the gap between Euler and the other RSs widens. This is expected and desirable.[8]

We observe that tokens in some systems (e.g., *probability*) can correspond to tactics (e.g., compare sizes) without corresponding to any specific tokens. This is interesting from the cognitive perspective, because these tokens and tactics are very different operationally. A cognitively focused analysis may be able to assess the impact of differences of this sort.

The trace analysis has many potential applications. We envision *tutoring systems* that can make specific recommendations (e.g., "maybe you can draw a region in space to represent the class of animals"), or explainable AI systems that can justify their decisions in a humanly-understandable manner.

Zero-Weight Properties. Some Q and RS properties make no contribution in terms of correspondence scores, for example, all the *circumstantial* and *noise* properties. Nevertheless, we chose to encode them in our framework because

---

[7] In Euler diagrams the cardinality of sets is abstracted away; the size of zones is meaningless.

[8] Note that the strength of the correspondences from *probability* to Pr and *compare sizes* was set to 1 (because in principle any probability function is representable in the Bayesian or Geometric systems), but it was set to 0.5 for Contingency because not every probability function is representable in Contingency tables.

they have potentially important effects on cognitive processes. For example, the total number of (circumstantial) tokens may be used to estimate the cognitive cost of registering a problem specification. Moreover, the inference power of an RS may make it more applicable from a formal point of view, but the cost of using it may be higher from a cognitive point of view.

An analysis of the correspondence between noise properties of Q and RS may be used for predicting human error or bias. For example, a novice user might be tempted to represent zoological facts given in the *Birds* problem, but they contribute to unnecessary cognitive costs.

5.3 Evaluating the Framework and Algorithm

To our knowledge, no work has been done on computationally modelling representation selection, so we have no benchmarks by which to judge our framework or algorithm. The execution of the algorithm presented here is a proof-of-concept application, but it shows that given our encoding of a problem Q and various representations RSs, we can compute interesting measures. Moreover, the approach that we take for encoding the description of problems, RSs and correspondences makes minimal assumptions about them. This makes it general. So far, we have encoded 9 different RSs and various problems.

One of the main limitations of our framework is the need for an analyst to encode the Q and RS properties, the correspondence strengths, and the importance that each Q property has relative to potential solutions. This clearly requires the analyst to understand the complexity of a problem, and to have at least some understanding of how a solution would look (e.g., identifying potentially instrumental facts). This poses a problem for automation. One way of tackling this is with the help of machine learning methods similar to the work of [17] for lemma selection.

5.4 Future Work

Our framework opens up many avenues for future research. Automating the generation of Q and RS tables and their importance is a clear goal to be achieved. We are currently including methods for analysing the cognitive properties of representations, and want to extend the framework to include user profiles next. We are curious to find out if representation selection based on our framework can promote problem solving or learning in humans, and want to incorporate it into a personalised multi-representation tutoring system.

6   Conclusion

We have presented a novel framework for computationally selecting suitable representations. We introduced the language, data structures, and methods for encoding and analysing the properties of problems, of representational systems, and the correspondences between them.

Our proof-of-concept algorithm ranks representational systems according to a measure of suitability given a problem. The algorithm analyses the problem's properties in terms of their informational contribution and estimates the likelihood that the problem's semantics can be recovered in each candidate RS. We see this work as an exciting foundation upon which we can build the machinery to analyse cognitive properties, so the user profile may be included to calculate a recommendation.

Acknowledgements. We thank the 3 anonymous reviewers for their comments, which helped to improve the presentation of this paper.

References

1. Ainsworth, S.: The functions of multiple representations. Comput. Educ. **33**(2–3), 131–152 (1999)
2. Barker-Plummer, D., Etchemendy, J., Liu, A., Murray, M., Swoboda, N.: Openproof - a flexible framework for heterogeneous reasoning. In: Stapleton, G., Howse, J., Lee, J. (eds.) Diagrams 2008. LNCS (LNAI), vol. 5223, pp. 347–349. Springer, Heidelberg (2008). https://doi.org/10.1007/978-3-540-87730-1_32
3. Bengio, Y., Courville, A., Vincent, P.: Representation learning: a review and new perspectives. IEEE Trans. Pattern Anal. Mach. Intell. **35**(8), 1798–1828 (2013)
4. Blackwell, A., Green, T.: Notational systems-the cognitive dimensions of notations framework. In: HCI Models, Theories, and Frameworks: Toward an Interdisciplinary Science. Morgan Kaufmann (2003)
5. Cheng, P.C.-H.: Unlocking conceptual learning in mathematics and science with effective representational systems. Comput. Educ. **33**(2–3), 109–130 (1999)
6. Cheng, P.C.-H.: Probably good diagrams for learning: representational epistemic recodification of probability theory. Top. Cogn. Sci. **3**(3), 475–498 (2011)
7. Cheng, P.C.-H.: What constitutes an effective representation? In: Jamnik, M., Uesaka, Y., Elzer Schwartz, S. (eds.) Diagrams 2016. LNCS (LNAI), vol. 9781, pp. 17–31. Springer, Cham (2016). https://doi.org/10.1007/978-3-319-42333-3_2
8. Chomsky, N.: Three models for the description of language. IRE Trans. Inf. Theory **2**(3), 113–124 (1956)
9. Chomsky, N.: On certain formal properties of grammars. Inf. Control **2**(2), 137–167 (1959)
10. Coquand, T.: Type theory. In: Stanford Encyclopedia of Philosophy (2006)
11. Harrison, J.: HOL light: an overview. In: Berghofer, S., Nipkow, T., Urban, C., Wenzel, M. (eds.) TPHOLs 2009. LNCS, vol. 5674, pp. 60–66. Springer, Heidelberg (2009). https://doi.org/10.1007/978-3-642-03359-9_4
12. Huffman, B., Kunčar, O.: Lifting and transfer: a modular design for quotients in Isabelle/HOL. In: Gonthier, G., Norrish, M. (eds.) CPP 2013. LNCS, vol. 8307, pp. 131–146. Springer, Cham (2013). https://doi.org/10.1007/978-3-319-03545-1_9
13. Jamnik, M., Bundy, A., Green, I.: On automating diagrammatic proofs of arithmetic arguments. J. Log. Lang. Inf. **8**(3), 297–321 (1999)
14. Jupyter. jupyter.org
15. Kaufmann, M., Moore, J.S.: ACL2: an industrial strength version of Nqthm. In: Proceedings of 11th Annual Conference on Computer Assurance, COMPASS 1996, pp. 23–34. IEEE (1996)

16. Kovács, L., Voronkov, A.: First-order theorem proving and VAMPIRE. In: Sharygina, N., Veith, H. (eds.) CAV 2013. LNCS, vol. 8044, pp. 1–35. Springer, Heidelberg (2013). https://doi.org/10.1007/978-3-642-39799-8_1

17. Kühlwein, D., Blanchette, J.C., Kaliszyk, C., Urban, J.: MaSh: machine learning for sledgehammer. In: Blazy, S., Paulin-Mohring, C., Pichardie, D. (eds.) ITP 2013. LNCS, vol. 7998, pp. 35–50. Springer, Heidelberg (2013). https://doi.org/10.1007/978-3-642-39634-2_6

18. Matlab. mathworks.com

19. Mossakowski, T., Maeder, C., Lüttich, K.: The heterogeneous tool set, HETS. In: Grumberg, O., Huth, M. (eds.) TACAS 2007. LNCS, vol. 4424, pp. 519–522. Springer, Heidelberg (2007). https://doi.org/10.1007/978-3-540-71209-1_40

20. Newell, A.: Human Problem Solving. Prentice-Hall Inc., Upper Saddle River (1972)

21. Nipkow, T., Paulson, L.C., Wenzel, M.: Isabelle/HOL: A Proof Assistant for Higher-Order Logic, vol. 2283. Springer, Heidelberg (2002). https://doi.org/10.1007/3-540-45949-9

22. GNU Octave. octave.org

23. Raggi, D., Bundy, A., Grov, G., Pease, A.: Automating change of representation for proofs in discrete mathematics (extended version). Math. Comput. Sci. **10**(4), 429–457 (2016)

24. SageMath. sagemath.org

25. Stapleton, G., Jamnik, M., Shimojima, A.: What makes an effective representation of information: a formal account of observational advantages. J. Log. Lang. Inf. **26**(2), 143–177 (2017)

26. Urbas, M., Jamnik, M.: A framework for heterogeneous reasoning in formal and informal domains. In: Dwyer, T., Purchase, H., Delaney, A. (eds.) Diagrams 2014. LNCS (LNAI), vol. 8578, pp. 277–292. Springer, Heidelberg (2014). https://doi.org/10.1007/978-3-662-44043-8_28

27. Urbas, M., Jamnik, M., Stapleton, G., Flower, J.: Speedith: a diagrammatic reasoner for spider diagrams. In: Cox, P., Plimmer, B., Rodgers, P. (eds.) Diagrams 2012. LNCS (LNAI), vol. 7352, pp. 163–177. Springer, Heidelberg (2012). https://doi.org/10.1007/978-3-642-31223-6_19

28. Winterstein, D., Bundy, A., Gurr, C.: Dr.Doodle: a diagrammatic theorem prover. In: Basin, D., Rusinowitch, M. (eds.) IJCAR 2004. LNCS (LNAI), vol. 3097, pp. 331–335. Springer, Heidelberg (2004). https://doi.org/10.1007/978-3-540-25984-8_24

29. WordNet (2010). wordnet.princeton.edu

A Plugin to Export Coq Libraries to XML

Claudio Sacerdoti Coen[(✉)]

Department of Computer Science and Engineering, University of Bologna,
Bologna, Italy
`claudio.sacerdoticoen@unibo.it`

Abstract. We introduce a plugin for the interactive prover Coq to
export its libraries to a machine readable XML format. The information
exported is the one checked by Coq's kernel after the input is elaborated,
augmented with additional data coming from the elaboration itself.

The plugin has been applied to the 49 Coq libraries that have an opam
package and that currently compile with the latest version of Coq (8.9.0),
generating a large dataset of 1,235,934 compressed XML files organized
in 18,780 directories that require 17 GB on disk.

1 Introduction

In recent years there is a renewed interest in exporting libraries of interactive
provers (ITP) in machine-readable formats that can be checked, mined and
elaborated independently of the ITP. Examples of possible applications are:
automatic alignment of concepts coming from different provers or from different libraries [MGK+17]; machine learning of premise-selection [ISA+16] or
automatic methods to advance in proofs [AGS+04]; implementation of hammers to blast away proof obligations [CK18]; system independent search &
retrieval [KS06]; independent verification.

Coq [Tea19] is one of the major ITPs in use and its libraries are huge. The first
XML export from Coq was presented at MKM 2003 by the author [Sac03] and
the exported library was heavily used in the European project MoWGLI (Math
on the Web: Get it by Logic and Interfaces) [AW02]. Since then both the logic
and the implementation of Coq were changed, in particular adding a complex
system of modules and functors to structure libraries. Therefore the exportation
code ceased to work a few years after. More recently several plugins have been
written independently to export libraries from Coq. None of the plugins attempt
to provide a complete exportation. For example, the ones implemented for the
Logipedia project [DT] and to implement a Coq Hammer [CK18] both ignore
modules and functors.

In this paper we introduce a new Coq plugin that resumes most of the func-
tionalities of the 2003 plugin, but extends them to cover all recent features of
Coq. The output of the plugin is already used as input to other projects. In particular, in [MRS19] the author and collaborators translate the generated XML

© Springer Nature Switzerland AG 2019
C. Kaliszyk et al. (Eds.): CICM 2019, LNAI 11617, pp. 243–257, 2019.
https://doi.org/10.1007/978-3-030-23250-4_17

files to the MMT language [RK13] preserving typeability and in [CKM+19] they automatically extract from the XML files a large set of RDF triples that can be used to perform system agnostic searches in the library.

2 Introduction to Coq and the XML Exportation Plugin

Following a rather standard architecture for an interactive theorem prover, user provided files are written in a source (also called external) language and are then elaborated by Coq to an internal language that is fed to the kernel. The kernel is only responsible for verifying that the input is correct according to the rules of the logic/type-system. The elaborator (also called refiner [ASTZ06]) is instead a much more complex piece of software that, among other things, is responsible for: inferring omitted types; resolving mixfix mathematical notation and typical ambiguity; patching the user input introducing subterms to promote values from a type to another; automatically search for missing proof terms necessary to interpret proof statements or single proof steps; elaborating high-level declarations in terms of a simpler language (e.g. implement canonical structures using records that are in turn implemented using inductive types).

Writing independent tools able to understand the external language of an interactive theorem prover is virtually impossible: not only the external language is subject to continuous changes, but to understand it one would need to reimplement all the algorithms of the elaborator, that are continuously improved, typically undocumented and based on a huge number of ever evolving heuristics. Therefore tools that address interoperability usually tackle the internal language understood by the kernel. This language is usually small, simple and well-documented (it is the syntax of the type theory or logic the system is based on) in order to reduce the trusted code base to a minimum. This is the so called De Brujin criterion. Moreover, since the logic evolves slowly, the code of the kernel is usually quite stable, making it easier to write exporters.

Unfortunately, the type system Coq is based on is all but small and simple, and more features are constantly added. The kernel of Coq is indeed about 13,000 lines of OCaml code and the one of Matita [ARST11], that implements a subset and a further simplification of the type theory of Coq, has more than 4,000 lines of OCaml code. For this reason in Sect. 2.2 we will present the grammar of the language without attempting to explain all the various constructors in detail.

Elaboration is a non invertible transformation: from the kernel language it is from hard to impossible to reconstruct the user input. In particular, all extra-logical information, i.e. information not necessary to implement type-checking, is not passed to the kernel. This complicates a lot the writing of an exporter, in particular for Coq. Indeed, in order for the exported library to be user-understandable or for tools that learn from the library to be able to apply knowledge to new theories, some extra-logical information is to be retained during the exportation. I list here a few, significant examples:

1. when the user introduces a definition, it flags it with an extra-logical flavor like theorem, lemma, corollary, fact, definition, let, etc.; similar synonyms can be used for axioms

2. some definitions are automatically generated by the system, e.g. when some tactics are applied or an inductive type is defined; those are indistinguishable from the user provided ones in the kernels

3. the user can explicitly name universes and add constraints over them; the system automatically generates hundreds of additional universes, automatically generating meaningless names, and the kernel cannot distinguish between the universes that the user named because they were meaningful to him, and the remaining ones

4. some definitions are flagged by the user to be used automatically in certain situations, e.g. as rewriting rules, as coercions to promote values to different types, as canonical structure instances to be used during proof search for an instance. If this information is forgotten, it becomes practically impossible to reuse the library in a different system

5. sections are a mechanism, similar to Isabelle's locales [KWP99], that allow to declare a logical context of declarations and assumptions, give definitions in this context and later automatically abstract all definitions over the variables of the context that were actually used. The kernel only receives the result of this abstraction, while a user looking at the library only sees the definition before the abstraction.

2.1 The XML Exportation Plugin

To address all the examples at the end of the previous section and a few more, we designed our plugin as follows: we have forked the latest official release of Coq (8.9.0) in the Git repository https://github.com/sacerdot/coq. Ideally, the fork should just add to the source code some hooks to the kernel and to the elaborator, so that the XML plugin could export all the required information. In practice, the fork does more and therefore it will take more time to negotiate with the Coq team how to incorporate the changes upstream.

First of all, to deal with the case of sections, when the occurrence of a constant is found the plugin needs to know if the constant was declared inside a section or not. The reason is that, to preserve sections in the output, the output of the plugin produces terms in a variation of the calculus where abstractions over variables in a section are explicitly instantiated by name (see [Sac03] or [Sac04] for details). To recover this information, Coq must remember it in the compiled files. The code to perform this recording is still present in the Coq code from the 2003 version of the plugin, but it does not work correctly any more. Therefore we have to patch it.

Second, the plugin must be automatically activated when Coq starts, in order to export all libraries, comprising the basic ones. The mechanism Coq uses to load and activate a plugin is to insert a special command in a script. However, that's too late: when the command is encountered, some information is already lost. Therefore the fork automatically registers and activate the plugin.

Third, there are some inconsistencies in the way Coq represents some information in the kernel. In practice, some information is recorded in a wrong way w.r.t. how it is supposed to be recorded and is recorded elsewhere, but the rest of the code is able to cope with it. Since two wrongs don't make a right, the data remains inconsistent and exporting it consistently would complicate the plugin code a lot. We prefer therefore to fix the representation in the code of Coq.

The need to patch some functions in the code of Coq partially explains why we did not try to use SerAPI [GA16] or a modification of it to implement XML serialization outside the system. The main reason, though, is another: some information that is not recorded by the kernel of Coq because it can be easily obtained by other parts of Coq calling various functions exported by the kernel; the same information is instead hard to obtain outside Coq, unless one complete reimplements the kernel of Coq, and therefore needs to be computed once and for all before exporting. For example, for every sub-term of a proof we export its type if it is proving a formula, i.e. when the sub-term is a proof step according to Curry-Howard (see [Sac01, Sac03] for details). This information has many interesting uses: first of all it allows to implement tools to explain the proof term in pseudo-natural language [Sac10]; secondly, by identifying the statement of all proof steps in every proof, it creates a formidable dataset for machine learning tools that try to automatically prove theorems.

Manual Plugin Activation. The plugin has only been tested on Linux. In order to activate the plugin, it is sufficient to set the `$COQ_XML_LIBRARY_ROOT` variable to point to a directory that will contain the extracted files. After that one can just run the Coq compiler `coqc` in the usual way on an input file to extract its content. For example, the command `coqc -R . mathcomp.field galois.v` runs the compiler on the file `galois.v` after declaring that all files rooted in the current directory . will be compiled in the logical prefix `mathcomp.field`. Thus, the content of the file `galois.v` will be exported on disk in the directory `$COQ_XML_LIBRARY_ROOT/mathcomp/field/galois/`. See Sect. 3 for details on the representation on disk of the extracted information.

Even if manual plugin activation is easy, it does not address the question of how to automate extraction of XML data from existing libraries. In order to solve the issue, we set up extraction scripts that exploit the opam system.

Opam Packages. There is a recent effort by the Coq team to push developers of libraries to release *opam* packages for them. Opam is a package manager for OCaml libraries that can be (ab)used to automatically download, compile and install Coq libraries as well, keeping track of versioned dependencies and automatically installing them on demand. Moreover, to release an opam package some Dublin-core like metadata like author and synopsis must be provided. Other interesting mandatory metadata are license and version. Finally, opam packages specify the exact Coq version they depend on, granting that compilation will succeed. At the time of writing of this paper, there are only 49 opam packages that compile with the recently released version 8.9.0 of Coq. More are under porting and will be available soon. However, there are also hundreds of additional libraries, many no longer maintained, that have no corresponding opam package.

With significant help by Tom Wiesing (FAU Erlangen-Nürnberg), we set up python scripts to automate the XML exportation from opam packages. In particular, for every opam package the scripts create a Git repository hosted at the following address: https://gl.mathhub.info/Coqxml. Each repository contains the $COQ_XML_LIBRARY_ROOT the package extracted to, plus Comma Separated Values (CSV) and Resource Description Framework (RDF) files automatically generated from the XML files (see [CKM+19]). Our idea is that further elaboration of the XML exportation by third parties could also in the future be committed to the repository. For example, we are planning to populate the repository also with the translation of the XML files to MMT (see [MRS19]).

In order to have one's library included, it is sufficient to release an opam package for it following the instructions on the website of Coq.

2.2 The Internal Language of Coq

The Calculus of (Co)Inductive Constructions, the type theory Coq is based on, is very complex and Coq extended it multiple times, e.g. with a module system inspired by the OCaml language. We briefly sketch here our enrichment of the internal language recognized by Coq 8.9.0, i.e. an abstract and simplified description of the language understood by the kernel of Coq enriched with additional information coming from the external syntax and preserved by our plugin by means of hooks and additional tables.

The grammar of the enriched internal language is in Table 1. Some additional constraints are not captured by the grammar. In detail, modules and module types cannot be nested inside sections and each extra-logical flavor is allowed to occur only in a subset of the positions where a flavor is expected.

The starting symbol of the grammar is *file*, that represents the content of a .v file. We represent a .v file as a set of type-theory-flags followed by a list of declarations. The flags are not actually written in the file by the user, but passed on the command line to coqc. They can be used to change the rules of the type theory to make the Set sort impredicative, to collapse the universe hierarchy (and obtain an inconsistent system) or to disable termination checking for functions (and also obtain an inconsistent system).

Due to space constraints we give only an extremely dense explanation of the language, focusing on the features relevant to the exportation.

Comments, Flavors and Requires. Comments and flavors are extra-logical data preserved from the user input. The plugin records as a flavor the exact keyword that was used to introduce a definition or declaration. Some flavors only carry the intent of the definition (e.g. to be a theorem or a lemma). Some others record information about the use of the definition during elaboration (e.g. as a coercion, type class instance, canonical structure).

The only comments preserved by the plugin are special comments in the source file that are meant to be elaborated by the coqdoc tool. These are the comments that the user expect to see in the automatically generated HTML description of a library. Therefore we assume those to be important.

An extra-logical **Requires** statement is used in a source file to ask Coq to elaborate another source file. Require statements force a direct acyclic graph

Table 1. The enriched internal language

file	::= type-theory-flags (decl)*
decl	::= — *extra logical commands*
	"a comment: some text + markup here"
	| **Requires** *file*
	— *base logic declarations*
	| $\mathcal{F}$ $\underline{e}@\{y^*\} : E[:= E]$
	| **Universe** $\underline{u}$
	| **Constraint** $u(< \mid \leq \mid =)u$
	| $\mathcal{F}$ (**Inductive** | **CoInductive**) $(\underline{e}@\{(y)^*\} : E := (\underline{e}@\{(y)^*\} : E)^*)^+$
	— *section declarations and variables in sections*
	| **Section** $\underline{s}$:= decl*
	| $\mathcal{F}$ **Variable** $x : E$
	| **Polymorphic Universe** y
	| **Polymorphic Constraint** $(u \mid y)(< \mid \leq \mid =)(u \mid y)$
	— *module (type) declarations*
	| **Module Type** $\underline{m}$ $(\underline{m} : T)^*$ <: T^* := $(T \mid \text{decl}^*)$
	| **Module** $\underline{t}$ $(\underline{m} : T)^*$ $[: T]$ <: T^* $[:= (M \mid \text{decl}^*)]$
E	::= — *base logic expressions*
	$e@\{(U)^*\} \mid x \mid \text{Prop} \mid \text{Set} \mid \text{Type}@\{U\} \mid \Pi x : E.E \mid \lambda x : E.E \mid E\,E$
	| $\text{Match}\,e\,E\,E\,E^* \mid (\text{Fix} \mid \text{CoFix})\,\mathbb{N}\,(\underline{e} : E := E)^* \mid \text{let}\ x : E := E\ \text{in}\ E$
	| $E.\mathbb{N} \mid (E : E)$
U	::= — *universes*
	$u \mid y \mid \max U\,U \mid \text{succ}\,U$
T	::= — *module type expressions*
	$[!]\,t\,m^* \mid T\ \text{with}\ e' := E \mid T\ \text{with}\ m' := M$
M	::= — *module expressions M*
	$[!]\,m\,m^*$
x, y	::= variables for term, universe respectively
e, u, m, t, s	::= qualified identifiers of expressions, universes, modules, module types
e', m'	::= relative qualified identifiers of expressions, modules
$\underline{e}, \underline{u}, \underline{m}, \underline{t}, \underline{s}$	::= fresh (unqualified) identifiers
$\mathbb{N}$	::= a natural number
$\mathcal{F}$	::= — *extra-logical flavours*
	Lemma | **Theorem** | **Corollary** | **Declaration** | **Definition** | **Axiom**
	| **Conjecture** | **Let** | **Example** | **Coercion** | **SubClass** | **Remark**
	| **CanonicalStructure** | **Fixpoint** | **CoFixpoint** | **Projection**
	| **IdentityCoercion** | **Scheme** | **Instance** | **Method** | **Fact** | **Property**
	| **Proposition** | **Record** | **Inductive** | **Coinductive** | **Assumption**
	| **Hypothesis** | **Conjecture** | **LocalDefinition** | **LocalLet** | **LocalFact**

(DAG) structure on Coq libraries. We preserve the statement because this structure is meaningful to the user and likely to be exploited also by automated tools.

Qualified Identifiers. The library is organized hierarchically. When forming base logic expressions E, module expressions M, and module type expressions T, declarations can be referred to by qualified identifiers e, m, resp. t formed from

1. The root path (sequence of identifiers) that is defined by the Coq package. This is the first argument of the `-R` option described above. Typically, but not necessarily, every package introduces a single unique root identifier.
2. One identifier each for every directory or file that leads from the package root to the respective Coq source file.
3. One identifier each (possibly none) for every nested module (type) inside that source file that contains the declarations.
4. The unqualified name e, u, m, resp. t.

Note that section identifiers do not contribute to qualified names: the declarations inside a section are indistinguishable from the ones outside the section. The only exception to this rule is for section variables: their qualified expressions follow the same rules as above, but after the identifier for the innermost module we have the list of identifiers of the sections that surround the section variable.

Universes are also assigned by Coq qualified identifiers u, but, since universes as considered to be globally declared anywhere, the module identifiers do not contribute: the identifier is obtained by putting a unique progressive number that carries no logical content after the file name.

Relative qualified names are always relative to a module type, i.e. they are missing the root identifiers and the directory identifiers parts.

Definitions, Declarations, Terms and Universes. Besides the usual λ-calculus with `let...in`, the expressions include dependent products $\Pi x : term.term$ (used to type λ-abstractions), sorts `Prop`, `Set`, `Type@{U}` (used to type types), casts $(E : E)$, (co)inductive types with primitive pattern-matching, (co)fixpoints definitions (i.e. terminating recursive functions) and record projections $(E.\mathbb{N})$. Notably, Coq maintains a partially ordered **universe hierarchy** (a direct acyclic graph) with consistent constraints of the form $U(< \mid \leq)U'$. Coq implements universe polymorphism, i.e. definitions and declarations of constants, inductive types and inductive constructors are abstracted over a list $(y)^*$ of universe variables that can occur in universe expression. Occurrences of constants are always fully applied to actual universe expressions: $e@\{(U)^*\}$. Universe polymorphism cohabits with template polymorphism, which is an older form of polymorphism where the sort `Type@{U}` of a (co)inductive type can become `Prop` or `Set` when the type is instantiated with parameters that are `Prop` or `Set`, according to some rules. The kernel does not record any ad-hoc information to implement template polymorphism and thus we do not export any. Finally, Coq has subtyping rules that include those used to compare (co)inductive types up to subtyping: when two occurrences of a (co)inductive type are compared, the formal universe parameters in corresponding position are compared according to the variance annotation associated to each actual universe parameter. The variance annotation, which is checked by the kernel to preserve logical consistency, is not explicitly shown in the grammar, but we will explicitly export it.

Module and Module Types. Module types and module are the main mechanism for grouping base logic declarations. Public identifiers introduced in **modules** are available outside the module via qualified identifiers, whereas **module types** only serve to describe what declarations are public in modules. We say that a module M *conforms* to the module type T if

- M declares every constant name that is declared in T and does so with the same type,
- M declares every module name that is declared in T and does so with a module type that conforms to the type (= the set of public declarations) of the module in T,
- if any such name has a definiens in T, it has the same definiens in M.

Conformation of a module *type* to a module type is defined accordingly.

Both modules and module types may be defined in two different ways: *algebraically* as an abbreviation for a module (type) expression (the definiens), or *interactively* as a new module (type) given by a list of declarations (the body). A module may also be abstract, i.e., have neither body nor definiens. Every module (type) expression can be elaborated into a list of declarations so that algebraic module (type) declarations can be seen as abbreviations of interactive ones. The $<:$ and $:$ operators may be used respectively to attach conformation conditions to a module or to restrict the interface of a module.

Module and module types can be abstracted over a list of module bindings $\underline{m} : T$, which may be used in the definiens or in the body, according to which one is given. When the list is not empty the module/module type is called respectively a *functor/functor type*. A functor must be typed with a functor type that has the same list of module bindings.

Module (type) expressions can be obtained by functor application, whose semantics is defined by β-reduction in the usual way, unless "!" annotations are used. According to complex rules that we will ignore in the rest of the paper for lack of space, the "!" annotations performs β-reduction and then triggers the replacement of constants defined in the actual functor argument with their definiens. Finally, the `with` operator adds a definition to an abstract field in a module type.

Sections. Coq files and module (type)s can be divided into nested **sections**. These are similar to module functors except that they abstract over base logic declarations, which are interspersed in the body and marked by the **Variable** and **Polymorphic** keywords. The section itself has no semantics: outside the section, all constant and inductive type declarations are $\lambda\Pi$-abstracted over all **Variable** that occur in the declaration and over all **Polymorphic** declarations.

3   The Exported Data

In this section we describe how the enriched internal language of Coq is mapped to disk.

URIs. We turn the qualified names of Coq to Uniform Resource Identifiers (URI) according to the following schema:

- A qualified module, module type or section identifier like *mathcomp.field.galois.SplittingFieldTheory* is turned into the URI `cic:/mathcomp/field/galois/SplittingFieldTheory` simply prepending `cic:/` and turning all dots into slashes
- A qualified variable/constant/mutual/(co)inductive/block identifier *path.id* is mapped to `uri/id.ext` where `uri` is the URI computed for *path* and `ext` belongs to the set {`var,con,ind`} according to what it refers to
- A qualified universe identifier is used as an URI without modifications. The reason is that all universes are considered to be global by Coq and there is no XML file on disk that declares them anyway because no information is attached to the universe. In other words, a qualified universe identifier is just a unique identifier with no attached meaning.

Namespaces. We assume the following invocation of `coqc`:

```
coqc -R physical_path logical_path path_to_file/filename.v
```

used to compile a `filename.v` file such that the absolute path of `physical_path` is a prefix of the absolute path `path_to_file` of the file. Then the logical path of the file is obtained replacing `physical_path` with `logical_path` in `path_to_file`, mapping all slashes to dots and removing the `.v` extension.

For example, `coqc -R . mathcomp field/galois.v` and `coqc -R field mathcomp.field field/galois.v` both determine the logical path `mathcomp.field.galois`.

The logical path is mapped to disk by creating a nested directory for each identifier but the filename. In the example above, we create `mathcomp/field` and enter the directory before exporting the file.

We call a directory obtained in this way a *namespace*. Namespaces can be identified on disk because they lack both a corresponding `.role` file (see module (type)s and sections below) and a corresponding `.theory` file (see files below).

Files. Each file `foo.v` is mapped to disk to two different structures: a directory `foo` that contains the logical entries of the file (excluding the type theory flags) and a `foo.theory.xml` file that contains the type theory flags and all the extra-logical information (comments, flavors, requires).

The `foo.theory.xml` file is an XHTML file obtained running `coqdoc` on the concatenation of the comments in the enriched internal language expression that the file is mapped to. Moreover, XML elements belonging to the "ht:" XML namespace are added to the XHTML file as follows:

- one `ht:TYPETHEORY` element whose attributes encode the type theory flags.
- one `ht:REQUIRE` element for each **Requires** in the file, with an attribute that holds the URI of the included file.
- one `ht:DEFINITION`, `ht:AXIOM`, `ht:THEOREM` or `ht:VARIABLE` for every declaration or definition of a constant, variable or mutual inductive types block that where explicitly provided by the user. The ones generated automatically are not recorded in the `.theory.xml` file. We use `ht:AXIOM` for declared constants that do not have a definiens and `ht:THEOREM` for defined constants

whose type is a proposition, i.e. it is typed by `Prop`. An attribute of the element specifies the URI of the declaration or definition while a second attribute gives the exact flavor.

– one `ht:UNIVERSE` for each (polymorphic) universe declaration that was explicitly provided by the user. The ones generated automatically are not recorded in the `.theory.xml` file. An attribute of the element specifies the URI of the declaration; a second attribute records the user provided universe name, that cannot be inferred from the URI; a third attribute whether the universe declaration is polymorphic or not.

– one `ht:CONSTRAINT` for each (polymorphic) universe constraint declaration that was explicitly provided by the user. The ones generated automatically are not recorded in the `.theory.xml` file. Three attributes specify the two sides of the constraint and the constraint relation.

– one `ht:SECTION` for each section. An attribute specify the section identifier. The context of the element is obtained recursively processing the content of the section.

– one `ht:MODULE` for each module declaration or module (type) definition. An attribute allow to distinguish between an interactive module, an algebraic module, an interactive module type, and an algebraic module type. Another attribute is the module (type) identifier. Finally the context of the element is obtained recursively processing the content of the section.

The next paragraphs describe the logical information that goes into the `foo` directory. With the exception of the type theory flags that are stored in the `foo.theory.xml` file only, all the logical information is inside the directory and a tool interested only into that (e.g. an independent verifier) could ignore the `foo.theory.xml` file completely.

On the other hand a tool that wants to stay close to the original input by the user will only consider the file in the `foo` directory that are referenced (by means of URIs) in the `foo.theory.xml`. In this way definitions automatically generated by Coq are ignored.

Modules and Module Types. We recall that modules and module types are declared or defined according to the following grammar:

$$\textbf{Module Type } \underline{m} \ (\underline{m} : T)^* <: T^* \ := (T \mid \texttt{decl}^*)$$
$$\textbf{Module} \qquad \underline{t} \ (\underline{m} : T)^* \ [: T] \ <: T^* \ [:= (M \mid \texttt{decl}^*)]$$

The exporter maps both to disc in a very similar way. Therefore it is useful for the sake of the discussion to unify the two entries using the generalized grammar

$$\textbf{Module [Type] } \underline{mt} \ (\underline{m} : T)^* [: T] \ <: T^* \ [:= (MT \mid \texttt{decl}^*)]$$

where $\underline{mt}$ can be either $\underline{m}$ or $\underline{t}$ and MT can be either M or T.

On disk we create:

1. a directory $\underline{mt}$ that contains all the logical declarations exported by $\underline{mt}$, i.e. the interface (or actual type) of $\underline{mt}$. Concretely, if the module type expression

$[\,:T\,]$ is provided, the exportation of its flattening will be the content of the directory $\underline{mt}$. Otherwise, if $\mathtt{decl}^*$ is provided, then it is the content of the directory. Otherwise, if the module (type) expression MT is provided, the exportation of its flattening will be the content of the directory.

In practice, tools that work on the XML files do not need to know anything about module (type) expressions and can just work on lists of logical declarations. Moreover, looking in the $\underline{mt}$ directory only, they will directly see the interface of the module (type), without having to re-implement the case reasoning above.

2. a directory $\underline{mt}.\mathtt{impl}$ if the module type expression $[\,:T\,]$ and $[\,:=M\mid\mathtt{decl}^*]$ are both provided. The directory $\underline{mt}.\mathtt{impl}$ contains all the logical declarations generated by the module definiens: if the definiens is a module expression M, then we export its flattening; otherwise we directly export the list of declarations $\mathtt{decl}^*$.

   Tools can inspect this directory to know what is the witness for the module type interface $\underline{mt}$. We call it a witness and not an implementation because the module system of Coq does not allow to recover the definiens in any way. This is counter-intuitive w.r.t. programming languages of the ML family where the implementation is the one that is actually run after linking when the program is invoked. The only reminiscent of this in Coq happens when OCaml code is extracted from the Coq development: Coq modules are extracted to OCaml modules and the witness becomes accessible to computation.

3. a file $\underline{mt}.\mathtt{role}$. The file is a textual file (not an XML file) that only contains one keyword to allow to distinguish the various uses of directories. In particular, for a module declaration the keyword is $\mathtt{DeclaredModule}$. It is $\mathtt{Module}$ for a module definition or $\mathtt{ModuleType}$ for a module type definition.

4. every module declaration in $(\underline{m}:T)^*$ is exported as if it were declared via **Module** $\underline{m}:T$ inside $\underline{mt}$ and also inside $\underline{mt}.\mathtt{impl}$, if the latter exists. The only difference that distinguish the parameter $\underline{m}$ from an actual module declaration is $\underline{mt}.\underline{m}.\mathtt{role}$ (and also $\underline{mt}.\mathtt{impl}.\underline{m}.\mathtt{role}$ if it exists) that uses the keyword $\mathtt{Parameter}$ in place of $\mathtt{DeclaredModule}$.

   This choice is perfectly coherent both with the naming scheme of Coq and with the semantics of functor type application: $\underline{t}\ \underline{m}'$ and $\underline{t}\ \mathtt{with}\ \underline{m}:=\underline{m}'$ yields exactly the same result respectively when $\underline{t}$ is a functor type abstracted over the parameter $\underline{m}:T$ and when $\underline{t}$ is a module type that begins with a declaration of $\underline{m}:T$. Indeed most tools are likely to ignore the distinction, that becomes relevant only when parameterized module types are used to type functors. Search for "covariant translation" in [MRS19] for a lengthy discussion of this issue.

5. if $\underline{mt}$ was obtained flattening a module expression or a module theory expression, then an XML file $\underline{mt}.\mathtt{expr}.\mathtt{xml}$ is generated to describe the expression.

6. if $\underline{mt}.\mathtt{impl}$ was obtained flattening a module expression, then an XML file $\underline{mt}.\mathtt{impl}.\mathtt{expr}.\mathtt{xml}$ is generated to describe the expression.

7. if the list of module theory expressions $<:T^*$ is not empty, a file $\underline{mt}.\mathtt{sub}.\mathtt{xml}$ is generated. It contains the list of description of module expressions.

   This is the only case where we do not export the flattened version of the module expression. Therefore it will be hard to write tools that exploit the

254 C. Sacerdoti Coen

$<: T^*$ construct. Note, however, that the only use of this in Coq is for users to check conformity with a module type in order to later feed the module to a functor. In other words, it is only used to catch errors earlier. Adding the flattening to disk just require a few lines of code, but it generates many more files when the construct is used. Therefore we plan to export the flattening only if somebody will require that information in the future.

Tools that want to parse the latter three entries are required to have full understanding of the flattening process of Coq. For the time being we do not know of any potential application requiring such a knowledge. Moreover, the expressions in XML ignore the "!" flags to functor applications: inside the kernel of Coq the flag are represented using abstract types that do not allow to recover the user provided information. To print it out we would need another invasive patch to the kernel. We leave it as future work in case some tools that care about module expressions will be created.

Sections. A section $\underline{s}$ is exported as a directory $\underline{s}$ plus a textual file $\underline{s}$.role containing the keyword `Section`. The sections and variables declared into the section $\underline{s}$ are recursively exported inside the directory $\underline{s}$. The constants and inductive types declared into $\underline{s}$, instead, are exported outside the sections surrounding them. The mapping between logical URIs and the physical path is therefore preserved, since sections names do not contribute in Coq to qualified identifiers (see Sect. 2.2). This choice is backward compatible with [Sac01].

Declarations and Definitions. We distinguish the case of variables, constants and blocks of mutual (co)inductive types.

- Case $\mathcal{F} \ \underline{e}@\{y^*\} : E[:= E']$: we create three or four files $\underline{e}$.con.xml.gz, $\underline{e}$.con.body.xml.gz, $\underline{e}$.con.types.xml.gz, $\underline{e}$.con.constraints.xml containing respectively: the name $\underline{e}$, type E, list of universe parameters $(y)^*$ and list of section variables that the constant depends on; the definiens E' of the constant, if given; the type of all subterms of E and E' that inhabits a proposition, together with pointers to the subterms in the uid.con.xml.gz and uid.con.body.xml.gz files; the list of all constraints between universes that need to hold for the constant to be well typed.
- Case $\mathcal{F}$ **Variable** $x : E$: the output is the same of the constant case, but .con is replaced by .var and the .con.body.xml.gz file is missing because a variable has no definiens.
- Case $\mathcal{F}$ (**Inductive** | **CoInductive**) $(\underline{e}@\{(y)^*\} : E := (\underline{e}@\{(y)^*\} : E)^*)^+$. Let $\underline{e}1$ be the $\underline{e}$ of the first type defined in the block. We generate the $\underline{e}1$.ind.xml.gz, $\underline{e}0$.ind.types.xml.gz and $\underline{e}1$.ind.constraints.xml files. The former contains all the logical information in the declaration. The latter contains both the set of constraints between universes that need to hold for the constant to be well typed and the variance information for every universe parameter.

The output is backward compatible with [Sac01], up to the changes to the exportation of terms inside the files and with the exceptions of universe polymorphism that was not there. In particular .`constraints.xml.gz` are new as well as the universe parameters $(y)^*$.

Terms. The encoding of terms to XML is rather straightforward: all the data available is just turned into XML elements and attributes. Moreover, at the level of terms the differences with the 2003 plugin are minimal: primitive record projection have been added to Coq; universe polymorphism has been added so that occurrences of constants are now applied to universes; finally we now export a precise description of universes whereas before we were just mapping to `Type` all universes—universes were handled differently by Coq at the time. Therefore we have just applied minimal changes to the DTD we were using in 2003.

Derived Information. Once the XML files are exported, we use python and bash scripts to add to the repository additional files containing data that can be inferred processing the XML files, but that require time to generate. This data is currently considered experimental and stored either in Comma Separated Values (CSV) or Resource Description Framework (RDF) formats.

In particular a `graph.csv` file collects all logical dependencies between variable/constant/inductive types in the form of "URI1 occurs in URI2". Additional dependencies are generated lifting the previous ones to directories: DIR2 depends on DIR1 iff DIR1 contains an object URI1 that occur in URI2 that is contained in DIR2. These dependencies can be used to automatically generate graphical representations of dependency graphs for libraries at different level of granularities (files, modules, objects).

The RDF files store many more additional triples, comprising the ones required by the Whelp search engine [AGS+04] and the ones that belong to the Upper Library Ontology (ULO) [CKM+19].

4   Statistics and Final Considerations

The new XML exportation plugin has been already applied to the 49 Coq libraries that have an opam package and that currently compile with the latest version of Coq (8.9.0), generating a large dataset of 1,235,934 compressed XML files organized in 18,780 directories that require 17 GB on disk. The library, which is already one of the largest dataset for formal libraries, consists in 16,322 variable declarations, 159,617 constants (143,165 of them have a definiens) and 2,712 blocks of mutual (co)inductive type declarations. Everything is organized in 1,889 theory files, 3,931 sections, 2,368 module definitions, 52 module declarations and 387 module type definitions. Among the constants there are 47,978 user declared theorems and we compute the statement of their 7,426,140 atomic proof steps. More packages are likely to be exported in the next weeks since the Coq developers are currently working on porting more Coq libraries to 8.9.0.

We hope that a large number of researchers will consider the library a good dataset to experiment with Mathematical Knowledge Management in the large, and will be able to build interesting tools over it. Search engines are an easy example, but we already have interesting proof of concepts since the early 2000s (see for example [AGS+04, GS03] that worked on the data exported by the old version of the plugin). We are more interested into more recent tools like hammers, automatic theory aligners and tools able to perform automatic refactoring, which are all promising to deliver to users tools that have an immediate value for the daily formalization activity.

Finally, we envision the generated Git packages as an open repository for data and we encourage all researchers that generate data derived from our XML files to contribute by committing their additional data to the repositories.

References

[ABD03] Asperti, A., Buchberger, B., Davenport, J.H. (eds.): MKM 2003. LNCS, vol. 2594. Springer, Heidelberg (2003). https://doi.org/10.1007/3-540-36469-2

[AGS+04] Asperti, A., Guidi, F., Coen, C.S., Tassi, E., Zacchiroli, S.: A content based mathematical search engine: whelp. In: Filliâtre, J.-C., Paulin-Mohring, C., Werner, B. (eds.) TYPES 2004. LNCS, vol. 3839, pp. 17–32. Springer, Heidelberg (2006). https://doi.org/10.1007/11617990_2

[ARST11] Asperti, A., Ricciotti, W., Sacerdoti Coen, C., Tassi, E.: The Matita interactive theorem prover. In: Bjørner, N., Sofronie-Stokkermans, V. (eds.) CADE 2011. LNCS, vol. 6803, pp. 64–69. Springer, Heidelberg (2011). https://doi.org/10.1007/978-3-642-22438-6_7

[ASTZ06] Asperti, A., Coen, C.S., Tassi, E., Zacchiroli, S.: Crafting a proof assistant. In: Altenkirch, T., McBride, C. (eds.) TYPES 2006. LNCS, vol. 4502, pp. 18–32. Springer, Heidelberg (2007). https://doi.org/10.1007/978-3-540-74464-1_2

[AW02] Asperti, A., Wegner, B.: MOWGLI – an approach to machine-understandable representation of the mathematical information in digital documents. In: Bai, F., Wegner, B. (eds.) ICM 2002. LNCS, vol. 2730, pp. 14–23. Springer, Heidelberg (2003). https://doi.org/10.1007/978-3-540-45155-6_2

[CK18] Czajka, L., Kaliszyk, C.: Hammer for Coq: automation for dependent type theory. J. Autom. Reasoning **61**(1–4), 423–453 (2018). https://doi.org/10.1007/s10817-018-9458-4

[CKM+19] Condoluci, A., Kohlhase, M., Müller, D., Rabe, F., Sacerdoti Coen, C., Wenzel, M.: Relational data across mathematical libraries. In: Kaliszyk, C., et al. (eds.) CICM 2019. LNAI, vol. 11617, pp. 61–76 (2019)

[DT] Dowek, G., Thiré, F.: Logipedia: a multi-system encyclopedia of formal proofs. http://www.lsv.fr/~dowek/Publi/logipedia.pdf

[GA16] Arias, E.J.G.: SerAPI: Machine-friendly, data-centric serialization for Coq, October 2016. Working paper or preprint. https://hal-mines-paristech.archives-ouvertes.fr/hal-01384408

[GS03] Guidi, F., Schena, I.: A query language for a metadata framework about mathematical resources. In: Asperti, et al. [ABD03], pp. 105–118. https://doi.org/10.1007/3-540-36469-2_9

[ISA+16] Irving, G., Szegedy, C., Alemi, A.A., Eén, N., Chollet, F., Urban, J.: DeepMath - deep sequence models for premise selection. In: Advances in Neural Information Processing Systems 29: Annual Conference on Neural Information Processing Systems, Barcelona, Spain, 5–10 December 2016, pp. 2235–2243 (2016). http://papers.nips.cc/paper/6280-deepmath-deep-sequence-models-for-premise-selection

[KS06] Kohlhase, M., Sucan, I.: A search engine for mathematical formulae. In: Calmet, J., Ida, T., Wang, D. (eds.) AISC 2006. LNCS, vol. 4120, pp. 241–253. Springer, Heidelberg (2006). https://doi.org/10.1007/11856290_21

[KWP99] Kammüller, F., Wenzel, M., Paulson, L.C.: Locales a sectioning concept for Isabelle. In: Bertot, Y., Dowek, G., Théry, L., Hirschowitz, A., Paulin, C. (eds.) TPHOLs 1999. LNCS, vol. 1690, pp. 149–165. Springer, Heidelberg (1999). https://doi.org/10.1007/3-540-48256-3_11

[MGK+17] Müller, D., Gauthier, T., Kaliszyk, C., Kohlhase, M., Rabe, F.: Classification of alignments between concepts of formal mathematical systems. In: Geuvers, H., England, M., Hasan, O., Rabe, F., Teschke, O. (eds.) CICM 2017. LNCS, vol. 10383, pp. 83–98. Springer, Cham (2017). https://doi.org/10.1007/978-3-319-62075-6_7

[MRS19] Müller, D., Rabe, F., Sacerdoti Coen, C.: The Coq library as a theory graph. In: Kaliszyk, C., et al. (eds.) CICM 2019. LNAI, vol. 11617, pp. 171–186 (2019)

[RK13] Rabe, F., Kohlhase, M.: A scalable module system. Inf. Comput. **230**, 1–54 (2013). https://doi.org/10.1016/j.ic.2013.06.001

[Sac01] Sacerdoti Coen, C.: Project IST-2001-33562 MoWGLI. Technical report D2.a Exportation Module, Information Society Technologies (IST) Programme (2001). http://mowgli.cs.unibo.it/misc/deliverables/transformation/D2a_exportation_module/report.pdf

[Sac03] Sacerdoti Coen, C.: From proof-assistants to distributed libraries of mathematics: tips and pitfalls. In: Asperti, et al. [ABD03], pp. 30–44. https://doi.org/10.1007/3-540-36469-2_3

[Sac04] Sacerdoti Coen, C.: Mathematical knowledge management and interactive theorem proving. Ph.D. thesis, Technical report UBLCS 2004-5. University of Bologna (2004). http://www.cs.unibo.it/~sacerdot/tesidott/thesis.ps.gz

[Sac10] Sacerdoti Coen, C.: Declarative representation of proof terms. J. Autom. Reasoning **44**(1–2), 25–52 (2010). https://doi.org/10.1007/s10817-009-9136-7

[Tea19] The Coq Development Team: The Coq Proof Assistant, version 8.9.0, January 2019. https://doi.org/10.5281/zenodo.2554024

Forms of Plagiarism in Digital Mathematical Libraries

Moritz Schubotz[1,2(✉)], Olaf Teschke[2], Vincent Stange[1], Norman Meuschke[1], and Bela Gipp[1]

[1] University of Wuppertal, Wuppertal, Germany
{schubotz,stange,meuschke,gipp}@uni-wuppertal.de
[2] FIZ Karlsruhe/zbMATH, Berlin, Germany
olaf.teschke@fiz-karlsruhe.de

Abstract. We report on an exploratory analysis of the forms of plagiarism observable in mathematical publications, which we identified by investigating editorial notes from zbMATH. While most cases we encountered were simple copies of earlier work, we also identified several forms of disguised plagiarism. We investigated 11 cases in detail and evaluate how current plagiarism detection systems perform in identifying these cases. Moreover, we describe the steps required to discover these and potentially undiscovered cases in the future.

1 Introduction

Plagiarism is 'the use of ideas, concepts, words, or structures without appropriately acknowledging the source to benefit in a setting where originality is expected' [5,7]. Plagiarism represents severe research misconduct and has strongly negative impacts on academia and the public. Plagiarized research papers compromise the scientific process and the mechanisms for tracing and correcting results. If researchers expand or revise earlier findings in subsequent research, papers that plagiarized the original paper remain unaffected. Wrong findings can spread and affect later research or practical applications.

Furthermore, academic plagiarism causes a significant waste of resources [6]. Reviewing plagiarized research papers and grant applications causes unnecessary work. For example, Wager [28] quotes a journal editor stating that 10% of the papers submitted to the respective journal suffered from plagiarism of an unacceptable extent. If plagiarism remains undiscovered, funding agencies may even award grants for plagiarized ideas or accept plagiarized research papers as the outcomes of research projects. Studies showed that some plagiarized papers are cited at least as often as the original [14]. This is problematic, since publication and citation counts are widely used as indicators of research performance, e.g., for funding or hiring decision. Moreover, universities and research institutions invest considerable resources to investigate and sanction plagiarism.

The waste of resources and the deterioration of academic quality due to plagiarism is also a pressing concern for zbMATH. The zbMATH abstracting

© Springer Nature Switzerland AG 2019
C. Kaliszyk et al. (Eds.): CICM 2019, LNAI 11617, pp. 258–274, 2019.
https://doi.org/10.1007/978-3-030-23250-4_18

and reviewing service organizes and reviews the world's literature in mathematics and related areas since 1931. zbMATH includes its predecessor *Jahrbuch für die Fortschritte der Mathematik*, which goes back to 1868. As of today, zbMATH comprises about 4 million publications, reviewed with the help of more than 7,000 international domain experts. These expert reviewers do not repeat the foregone peer-review process of the venue publishing the article in question. Rather the zbMATH reviewers provide an unbiased view on the originality and innovative potential of articles for their subject areas, i.e., across venues. Ensuring the quality of articles is an integral part of zbMATH's mission statement and central to the usefulness of the service.

However, so far zbMATH's reviewing process for articles is conducted manually without the help of automated originality checks. Quality and originality insurance relies entirely on the knowledge of the expert reviewers who have to identify potential content overlap with other papers. The ability to spot such similarities requires reviewers to be closely familiar with similar articles. If an article exhibits significant overlap with prior works without discussing this fact, the reviewers will assign an editorial remark to the article.

The growth in publications indexed by zbMATH has raised concerns regarding the viability of the entirely manual reviewing process. Thus, zbMATH is investigating the use of automated approaches to support their reviewers. To guide and support this process, we performed an exploratory analysis of cases for which zbMATH reviewers questioned the originality of articles or identified plagiarism with certainty. Our goal is to develop an understanding of the typical characteristics of mathematical articles with questionable originality to derive the requirements for an automated system that can detect such cases.

We structure our report on this investigation as follows. Section 2 discusses related work before Sect. 3 presents the methodology of our investigation. Section 4 describes our findings and discusses their implications. Section 5 summarizes our results and gives an outlook on the next steps of the project.

2   Background and Related Work

The problem of academic plagiarism has been present for centuries [29]. However, the advancement of information technology has made plagiarizing easier than ever [6]. Forms of academic plagiarism range from copying content (*copy&paste*) over "patch-writing", i.e., interweaving text from multiple sources with moderate adjustments, to heavily concealing content reuse, e.g., by paraphrasing or translating text, and reusing data or ideas without proper attribution [29]. The easily recognizable copy&paste-type plagiarism is more prevalent among students whose main motivation for plagiarizing is typically to save time [15]. Concealed forms of plagiarism are more characteristic of researchers, who have strong incentives to avoid detection [2].

While making plagiarizing easier, information technology also facilitated the detection of plagiarism. Researchers proposed many plagiarism detection approaches that employ lexical, semantic, syntactical, or cross-lingual text analysis [4, 17, 27]. Such approaches typically employ a two-stage process consisting of candidate retrieval and detailed analysis [17,24]. In the candidate retrieval stage, the approaches employ computationally efficient retrieval methods to limit the collection to a set of documents that may have been the source for the content in the input document. In the detailed analysis stage, the systems perform computationally more demanding analysis steps to substantiate the suspicion and to align components in the input document and potential source documents that are similar [2,6,17].

Current plagiarism detection approaches reliably detect copied or moderately altered text; some approaches are also effective for finding paraphrased and translated text. Most plagiarism detection systems available for productive use focus on reliably and efficiently identifying plagiarism forms with little to no obfuscation, which are characteristic of students. We conjecture that student plagiarism is a more profitable market segment for commercial providers of plagiarism detection services. Arguments in favor of this hypothesis are the higher number of students compared to researchers, the higher frequency of plagiarism among students than among researchers [15,26] and the availability of well-established, efficient methods to find literal text reuse [4,17,27].

The market leader for plagiarism detection services, *iParadigms LLC*[1], offers its products under several brand names. The system *turnitin*[2] is tailored to providing originality checks and academic writing training for students. The *iThenicate*[3] service is mainly offered to academic publishers and conference organizers for checking research publications. The iThenticate service is also licensed to other academic service providers, such as *Crossref* who offers the service to its members as *Similarity Check*[4].

The detection methods employed by commercial systems, such as turnitin and iThenticate, are trade secrets. However, the performance of the systems in benchmark evaluations [30] suggests that they mainly use efficient text retrieval methods, such as word-based fingerprinting and vector space models. Text fingerprinting approaches first split a document into (possibly overlapping) word or character n-grams, which are used to create a representation of the document or passage (the 'fingerprint') [17]. To enable efficient retrieval, most approaches select a subset of the fingerprints, which they store in an index. To speed up the comparison of fingerprints, some approaches hash or compress the fingerprints, which reduces the lengths of the strings to compare and allows for computationally more efficient numerical comparisons [6].

To complement the many text analysis approaches and to improve the detection capabilities of concealed forms of academic plagiarism, researchers proposed approaches that analyze nontextual content features, such as academic citations [7–11,16,23] and images [18]. Nontextual content features in academic documents are a valuable source of semantic information that are largely independent of natural language text. Considering these sources of semantic information for

---

[1] https://www.crunchbase.com/organization/iparadigms-inc.
[2] https://www.turnitin.com.
[3] https://www.turnitin.com/products/ithenticate.
[4] https://www.crossref.org/services/similarity-check/.

similarity analysis raises the effort plagiarists must invest for obfuscating reused content [16, 22].

Nontextual feature analysis appears to be a promising approach to plagiarism detection for mathematics and related fields. In these fields, much of the semantic content of publications is expressed in terms of mathematical notation. Research showed that classical text retrieval methods, which are similar to the methods employed by commercial plagiarism detection services, are less effective for documents in mathematics, physics and other domains that routinely interweave natural language and mathematical notation [31].

However, only a few studies have addressed the detection of plagiarism in digital mathematical libraries [19, 21, 22] regardless of the detection approach. We briefly describe the main findings of these studies hereafter.

Following up on discussions at the doctoral consortium of the SIGIR conference 2015, Meuschke et al. [19, 20] described mathematics-based plagiarism detection (MathPD) as a discrete sub-problem within mathematical information retrieval. The authors argued that the different approaches to query formulation and query processing distinguish MathPD from the mathematical document retrieval problem as defined by Guidi and Sacerdoti Coen [12].

To test whether an exclusive analysis of mathematical similarity holds promise for plagiarism detection, Meuschke et al. [19, 20] gathered documents that have been retracted for plagiarism and contain significant amounts of mathematical content from three sources. The first source was an earlier study on retracted publications by Halevi and Bar-Ilan [13]. This study had queried Elsevier's full text database *Science Direct* for the term "RETRACTED" in October 2014. The search yielded 988 retracted articles, of which 276 had been retracted for plagiarism [13]. Meuschke et al. limited these 276 publications to a set of 39 publications that contain significant amounts of mathematical content. The second source was the blog *Retraction Watch*[5] from which Meuschke et al. obtained two confirmed cases of plagiarism. The third source was the crowd-sourced project *VroniPlag*[6], from which Meuschke et al. obtained three additional cases. The authors then limited the 44 cases they had gathered to cases that matched their area of expertise, i.e., mathematics, physics, and computer science, which resulted in 19 cases the authors then investigated manually. They categorized the types of shared mathematical content they observed in the analysis of these 19 cases into six broad categories [19]:

Identical: an exact copy of math in the source document.
Equivalent: equivalent forms, e.g., due to commutativity or distributivity.
Order changes: order of expressions within document differs.
Different presentation: structurally and semantically identical.
Splits or merges: of expressions that are semantically identical.
Different concepts: different, yet semantically (nearly) identical, concepts, e.g., summation over vector components instead of matrix multiplication.

---

[5] http://www.retractionwatch.com.
[6] http://www.vroniplag.wikia.com.

Of the 19 cases reviewed manually, Meuschke et al. selected 10 cases that were most representative of the types of content similarity they observed. The authors converted the ten source documents and ten retracted documents of those cases from PDF to LaTex using InftyReader [25] and subsequently from LaTeX to XHMTL using LaTexML[7]. They embedded the converted documents in the dataset of the NTCIR-11 Math task [1] (105,120 arXiv documents). Using pairwise document comparisons, Meuschke et al. evaluated the retrieval effectiveness of similarity measures that consider basic representational math features, i.e., identifiers, numbers, operators, and combinations thereof. The best performing approach, a set-based comparison of the frequency of mathematical identifiers, retrieved eight of ten test cases at the top rank and achieved a mean reciprocal rank of 0.86.

In a follow-up study, Meuschke et al. introduced similarity measures that consider the order of mathematical identifiers and presented a two-stage retrieval process consisting of a candidate retrieval and a detailed analysis stage that replaced the exclusive use of pairwise document comparisons [22]. They implemented the process in the HyPlag prototype that also offers a user interface to investigate the identified similarities [21]. The candidate retrieval stage employs efficient index-based retrieval methods based on mathematical features. The candidate documents retrieved in the first stage then undergo pairwise comparisons in the detailed analysis stage of the process. The authors compared the effectiveness of their math-based analysis to citation-based and text-based approaches. They found that the order-observing similarity measures for mathematical identifiers achieved better results than the order-agnostic measures in their previous study [19]. Most of their ten test cases also exhibit a high textual similarity. A combined analysis of math-based and citation-based similarity performed equally well as the text-based analysis for the ten test cases. In an analysis of all 105K documents in their dataset, Meuschke et al. demonstrated that the combined analysis of math-based and citation-based similarity has advantages over a text-based analysis by identifying interesting instances of content reuse that a text-based analysis could not detect.

In summary, Meuschke et al. [22] demonstrated that the combined analysis of text-based and nontextual similarity, e.g., the similarity of mathematical content and citations, achieves promising results for retrieving confirmed cases of plagiarism that involve mathematical content. However, the set of documents they analyzed is small and likely does not reflect the full spectrum of possible content reuse in digital mathematical libraries. To aid in the advancement of plagiarism detection methods for mathematics and related disciplines, we analyze a larger set of cases obtained from the zbMATH collection. An interesting property of this collection is that it exclusively includes published work since 2007, i.e., from a period in which larger publishers already employed services like CrossRef's Similarity Check. Also digitization has reached maturity during this period, so we can expect that these examples were not detected by standard tools.

---

[7] http://dlmf.nist.gov/LaTeXML/.

3   Method

Subsection 3.1 describes our approach to identify cases of *noticeable content reuse* (NCR). Subsection 3.2 presents the challenges we faced in regard to processing the cases using the HyPlag detection system. Lastly, Subsect. 3.3 defines the properties we evaluate for a small number of example cases.

3.1   Identification of Noticeable Content Reuse

The zbMATH collection currently[8] contains 3'981'836 publications. Since 2007, zbMATH follows a intra-organizational procedure for marking publications that exhibit noticeable content reuse. The managing editor and the deputy editor-in-chief decide on a case-by-case basis on the actions to be taken if illegitimate content reuse is observed. From 2007 to 2018, 1,226,203 new publications have been added to the zbMATH database. Although all publications underwent peer-review by the publishing venue before being submitted to zbMATH, 446 cases of questionable content reuse have been reported to the managing editor of zbMATH. After careful investigation of these reports, 144 cases received an editorial note about NCR. This list includes cases of content reuse by the same authors in different papers as well as content reuse by different authors. Moreover, in contrast to Meuschke et al. [22], this dataset includes both true positives (144), i.e., suspicious documents, and false positives (302).

The list of the 144 suspicious cases is openly available from the zbMATH website[9] using the query shown in Listing 1.1. The logic of the query is as follows: Line 1 filters for publications that appeared between 2007 and 2018, which matches the period investigated in this paper. 'py' is the query term for publication year. Line 2 filters the abstracts (ab) for the keywords 'editorial remark' or 'editorial note.' Line 3 filters for remarks that indicate plagiarism. Examples for excluded editorial notes are incorrect results, conceptual flaws, or organizational comments. Note that we applied this filter to all fields, not just the abstract, since sometimes the indicator for an editorial note is included in other fields, e.g., the keywords. For example the, document 1191.35223[10] is in the category 'suspected plagiarism,' although this is not indicated in the abstract of the document. Line 4 corrects the search result and excludes false positives.[11]

---

[8] As of 2019-03-19 see https://zbmath.org/about/#id_4 for updated numbers.

[9] https://zbmath.org.

[10] We use zbMATH identifiers for referring to cases throughout the paper. The identifiers resolve via, e.g., https://zbmath.org/1191.35223 to documents accessible without subscription.

[11] See https://zbmath.org/general-help/ for the details of the search syntax.

Listing 1.1. zbMATH search query to retrieve papers with a noticeable amount of content reuse. Click here to execute the query. Subscription required for full display!

```
1  py:2007−2018 &
2  ( ab:"editorial remark" | ab:"editorial note" ) &
3  ( "very similar" | "high similarity" | overlap
        |plagiari* | identical | substantial* | essentially )
4  !( so:ieee
        |se:00000250 | se:00001661 | pu:AIP | an:0584.10010
        |an:0712.35001 | an:0597.14041 | an:1375.14126
        |an:0156.05104 | an:1345.15011 | an:1262.11083)
```

3.2 The Challenge of Full Text Availability

After having identified the set of cases to investigate, we had to import the documents to our plagiarism detection system HyPlag (cf. Sect. 2), which requires text encoding initiative (TEI) format as input. Unfortunately, the zbMATH dataset does not include full texts. The full texts might be obtained by following the DOI, an arXiv link, or a link to another digital repository. Yet, in most cases (except for arXiv) the LaTeX sources of the documents are unavailable. While HyPlag includes a conversion procedure that generates the TEI input format from PDF files via the PDF processor GROBID[12], this procedure cannot process mathematical formulae. As a result, TEI documents generated from PDF documents miss mathematical formulae.

In a previous study [19], we employed the image to formula conversion tool InftyReader (cf. Sect. 2). However, the results were unsatisfactory. While InftyReader extracted parts of the formulae correctly, its extraction accuracy regarding the structure of the document was significantly worse than that of GROBID. We also evaluated several alternative tools, including the combination of maxtract [3] and pdfminer[13]. We also discovered and tested new machine learning based approaches[14]. However, these approaches only worked in a few exceptional cases.

Eventually, we were unable to identify a tool capable of converting the zbMATH documents including all essential features, i.e, text, formulae and figures. Consequently, we modified the setup of our study and decided to investigate only a small sample of the collected documents. To still analyze a diverse and representative test dataset, we decided to use a semi-random method. The managing editor of zbMATH manually selected interesting cases that had undergone extended internal discussions, which we see as an indicator that the potential overlap was not initially obvious. Due to the diversity of the cases and the different decisions zbMATH reviewers made regarding the legitimacy of the observed similarities, the documents can form an interesting test collection for PD systems in mathematics. The small test collection consists of the 11 items listed in Table 1.

---

[12] https://grobid.readthedocs.io.

[13] https://pypi.org/project/pdfminer/.

[14] For example: http://cs231n.stanford.edu/reports/2017/pdfs/815.pdf.

3.3   Properties to Investigate

After choosing the test cases, we specified the following properties to investigate:

1. Which type of plagiarism is observable in the article?
2. Is the article digitally available? Has it been retracted?
3. How important were the text, the figures, the references, and the formulae during the discussion about issuing an editorial remark?
4. When were the articles published? What are the languages of the documents?
5. What is the impact of the case? Has the article that received an editorial remark been cited. Does other statistical data on the use of this article exist?
6. Which requirements on a plagiarism detection system derive from this case?

4   Results

In this section, we first present descriptive statistics for the cases exhibiting noticeable content reuse. Second, we describe the 11 selected test cases in detail. Third, we derive requirements on a plagiarism detection system from the exemplary results of our analysis.

4.1   Distribution of the Source Documents

The 144 publications that received an editorial remark for NCR consist of 139 journal articles and 5 books. The 139 articles originate from 101 journals. Two journals published 6 articles with editorial remarks each (cf. Fig. 1), while 76 journals published only one such article. The 144 documents have 215 authors. One person was an author of 6 publications that received an editorial remark, while 173 authors were involved in only one case (cf. Fig. 1). For 78 of the 144 documents, the full texts are available from at least one source (DOI (76), arXiv (3), eudml (4), or emis (3)). See Appendix A for the complete list of cases.

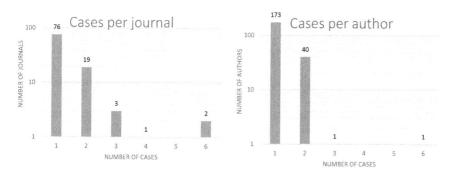

Fig. 1. Distribution of journal (left) and author (right) frequencies on a logarithmic scale.

Table 1. Overview of manually investigated cases. The similarity scores were computed using HyPlag. l_i denotes the later document of case i and $e_{i,j}$ the j-th earlier document of case i.

#	l_i	$e_{i,j}$	Retr.	Avail. via	Text sim	Cit sim	Spread
1	1349.46021 (2015)	06696052 (2015) 1353.46015 (2014)	-	doi, eudml, ams	**.23**	-	40 reads on researchgate
2	1381.51005 (2008)	1162.51304 (2007)	Yes	ams	.03	-	-
3	1119.11307 (2001)	1062.11019 (2000)	Yes	doi, ams	**.33**	-	40 reads on researchgate, 21 downloads on springer link
4	1112.35034 (2005)	0632.65108 (1987)	-	doi, ams	**.33**	-	6 reads on researchgate
5	1183.05037 (2008)	0247.05143 (1972)	-	doi, ams	.0	**.75**	5 reads on researchgate
6	1121.35118 (2005)	1062.81046 (2004)	-	doi, eudml, arXiv	.06	-	5 reads & 3 cits. on researchgate, 61 downloads on springer link
7	1176.08001 (2009)	1036.08001 (2003)	-	-	-	-	-
8	1219.30004 (2011)	1040.30002 (2004)	-	doi, eudml	.14	.19	21 reads & 4 cits. on researchgate
9	0946.35085 (1999)	0816.47056 (1994)	-	doi	.09	-	4 reads & 1 cit. on researchgate, 27 downloads on springer link
10	1155.35429 (2006)	1142.35593 (2004)	-	doi	.16	-	112 reads & 41 cit. on researchgate, 38 cits. on ScienceDirect
11	1360.81259 (2017)	1185.81005 (2009) - (-)	-	doi	0.1	-	-

4.2 Manual Investigation

Hereafter, we present our findings from manually analyzing the 11 test cases:

Case 1 (legitimate content reuse) consists of the inspected document l_1 and the earlier works $e_{1,1}$ and $e_{1,2}$.

While the zbMATH editorial remark just reads: "Almost the same results were previously obtained in $(e_{1,1})$", more information is available through the reviews at https://mathscinet.ams.org/mathscinet-getitem?mr=3390281:

- Theorem 2.3(2) is Theorem 2.4(7)
- Corollary 2.4 is Corollary 2.6
- Corollary 2.5(2), (4) and (5) is Corollary 2.5(5), (3) and (7)
- Theorem 2.7 and its Corollary 2.8 are respectively Theorem 2.11 and Corollary 2.12 of the older document (by noting from Theorem 2.11 of the older

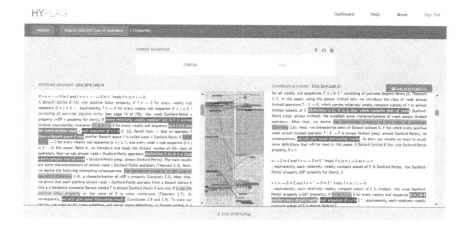

Fig. 2. Visualization of case 1 in HyPlag prototype.

document that the order bounded operators $T : E \to E$ in Corollary 2.12 may be replaced by positive ones).

Moreover, the reviewer states for the second prior document $e_{1,2}$

– Note also that Theorem 2.3(5) and Corollary 2.5(8) are respectively Theorem 2.7(8) and Corollary 2.10(5) of the second prior document. The proofs of the results that are republished in the paper under review are similar to those of the other publication.

Despite the overlap in content, the editor decided to publish the article. The rationale of this decision is that the similar structure seems to be the obvious solution to the given problem. However, this explanation does not justify the high textual similarity (0.23) that HyPlag computed for l_1 and $e_{1,1}$. Despite this moderately high value[15] for the overall textual similarity, the HyPlag visualization[16] (cf. Fig. 2) shows that the text similarity in the section described by the reviewers is particularly high. To our knowledge, neither the reviewer, nor the editor had access to a text similarity visualization such as the one of HyPlag when they decided not to retract the article.

Note that 1394.47040 also used theorems from $e_{1,1}$ in combination with results from 1336.46019. The authors published an erratum 06644537 and acknowledged that 'some results' have been proven by $e_{1,1}$ and 1336.46019. They 'feel sorry' that they have ignored the original sources. In contrast to the other sources 1394.47040 draws upon, We did not identify a textual similarity of 1394.47040 with $e_{1,1}$ and 1336.46019.

---

[15] A value above 0.2 is considered as suspicious.
[16] https://www.hyplag.org/ user cicm@hyplag.org pw: cicm2019.

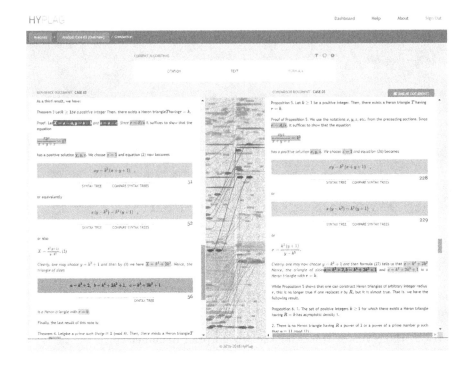

Fig. 3. Visualization of case 3 in HyPlag prototype.

Case 2 (retracted) consists of the retracted paper l_2 which overlaps with e_2. The retraction note states 'The author and the editor regret an oversight that this paper has significant overlap with the prior publication.'

From a plagiarism detection perspective, this case is particularly interesting since the later paper does not reuse text from the earlier paper (text similarity score 0.03). Moreover, the documents do not have common citations. However, many formulae and figures in the documents can be used to identify the overlap.

Unfortunately, the extraction of the figures from the PDF was challenging. State of the art image extraction technology was unable to identify the images. The internal representation of the figures in the PDF object stream prevents the identification of the basic geometric objects as a meaningful figure.

Case 3 (retracted) consists of the paper l_3 which is similar to e_3 without citing the earlier work. The later paper reuses several identical formulae and has a significant text overlap (text similarity score 0.33). The paper was published in 2001 and retracted in 2007. In the meantime, it received 2 citations in zbMATH - interestingly, by two papers that also cited e_3.

For this case, the LaTeX sources were available to us. Thus, we can visualize the formula similarity using HyPlag. Despite the high text similarity, the identical formulae are apparent within the visualization (cf. Fig. 3).

Fig. 4. Visualization of case 5 in HyPlag prototype

Case 4 (plagiarism). In this case, the authors of 1253.35026, which they also published as l_4, copied results from e_4 published in 1987. The papers have a high text similarity of 0.33, even though we extracted the text from the earlier paper using OCR. However, one may speculate that the limited availability of the original in digital form (only available as a scan) contributed to the late discovery of the case. The republished version of the article l_4 is unavailable in digital form. 1253.35026 has been cited once. The case illustrates the limitations resulting from insufficient digitisation.

Case 5 (translation) is a prototypical example for translation plagiarism. The original work e_5 written in French and published 1972 was translated to l_5 published in 2008 without acknowledging the original source.

This case likewise illustrates the limitations induced by sub-optimal digitisation. While both papers are available via DOI, the scan of the original only allows for an OCR quality that is insufficient for matching the citations in both documents. For instance, using Adobe Acrobat version 11.0.0, one receives the following representation of the references:

[1] A. RÉNYI, On oonnected gl'aphs, Magyar Tud. Aka.d. Mat. Kutato Iut. Ki)zl., 4, 1959, p. 385−388.
[2] G. FORD, G. UHLENBECK, Combinatorial problems in the tlteor·y of graphs, Proceedings of the National Acttdemy of Sciences of the U. S. A., 42, 1956, p. 122−128.
[3] J. \\V. MooN, En!mterating Labeled 1'rees, dans: Graph Theory an●l Theoretica.l Physic\˜, editor F. Httrary, Academie Press, New York−London, 1967, p. 261−271.

The quality of the extracted references was too low to match references and in-text citations in the documents. To demonstrate the potential of the approach, we manually corrected the OCR text. Figure 4 shows the result: the first three citations appear in identical order in both documents resulting in a high citation-based similarity score. e_5 has been neither retracted nor cited so far.

Case 6 (topical relatedness) consists of l_6. The main result of this paper had been proven by an earlier article e_6 using similar methods (or, as https://mathscinet.ams.org/mathscinet-getitem?mr=2177689 states: "The same theory can be found in an essentially identical presentation in [the] earlier paper [...] not cited by the present author."). A subsequent discussion by expert reviewers remained inconclusive; thus, the paper has not been retracted. Technical PD tools fail to detect any significant similarity of the articles. Perhaps due to the awareness created by the reviewers' discussion, l_6 received only two (self-)citations, while e_6 is cited frequenlöy.

Case 7 (distribution stopped) represents the translation of a book. The German original e_7 from 2003 was translated to English and published in 2009 as l_7. The publisher stopped the distribution of the English version[17], which therefore was digitally unavailable to us. Despite its short period of availability, l_7 has been cited at least three times, while only one citation of e_7 is known so far.

Case 8 (identical) is an example for a work that reuses an earlier work, changes the mathematical notation, and presents a weaker result. The later paper l_8 which reused content from e_8 is still online without referencing the original work. The later paper received three citations according to Google scholar, was downloaded 4013 times, and viewed 7615 times according to the publisher[18]. Despite the significant overlap, the publisher did not issue a retraction but only a statement of priority for the original result. The statement appeared inconspicuously in a later issue and is not linked from the article itself. The similarity of the text and the references, although slightly below a critical threshold, should have issued at least a warning by a PD system.

Case 9 (unclear) comprises l_9 which adopted content from the earlier work e_9. The notation was changed and the text differs (text similarity 0.09). However, expert reviewers qualified the later article as: "derivative work". So far, no retraction has been issued. According to the publisher[19], the derived work was downloaded 27 times and received one citation.

Case 10 (unclear) consists of the paper l_{10}, parts of which reuse material from e_{10} literally identical. However, the overall text similarity is below the critical threshold (score 0.16). Another noticeable difference is that one paper uses the computer algebra system Maple while the other paper uses Mathematica. No retraction has been issued. According to a later comment[20], the later article derives incorrect formulae. Nevertheless, both articles achieved citation counts that are well above the average for math articles. The citations seem to originate from a rather peculiar community. A PD system allowing for a uniform representation of Maple/Mathematica content would have facilitated a clear detection of the similarities. However, such as system is a distant prospect.

---

[17] https://www.emis.de/misc/articles/ext05526289.html.

[18] https://www.scirp.org/journal/PaperInformation.aspx?PaperID=3820.

[19] https://link.springer.com/article/10.1007%2FBF02463791.

[20] https://doi.org/10.1016/j.camwa.2011.01.043.

Case 11 (compilation of text elements) consists of paper l_{11} which combines material from $e_{11,1}$ and a paper[21] not part of the zbMATH corpus. A reviewer who had critically noted the authors' way of working before indicated the case to zbMATH. So far, the journal has not reacted on the comments in any way. Due to the low visibility of the journal, the compilation seem to have had little impact so far. The comparably low text similarity of the article derives intrinsically from being a compilation of two sources. For such cases, an adapted measure resulting in an adequate warning would be desirable. Humans spot the respective adaptations quickly.

4.3 Requirements for a Plagiarism Detection System at zbMATH

The investigation of the selected cases indicates that the application of a purely text-based system, such as the commercial service of iThenticate, appears insufficient for analyzing content overlap in mathematical publications. Many publishers already use iThenticate as part of their submission pipelines.

The major obstacle for using the open source solution HyPlag is the availability of high quality sources. While PDF files were often available, the mathematical formulae could not be extracted from these PDFs. Therefore, the math-based similarity detection of HyPlag [20] could not be evaluated in this paper. Moreover, some PDFs are of a low quality ans resulted in OCR text that is too erroneous for citation matching. Another problem with the PDF sources was that figures could not be identified.

5 Conclusion and Outlook

We created an openly accessible dataset of 144 papers with noticeable content reuse in zbMATH. The dataset can serve as a training set or test set, e.g., for plagiarism detection competitions, such as PAN. In a second step, we extended the 144 confirmed cases of NCR with cases for which the content similarity was eventually rated as legitimate. To not discredit authors who were incorrectly accused of wrongdoing, we refrain from publishing the complete dataset of 446 cases. Instead, we composed a list of 11 typical cases that illustrate the spectrum of reported content reuse. Moreover, we will continue our analysis with more cases to derive general patterns.

Using the 11 cases, we investigated how the plagiarism detection system HyPlag would perform in identifying the documents as suspicious. In a recent study [22], we applied the system to a large test collection producing only a small number of false positives. However, nine of ten test cases in [22] could have been discovered using traditional text-based detection methods. In contrast, for the zbMATH collection, this number is only three of eleven. For the text-based and the math-based detection methods, we needed to transcribe the test data manually since the sources were unavailable and the quality of formulae,

---

[21] https://math.berkeley.edu/~kwray/papers/string_theory.pdf.

citations, and figures extracted from PDF was insufficient for reliably matching these features. However, we demonstrated that our detection system would have discovered the similarities in content if the data would be available in LaTeX or XHTML format.

The dataset of 446 cases supports zbMATH's work towards the goal of installing a system that supports the editor in identifying potentially suspicious documents, even if the final decision is not to issue a public note on content reuse. In other words, the notification threshold of the system needs to be lower than for most plagiarism detection systems. Furthermore, the system must enable the zbMATH editor to easily understand why a document has been retrieved as potentially suspicious. This requirement is even more important than automatically performing a highly accurate binary classification of documents as suspicious or unsuspicious. To achieve this goal, visualizing the topical similarity is a key features required of the future system.

The next steps for realizing such a system are to establish an automated workflow for receiving the full-texts of the papers submitted to zbMATH. Moreover, we need to obtain mathematical formulae in a machine-readable format for at least a fraction of the zbMATH collection. We will continue our efforts to extract LaTeX formulae from PDF documents and are looking forward to the results of this years CHROME competition[22]. Especially the results for machine-readable formulae will be the foundation to conceive more sophisticated math-based detection methods. In the long run, we plan to lower the notification threshold for content reuse, which will undoubtedly require more sophisticated detection methods for formula similarity. The idea is to also identify papers that did not plagiarize but have limited novelty.

Acknowledgements. This work was supported by the German Research Foundation (DFG grant GI-1259-1).

A   List of Documents with Noticeable Content Reuse

1360.53021, 1357.30013, 1353.39029, 1353.30019, 1345.15011, 1359.62073, 1356.01026, 1337.16003, 1354.47018, 1340.90030, 1360.47003, 1345.92082, 1318.46035, 1400.34041, 1388.42037, 1388.42036, 1343.65150, 1330.35490, 1322.93076, 1321.81036, 1307.65177, 1308.81133, 1358.47017, 1309.65163, 1304.57008, 1325.47059, 1301.16002, 1293.65167, 1359.62055, 1291.30077, 1323.65125, 1328.47074, 1328.47073, 1299.65168, 1295.35151, 1294.35189, 1290.26023, 1282.91334, 1279.91096, 1281.35058, 1306.90186, 1311.90164, 1273.91086, 1287.81012, 1386.18011, 1301.45006, 1290.18001, 1278.68235, 1278.53033, 1271.54029, 1271.39024, 1266.65214, 1266.33002, 1264.34048, 1342.34118, 1266.30001, 1265.39016, 1264.81239, 1257.11089, 1250.78038, 1246.90035, 1246.90034, 1250.78039, 1252.68177, 1234.34034, 1364.47004, 1399.35153, 1274.76184, 1252.83109, 1288.49015, 1249.60023, 1250.47059, 1231.83033, 1227.34015, 1219.30004, 1236.58009, 1230.46033, 1213.60020, 1211.34093, 1211.34092, 1295.91090, 1242.49079, 1234.60021, 1262.11083, 1221.81113, 1234.60020, 1211.46021, 1217.34137, 1211.11127, 1203.06007, 1203.06006, 1212.49026, 1193.35074, 1191.35223, 1253.60034, 1235.37020, 1186.54007, 1189.35123, 1188.16002, 1183.37156, 1371.91006, 1371.91005, 1258.74210, 1257.78018, 1192.34093, 1195.55004, 1212.60016, 1201.60017, 1184.20030, 1176.91147, 1173.90327, 1206.34097, 1177.35217, 1170.34353, 1173.34354, 1279.90096, 1153.91544, 1189.35124, 1177.35218, 1175.86006, 1162.30319, 1170.42304, 1165.35336, 1162.30309, 1153.86318, 1154.94319, 1250.49003, 1166.47308, 1153.91523, 1155.26016, 1157.05036, 1162.83357, 1139.81335, 1213.35364, 1169.46304, 1169.42310, 1144.81475, 1141.90010, 1231.93121, 1132.14304, 1144.46044, 1134.60382, 1129.83326, 06921286.

---

[22] https://www.cs.rit.edu/~crohme2019/index.html.

References

1. Aizawa, A., et al.: NTCIR-11 Math-2 task overview. In: Proceedings of NTCIR Conference on Evaluation of Information Access Technologies (2014)
2. Alzahrani, S.M., Salim, N., Abraham, A.: Understanding plagiarism linguistic patterns, textual features, and detection methods. IEEE Trans. Syst. Man Cybern. C Appl. Rev. **42**(2) (2012). https://doi.org/10.1109/TSMCC.2011.2134847
3. Baker, J.B., Sexton, A.P., Sorge, V.: MaxTract: converting PDF to LaTeX, MathML and text. In: Jeuring, J., et al. (eds.) CICM 2012. LNCS, vol. 7362, pp. 422–426. Springer, Heidelberg (2012). https://doi.org/10.1007/978-3-642-31374-5_29
4. Eisa, T.A.E., Salim, N., Alzahrani, S.M.: Existing plagiarism detection techniques: a systematic mapping of the scholarly literature. Online Inf. Rev. **39**(3), 383–400 (2015)
5. Fishman, T.: 'We know it when we see it'? is not good enough: toward a standard definition of plagiarism that transcends theft, fraud, and copyright. In: Proceedings of Asia Pacific Conference on Educational Integrity (2009)
6. Foltynek, T., Meuschke, N., Gipp, B.: Academic plagiarism detection: a systematic literature review. Journal article in review (2019)
7. Gipp, B.: Citation-Based Plagiarism Detection - Detecting Disguised and Cross-Language Plagiarism Using Citation Pattern Analysis. Springer, Wiesbaden (2014). https://doi.org/10.1007/978-3-658-06394-8
8. Gipp, B., Meuschke, N.: Citation pattern matching algorithms for citation-based plagiarism detection: greedy citation tiling, citation chunking and longest common citation sequence. In: Proceedings of ACM Symposium on Document Engineering (DocEng) (2011). https://doi.org/10.1145/2034691.2034741
9. Gipp, B., Meuschke, N., Beel, J.: Comparative evaluation of text- and citation-based plagiarism detection approaches using GuttenPlag. In: Proceedings of ACM/IEEE-CS Joint Conference on Digital Libraries (JCDL) (2011). https://doi.org/10.1145/1998076.1998124
10. Gipp, B., Meuschke, N., Breitinger, C.: Citation-based plagiarism detection: practicability on a large-scale scientific corpus. JASIST **65**(2) (2014). https://doi.org/10.1002/asi.23228
11. Gipp, B., et al.: Web-based demonstration of semantic similarity detection using citation pattern visualization for a cross language plagiarism case. In: Proceedings of International Conference on Enterprise Information Systems (2014). https://doi.org/10.5220/0004985406770683
12. Guidi, F., Sacerdoti Coen, C.: A survey on retrieval of mathematical knowledge. Math. Comput. Sci. **10**(4) (2016). https://doi.org/10.1007/s11786-016-0274-0
13. Halevi, G., Bar-Ilan, J.: Post retraction citations in context. In: Proceedings of BIRNDL Workshop at JCDL (2016). https://doi.org/10.1007/s11192-017-2242-0
14. Long, T.C., et al.: Responding to possible plagiarism. Science **323**(5919) (2009). https://doi.org/10.1126/science.1167408
15. McCabe, D.L.: Cheating among college and university students: a North American perspective. Int. J. Educ. Integrity **1**(1) (2005). https://doi.org/10.21913/IJEI.v1i1.14
16. Meuschke, N., Gipp, B.: Reducing computational effort for plagiarism detection by using citation characteristics to limit retrieval space. In: Proceedings of IEEE/ACM Joint Conference on Digital Libraries (JCDL) (2014). https://doi.org/10.1109/JCDL.2014.6970168

17. Meuschke, N., Gipp, B.: State of the art in detecting academic plagiarism. Int. J. Educ. Integrity **9**(1) (2013). https://doi.org/10.21913/IJEI.v9i1.847
18. Meuschke, N., et al.: An adaptive image-based plagiarism detection approach. In: Proceedings of ACM/IEEE-CS Joint Conference on Digital Libraries (JCDL) (2018). https://doi.org/10.1145/3197026.3197042
19. Meuschke, N., et al.: Analyzing mathematical content to detect academic plagiarism. In: Proceedings of ACM Conference on Information and Knowledge Management (CIKM), pp. 2211–2214 (2017). https://doi.org/10.1145/3132847.3133144
20. Meuschke, N., et al.: Analyzing semantic concept patterns to detect academic plagiarism. In: Proceedings of WOSP Workshop held at ACM/IEEE-CS Joint Conference on Digital Libraries (JCDL) (2017). https://doi.org/10.1145/3127526.3127535
21. Meuschke, N., et al.: HyPlag: a hybrid approach to academic plagiarism detection. In: Proceedings of International ACM SIGIR Conference on Research and Development in Information Retrieval (SIGIR) (2018). https://doi.org/10.1145/3209978.3210177
22. Meuschke, N., et al.: Improving academic plagiarism detection for STEM documents by analyzing mathematical content and citations. In: Proceedings of ACM/IEEE-CS Joint Conference on Digital Libraries (JCDL) (2019). https://doi.org/10.1109/JCDL.2019.00026
23. de Lurdes Pertile, S., Moreira, V.P., Rosso, P.: Comparing and combining Content- and Citation-based approaches for plagiarism detection. JASIST **67**(10), 2511–2526 (2016)
24. Stein, B., zu Eissen, S.M., Potthast, M.: Strategies for retrieving plagiarized documents. In: Proceedings of International ACM SIGIR Conference on Research and Development in Information Retrieval (SIGIR) (2007). https://doi.org/10.1145/1277741.1277928
25. Suzuki, M., Kanahori, T., Ohtake, N., Yamaguchi, K.: An integrated OCR software for mathematical documents and its output with accessibility. In: Miesenberger, K., Klaus, J., Zagler, W.L., Burger, D. (eds.) ICCHP 2004. LNCS, vol. 3118, pp. 648–655. Springer, Heidelberg (2004). https://doi.org/10.1007/978-3-540-27817-7_97
26. Swazey, J.P., Anderson, M.S., Louis, K.S.: Ethical problems in academic research. Am. Sci. **81**(6), 542–553 (1993)
27. Vani, K., Gupta, D.: Study on extrinsic text plagiarism detection techniques and tools. J. Eng. Sci. Technol. Rev. **9**(4) (2016)
28. Wager, E.: Defining and responding to plagiarism. Learn. Publ. **27**(1) (2014). https://doi.org/10.1087/20140105
29. Weber-Wulff, D.: False Feathers: A Perspective on Academic Plagiarism. Springer, Heidelberg (2014). https://doi.org/10.1007/978-3-642-39961-9
30. Weber-Wulff, D.: Portal Plagiat - Tests of Plagiarism Software. Online Source (2019). http://plagiat.htw-berlin.de/software-en/. Accessed 12 Mar 2019
31. Wolska, M.: A language engineering architecture for processing informal mathematical discourse. In: Proceedings of DML WS Towards Digital Mathematics Library (2008)

Integrating Semantic Mathematical Documents and Dynamic Notebooks

Kai Amann[1], Michael Kohlhase[1], Florian Rabe[1,2], and Tom Wiesing[1(✉)]

[1] Computer Science, FAU Erlangen-Nürnberg, Erlangen, Germany
tom.wiesing@fau.de
[2] LRI, Université Paris Sud, Orsay, France

Abstract. Mathematical software systems offer two major paradigms for interacting with mathematical knowledge. One is static files with semantically annotated representations that define mathematical knowledge and can be compiled into documents (PDF, html, etc.), and the other dynamically build mathematical objects in interactive read-eval-print loops (REPL) such as notebooks. Many author-facing interfaces offer both features in some way. However, reader-facing interfaces usually show only one or the other.

In this paper we present an integration of the approaches in the context of the MMT system. Firstly, we present a Jupyter kernel for MMT which provides web-ready REPL functionality for MMT. Secondly, we integrate the resulting Jupyter notebooks into MathHub, a web-based frontend for mathematical documents. This allows users to context-sensitively open a Jupyter notebook as a dynamic subdocument anywhere inside a static MathHub document. Vice versa, any such highly interactive and often ephemeral notebook can be saved persistently in the MathHub backend at which point it becomes available as a static document. We also show how Jupyter widgets can be deeply integrated with the MMT knowledge management facilities to give semantics-aware interaction facilities.

1 Introduction

Mathematical software systems need to support two kinds of user interface paradigms. Firstly, mathematical *documents* have been very successful for presenting mathematical knowledge. While there have been efforts to make them modular and interactive, they predominantly remain in the mode of archiving and transporting knowledge in Mathematics. Secondly, *notebook* interfaces focus on REPL (Read/Eval/Print Loop) interaction leading to documents consisting of a sequence of computational cells within which the mathematical discourse is interspersed in the form of rich comments. A "literate programming" version of notebooks which gives mathematical discourse structural precedence is possible in principle but has not been supported consistently at the system level.

A combination of both of these paradigms almost immediately leads to new applications. One such application is the interaction with document-based systems, such as MMT, within a REPL. The MMT tool ecosystem only really

© Springer Nature Switzerland AG 2019
C. Kaliszyk et al. (Eds.): CICM 2019, LNAI 11617, pp. 275–290, 2019.
https://doi.org/10.1007/978-3-030-23250-4_19

supported IDE-interaction with MMT libraries via Edit and (recently) IntelliJ IDEA plugins. While the MMT system provides a simple shell for interaction, this was only used for configuration and setup of the MMT process. We anticipate that the REPL-like interaction will feel more natural for users of interactive theorem provers and computer algebra systems.

Goals and Challenges. Static documents do not allow for interactivity, and notebook approaches require significant programming knowledge to use. Our goal is to overcome these restrictions to enable domain experts to created interactive documents declaratively. This leads us to two challenges

(*i*) How can we combine the notebook and document paradigms?
(*ii*) How can we support flexible interactions without forcing authors to program?

Traditionally, flexible interactions in (web) documents are handled by applets, small, document-embedded programs providing specialized functionality. Modern notebook systems such as Jupyter, which we introduce in more detail below, provide the concept of widgets which provide applet-like functionality, but their combination into interactions still requires non-trivial programming.

Contribution. We present an integration of Jupyter Notebooks into the MathHub platform for hosting semantic, active documents. MathHub offers versioned persistent storage for semantically enhanced mathematical documents and knowledge representations. These are unified into the OMDoc/MMT format and loaded into a cross-document-format mathematical knowledge space managed by the MMT system (written in Scala). MathHub is a web frontend for showing OMDoc/MMT content as (largely static) mathematical documents. Jupyter offers a uniform interface to various computation facilities in the form of a read-eval-print loop (REPL), which can be seen as dynamic, ephemeral documents. The system consists of a general, feature-rich browser-based REPL interface that communicates to a system-specific backend, called a Jupyter kernel that supplies the computational capabilities. Such a kernel either connects the native system REPL via a generic Python kernel or uses language-specific network libraries.

Generally, the integration of MathHub and Jupyter consists of two challenges:

(*i*) the integration of the document paradigms and user interfaces and
(*ii*) the integration of the knowledge management and computation services.

The latter requires defining the semantics of the mathematical knowledge maintained in the user interfaces, and both Jupyter and MathHub are parametric in this semantics. In Jupyter, a separate kernel must be provided for each concrete language. In particular there are separate kernels for all computation systems used in OpenDreamKit. In MathHub, the determination of the semantics is delegated to the MMT system. This paper describes progress in both integration challenges.

Overview. In Sect. 2, for the integration of services, we present an MMT kernel for Jupyter. This not only makes the MMT functionality available at the Jupyter level, but also deeply integrates Jupyter widgets with the MMT Scala level. Widgets are a key Jupyter feature that reaches far beyond the standard REPL interaction. For instance, the Jupyter community has developed a large array of widgets for interactive 2D and 3D visualization of data in the form of charts, maps, tables, etc.

In Sect. 3, for the integration of document paradigms, we first show how to extend MathHub with a Jupyter server that allows viewing notebooks stored in MathHub. Then we present a MathHub feature that allows using interactive, ephemeral Jupyter Notebooks as subdocuments of static mathematical documents, e.g., HTML pages generated from scientific articles.

In Sect. 4, we present two case studies that evaluate our results: in-document computing facilities in active documents and a knowledge-based specification dialog for modeling and simulation. Section 5 concludes the paper.

2 Jupyter Notebooks for MMT

Jupyter notebooks consist of a sequence of cells; each of which contains either rich text or code that can be evaluated. The Jupyter user interface is implemented using TypeScript in the browser. The backend is implemented in Python and delegates the programming-language specific features to so-called kernels via a networking protocol. Each kernel works exactly like a REPL, that is to say they receive the user input of the code cells and produce output to be presented to the user. Additionally, kernels can implement custom interactions using widgets, consisting of re-usable user interface components that communicate directly with the kernel. Kernels for a specific programming language are typically implemented in that programming language, to ease implementation and make use of existing tool support. For details we refer the reader to [JD].

We designed and implemented a Jupyter kernel for MMT. The source code is available at [MMTJup17]. We describe the requirements of an MMT REPL in Sect. 2.1, its interface in Sect. 2.2, the implementation in Sect. 2.3 and our conversion between MMT data structures and notebook in Sect. 2.4. In Sect. 2.5, we describe and discuss our implementation of widgets within our kernel.

2.1 A REPL for MMT

MMT differs from typical computational engines in Jupyter in that it does not only (and not even primarily) perform computation but also handles symbolic expressions with uninterpreted function symbols whose semantics is described by logical axioms. Another important difference is how MMT handles context and background knowledge. Kernels for (mathematics-oriented or general purpose) programming languages, as typical in Jupyter, build and maintain a dynamic context of declarations with imperative assignment and stack-oriented shadowing and rely on a fixed—often object-oriented—background library of computational functionality. MMT, on the other hand, uses graphs of inter-connected theories to represent a multitude of possible contexts and background libraries to move knowledge between contexts. To adequately handle these subtleties, we systematically specified a new interface for Jupyter-style interactions with MMT.

Example. MMT uses theory graphs to model mathematical knowledge (see Fig. 1). This theory graph shows two kinds of inheritance mechanisms in MMT: commutative groups (theory CGrp) include monoids (Monoid), inheriting all Monoid objects (the universe U, the operation op, and the unit element e) and the unit axiom unit. Rings are formed by combining a (multiplicative) monoid with an (additive) commutative group. Inclusion

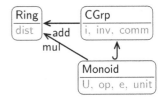

Fig. 1. Rings in MMT

roughly corresponds to class inheritance in object-oriented programming, while MMT structures duplicate material. Here the operation op from Monoid forms both addition ($+$ = add/op) and multiplication ($*$ = mul/op) in a ring and the Monoid unit becomes both zero (add/e) and the one elements (mul/e) of the ring.

The MMT system is usually used to answer queries such as computing particular, inherited ring axioms: $x + 0 = x$ and $x * 1 = x$ or determining the theorems and axioms of (i.e. inherited into) a theory.

2.2   Interface and Sessions

On top of the notebook abstraction, Jupyter interactions are managed in **sessions**: every browser page opening a notebook creates a new session.

MMT already has an abstraction that can closely model a notebook, called a document. In MMT terms, a document is a narrative construct that contains a sequence of declarations. For details, see the MMT documentation at [MMT]. Each input within the Jupyter session can be represented as a single declaration within the corresponding document; see Sect. 2.4 for further applications of this mapping.

Thus it makes sense to represent each session as an ephemeral MMT document. We call an MMT document **ephemeral**, iff it is (at least initially; it can be serialized and saved) created only in memory in the MMT process; apart from this, it behaves like any other MMT document. This gives each session a unique MMT URI, which in turn allows full referencing of all document components. All commands executed within a session manipulate the associated document, most importantly by interactively creating new theories and then calling MMT algorithms on them. The latter include but are not limited to computation.

Input. The possible inputs accepted by the MMT kernel come in three groups.

1. **Global management commands** allow displaying and deleting all current sessions. In practice, these commands are typically not available to common users, which should only have access to their own session.

2. **Local management commands** allow starting, quitting, and restarting the current session. These are the main commands issued by the frontend in response to user action.
3. **Content commands** are the mathematically meaningful commands and described below.

The content commands are again divided into three groups:

1. **Write-commands** send new content to the MMT backend to build the current MMT document step by step. The backend maintains one implicit, ephemeral MMT document for each session, and any write command changes that document.
2. **Read-commands** retrieve information from the backend without changing the session's document. These include lookups (both in the session document and in any other accessible document) or computations.
3. **Interactive-commands** that create a new user interface component allowing the user to interactively read and write MMT content. In the Jupyter system these are implemented as widgets which extend the REPL-paradigm; see Sect. 2.5.

A write-command typically consists of a single MMT declaration roughly corresponding to a line in a typical MMT source file. However, the nesting of declarations is very important in MMT. This is in contrast to many programming language kernels where nesting is often optional, e.g., to define new functions or classes; for many current kernels, it makes sense to simplify the implementation by requiring that the entire top-level command, including any nesting, be contained in a single cell.

In our MMT kernel, all declarations that may contain nested declarations (most importantly all MMT documents and theories) are split into parts as follows: the header, the list of nested declarations, and a special end-of-nesting marker. Each of these is communicated in a separate write-command. The semantics of MMT is carefully designed in such a way that (i) any local scope arising from nesting has a unique URI, and (ii) if a well-formed MMT document is built incrementally by appending individual declarations to a currently open local scope, any intermediate document is also well-formed. This is critical to make our implementation feasible: the MMT kernel maintains the current document as well as the URI of the current scope; any write-command affects the current scope, possibly closing it or creating new subscopes. This ensures that all nested declarations are parsed and interpreted in the right scope.

For example, the sequence of commands on the left of Fig. 2 builds two nested theories, where the inner one refers to the type a declared in the outer one. The right-hand side of Fig. 2 shows the equivalent MMT surface syntax on the right. Semantically, there is no difference between entering the left-hand side interactively via our new kernel or processing the write commands on the right with the standard MMT parser.

An additional special write-command is `eval T`. It interprets T in the current scope, infers its type A, computes its value V, and then adds the declaration

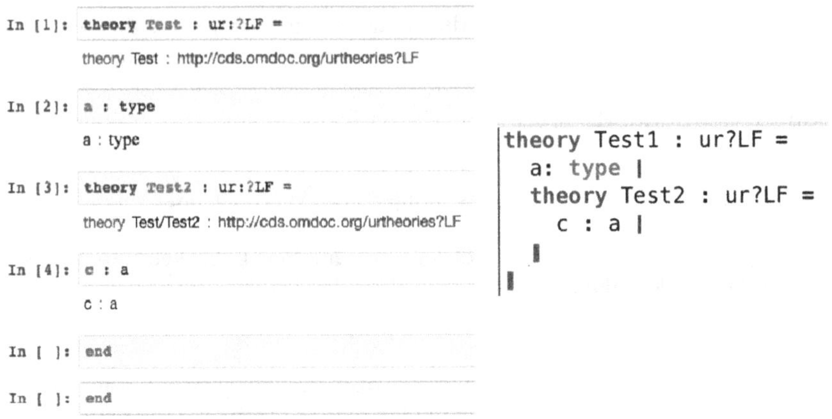

```
In [1]:  theory Test : ur:?LF =

         theory Test : http://cds.omdoc.org/urtheories?LF

In [2]:  a : type

         a : type

In [3]:  theory Test2 : ur:?LF =

         theory Test/Test2 : http://cds.omdoc.org/urtheories?LF

In [4]:  c : a

         c : a

In [ ]:  end

In [ ]:  end
```

```
theory Test1 : ur?LF =
  a: type |
  theory Test2 : ur?LF =
    c : a |

I
I
```

Fig. 2. Content commands for building theory graphs

resI:A=V to the current theory, where I is a running counter of unnamed declarations. This corresponds most closely to the REPL functionality in typical Jupyter kernels.

While write-commands correspond closely to the available types of MMT declarations, the set of read-commands is extensible. For example, the commands get U where U is any MMT URI returns the MMT declaration of that URI.

Output. The kernel returns the following kinds of return messages:

1. **Admin messages** are strings returned in response to session management commands.
2. **New-element messages** return the declaration that was added by a write-command.
3. **Existing-element messages** return the declaration that was retrieved by a get command.

Like read-commands, the set of output messages is extensible. The new-element and existing-element messages initially return the declaration in MMT's abstract syntax. A post-processing layer specific to Jupyter renders them in HTML5+MathML (presentation). That way, the core kernel functionality can be reused easily in frontends other than Jupyter.

2.3 Implementation

Generally, Jupyter emphasizes protocols that specify the communication between frontend and backend.

Executing the user commands requires a strong integration with the MMT system, which is implemented in Scala. Even though a Jupyter Scala kernel exists, we implement the MMT kernel on top of the Jupyter Python kernel infrastructure which is by far the best developed one. We implement all Jupyter-specific functionality, especially the communication and management, in Python, while all mathematically relevant logic is handled in Scala.

Our implementation consists of three layers. The top layer (depicted on the left of Fig. 3) is a Python module that implements the abstract class for Jupyter kernels. The bottom layer is a Scala class adding a general-purpose REPL to MMT that handles all the logic of MMT documents. This can be reused easily in other frontends e.g., the IntelliJ IDE plugin for MMT. User commands are entered in the front-end and sent to the top layer, which forwards all requests to the bottom layer and all responses from the bottom layer to the client. The communication between the top and bottom layer is handled by a middle layer which bridges between Python and MMT, formats results in HTML5, and adds interactive functionality via widgets.

This bridging of programming languages is a generally difficult problem. We chose to make use of the Py4J library [P4J], a Python-JVM bridge that allows seamless interaction between Python and any JVM-based language (such as Scala). Thus, our Python kernel can call MMT code directly. Valuable Py4j features include callbacks from MMT to Python, shared memory (by treating pointers to JVM objects as Python values), and synchronized garbage collection. That allows our kernel to directly and easily benefit from future improvements to the MMT backend, without needing to duplicate these improvements in kernel-specific code.

As Py4J works at the Java/JVM level, we provide a Python module that performs the bureaucracy of matching up advanced Python and Scala features. This is distributed along with the Jupyter Kernel.

2.4   Converting Between Jupyter Notebooks and MMT Documents

Recall that we were to closely model each notebook as an MMT document. To integrate Jupyter notebooks and MMT documents, we make use of two fortunate design properties:

Firstly, the Jupyter notebook format is well-documented [JND]. We implemented an **OMDoc/NB** API in MMT that can extract the MMT content of a notebook and generate a notebook pre-filled with some MMT content.

Secondly, MMT abstracts from the file formats for MMT documents – e.g. MMT's native surface syntax, sTEX, or prover libraries – and maintains a cross-format document space of any document that can be converted into OMDoc. The OMDoc/NB API to adds Jupyter notebooks into this. Thus, we can support the following workflow:

1. MMT content is written in any format and available as OMDoc.
2. A new interactive notebook is written, using some of that content.
3. The notebook is stored as a file and MMT extracts the relevant content as OMDoc.
4. Any other MMT document (including other notebooks) can now use this content.

2.5 Graphical User Interfaces via Jupyter Widgets

Jupyter widgets are interactive GUI components (e.g., input fields, sliders, etc.) that allow Jupyter kernels to provide graphical interfaces. While the concept is general, it is most commonly used to refer to the Python-based widget library developed for the Python kernel. A widget encapsulates state that is maintained in an instance of a Python class on the server and displayed via a corresponding Javascript/HTML component on the client. A major advantage of our kernel design is that we can reuse these widgets directly in Scala using PY4J (in the top layer)

As our kernel's intelligence is maintained in MMT and thus Scala, we had to write some middle layer code to allow our kernel to create widgets. This code uses Py4J to expose the widget-management functionality of the top layer to the lower layers. This is done via a class of callback functions C that are passed along when the former calls the latter.

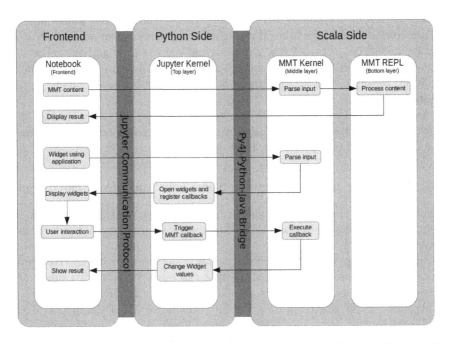

Fig. 3. Architecture diagram. Steps that simply forward data from one layer to the next are not shown explicitly.

Figure 3 shows the details of the communication. The upper part shows the simplest (widget-less) case: MMT content is entered in the frontend and forwarded to the bottom layer, and the response is forwarded in the opposite direction.

The lower part shows a more complex widget-based interaction. First of all, we add special management commands that are not passed on to the GUI-agnostic bottom layer. Instead, they are identified by the middle layer, which responds by delegating to a GUI application. This application then builds its graphical interface by calling the callbacks passed along by the top layer. This results in a widget object in Python that is returned to the top layer and then forwarded to the frontend.

As usual, GUI components may themselves carry callback functions for handling events that are triggered by user interaction with the GUI in the frontend. While conceptually straightforward, this leads to an unusually deep nesting of cross-programming language callbacks. When creating a widget, the Scala-based GUI application may pass Scala callbacks whose implementation makes use of the callbacks provided by the top layer. Thus, a user interaction triggers an MMT callback in the Python top layer, which is executed on the Scala side via Py4J, which in turn may call the Python callbacks exposed via Py4J.

Example: In-Document Computation We present an example of a GUI application inside of a notebook. We will later use this widget for active in-document computation. Figure 4 presents a simple example.

This notebook first defines a new theory (in In[1]), called AddionExample. This theory makes use of the MMT implementation of real number arithmetics.

Our widget is then triggered in In[2] by the special command active computation. It takes two parameters, a list of variables (here a and b) and a term (here $a + b$).

Fig. 4. An active computation widget in a notebook via Jupyter/MMT widgets

These parameters are sent to the middle layer of our MMT kernel (see again Fig. 3). This Scala code then parses the parameters (using the bottom layer), and instructs the middle layer to create a label and a text field for each variable. Furthermore, it also instructs the python code to create a button labeled Simplify and registers a callback inside the Scala code to be executed when the button is pressed. The labels, input fields and the button being used here are standard Jupyter widgets.

In our case the user has already entered some terms, 1.2 for a and 2.3 for b, and already clicked the Simplify button. This triggered the previously registered callback in the middle layer. The function first used the bottom layer to parse the terms inside the input fields. It then substituted the results into the original term $a + b$. The result of this substitution (in this case $1.2 + 2.3$) was then simplified (again using bottom layer code). This resulted in the final output of 3.5.

The important take-away here is not the difficulty of the computation[1]; it is the seamless integration between the frontend, top, middle and bottom layer code. This example demonstrates that our design makes it very easy to build and deploy simple GUI applications for MMT—we still have the full power of Jupyter widgets at our fingertips.

3   Jupyter Notebooks in MathHub

We now discuss the integration of Jupyter Notebooks into the MathHub system.

3.1   Overview

The Jupyter-extended MathHub system consists of four components:

1. A GitLab repository hosting server https://gl.mathhub.info that provides persistent storage of documents in any format, including their OMDoc representation.
2. A Jupyter Notebook server https://jupyter.mathhub.info provides web-based IDE for editing interactive documents
3. An MMT instance which uses the OMDoc representations to provides the shared knowledge space and provides a high-level API for it[2].
4. The MathHub frontend https://mathhub.info that serves as the main entry point and delegates some subtasks to the former. We have extended MathHub front-end with a new document type presenter for notebooks that gives access to the source, context, statistics, and metadata of notebooks, and provides a "preview" and "interact inline" views.

The Jupyter server is an out of the box installation of Jupyter except for additionally supporting our new MMT kernel and a small plugin enabling smoother opening of notebooks via a URL. Consequently, the integration between the Jupyter and the MathHub frontends is shallow: MathHub opens Jupyter Notebooks in separate tabs or iframes using URLs served by Jupyter.

---

[1] In our current implementation we compute using MMT, which models it of using term simplification. However in principle it is possible to use any kind of computation engine here. We want to integrate the active computation widget with our work on the Math-In-The-Middle paradigm (such as in [D6.518]) which would be ideally suited for further applications.

[2] Technically, each kernel has a separate MMT instance in addition to the primary one. Except for the ephemeral document representing each Notebook, these are identical to the main instance. These exist only to isolate different users from one another, and prevent scenarios where they could unintentionally break each others notebook sessions.

3.2   Notebooks as Parts of Semantic Documents

To interact dynamically with content in arbitrary MathHub documents, we can make use of the active computation widget presented in Sect. 2.5. For this purpose we implemented a new feature that creates a new ephemeral Jupyter Notebook and allows accessing it from the current document. Importantly, the new Notebook is pre-filled with an import of the current context.

Mass-energy equivalence

The energy E is the quantitative property that must be transferred to an object in order to perform work on, or to heat the object. The mass m is both a property of a physical body and a measure of its resistance to acceleration (a change in its state of motion) when a net force is applied.

The speed of light in vacuum, commonly denoted c, is a universal, physical constant inportant in many areas of physics. Its exact value is 299,792,458 meters per second (approximately 300,000 km/s (186,000 mi/s)).

Combining these quantities we now can define Einsteins formula as $E = mc^2$.

```
<h2>Mass−energy equivalence</h2>
<div data−theory="?MEC">
 <p>The energy
  <math data−declares="E"><mi>E</mi></math>
  ... The speed of light in vacuum ...
  <math data−declares="c"><mi>c</mi></math> ...
 </p>
 <p>We can now define Einsteins formula as
  <math data−declares="m,c">E=mc^2</math>.</p>
</div>
```

Fig. 5. A semantic HTML document and an abbreviated version of the source code

Figure 5 shows a (simplified) scientific HTML document (on the left) and an extract of its source code (on the right). The document contains the equation $E = mc^2$. The user can use the context menu to trigger the notebook generation on this formula.

This scientific document is semantically annotated. Most notably, the formula that the user can interact with defines the variables that the user might want to interactively change using the **data-declares** attribute. Furthermore, the document contains a reference to an MMT context (using the **data-theory** attribute). This gives semantic meaning to the formula.

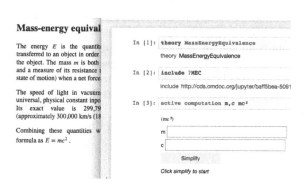

Fig. 6. The resulting Jupyter notebook/widget

The context menu is generated using JavaScript that picks up on these annotations. Currently the author has to manually create the formula and context annotations, but we are working on a mechanism to automatically create it from the document context. The data is then sent to our Jupyter installation using appropriate URL parameters.

Figure 6 shows the notebook created by our tool. This notebook starts with an `include` declaration of the document context. These are generated by our tool to obtain a minimal standalone MMT theory in which the respective formula is well-formed. The notebook then directly instantiates the active computation widget we presented above using the parameters extracted from the document.

In this demonstration we directly show the Jupyter Notebook to the user in a separate window. If desired, the notebooks can be easily uploaded to the Jupyter server, stored persistently in the repository server, or evaluated in a locally deployed version of the system per drag-and-drop.

4   Applications

The immediate application of the Jupyter/MMT integration presented in this paper is interacting with MMT in a REPL. The MMT tool ecosystem only really supported IDE-interaction with MMT libraries via JEdit and (recently) IntelliJ IDEA plugins. While the MMT system provides a simple shell for interaction, this was only used for configuration and setup of the MMT process. We anticipate that the REPL-like interaction will feel more natural for users of interactive theorem provers and computer algebra systems. Even for the new MathScheme-style of specifying theory graph libraries via theory combinators [SR] e.g.,

semigroup = extend magma by $\{\mathsf{assoc}: \vdash \forall a, b, c : G.a \circ (b \circ c) = (a \circ b) \circ c\}$

is well-suited to development/experimentation in a REPL followed by generating an OMDoc file from the recorded notebook.

4.1   Towards a Virtual Research Environment Based on the Math-in-the-Middle Paradigm

Another direct application is in the context of the OpenDreamKit project, which integrates various independently developed computational engines into a mathematical virtual research environment following the Math-in-the-Middle (MitM) approach [Deh+16]. This uses the MMT language for formalizing mathematical background knowledge (which we store in MathHub documents of type MMT) and the MMT system for integrating computation tools. Therefore, Jupyter-MMT notebooks can serve as a unified user interface for MitM systems.

For example, consider the theory[3] in Fig. 7, which serves as our standard example for the interaction between MMT and LMFDB (a large database of mathematical objects that was integrated with MMT in previous deliverables of OpenDreamKit). We can now rewrite it as a notebook.

A screenshot of the resulting notebook, as displayed by a Jupyter server running our MMT kernel, is shown in Fig. 8.

---

[3] Available at https://gl.mathhub.info/ODK/lmfdb/blob/master/source/schemas/tutorial_example.mmt.

The selected declaration of `mycurve` accesses the elliptic curve `11a1` that is stored in LMFDB. When the Jupyter kernel for MMT processes this command, the bottom layer of the kernel dynamically retrieves this curve from LMFDB and builds from it an object of type `elliptic_curve` in the MitM ontology.

```
theory Example : MitM:/Foundation?Logic =
  include MitM:/smglom/elliptic_curves?Elliptic_curve |
  include MitM:/smglom/elliptic_curves?Conductor |

  include db/elliptic_curves?curves |
  /T get elliptic curve 11a1 from LMFDB |
  mycurve: elliptic_curve | = `db/elliptic_curves?curves?11a1 |
  /T let c be its conductor (as stored in the LMFDB) |
  c: int_lit | = conductor mycurve |

  include db/transitivegroups?groups |
  /T get transitive group with label 8T3 from LMFDB |
  mygroup: group | = `db/transitivegroups?groups?8T3 |
  /T let d be its number of automorphisms (as stored in the LMFDB) |
  d : ℕ | = automorphisms mygroup |

  /T Same for a Hilbert Newform |
  include db/hmfs?hecke |
  hecketest : hilbertNewform | = `db/hmfs?hecke?4.4.16357.1-55.1-c |
  dimtest : ℕ | = dimension hecketest |

∎
```

Fig. 7. A theory for LMFDB/MMT interaction

```
In [ ]:  theory Example : http://mathhub.info/MitM/Foundation?Logic

In [ ]:  include http://mathhub.info/MitM/smglom/elliptic_curves?Elliptic_curve

In [ ]:  include http://mathhub.info/MitM/smglom/elliptic_curves?Conductor

In [ ]:  include http://lmfdb.org/db/elliptic_curves?curves

In [ ]:  include http://lmfdb.org/db/transitivegroups?groups

In [ ]:  mycurve: elliptic_curve = `http://lmfdb.org/db/elliptic_curves?ec_curves?11a1

In [ ]:  c: int_lit = conductor mycurve

In [ ]:  mygroup: group = `http://lmfdb.org/db/transitivegroups?groups?8T3
```

Fig. 8. The beginning of the notebook for the theory from Fig. 7

4.2 Domain Specific Applications e.g., MoSIS

Our second case study addresses a *knowledge gap* that is commonly encountered in computational science and engineering: To set up a simulation, we need to combine domain knowledge (usually in terms of physical principles), model knowledge (e.g., about suitable partial differential equations) with simulation (i.e., numerics/computing) knowledge. In current practice, this is resolved by intense collaboration between experts, which incurs non-trivial translation and communication overheads. With the infrastructure presented in this paper, we can do better. In fact, the MoSIS application was developed in parallel to our Jupyter/MathHub integration and MoSIS requirements helped inform the the development. We have ported the original version [PKK18] to the new infrastructure, simplifying and extending it in the course. All in all, the interaction part of the MoSIS project would now be a straightforward software development exercise instead of a contribution of its own.

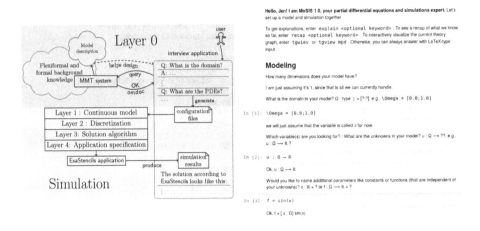

Fig. 9. MoSIS information architecture and dialogue

Concretely, MoSIS uses a Jupyter notebook that has access to an MMT theory graph on MathHub.info. Our Jupyter/MMT/MathHub integration enabled building an interview application that hides these mathematical details from the user.

Based on this theory graph, we built a targeted knowledge acquisition dialog that supports the formalization of domain knowledge, combines it with simulation knowledge and finally drives a simulation run—all integrated into a Jupyter Notebook. Figure 9 shows the general architecture: The left side shows the simulation engine ExaStencils [EXA] and the MMT system that acts as the theory graph interface. The right hand side shows the interview—a Jupyter notebook—as the active document and how it interacts with the MMT kernel. The user only sees the notebook. She answers the knowledge acquisition questions presented by MoSIS until MoSIS can generate a configuration file for ExaStencils. The latter builds efficient code from it through the ExaSlang layers and computes the results and visualizations, which MoSIS in turn incorporates into the notebook.

5   Conclusion and Future Work

We have presented an integration of two interaction paradigms in mathematical software systems: document-based and computation-oriented interactions. Concretely, we have implemented an integration of three systems: Jupyter for computation/experimentation in notebooks and MathHub for interactive mathematical documents as well as MMT for describing the semantics of the knowledge contained in the former. We have evaluated the reach of the evaluation in several case studies.

Even though the work presented in this paper lays the foundation towards an integration of the static/dynamic paradigms for the interaction with mathematical knowledge, at lot of practical enhancements remain for future work. We sketch the most important ones here:

Deeper MathHub/Jupyter Integration. E.g., using Jupyter simply as a JavaScript library in MathHub. This would have been preferable to the current iFrame-based integration, but is infeasible because Jupyter is primarily designed as a monolithic system. Recent versions of Jupyter are working towards a Jupyter-as-a-module design, so we leave deep integration to future work.

IDE Support for Documents with Active Computation. Currently, the semantic documents like the one in Fig. 5 have to be manually extended by the pertinent semantic annotations. An extension of the sTEX framework would allow authors e.g., of educational documents to directly manage the annotations in the LATEX sources.

REPL Cells/Documents as First-Class Citizens in MMT. We already use the notebook-to-MMT-document isomorphism in our system. A first-class model of REPL cells in MMT – this will need a considerable language design effort – would allow to strengthen this isomorphism and refactor our system. We expect that first-class REPL cells in MMT would allow enhanced IDE support for MMT notebooks.

More Flexible Active Computation. The current widget is relatively inflexible in terms of the objects it allows to change for computation. In principle, all variables and constants from the context could be used. We will need more user experience to generalize our current design.

TGView/Notebook Integration. The MMT Jupyter kernel is fundamentally co-dependent on the background theory graph. Therefore we want to explore an integration of the TGView graph viewers [MKR] into the Jupyter front-end. Both Jupyter and TGView are based on REACT.JS, so this should be feasible

Mathematical Search on Notebooks. Last, but not least, we want to extend mathematical search on MathHub to Jupyter notebooks by extending the MathWebSearch harvester accordingly.

Acknowledgements. We acknowledge financial support from the OpenDreamKit Horizon 2020 European Research Infrastructures project (#676541). The authors gratefully acknowledge the support of the Jupyter team and in particular the advice of Benjamin Ragan-Kelly. The MoSIS system was developed in collaboration with Theresa Pollinger [PKK18].

References

[D6.518] Cremona, J., et al.: Report on OpenDreamKit deliverable D6.5: GAP/SAGE/LMFDB interface theories and alignment in OM-Doc/MMT for system interoperability. Deliverable D6.5. Open-DreamKit (2018). https://github.com/OpenDreamKit/OpenDream Kit/raw/master/WP6/D6.5/report-final.pdf

[Deh+16] Dehaye, P.-O., et al.: Interoperability in the OpenDreamKit project: the math-in-the-middle approach. In: Kohlhase, M., Johansson, M., Miller, B., de de Moura, L., Tompa, F. (eds.) CICM 2016. LNCS (LNAI), vol. 9791, pp. 117–131. Springer, Cham (2016). https://doi.org/10.1007/978-3-319-42547-4_9. ISBN 978-3-319-08434-3, https://github.com/OpenDreamKit/OpenDreamKit/blob/master/WP6/CICM2016/published.pdf

[EXA] Advanced Stencil-Code Engineering (ExaStencils). http://exastencils.org. Accessed 25 Apr 2018

[JD] What is Jupyter. http://jupyter-notebook-beginner-guide.readthedocs.org/en/latest/what_is_jupyter.html. Accessed 22 Aug 08 2017

[JND] The Jupyter Notebook Format. https://nbformat.readthedocs.io/en/latest/. Accedded 13 Mar 2018

[MKR] Marcus, R., Kohlhase, M., Rabe, F.: TGView3D system description: 3-dimensional visualization of theory graphs. Submitted to CICM (2019). https://kwarc.info/kohlhase/submit/cicm19-tgview.pdf

[MMT] Rabe, F.: The MMT system. https://uniformal.github.io/doc/. Accessed 16 July 2014

[MMTJup17] Wiesing, T., Amann, K.: MMT jupyter kernel: a jupyter kernel for MMT, 16 October 2017. https://github.com/UniFormal/mmt_jupyter_kernel. Accessed 08 Nov 2017

[P4J] Py4J. https://www.py4j.org/. Accessed 16 July 2018

[PKK18] Pollinger, T., Kohlhase, M., Köstler, H.: Knowledge amalgamation for computational science and engineering. In: Rabe, F., Farmer, W.M., Passmore, G.O., Youssef, A. (eds.) CICM 2018. LNCS (LNAI), vol. 11006, pp. 232–247. Springer, Cham (2018). https://doi.org/10.1007/978-3-319-96812-4_20

[SR] Sharoda, Y., Rabe, F.: Diagram combinators in MMT. In: Kaliszyk, C., et al. (eds.) CICM 2019. LNAI, vol. 11617, pp. 211–226. Springer, Heidelberg (2019)

Explorations into the Use of Word Embedding in Math Search and Math Semantics

Abdou Youssef[1,2(✉)] and Bruce R. Miller[2]

[1] The George Washington University, Washington, D.C., WA, USA
`ayoussef@gwu.edu`
[2] Applied and Computational Mathematics Division, NIST, Gaithersburg, MD, USA
{`youssef,miller`}`@nist.gov`

Abstract. Word embedding, which represents individual words with semantically rich numerical vectors, has made it possible to successfully apply deep learning to NLP tasks such as semantic role modeling, question answering, and machine translation. As math text consists of natural text as well as math expressions that similarly exhibit linear correlation and contextual characteristics, word embedding can be applied to math documents as well. On the other hand, math terms also show characteristics (e.g., abstractions) that are different from textual words. Accordingly, it is worthwhile to explore the use and effectiveness of word embedding in math language processing and MKM.

In this paper, we present exploratory investigations of math embedding by testing it on some basic tasks such as (1) math-term similarity, (2) analogy, (3) basic numerical concept-modeling using a novel approach based on computing the (weighted) centroid of the keywords that characterize a concept, and (4) math search, especially query expansion using the weighted centroid of the query keywords and then expanding the query with new keywords that are most similar to the centroid. Due to lack of benchmarks, our investigations were done using carefully selected illustrations on the DLMF. We draw from our investigations some general observations and lessons that form a trajectory for future statistically significant testing on large benchmarks. Our preliminary results and observations show that math embedding holds much promise but also point to the need for more robust embedding.

1 Introduction

Word embedding [22] has made it possible to apply deep learning in natural language processing (NLP) with great effect. That is because embedding represents individual words with numerical vectors that capture contextual and relational semantics of the words. Such representation enables inputting words and sentences to a (deep) neural network in numerical form. This allows the training of NNs and using them as predictive models for various NLP tasks and

This is a U.S. government work and not under copyright protection in the United States; foreign copyright protection may apply 2019
C. Kaliszyk et al. (Eds.): CICM 2019, LNAI 11617, pp. 291–305, 2019.
https://doi.org/10.1007/978-3-030-23250-4_20

applications, such as semantic role modeling [12,34], word-sense disambiguation [13,29], sentence classification [14], sentiment analysis [32], coreference resolution [19,33], named entity recognition [5], reading comprehension [7], question answering [20], natural language inferencing [8,11], and machine translation [9]. The performance of word embedding in NLP tasks has been measured and shown to deliver fairly high accuracy [22,27,28].

As math text consists of natural text as well as math expressions that exhibit linear and contextual correlation characteristics that are very similar to those of natural sentences, word embedding applies to math text much as it does to natural text. Accordingly, it is worthwhile to explore the use and effectiveness of word embedding in math language processing (MLP) and math knowledge management (MKM). Yet, math expressions and math writing styles are different from natural text to the point that NLP techniques have to undergo significant adaptations and modifications to work well in math contexts.

While some efforts have started to apply word embedding to MLP, such as equation embedding [10,16], there is a healthy skepticism about the use of deep learning (DL) in MLP and MKM, and much work will need to be done to prove the effectiveness of DL in MLP, and to learn how to adapt and apply DL to MLP/MKM. Most applications of DL in MLP/MKM rest on the effectiveness of word/math-term embedding (henceforth *math embedding*), because the latter is the most basic foundation in language DL. Therefore, it behooves us to start to look at the effectiveness of math embedding in basic tasks, such as term similarity, analogy, and basic math search, to learn their powers and limitations, and more importantly, to learn how to refine and evolve math embedding to become accurate enough for more serious applications. That is the primary focus of this paper.

Examples of math similarity include not only math synonyms but also math relatedness, such as: 'Airy' (functions) is "similar", i.e., related to, 'Bessel' (functions); 'Fourier' is similar to 'transform'; 'Euler' is similar to 'Gamma' and 'Beta'; and so on. Math analogies are a little different and include such patterns as: 'x' is to 'real' what 'z' is to 'complex', 'cos' is to 'cosh' what 'sin' is to 'sinh', 'cos' to 'arccos' is what 'log' is to 'exp', 'arcsin' is to 'sin' what 'integral' is to 'derivative', and so on. Being able to detect such similarities and analogies serves as fundamental validation that the underlying math embedding technique is capturing true, relational semantics. Of course, they can serve other purposes in applications such as similarity search, concept modeling, query expansion, and so on. Math similarity, analogy, and applications to search, are the main emphasis of this paper as the basic way to begin to explore the effectiveness of math embedding.

To that effect, there is a fundamental need for datasets and benchmarks, preferably standard ones, to allow researchers to measure the performance of various math embedding techniques and ideas in an objective and statistically significant way, and to measure improvements and comparative progress. Such resources are abundant in the natural language domain, but terribly lacking in the MLP domain. The authors plan to develop some of such benchmarks, which, it is hoped, will form the nucleus for further development by the community in order to facilitate research and speed up progress in this vital area of research.

The task is quite demanding. Much as in NLP, math embedding requires training on large corpora of math documents in order for the resulting term embedding vectors to capture representative relational semantics about the terms to the point where term similarities and analogies (like the ones in the previous examples) can be detected with high accuracy. Therefore, the resource development efforts must extend to creating very large corpora. On the other hand, certain similarities and analogies are domain-specific. For example, the concept of "the inverse of integral" being a "derivative" is specific to calculus, and thus may only be captured if the corpus is a calculus corpus. Similarly, the analogy that " 'x' is to 'z' what 'real' is 'complex' " is specific to real and complex analysis. Thus, the corpora collection and the similarities/analogies benchmark development must go hand in hand in a coordinated and mutually informed fashion.

To appreciate more the magnitude and dimensions of creating such benchmarks, it is instructive to look at some of those developed for NLP whose tasks can beneficially inform and guide corresponding tasks in MLP. The NLP benchmarks include one for natural language inference [2], one for machine comprehension [30], one for semantic role modeling [25], and one for language modeling [4], to name a few. With such benchmarks, which are often *de facto* standards for the corresponding NLP tasks, the NLP research community has been able to (1) measure the performance of new techniques up to statistical significance, and (2) track progress in various NLP techniques, including deep learning for NLP, by easily comparing the performance of new techniques to others and to the state of the art.

While the task of creating such resources for DL applications in MLP is monumental and will take time, the examination of math embedding should not wait but should proceed right away, albeit in an exploratory fashion, at least to ascertain the value of math embedding for MLP/MKM and to inform the process and trajectory of creating the corpora and benchmarks. Admittedly, until adequate datasets and benchmarks become available for MLP, we have to resort to less systematic performance evaluation, and rely on performing preliminary tests on the limited resources available. The DLMF [24] is a good resource to start our exploratory embedding efforts due to its high quality and the authors' familiarity with its contents, which aid in crafting some of the tests. In that spirit, this paper is such an early exploratory investigation of the effectiveness and use of word embedding in MLP and MKM.

The paper is organized as follows. Next section gives a quick survey of the foundations and of prior work related to word embedding. Section 3 presents preliminary experiments and uses of (math) term similarity, and draws early lessons. Section 4 does the same for math analogies. In Sect. 5, we present a novel embedding-based technique for concept modeling and query expansion, using the combined notions of (weighted) word centroids and similarity. The section provides some preliminary illustrations and draws some observations. Finally, Sect. 6 concludes the paper and outlines future directions.

2   Foundations and Related Work

The advances most relevant to our work are the recent developments in *word embedding* [1,3,6,17,18,21–23,26–28,31]. Word embedding takes as input a text collection, and generates a numerical feature vector (typically 100D or 300D) for each word in the collection. This vector captures latent semantics of a word from the contexts of its occurrences in the collection; in particular, words that co-occur often in close proximity tend to have similar feature vectors (where similarity is measured by the cosine similarity, the Euclidean distance, etc.).

In this paper, we will apply Word2Vec on the DLMF [24] for generating embedding vectors for various math symbols and terms, and test various tasks, such as term similarity, term analogy, and query expansion.

Note that applications of embedding to MLP have started to emerge, such as equation embedding [10,16]. Equation embedding is useful for identifying similar equations and contextual descriptive keywords. In our work, we are addressing term embedding at a more basic level to determine its power and limitations, and draw lessons and identify factors for how to derive better term embeddings that can enable doing the higher tasks at higher levels of performance.

Observe that co-occurrence matrices could be used for finding similar words, and they are worth investigating and comparing with word-embedding-based similarity detection, to see which gives better performance. However, co-occurrence matrices are not useful for other tasks (like detecting math analogies). Also, co-occurrences are not as close to "semantics" as word embeddings are because the latter is locality sensitive (i.e., proximity sensitive) whereas the former is locality agnostic. Due to the limitations of co-occurrences matrices, and since they are quite far from the focus of this work on word embedding, they will not be explored any further in this paper (except for brief comparative mentions), but instead they will be the focus of future comparative work.

3   Term Similarity

Identifying similar words (to a given keyword) can:

1. serve as an indicator of the semantics-capturing capabilities of the underlying word embedding technique;
2. enrich search queries (by combining the keyword with its semantic/related neighbors into an expanded query);
3. find related concepts that could not be found as efficiently and conveniently as through embedding-based word similarity.

We applied Word2Vec on the entire DLMF, and ran preliminary experiments for term similarity (and for other tasks explained later). Table 1 presents the results of searching for the 20 most similar words for four math terms. The results show that many of the returned "hits" are quite what a mathematician would expect (especially hits for the words 'Bessel' and 'hypergeometric' in columns 3 and 4), but at the same time, certain similar/related terms failed to be returned. For example, considering the hits for 'transform' (1st column of the table), we observe:

- the top-20 hits showed some synonyms (e.g., 'transformation') and related terms like 'convolution', 'Mellin' and 'Hilbert' (the latter two are due probably to 'Mellin transform' and 'Hilbert transform'), which are all good;
- the top-20 hit list failed to include 'Fourier', despite the fact that it is arguably the most famous transform;
- another drawback is the fact that certain irrelevant words, e.g., 'By' and 'allows', ranked higher than what is actually the more similar word 'convolution'.

Also, looking at the 2nd column, the hits of words similar to 'Fourier' include many other terms that are truly related to the keyword 'Fourier', where in several instances (e.g., 'Stieltjes' and 'Hilbert'), the similarity could perhaps be attributed to the fact there are transforms associated with those terms. Unlike in the previous column, the word 'Transform' rightly appears in the top-20 similar words of 'Fourier'. This lack of symmetry, though understandable, shows that similarity, or rather *dissimilarity*, (based on Word2Vec embedding), is a not a measure in the mathematical sense, which can be a serious shortcoming.

Obviously, these four similarity exercises are awfully too few to draw any generalizable conclusions, but they illustrate the drawbacks and the promises of embedding for MLP, and press the need for benchmarks to achieve generalizable, statistically significant results.

4 Term Analogy

Finding mathematical analogies is a powerful tool for crafting queries for analogy search, which cannot be performed by mere keyword search. Here are some examples: 'x' is to 'real' what 'z' is to 'complex', 'cos' is 'cosh' what 'sin' is to 'sinh', 'cos' to 'arccos' is what 'log' is 'exp', 'arcsin' is to 'sin' is what 'integral' is to 'derivative', and so on. To illustrate the use of analogies, consider this simple example of a math student who has taken courses on real analysis and is just starting to learn complex analysis. That student is likely curious to know the common notation for a complex variable, as the counterpart of 'x' being the common notation for a real variable. In plain English, the student can formulate that information need as a query/question of the form: What is to 'complex' as 'x' is to 'real'? With powerful word embedding, the unknown term being searched for satisfies the following relation:

$$V(\text{Unknown}) - V(\text{'complex'}) \approx V(\text{'x'}) - V(\text{'real'})$$

or equivalently

Table 1. Keywords and their top-20 most similar words, by the Euclidean distance.

transform	Fourier	Bessel	hypergeometric
transform	Fourier	Bessel	hypergeometric
Mellin	power	Airy	generalized
Transform	Hilbert	Hankel	confluent
Transforms	Heun	modified	multivariate
extend	Maclaurin	Struve	generating
By	Stieltjes	Modified	Olver's
defining	radii	Generalized	Lauricella's
Stieltjes	joining	Spherical	Heun
Hilbert	summable	Coulomb	Appell
allows	noninteger	Many	gamma
convolution	Transform	Inverse	bilateral
standard	Laurent	products	basic
rise	Every	Kelvin	elementary
group	trapezoidal	Mathieu	Gauss
us	geometric	spheroidal	Kummer
summable	rules	Weber	Inverse
transformation	iterative	spherical	Many
ellipsoids	Lagrange	gamma	plays
solve	vacuum	Lamé	Coulomb
Since	construction	Contiguous	beta

$$V(\text{Unknown}) \approx \boxed{V(\text{`x'})} + \boxed{(V(\text{`complex'}) - V(\text{`real'}))},$$

where $V(t)$ is the embedding vector of term t. Accordingly, to find the *unknown term*, find the closest vectors to the vector $V(\text{`x'}) + (V(\text{`complex'}) - V(\text{`real'}))$, and retrieve the corresponding words. Ideally, with good embedding, the unknown term should be the top match or at least among the top few matches. Note that in the equation above, the vector on the right hand side of the approximation is the sum of the vector for the *known term* (i.e., first box) and the vector (in the second box) that captures the relation between the known term and the unknown term. We will call the second-box vector the *relation vector*.

We tested this analogy capability using several analogy queries, as shown in Table 2 where **Term** stands for the unknown term being searched for. The query illustrated above about the complex variable notation was formulated in two different flavors (top half of the first two columns), and, for extra measure, the question was modified to search for the real variable given the complex variable (top half of the third column); the purpose of varying the question is to test for robustness. Examining the results in the table, one can observe the following:

- In all three queries, the desired answer was the second topmost match, which, though not ideal, is quite impressive.
- The topmost match for the unknown term is, interestingly, the known term, in all three queries. That indicates that the relation vector is, at least in these queries, of very small magnitude. This could result from one or two factors: (1) the vectors of 'complex' and 'real' are quite similar due to the strong inter-relatedness, making their difference quite small, or (2) those two vectors are of small magnitude, causing their difference to be small as well. The 1st factor is mitigated when the relation is between two disparate (i.e., not so correlated) concepts, while the 2nd factor can be remedied by taking *normalized* embedding, resulting in unit-length vectors.

The bottom half of Table 2 shows the results for three other analogy queries. The first query tests for analogy between trigonometric $((\sin, \cos))$ and hyperbolic functions $((\sinh, \cosh))$, the second query tests for inverse function relation in trigonometry, i.e., analogy between $(\sin, \arcsin)$ and $(\cos, \arccos)$, and the third query also tests for inverse function relation but this time between functions from different areas (one pair from trigonometry, namely, $(\cos, \arccos)$, and the other pair being $(\exp, \log)$). One can observe the following about the results of those queries:

- for the first 2 queries, we observe the same as above: the desired match ranks second, and the topmost match is (wrongly) identical to the known term.
- For the third query, the desired match is not even in the top-10 list.

All those observations, but especially the last one, point to the urgent need for mass testing on large benchmarks, to assess accurately the power and limitations of embedding in MLP applications, and for better diagnosis of shortcomings so that more targeted remedies or adjustments can be made. For example, is it the case that, when analogies are being drawn from two rather different areas, the analogy search is not as accurate? The preliminary few tests performed in this paper do not give us a strong basis for answering such a question, but further tests on large benchmarks will almost certainly provide an answer.

5   Concept Modeling and Query Expansion

Many concepts can be "described" by a (sub)set of keywords that capture different aspects of the concept, and serve as "axes" that characterize the concept. For example, the concept of "dog" can be described (at least partially) by keywords like "animal", "domestic", "friendly", "loyal", etc. Note that when a concept has no name, the characterizing keywords form the fundamental pieces of an implicit definition of the unnamed concept. In any case, numerical modeling of a concept can be achieved by taking the centroid of the keywords that characterize the

Table 2. Analogies of the form: find term where term is to X what Y is to Z. The similarity measure is cosine similarity.

Top 10 best **Term**'s where		
Term is to "**complex**" what "**x**" is to "**real**"	**Term** is to "**x**" what "**complex**" is to "**real**"	**Term** is to "**z**" what "**real**" is to "**complex**"
x	x	z
z	z	x
\left(	\left(	2
\right)	\right)	t
,	,	-
1	1	1
=	=	\right)
-	-	n
\pi	\pi \pi	
-	-	+
Term is to "**sin**" what "**cosh**" is to "**cos**"	**Term** is to "**sin**" what "**arccos**" is to "**cos**"	**Term** is to "**exp**" what "**arccos**" is to "**cos**"
cosh	arccos	arccos
sinh	arcsinh	arccosh
sin	arctan	arctan
tanh	arctanh	arctanh
csch	arccosh	arcsinh
cot	arcsin	exp
coth	arccsc	arcsin
mt	arcsec	erfc
zs	arccoth	sign
sech	arccsch	xyz

concept, i.e., by taking the average of the embedding vectors of the characterizing keywords. The centroid can also be viewed as capturing the commonalities between the concepts represented by the component keywords.

We tested the centroid-based concept modeling technique using several examples. The results are shown in Tables 3, 4 and 5.

In Table 3, we show the most similar words to the centroid of {'Fourier', 'Mellin'}. Observe that although 'transform' did not appear in the top-20 similarity matches of 'transform' in Table 1, it appears in the centroid matches, probably because 'transform' is a central commonality between 'Fourier' and 'Mellin'. This illustrates the conceived power of this simple centroid-based technique. By the same token, and indirectly through 'transform', other transforms appear in the top list of centroid matches, such as Laplace, Hilbert, Kontorovich-Lebedev, and so on.

Tables 4 and 5 show more examples, where the top-20 matches are populated by mostly relevant terms. One striking yet unexplainable observation is that the matches tend to be of lengths comparable to those of the component keywords of the centroid. For example, nearly all the matches of centroid({'se', 'ce'}) in Table 4 are of length 2 characters and the remaining matches are all of length just 3 characters. Likewise, in Table 5, the top-20 matches for the centroid of {'Bessel', 'Struve'} are the names of various similar functions, where the names are of length comparable to (or larger than) that of the two component keywords, even though the one-letter names of specific Bessel functions (e.g., I, J and K) should be on/near the top of the list. In future work, this phenomenon will be investigated further, and, if length-bias is confirmed, length-agnostic embedding techniques will be sought.

Table 3. The words/lemmas most similar to the centroid of "Fourier" and "Mellin", by cosine similarity.

Top 20 Most Similar Words for Centroid of {'Fourier', 'Mellin'}		Top 10 Most Similar Lemmas for Centroid of {'Fourier', 'Mellin'}
Mellin	Stieltjes	Mellin
Fourier	Leading	Fourier
Hilbert	convolution	Hilbert
Laplace	many-body	Laplace
Transform	summable	Transform
Kontorovich-Lebedev	ease	Kontorovich-Lebedev
transform	collections	products
products	FFT	Stieltjes
Transforms	us	Leading
transforms	Convergence	convolution

5.1 Weighted Centroids

The notion of centroids is flexible enough to allow the user to put more, or less, emphasis on certain aspects/keywords in the component list, so as to represent a different concept, or a different gradation of a concept. This is achieved through weighted centroids, where more emphasis is put by giving a larger weight to the corresponding keyword, and vice versa. One can even de-emphasize certain aspects/dimensions/keywords by giving them negative numerical weights.

Table 6 illustrates the power of weighted centroids. In the 1st column, by giving weight 0 to 'Gamma', effectively finding the words similar to 'Euler', the search failed to uncover the relevant Beta (function) in the top 20 hits. By including 'Gamma' with equal weight as 'Euler' (2nd column), 'Beta' was returned (as the 7th hit). Disappointingly, 'Gamma' itself was not returned, and

Table 4. Similarities to the centroids of 4 subsets of words, by cosine similarity.

Top 20 most similar words for the centroid of			
{'se', 'ce'}	{'Si', 'Ci'}	{'Ai', 'Bi'}	{'sin', 'cos', 'tan'}
ce	Ci	Bi	sin
se	Si	Ai	cos
fe	Ei	envAi	tan
ge	nt	envBi	cot
Se	ez	Hi	cosh
Fe	sec	Gi	sinh
Ce	Arctan	envelope	tanh
Ge	xe	Airy	uv
Io	xM	xe	Arctanh
Gey	Shi	1535	csch
Ko	Gi	Chi	pm
me	Chi	'	si
Ke	ie	54703	Ein
Fey	Ein	Shi	ir
Ds	zn	implicitly	Arccsc
Dc	6144	derivative	sec
mz	Cin	Ein	Arccosh
Ie	xJ	1797	coth
Me	arccot	ie	csc
inh	1797	Ei	rh

that is because the vector of 'Euler' has a relatively much larger magnitude than the vector of 'Gamma'. This points to the need to use **normalized** embedding vectors instead. In the third column, more weight is given to 'Gamma' than to 'Euler'; as a result, two things were observed: (1) 'Gamma' is in the hit list and near the top, and (2) 'Beta' now ranks higher than when both query words are of equal weight.

Weighted centroids show much promise and potential, and call for further studies to determine techniques for systematically selecting weights to meet certain objects. One of the applications of centroids, whether weighted or unweighted, is query expansion for a more effective search. This is addressed in the next subsection.

5.2 Query Expansion

One limitation of keyword/keyphrase search is that it is based on the literal occurrence of the query keywords/keyphrases, regardless of the underlying semantics. Incorporating synonym search does not eliminate this deficiency. The

Table 5. Similarities to the centroids of three subsets of words, by Cosine Similarity.

Top 20 most similar words for the centroid of		
{'Legendre', 'Hypergeometric'}	{'Bessel', 'Struve'}	{'Legendre', 'Hypergeometric', 'Bessel', 'Struve'}
Legendre	Bessel	Struve
Hypergeometric	Struve	Bessel
Generalized	Kelvin	Generalized
Struve	Hankel	Hypergeometric
Gamma	Modified	Weber
Generating	Weber	Contiguous
dilated	Noninteger	Modified
Associated	Airy	Gamma
Arguments	Spherical	Legendre
Confluent	Contiguous	Kelvin
Products	Anger-Weber	Hankel
Ferrers	Many	Associated
Contiguous	Generalized	Anger-Weber
Number-Theoretic	Inverse	Many
Incomplete	Half-Integer	Noninteger
Parabolic	Functions-Real	Generating
Kind	Functions-Complex	Confluent
Mittag-Leffler	Gamma	Spherical
-Function	Incomplete	Incomplete
Elementary	gamma	Arguments

"integrated" semantic notions represented by conjoining a number of character-izing keywords cannot be identified by the mere occurrence of those keywords in a document. Rather, it is more effective to first determine new keywords that pertain very closely to the concept represented/shared by certain characterizing keywords, and then add those new keywords to the original keywords to form an expanded query. In other terms, it is significantly more effective to "**explicitize**" the concept that is underlying a set of keywords into new keywords to add to the search query.

This query expansion process is quite straightforward thanks to the embedding-based centroid concept introduced earlier in this section. Specifically, the query expansion is done through the following steps:

1. **Embedding:** Retrieve the embedding vectors of the keywords of the query;
2. **Centroid:** Compute the (weighted) centroid C of those vectors;
3. **Similarity Search:** Find the top N most similar vectors to C (N is preset);
4. **Expansion Keywords:** Retrieve the words corresponding to those vectors;

Table 6. The words most similar to the weighted centroids of {'Euler', 'Gamma'}, by cosine similarity. (Note: certain matches like ':sec:LA.F2.DC' are obviously wrong and a result of tokenizer artifacts which will be fixed in future versions)

Top 20 most similar words to the centroid of {'Euler', 'Gamma'} using different weights w_1 and w_2		
$(w_1, w_2) = (1, 0)$	$(w_1, w_2) = (1, 1)$	$(w_1, w_2) = (1, 2)$
Euler	Euler	Euler
Bernoulli	LA4	Gamma
belonging	Bernoulli	Beta
cyclotomic	Numbers	Generating
polynomials	exponentials	Periodic
splines	Periodic	Parabolic
Numbers	splines	Cylinder
LA4	Beta	LA4
generating	belonging	exponentials
Stirling	Gamma	Number-Theoretic
:sec:LA.F2.DC	15-point	Generalized
quotients	:sec:LA.F2.DC	Unmodified
Splines	5-point	Numbers
1851	Curve	Modular
Genocchi	cyclotomic	Exponential
Hermite	Cylinder	Toroidal
Factorization	generating	Trigonometric
Computer	Factorization	Elementary
exponentials	Gauss-	Contiguous
15-point	Generating	Associated

5. **Expansion-keywords Selection** [optional]: In human-in-the-middle situations, where the user has domain expertise, the user selects from the list of the previous step the words that truly pertain to the keywords of the query;
6. **Expanded Query:** Add the words of the previous step to the keywords of the original query, conjoined by the OR or the AND Boolean operator;

We performed several preliminary tests of query expansion on 4–5 queries using DLMF and its math search capability, and following the steps outlined above. We carefully selected the expansion keywords using our familiarity with DLMF and Special Functions. Table 7 shows the original queries and the expanded queries, and reports the recall as *P-Recall* and *E-Recall*, corresponding to page search and equation search, respectively. The recall of the OR-expanded queries increases, and this increase indicates that this expansion is not superfluous, i.e., the new keywords are not subsumed by the original query, but it is

Table 7. Query expansion using centroids and similarity. The reported recalls are derived from running the queries on the DLMF [24] in two modes: (1) page search (for P-Recall) and (2) equation search (for E-Recall)

Query	P-Recall	E-Recall
Original Query: Bessel	195	858
1st Expansion: Bessel OR Airy	234	1061
2nd Expansion: Bessel OR Spherical	220	909
3rd Expansion: Bessel OR Airy OR Spherical	259	1112
Original Query: Fourier OR Mellin	84	54
1st Expansion: Fourier OR Mellin OR transform	189	90
2nd Expansion: Fourier OR Mellin OR transform OR Convolution	192	92
Original Query: Euler	381	1513
Original Query: Gamma	220	879
"Inspired" Query: Beta	179	543
1st Expansion: Euler OR Gamma	381	1515
2nd Expansion: Euler OR Beta	420	1817
3rd Expansion: Euler OR Gamma OR Beta	420	1819
4th Expansion: Euler AND Gamma	220	877
5th Expansion: Euler AND Beta	79	543
6th Expansion: Euler AND Gamma AND Beta	62	38

a judicious expansion that helps the user uncover new, relevant hits that the original query could not match.

Note that there are applications where users have domain expertise for a judicious selection of expansion keywords. For example, frequently, users of math search are domain experts in their disciplines. Another example is patent search, where patent examiners are domain experts who search for "prior art" through a sequence of queries that they evolve by expansion. Our proposed query expansion method suggests valuable keywords to add, and the patent examiners have the expertise to wisely choose from the suggested keywords to form better queries for more effective and more efficient search of prior arts. This method has already been tested by the US Patent & Trademark Office (US PTO), and has shown good results [15].

The expansion is not limited to OR expansion for an increased recall, but it can suggest valuable new keywords to intersect with the old keywords using AND-expansion, leading to better precision.

Another use of weighted centroids is relevance ranking, especially in search systems that do not allow weighting the query keywords. For example, to give more, or less, emphasis to some keywords in the query, one can compute an appropriately weighted centroid of the query keywords. The new keywords resulting from Step 3 of the algorithm capture the inherent emphasis. By expanding the original query with those properly biased new keywords, the hits will be ranked in a way that reflects that bias, leading to better relevance ranking and higher user satisfaction.

Of course, further, more extensive, and more systematic study of this novel form of query expansion is needed and will be conducted in future work.

6 Conclusions

In this paper, we explored the use and effectiveness of word embedding for MLP on three fundamental tasks, namely, term similarity, analogy, and math search using a novel centroid-based query-expansion technique that we introduced. While our exploratory studies need extensive future experimentation for statistically significant validation on large datasets and benchmarks, they preliminarily show some of the promise and limitations of word embedding in math (MLP) applications.

As suspected at the outset, our preliminary results stress the urgent need for creating large math-specific benchmarks for testing math embedding techniques on math-specific (MLP) tasks. The authors plan to begin developing some of such benchmarks, and to pursue further investigations of the some of the lines of inquiry indicated in the paper.

Future investigations will also examine the effectiveness of other embedding techniques, as well as more MLP tasks and applications such as part of math tagging, math-term disambiguation, and representation-to-computation deep learning models, to name a few.

References

1. Bordes, A., et al.: Joint learning of words and meaning representations for open-text semantic parsing. In: AISTATS (2012)
2. Bowman, S.R., Angeli, G., Potts, C., Manning, C.D.: A large annotated corpus for learning natural language inference. In: EMNLP (2015)
3. Cer, D., et al.: Universal sentence encoder. CoRR arXiv:1803.11175 (2018)
4. Chelba, C., et al.: One billion word benchmark for measuring progress in statistical language modeling. In: INTERSPEECH (2014)
5. Chiu, J., Nichols, E.: Named entity recognition with bidirectional LSTM-CNNs. Trans. Assoc. Comput. Linguist. 4, 357–370 (2016)
6. Cho, K., et al.: Learning phrase representations using RNN encoder-decoder for statistical machine translation. In: EMNLP (2014)
7. Clark, C., Gardner, M.: Simple and effective multi-paragraph reading comprehension. In: ACL 2018, Melbourne, Australia, 15–20 July 2018, pp. 845–855 (2018)
8. Chen, Q., et al.: Enhanced LSTM for natural language inference. In: ACL (2017)
9. Devlin, J., et al.: Fast and robust neural network joint models for statistical machine translation. In: Proceedings of the ACL (2014)
10. Gao, L., et al.: Preliminary exploration of formula embedding for mathematical information retrieval: can mathematical formulae be embedded like a natural language? arXiv:1707.05154 (2017)

11. Gong, Y., Luo, H., Zhang, J.: Natural language inference over interaction space. In: ICLR (2018)
12. He, L., Lee, K., Lewis, M., Zettlemoyer, L.S.: Deep semantic role labeling: what works and what's next. In: ACL (2017)
13. Iacobacci, I., Pilehvar, M.T., Navigli, R.: Embeddings for word sense disambiguation: an evaluation study. In: ACL (2016)
14. Kim, Y.: Convolutional neural networks for sentence classification. In: EMNLP, Doha, Qatar, pp. 1746–1751, October 2014
15. Krishna, A., Youssef, A., et al.: Query Expansion for Patent Searching using Word Embedding and Professional Crowdsourcing (in submission)
16. Kstovski, K., Blei, D.M.: Equation embeddings. arXiv:1803.09123, March 2018
17. Lai, S., Liu, K., He, S., Zhao, J.: How to generate a good word embedding. IEEE Intell. Syst. **31**(6), 5–14 (2016)
18. Le, Q., Mikolov, T.: Distributed representations of sentences and documents. In: International Conference on Machine Learning, pp. 1188–1196, January 2014
19. Lee, K., He, L., Lewis, M., Zettlemoyer, L.S.: End-to-end neural coreference resolution. In: EMNLP (2017)
20. Liu, X., Shen, Y., Duh, K., Gao, J.-F.: Stochastic answer networks for machine reading comprehension. arXiv:1712.03556
21. Mikolov, T., et al.: Efficient estimation of word representations in vector space. In: Workshops Track, International Conference on Learning Representations (2013)
22. Mikolov, T., et al.: Distributed representations of words and phrases and their compositionality. In: NIPS, pp. 3111–3119 (2013)
23. Nickel, M., Kiela, D.: Poincare embeddings for learning hierarchical representations. In: Advances in NIPS (2017)
24. Olver, F.W.J., et al., (eds.): NIST Digital Library of Mathematical Functions. https://dlmf.nist.gov/, Release 1.0.18 of 27-03-2018
25. Palmer, M., et al.: The proposition bank: an annotated corpus of semantic roles. Comput. Linguist. **31**, 71–106 (2005)
26. Piotr, B., Grave, E., Joulin, A., Mikolov, T.: Enriching word vectors with subword information. Trans. ACL **5**, 135–146 (2017)
27. Peters, M.E., et al.: Deep contextualized word representations. In: Proceedings of NAACL-HLT, pp. 2227–2237 (2018)
28. Pennington, J., Socher, R., Manning, C.D.: GloVe: global vectors for word representation. InL EMNLP, 25–29 October 2014, pp. 1532–1543 (2014)
29. Raganato, A., Bovi, C.D., Navigli, R.: Neural sequence learning models for word sense disambiguation. In: EMNLP (2017)
30. Rajpurkar, P., Zhang, J., Lopyrev, K., Liang, P.: SQuAD: 100,000+ questions for machine comprehension of text. In: EMNLP (2016)
31. Rudolph, M., Ruiz, F., Athey, S., Blei, D.M.: Structured embedding models for grouped data. In: NIPS, pp. 250–260 (2017)
32. Socher, R., et al.: Recursive deep models for semantic compositionality over a sentiment treebank. In: EMNLP (2013)
33. Wiseman, S., Rush, A.M., Shieber, S.M.: Learning global features for coreference resolution. In: HLT-NAACL (2016)
34. Zhou, J., Xu, W.: End-to-end learning of semantic role labeling using recurrent neural networks. In: ACL (2015)

Author Index

Printed in the United States
By Bookmasters